GW00724765

Visual Basic®

Your visual blueprint for building
versatile programs on the .NET Framework

by Richard Bowman

Visual

From

maranGraphics®

&

Hungry Minds™

Best-Selling Books • Digital Downloads • e-Books • Answer Networks • e-Newsletters • Branded Web Sites • e-Learning

New York, NY • Cleveland, OH • Indianapolis, IN

Visual Basic® .NET: Your visual blueprint for building versatile programs on the .NET Framework

Published by
Hungry Minds, Inc.
909 Third Avenue
New York, NY 10022
www.hungryminds.com

Copyright © 2002 Hungry Minds, Inc.

Certain designs and illustrations are copyright © 1992-2002 maranGraphics, Inc., used with maranGraphics' permission. All rights reserved. No part of this book, including interior design, cover design, and icons, may be reproduced or transmitted in any form, by any means (electronic, photocopying, recording, or otherwise) without the prior written permission of the publisher.

maranGraphics, Inc.
5755 Coopers Avenue
Mississauga, Ontario, Canada
L4Z 1R9

Library of Congress Control Number: 2001097474

ISBN: 0-7645-3649-4

Printed in the United States of America

10 9 8 7 6 5 4 3 2 1

1V/SY/RS/QR/IN

Distributed in the United States by Hungry Minds, Inc.

Distributed in Canada by CDG Books Canada Inc. for Canada; by Transworld Publishers Limited in the United Kingdom; by IDG Norge Books for Norway; by IDG Sweden Books for Sweden; by IDG Books Australia Publishing Corporation Pty. Ltd. for Australia and New Zealand; by TransQuest Publishers Pte Ltd. for Singapore, Malaysia, Thailand, Indonesia, and Hong Kong; by Gotop Information Inc. for Taiwan; by ICG Muse, Inc. for Japan; by Intersoft for South Africa; by Eyrolles for France; by International Thomson Publishing for Germany, Austria and Switzerland; by Distribuidora Cuspide for Argentina; by LR International for Brazil; by Galileo Libros for Chile; by Ediciones ZETA S.C.R. Ltda. for Peru; by WS Computer Publishing Corporation, Inc., for the Philippines; by Contemporanea de Ediciones for Venezuela; by Express Computer Distributors for the Caribbean and West Indies; by Micronesia Media Distributor, Inc. for Micronesia; by Chips Computadoras S.A. de C.V. for Mexico; by Editorial Norma de Panama S.A. for Panama; by American Bookshops for Finland.

For U.S. corporate orders, please call maranGraphics at 800-469-6616 or fax 905-890-9434.

For general information on Hungry Minds' products and services please contact our Customer Care Department within the U.S. at 800-762-2974, outside the U.S. at 317-572-3993 or fax 317-572-4002.

For sales inquiries and reseller information, including discounts, premium and bulk quantity sales, and foreign-language translations, please contact our Customer Care Department at 800-434-3422, fax 317-572-4002, or write to Hungry Minds, Inc., Attn: Customer Care Department, 10475 Crosspoint Boulevard, Indianapolis, IN 46256.

For information on licensing foreign or domestic rights, please contact our Sub-Rights Customer Care Department at 212-884-5000.

For information on using Hungry Minds' products and services in the classroom or for ordering examination copies please contact our Educational Sales Department at 800-434-2086 or fax 317-572-4005.

For press review copies, author interviews, or other publicity information, please contact our Public Relations department at 317-572-3168 or fax 317-572-4168.

For authorization to photocopy items for corporate, personal, or educational use, please contact Copyright Clearance Center, 222 Rosewood Drive, Danvers, MA 01923, or fax 978-750-4470.

Screen shots displayed in this book are based on pre-released software and are subject to change.

LIMIT OF LIABILITY/DISCLAIMER OF WARRANTY: THE PUBLISHER AND AUTHOR HAVE USED THEIR BEST EFFORTS IN PREPARING THIS BOOK. THE PUBLISHER AND AUTHOR MAKE NO REPRESENTATIONS OR WARRANTIES WITH RESPECT TO THE ACCURACY OR COMPLETENESS OF THE CONTENTS OF THIS BOOK AND SPECIFICALLY DISCLAIM ANY IMPLIED WARRANTIES OF MERCHANTABILITY OR FITNESS FOR A PARTICULAR PURPOSE. THERE ARE NO WARRANTIES THAT EXTEND BEYOND THE DESCRIPTIONS CONTAINED IN THIS PARAGRAPH. NO WARRANTY MAY BE CREATED OR EXTENDED BY SALES REPRESENTATIVES OR WRITTEN SALES MATERIALS. THE ACCURACY AND COMPLETENESS OF THE INFORMATION PROVIDED HEREIN AND THE OPINIONS STATED HEREIN ARE NOT GUARANTEED OR WARRANTED TO PRODUCE ANY PARTICULAR RESULTS, AND THE ADVICE AND STRATEGIES CONTAINED HEREIN MAY NOT BE SUITABLE FOR EVERY INDIVIDUAL. NEITHER THE PUBLISHER NOR AUTHOR SHALL BE LIABLE FOR ANY LOSS OF PROFIT OR ANY OTHER COMMERCIAL DAMAGES, INCLUDING BUT NOT LIMITED TO SPECIAL, INCIDENTAL, CONSEQUENTIAL, OR OTHER DAMAGES.

Trademark Acknowledgments

Hungry Minds, the Hungry Minds logo, Visual, the Visual logo, Read Less - Learn More and related trade dress are registered trademarks or trademarks of Hungry Minds, Inc., in the United States and/or other countries and may not be used without written permission. The maranGraphics logo is a registered trademark or trademark of maranGraphics, Inc. Visual Basic® .NET is a registered trademark of Microsoft Corporation. All other trademarks are the property of their respective owners. Hungry Minds, Inc. and maranGraphics, Inc. are not associated with any product or vendor mentioned in this book.

FOR PURPOSES OF ILLUSTRATING THE CONCEPTS AND TECHNIQUES DESCRIBED IN THIS BOOK, THE AUTHOR HAS CREATED VARIOUS NAMES, COMPANY NAMES, MAILING, E-MAIL AND INTERNET ADDRESSES, PHONE AND FAX NUMBERS AND SIMILAR INFORMATION, ALL OF WHICH ARE FICTITIOUS. ANY RESEMBLANCE OF THESE FICTITIOUS NAMES, ADDRESSES, PHONE AND FAX NUMBERS AND SIMILAR INFORMATION TO ANY ACTUAL PERSON, COMPANY AND/OR ORGANIZATION IS UNINTENTIONAL AND PURELY COINCIDENTAL.

Permissions

maranGraphics

Certain text and illustrations by maranGraphics, Inc., used with maranGraphics' permission.

 is a trademark of Hungry Minds, Inc.

U.S. Corporate Sales	U.S. Trade Sales
Contact maranGraphics at (800) 469-6616 or fax (905) 890-9434.	Contact Hungry Minds at (800) 434-3422 or (317) 572-4002.

Visual Basic® .NET

*Your visual blueprint for building
versatile programs on the .NET Framework*

**maranGraphics is a family-run business
located near Toronto, Canada.**

At **maranGraphics**, we believe in producing great computer books — one book at a time.

maranGraphics has been producing high-technology products for over 25 years, which enables us to offer the computer book community a unique communication process.

Our computer books use an integrated communication process, which is very different from the approach used in other computer books. Each spread is, in essence, a flow chart — the text and screen shots are totally incorporated into the layout of the spread. Introductory text and helpful tips complete the learning experience.

maranGraphics' approach encourages the left and right sides of the brain to work together — resulting in faster orientation and greater memory retention.

Above all, we are very proud of the handcrafted nature of our books. Our carefully-chosen writers are experts in their fields, and spend countless hours researching and organizing the content for each topic. Our artists

rebuild every screen shot to provide the best clarity possible, making our screen shots the most precise and easiest to read in the industry. We strive for perfection, and believe that the time spent handcrafting each element results in the best computer books money can buy.

Thank you for purchasing this book. We hope you enjoy it!

Sincerely,

Robert Maran

President

maranGraphics

Rob@maran.com

www.maran.com

www.hungryminds.com/visual

CREDITS

Acquisitions, Editorial, and Media Development

Project Editor
Maureen Spears

Acquisitions Editor
Jen Dorsey

Product Development Supervisor
Lindsay Sandman

Copy Editors
Timothy J. Borek, Jill Mazurczyk

Technical Editor
Todd Meister, Garrett Pease

Editorial Manager
Rev Mengle

Media Development Manager
Laura Carpenter Van Winkle

Senior Permissions Editor
Carmen Krikorian

Media Development Specialist
Angela Denny

Editorial Assistant
Amanda Foxworth

Production

Book Design
maranGraphics®

Production Coordinator
Dale White

Layout
Kristin McMullan,
LeAndra Johnson, Jill Piscitelli

Screen Artists
David Gregory, Mark Harris,
Jill A. Proll

Cover Illustration
David E. Gregory

Proofreaders
John Bitter, Joanne Keaton,
Carl Pierce

Indexer
TECHBOOKS Production Services

Special Help
Microsoft Corporation
Sarah Hellert
Mica Johnson

ACKNOWLEDGMENTS

Hungry Minds Technology Publishing Group: Richard Swadley, Senior Vice President and Publisher; Mary Bednarek, Vice President and Publisher, Networking; Joseph Wikert, Vice President and Publisher, Web Development Group; Mary C. Corder, Editorial Director, Dummies Technology; Andy Cummings, Publishing Director, Dummies Technology; Barry Pruett, Publishing Director, Visual/Graphic DesignHungry Minds Manufacturing: Ivor Parker, Vice President, Manufacturing

Hungry Minds Marketing: John Helmus, Assistant Vice President, Director of Marketing

Hungry Minds Production for Branded Press: Debbie Stailey, Production Director

Hungry Minds Sales: Michael Violano, Vice President, International Sales and Sub Rights

ABOUT THE AUTHOR

Richard Bowman owns and operates BowmanSoft, Inc., which specializes in software consulting and Internet development technolgies.

Richard is also the editor and owner of the Visual Basic Web Magazine, a Web resource site focusing on Visual Basic and ASP programming. You can visit VBWM at http://www.vbwm.com/. You can reach the author at richard@bowmansoft.com.

AUTHOR'S ACKNOWLEDGMENTS

The last few months have been a long and arduous journey. I never knew how stressful a project could be until I took on the process of writing this book. I would like to thank all of the people that helped me keep my sanity and told me I could do it. My family — Debbie, Richard, and Megan — provided me with love and assistance from proposal to production. Special thanks go to my friends and colleagues Aaron, Chris, Christina, Katie, and Stephanie, who provided enourmous encouragement and support throughout the process.

Thanks goes to the authors and developers of the VBWM.COM site for their understanding and patience when I missed deadlines. Special thanks go to my editors — Maureen, Jen, Rev, Tim, Mica, Todd, and Garrett — who kept me on track and always held out a helping hand when I was stuck.

To my family, who put up with so much.

TABLE OF CONTENTS

VISUAL BASIC .NET:
Your visual blueprint for building
versatile programs on the .NET Framework

3) WORK WITH CONTROLS

4) PROGRAMMING IN VISUAL BASIC .NET

TABLE OF CONTENTS

5) PROVIDE INPUT AND OUTPUT

6) CREATE GRAPHICS AND MULTIMEDIA

7) WORK WITH CLASSES

VISUAL BASIC .NET:
Your visual blueprint for building
versatile programs on the .NET Framework

8) USING ADVANCED OOP TECHNIQUES

9) ACCESS ADO.NET

TABLE OF CONTENTS

10) USING WEB FORMS

11) USING WEB SERVICES

12) DEVELOPING COMPONENTS

VISUAL BASIC .NET:
Your visual blueprint for building
versatile programs on the .NET Framework

13) PACKAGE YOUR APPLICATION

APPENDIX

INDEX

Visual Basic .NET: Your visual blueprint for building versatile programs on the .NET Framework uses simple, straightforward examples to teach you how to create powerful and dynamic programs.

To get the most out of this book, you should read each chapter in order, from beginning to end. Each chapter introduces new ideas and builds on the knowledge learned in previous chapters. When you become familiar with *Visual Basic .NET: Your visual blueprint for building versatile programs on the .NET Framework*, you can use this book as an informative desktop reference.

Who This Book Is For

If you are interested in writing applications for Windows computers and the Internet using the Visual Basic .NET programming environment, *Visual Basuc .NET: Your visual blueprint for building versatile programs on the .NET Framework* is the book for you.

This book takes you through the process of installing and using the Development Studio, writing advanced Windows Applications, and developing Web applications. The book also provides detailed coverage to develop reusable components and package your application or component.

Although this book requires no prior experience with Visual Basic programming, a familiarity with the Microsoft Windows operating system installed on your computer, and programming languages in general is recommended.

What You Need to Use This Book

To perform the tasks in this book, you need a computer with Microsoft Windows NT 4.0, 2000, or XP installed, as well as Microsoft Visual Studio .NET. You do not require any special development tools, because all the tools are part of the Visual Studio .NET Development Environment.

The Conventions in This Book

A number of typographic and layout styles have been used throughout *Visual Basic .NET: Your visual blueprint for building versatile programs on the .NET Framework* to distinguish different types of information.

Courier Font

Indicates the use of Visual Basic for Applications (VBA) code such as tags or attributes, scripting language code such as statements, operators, or functions, and Excel Object Model code such as objects, methods, or properties.

Bold

Indicates information that you must type.

Italics

Indicates a new term.

Apply It

An Apply It section usually contains a segment of code that takes the lesson you just learned one step further. Apply It sections offer inside information and pointers that you can use to enhance the functionality of your code.

Extra

An Extra section provides additional information about the task you just accomplished. Extra sections often contain interesting tips and useful tricks to make working with Excel macros easier and more efficient.

VISUAL BASIC .NET:
Your visual blueprint for building
versatile programs on the .NET Framework

The Organization of this Book

Visual Basic .NET: Your visual blueprint for building versatile programs on the .NET Framework contains 13 chapters and one appendix.

The first chapter, "Getting Started with Visual Basic .NET," familiarizes you to the features and functions you use throughout the book. You learn how to install Visual Studio .NET, how to create a new project, how to save and open project files, and how to upgrade Visual Basic 6.0 projects.

Chapter 2, "Getting Started with Windows Forms," shows you how to build and manage the development of a Windows application. This chapter focuses on how to work in the Visual Development environment and how to build menus and various windows.

Chapter 3, "Work with Controls," shows you how to build various types of controls, such as buttons, radio buttons, check boxes, list boxes, and toolbars onto your Windows forms applications.

The fourth chapter, "Programming in Visual Basic .NET," shows you how to work with the Visual Basic language to declare and use variables, strings, arrays, collections, use operators, arguments, conditional blocks, and loops.

Chapter 5, "Provide Input and Output," shows you how to read and write from files, detect changes in the file system, and retreive file and directory listings. This chapter also covers how to add printing and print preview support, and how to download information from a network or the Internet. You also learn how to building your own server.

Chapter 6, "Create Graphics and Multimedia," shows you how to add graphics commands to your application. This chapter shows you how to draw lines, shapes, and text, in various fills and patterns. This chapter shows you how to build a custom shape and apply it to the form to make a custom-shaped form of any dimension or shape.

Chapters 7, "Work with Classes," and 8, "Using Advanced OPP Techniques" illustrate how to build and use classes effectively. This includes how to develop a set of properties, methods, and events in your classes. It also continues to explore more advanced techniques for class development, including inheritance, overloading, and using threads.

The ninth chapter, "Access ADO .NET," introduces you to the ADO .NET database-programming tools, and shows you how to build data-bound controls, how to use data grids, and how to develop data validation

Chapter 10, "Using Web Forms," illustrates the development of Web forms server applications. The chapter shows you how to use the Web interface designer, and how to work with controls and the event model to build applications that run in any standard Web browser.

Chapter 11, "Using Web Services," shows you how to build service applications, export functionality from Web services over the Internet, and how to monitor services.

Chapter 12, "Developing Components," shows you how to build your own components, controls, Web controls, and user controls.

Chapter 13, "Package Your Application," illustrates how to package your application to distribute, how to catch and handle errors, and how to provide features for disabled users.

What's on the CD-ROM

The CD-ROM included in this book contains the sample project code from each of the two-page lessons throughout the book. This saves you from having to type the code and helps you quickly get started creating VB .NET code. The CD-ROM also contains several evaluation versions of programs that you can use to work with *Visual Basic .NET: Your visual blueprint for building versatile programs on the .NET Framework*. An e-version of the book and all the URLs mentioned in the book are also available on the disc.

AN INTRODUCTION TO VISUAL BASIC .NET

Visual Basic .NET is part of Microsoft Visual Studio .NET, the latest development environment from Microsoft. With Visual Basic .NET, or VB .NET for short, you can create powerful Windows and Internet applications using a unified toolkit. See the section "Understanding the Framework" for more information on the .NET Framework.

With the release of VB .NET, Visual Basic received advanced language features on par with languages like C++, C#, and Java. Powerful new features give VB .NET the simplicity of its predecessors, but with the power of creating full-fledged applications that take advantage of the computing field's latest innovations.

FEATURES

Easy to Use

The Visual Basic language implements an updated version of the original BASIC language, developed in 1964. The focus of the BASIC language was to provide a high-level programming language that hid much of a computer's complexity from the developer.

Automatic Memory Management

Visual Basic .NET uses a system called garbage collection to manage your application's memory. Garbage collection is an important feature that VB .NET shares with languages like C# and Java. Garbage collection does not explicitly require you to delete objects from memory. VB .NET finds objects that are no longer referenced and removes them from memory automatically when your application is idle.

Fully Object-Oriented

Visual Basic .NET, unlike Visual Basic 6.0 and earlier versions, supports full object-oriented programming, with support for polymorphism, true inheritance, and interfaces. Full object-oriented programming enables VB .NET to communicate and extend other high-level languages such as Visual C++ and C#. In fact, because of the power of the .NET Framework, Visual Basic .NET can utilize source files from another language, inheriting a class created in C# or providing true objects for use in C++. For more information on using objects, see Chapter 7.

Powerful Database Support

VB .NET extends the strong support for which the Visual Basic language is known when developing high-level, multi-tier database applications. Supporting a new version of ADO and ADO.NET, VB .NET can create powerful Web-enabled database applications with better performance and more functions than ever before.

Visual Development

The advent of the Graphical User Interface (GUI) promised easier-to-use computers. But developing applications for the GUI environment was more difficult than expected. Visual Basic was the first Windows programming language that successfully used drag and drop and a powerful integrated development environment (IDE) to enable users to develop applications in record time.

Today, the Visual Studio.NET suite shares one IDE that performs an enormous array of functions. The IDE design allows it to expand to support various languages and toolkits. The integration of languages also means you do not have to learn multiple development environments if you work with more than one language.

True Web Development

Visual Basic .NET uses the new ASP.NET objects to create fully compiled server-side applications that use the full power of the Visual Basic language and the .NET Framework while still interfacing with standard browsers. ASP.NET, combined with Visual Basic .NET, provides a unique development system called *Web Forms* that brings the drag-and-drop ease of Visual Basic to Web development.

Web Services, possibly one of the most important features of the .NET Framework, provides a method of accessing remote objects over the Internet using the SOAP standard, which relies on XML. You can store an object on a Web server and enable any application to access this object directly over the Internet transparently. For example, you can create a Windows application that uses an object stored on a centralized Web server the same as you use a component on the local machine. Visual Basic .NET takes full advantage of this functionality and creates Web-enabled objects.

DEVELOPMENT SUPPORT

Native Windows Applications

You can use the Windows Forms technology present in VB .NET to develop applications that take full advantage of the Windows operating systems. A powerful form designer lets you click, drag, and drop your way to a complete Windows interface. See Chapter 2 to develop Windows applications.

Games and Multimedia Applications

Visual Basic .NET accesses the same class library as other languages in Visual Studio.NET, providing VB .NET access to powerful GDI+ and DirectX functions. The .NET Framework Library wraps a complete class library around all Windows drawing functions, enabling you to use graphic commands just like other components in the Visual Basic .NET system without calling complex system calls. See Chapter 5 for information on graphics commands.

Database Applications

Data access has been a strong point of the Visual Basic language since its inception, and Visual Basic .NET carries the tradition by providing the most sophisticated data access tools to date. You can drag and drop tables onto your forms and point-and-click to create automatically connected controls. With Microsoft's Active Data Objects library (ADO.NET), you can access a variety of database systems through one powerful environment. You can use standard classes in ADO.NET to easily transport your application from Microsoft Access to Microsoft SQL Server to Oracle servers with little-to-no change in code. See Chapter 9 to develop database applications.

Console Applications

New to Visual Basic .NET, you can create console applications that run in standard text consoles. These console applications let you create utilities that a user can access from the command line and create quick programs to test programming functions. See Chapter 4 for more information on creating console applications.

Create Windows Services

Visual Basic .NET can create true Windows services, the software that maintains background tasks on a Windows NT, Windows 2000, or Windows XP system. Windows includes a number of services that let the system index files on disks for faster searching, run Internet servers, and pass messages from application to application. Services enable you to easily create servers and utilities that integrate with Windows to provide transparent background functions. VB .NET is the first version of Visual Basic to support the creation of service applications. See Chapter 11 to develop your own Windows services.

Create Web Applications

New Web Forms technology in VB .NET lets you create interactive applications that run over the Web. These applications run completely on the server using Microsoft Internet Information Server (IIS). You can create applications that function with any browser and allow Web Forms to maintain variables and state information across pages automatically, creating a seamless application development process for you. See Chapter 10 to develop Web applications.

Create Web Services

Web Services use the power of .NET technologies to export functions across the Internet in a secure manner. Any .NET enabled application, whether a Web Forms application or a Windows Forms application, can access the Web Service as if it is present on the same machine. See Chapter 11 to develop your own Web service.

INSTALL VISUAL STUDIO .NET

The first step in using VB .NET involves installing the Development Studio and compilers. The Visual Studio .NET application suite includes Visual C++, Visual C#, Visual Basic .NET, an enormous help library courtesy of the Microsoft Developers Network (MSDN), and various tools.

A full installation of Visual Studio .NET recommends 500MB of space on a system drive and 2.5GB of space on an application drive. Visual Studio .NET does not support Windows 95, Windows 98, or Windows ME operating systems. If you plan to use the Web development tools, you can install Visual Studio on Windows 2000 Server, although Visual Studio .NET can work with remote Windows 2000 servers. Visual Studio .NET requires a minimum of 96MB of RAM to install on Windows 2000 Professional and recommends 128MB. For Windows 2000 Server, Visual Studio .NET requires 192MB of RAM and recommends 256MB.

When you install Visual Studio .NET, you may need to update a number of Windows components. The Visual Studio .NET installation prompts you to insert the Windows Component Update CD-ROM included in the package, and it updates your system with Windows Service Packs and other components. The installation automatically reboots during this installation. The installation then asks you to optionally enter log in information so it can log in automatically and continue the installation.

The Visual Studio installation itself spans multiple CD-ROMs or a single DVD, but automates most of the installation process. It enables you to select different drives for different components of the installation, which helps to lessen the extreme disk space requirements. By default, the installation installs all three programming languages and runs the help from the CD-ROM. The MSDN help libraries are a very important resource, so if you have enough disk space, you can set the MSDN help selection to install to disk to make it more readily accessible.

INSTALL VISUAL STUDIO

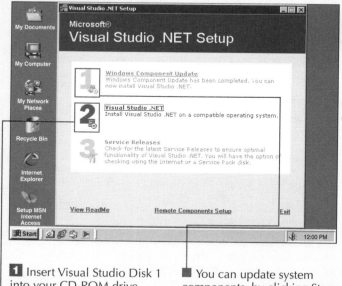

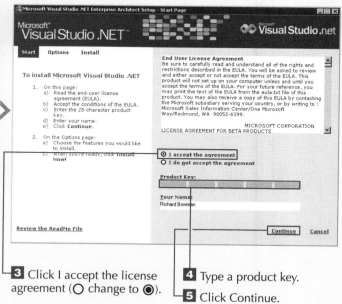

■1 Insert Visual Studio Disk 1 into your CD-ROM drive.

■2 Click Step 2 to begin installing Visual Studio. NET.

■ You can update system components, by clicking Step 1 and follow the directions.

■ You can click Step 3 to check for the latest Service Releases.

■3 Click I accept the license agreement (○ change to ◉).

■4 Type a product key.

■5 Click Continue.

Extra

You can use the installation program to install various parts of the application in different locations. For example, you can install the .NET Framework files on one drive and the main development files on another drive. To alter the install paths of individual parts of the installation, click the item in the tree shown in the installation program and modify the installation path by clicking 🔲 to the right of the installation path.

You can install the MSDN help files using the installation program for easy access. The MSDN help files contain all of the documentation for the languages present in the package as well as a number of books and articles Microsoft publishes in electronic form. To install the MSDN to disk instead of running it from CD-ROM drive, click the CD icon beside the MSDN Documentation item and click Install to Disk.

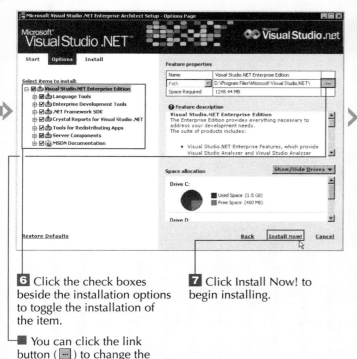

6 Click the check boxes beside the installation options to toggle the installation of the item.

■ You can click the link button (🔲) to change the installation directory if desired.

7 Click Install Now! to begin installing.

■ The Visual Studio Setup installs the desired options.

USING THE DEVELOPMENT STUDIO

The Development Studio provides an integrated user interface for nearly every facet of development, including visual design tools, code editors, integrated MSDN help system, debugging, and add-in support. You use the Development Studio to create and manage all of the .NET applications you create.

Across the top of the Development Studio, you find a standard layout for menus and toolbars. Around the window, you can see various tool windows attached to the main window. You can move and customize all of the menus, toolbars, and tool windows.

When you start the Development Studio, it presents you with an opening Start Page. This page lets you open recent projects, search the product and support pages, check the What's New area, and browse the online community.

When you open the Development Studio for the first time, it displays the My Profile section of the start page, giving

you access to a set of standard setups for the studio. Assuming you choose the Visual Basic Developer setup, you find the Toolbox attached to the left side of the window. The Toolbox provides the components you use to design Windows Forms, Web Forms, Database applications, and other types of applications.

On the right side of the Development Studio, you find the Solution Explorer. The Solution Explorer holds the contents of a single solution. A solution, however, can hold multiple projects of different types that combine together into one application.

The New Project button on the Start Page lets you begin a new application. This dialog provides the list of available project types. You can learn more about creating a project in the section "Create a Project." The Open Project button provides a list of folders in the Visual Studio project folder to open. To learn more about opening existing projects, see the section "Work with Projects."

USING THE DEVELOPMENT STUDIO

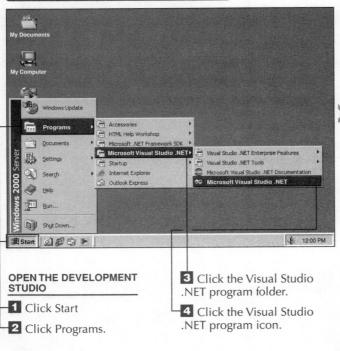

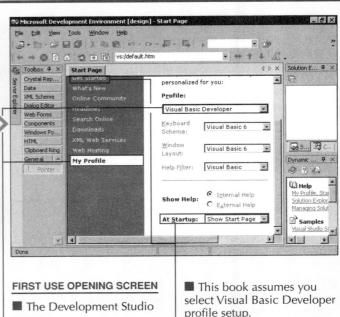

OPEN THE DEVELOPMENT STUDIO

1 Click Start

2 Click Programs.

3 Click the Visual Studio .NET program folder.

4 Click the Visual Studio .NET program icon.

FIRST USE OPENING SCREEN

■ The Development Studio opens.

5 Click My Profile.

6 Click the Profile list ☑ and click an appropriate style for the Development Studio.

■ This book assumes you select Visual Basic Developer profile setup.

■ You can click ☑ and click another startup options.

7 Click Get Started to open the default home page for the environment.

Extra

You can return to the Start Page at any time by clicking Help and then Show Start Page. The Start Page provides common starting point resources for you to use in the environment.

If you close any of the tool windows or cannot find them, click View. The menu lists all of the parts of the Development Studio. The Other Windows menu item has a submenu with more tool windows if you cannot find the one you need on the main View menu.

You can access the searchable MSDN library inside of the environment. Click Help and then Search. A Search tool window appears and lets you specify search terms. You can also filter the results to a particular area of help. Because the help covers all aspects of development, from articles and references, to online books, you most likely want to filter the results using the Visual Basic and Related item. This narrows your search to access reference information in the Visual Basic subsection and includes the .NET Framework reference. When you click Search, a Results tool window appears along the bottom of the environment.

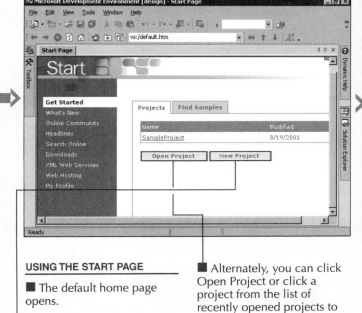

USING THE START PAGE

■ The default home page opens.

■ You can click New Project to start a new project.

Note: To create a new project, see the section "Create a Project."

■ Alternately, you can click Open Project or click a project from the list of recently opened projects to open an existing project.

Note: To open and save projects, see the "Work with Project Files" section.

■ The Start Page provides access to the common areas of the Development Studio.

OBJECT-ORIENTED CONCEPTS

Visual Basic .NET provides a fully object-oriented environment, which means it bases its functionality around sets of objects. Many languages, such as C++, C#, Java, and others are considered object-oriented as well, and offer many of the same features. You can use object-oriented programming (OOP) to create code you can easily reuse and extend.

Visual Basic versions 6.0 and earlier offered partial implementations of OOP, but VB .NET is the first version of Visual Basic primarily designed around objects.

CLASS

A *class*, which contains a set of data, is the primary building block of an object-oriented application. Instead of manipulating data directly as you might in a non-object-oriented language, the class controls how you can access that data from the outside. You can think of a class as having two distinct parts, the interface and the implementation, that provide the ease of use and reusability that are key to development in an OOP language. For more information on classes, see Chapter 7.

In many ways, a class attempts to mimic the way you define things in the real world. For example, you may want to create a program where a ball bounces on the screen. You can place all of the code to define the shape, size, and actions of the ball together with the code to draw and manipulate the user interface. But in an object-oriented language, it makes more sense to create a class to represent the ball.

OBJECTS

An *object* is the actual representation you create from your class. A class provides the code and definition that makes up an object. When you create an object, you create a usable version of the class that stores independently in memory. Then you can access the parts of the object, set properties, and work with the abilities its methods provide. You can create any number of objects based on the information from a class. No matter the number of objects you define from a single class, all of the properties and data associated with that object are unique to the individual object.

For example, in your application, assume you want to create a bouncing ball on screen. You define a class that represents a ball. You then create a single instance of the ball in your application, set attributes of the ball, and tell it to bounce. The ball bounces appropriately on screen. You can easily go back to your code for the application, not touching the class defined for the ball, and create a new instance of the class. This ball bounces independently, knowing nothing about the existence of the other balls.

INTERFACE

The interface of the class provides a way for other parts of the application to access an object. When you define the class, you determine what needs users have for the class and create an interface of properties, methods, and events to make the class usable. When you or

someone else creates an object using the class, you do not need to understand its internal functionality. The class internalizes all of its functionality and allows interaction.

IMPLEMENTATION

The *implementation* of the class is the code behind the properties and methods that enable the class to work. When you use an object, you work with the implementation to access the abilities of the class.

The actual implementation of the class is hidden from you so you can focus on using the class rather than on how it works.

PROPERTIES

A part of a class, you can think of a *property* as the attributes that define the details of a class. You use properties to define the data that makes up the characteristics of the class. Each property stores a single data type and can contain a piece of text, a number, or a whole other object.

Using the example of a class representing a ball, you use properties to define the shape, size, color, weight, and position of the ball. A property makes the object you create from a class unique.

METHODS

Methods enable a class to define the actions that make the object functional. A method is made up of a block of code that performs one specific action. You can define any number of methods to make up a class. You can think of a method as a definition of something an object does or can have done to it.

For example, you can perform one of many actions on a ball, such as throw, toss, or roll. Of course, a computer-simulated ball also needs methods to make it move, draw on screen, and bounce in an onscreen boundary.

EVENTS

An object uses events to send information back to the user of the object. An event normally represents a response to a method the owner of the class calls. An event can send back data through arguments. The owner of the class optionally responds to the event by creating a method called an event handler, which the owner of the object must set up.

For example, when you throw, toss, or roll a ball, many event can occur in response to your actions. The ball can hit the ground, hit a wall, or pop. In a computer environment, a ball hits a defined boundary, and lets the owner of the object respond to this occurrence. You often use an event to simply send status information back to the owner of the object, for example, the current position of the ball, or a change in course that the class handled itself.

UNDERSTANDING THE FRAMEWORK

The .NET Framework provides an enormous class library that contains much of the functionality available to VB .NET. You can use this guide as a starting point for understanding the underlying structure of a .NET application.

THE .NET FRAMEWORK

Features

The .NET Framework is an enormous environment that represents much of the functionality contained in Visual Studio .NET. The base of the framework consists of the Common Language Runtime, or CLR, the engine that drives the entire system. The CLR provides a standard system of data types and objects, and makes cross-language and cross-platform development possible.

The middle layer of the Framework includes next-generation system services such as ADO.NET, ASP.NET, and XML. Unlike previous versions of these tools, the Framework manages these tools, making their availability universally consistent across languages.

The top-most layer includes user and program interfaces. Windows Forms provides the interface to create standard Win32 applications. Web Forms provides a powerful server side visual development tool wrapped around ASP.NET. Web Services provides a mechanism for programs to communicate directly over the Internet. Also, a console interface allows creation of simple text-based applications.

CLR

The purpose of the CLR is to create an easier and faster development system with automatic handling of low-level details such as memory management and process communication. Other important features for the CLR include a simpler and safer deployment environment and scalability.

The CLR transparently supports any number of languages, not limited to those Microsoft develops. This integration enables many languages to take advantage of the built-in debugging system and memory management. The integration with the CLR required the VB language to change signficantly, but gives it the ability to work with other languages much more effectively.

Versioning

The CLR offers significant improvements for application deployment and component versions. Unlike previous component models, like COM, the CLR can find and reference components without the use of ProgIDs, CLSIDs, and type libraries. The CLR supports side-by-side deployment, and therefore can load and use multiple versions of the same assembly. This lets a program work with a certain version of a DLL while another program uses a newer version of the DLL simultaneously, removing problems of non-backwards compatible DLLs.

When you compile an application that references a DLL, or shared assembly, the compiler stores the assembly's name and version number into your application.

Assemblies

A set of one of more modules makes up a single unit called an assembly. This assembly contains the necessary information for you to deploy it on multiple computers. The assembly contains a catalog of component metadata known as a manifest. This manifest holds critical information about type visibility, component versioning, and security. Every type must exist with the scope of an assembly. In Visual Basic .NET, a single project represents a single assembly. A solution holds multiple projects, and therefore relates multiple assemblies together for deployment.

When you create an assembly for others to use, you must decide which types should appear outside of the assembly. You use the `Public` and `Private` keywords to expose or hide a class or interface from outside users. You can also use the `Friend` keyword to hide a method from outside of the assembly, but make it usable throughout the assembly.

The .NET Class Framework libraries implement the functions you use in .NET enabled languages. The Class Framework consists of hundreds of classes and interfaces. It wraps class functionality around most of the Windows system libraries and provides extra functionality not available in standard Windows libraries.	**Features** The .NET class framework includes functions over a broad set of needs. These functions include: • **Data access and manipulation:** data access through ADO.NET, robust XML support, and file and directory tools • **Standard language functions:** math commands, arrays, collections, and strings • **Creation and management of threads:** free-threading libraries and process management • **Interfaces to Windows functions:** Windows Forms, Web Forms, Web Services, and console applications • **Management and enforcement of application security** • **Application configuration** • **Working with Windows Directory Services, event logs, message queues, and timers** • **Support for a number of network protocols**

System Namespace

The `System` namespace holds much of the functionality in the .NET Framework. The table explains some of the major subsections of `System`. You can use this list as a starting point to find a particular function in the library.

NAMESPACE	DESCRIPTION	EXAMPLE CLASSES
`System.Collections`	Classes representing various sorts of collections.	`ArrayList, HashTable, SortedList`
`System.Data`	Classes that constitute the ADO.NET architecture.	`DataRow, DataTable, DataColumn, DataSet`
`System.Diagnostics`	Classes that enable you to debug your application and to trace execution of your code.	`Debug, EventLog, FileVersionInfo, Trace`
`System.Drawing`	Provides access to the GDI+ basic graphics functionality.	`Brush, Font, Image, Pen, Region, SystemColors`
`System.Drawing.Printing`	Provides printing functions and printer and page settings.	`PageSettings, PrintDocument, PrinterSettings`
`System.IO`	Contains types for reading and writing data streams and files.	`DirectoryInfo, FileInfo, FileStream, StreamReader, StreamWriter`
`System.Net`	Provides an interface to many common Web protocols.	`Cookie, Dns, FileWebRequest, IPAddress, WebClient`
`System.Resources`	Manage the creation and storage of various culture-specific resources in an application.	`ResourceManager, ResourceReader, ResourceWriter`
`System.Security`	Provides the underlying security structure of the CLR.	`PermissionSet, SecurityManager`
`System.Security.Cryptography`	Provides data encoding and decoding routines, and functions like hashing, random number generation, and message authentication.	`CryptoStream, DES, DSACryptoServiceProvider, MD5CryptoServiceProvider, RSACryptoServiceProvider`
`System.Text`	Contains classes representing ASCII, Unicode, other character encodings, and classes for conversion between formats.	`ASCIIEncoding, StringBuilder, UnicodeEncoding, UTF7Encoding`
`System.Threading`	Enables multi-threaded programming. Includes classes to manage individual threads, pools of threads, and synchronization issues.	`Monitor, Mutex, Thread, ThreadPool, Timer`
`System.Web`	Supplies classes that enable browser and server communication for ASP.NET applications.	`HttpApplication, HttpPostedFile, HttpRequest, HttpResponse, HttpWriter`
`System.Windows.Forms`	Provides classes to create complete Windows applications.	`Button, CheckBox, Clipboard, Form, ListView, MessageBox`
`System.Xml`	Provides standards-based support for processing XML.	`NameTable, XmlAttribute, XmlNode, XmlReader, XmlText, XmlValidatingReader`

LANGUAGE BASICS

Visual Basic .NET is a simple language that uses many plain English words. To use the language effectively, you need to learn certain common conventions. For

more information on conventions, consult the Visual Basic Programmer's Guide in the help system.

INDENTING

Indenting code is the practice of inserting spaces to make code more readable. While some languages require certain indentations to build the code properly, indentation is completely optional in Visual Basic .NET.

Highly recommended, indentation makes code much easier to read and understand. You use four spaces, the default amount in VB .NET, to indent code inside a block.

Non-Indented code:
```
Sub MyMethod(argument As String)
Dim counter As Integer
If argument = "Test" Then
For counter = 1 To 10
ProcessData()
Next
End If
End Sub
```

Properly Indented code:
```
Sub MyMethod(argument As String)
    Dim counter As Integer
    If argument = "Test" Then
        For counter = 1 To 10
            ProcessData()
        Next
    End If
End Sub
```

COMMENTS

Lines in a code file that VB .NET does not process, comments let you make plain-English descriptions of code. This makes it easier to debug and understand code at a later date. To comment code, place a single

apostrophe at the end of a code line or on a new line. VB .NET ignores anything after the apostrophe, so you can "comment out" code during testing and VB .NET does not run the code behind the apostrophe.

Non-Commented Code:
```
Sub Main()
    Setup()
    ShowInitialScreen()
    ProvideUserFeedback()
End Sub
```

Commented Code:
```
Sub Main()                      ' program begins here.
    ' initalize variables to default values and load
    ' the configuration file CONFIG.INI
    Setup()
    ' create an instance of the MainForm form and
    ' show it to the user.
    ShowInitialScreen()
    ' when the user exits the form, allow them to
    ' provide feedback about their experience
    ProvideUserFeedback()
End Sub
```

LINE BREAKS

You can break a single statement in VB .NET into multiple lines of code using the underscore (_) character. You can only break lines where you normally have a space in the line, and therefore cannot break lines in the middle of strings. You can break a line in a string, thus separating it, by creating two strings and splitting the line between the parts. You also normally indent the extra lines of the statement to increase readability. The book uses the underscore character in the task screens often so that you can see the lines of code.

```
Example:
Sub Method1()
    ' call method 2
    Method2(New Point(5. 5), _
        New Rectangle(10, 10, _
        20, 20), New Point(15, 15)
End Sub
```

CLASSES

When you access namespaces and elements of classes, you separate the various components with a period (.).

```
Example:
' declare a new Point object from the Point
' class located in the Drawing namespace
' located in the System namespace.
Dim a As New System.Drawing.Point()
' set the X and Y properties of the Point
a.X = 100
a.Y = 100
```

CONSTANTS

You can declare constants, named values, in your program using the Const keyword in the base of any module. Constants create more readable code. Also, you can change the value of the constant to affect all code that uses the constant.

```
Example:
Const MyFavoriteNumber As Integer = 9
Const DefaultErrorMessage As String = "Error!"
```

REGIONS

You can use regions to separate parts of the code in the module to make it more readable. When you declare a region of code, the code editor provides a plus/minus button to expand or collapse the section. For long code that rarely changes, a region can make using the code editor much simpler.

```
Example:
#Region "Calculation functions"
    Sub Add()
    ...
    End Sub
...
#End Region
```

KEYWORDS

The list of keywords below is not complete; search help for "keywords" for the full list.

Alias	And	AndAlso	Assembly	Ansi
As	Auto	Boolean	ByRef	Byte
ByVal	Case	Catch	Char	Class
Const	Date	Decimal	Declare	Default
Delegate	Dim	Do	Double	Each
Else	ElseIf	End	Enum	Erase
Error	Event	Exit	False	Finally
For	Friend	Function	Get	Handles
If	Imports	In	Inherits	Integer
Interface	Is	Let	Lib	Like
Long	Loop	Me	Mod	Module
MyBase	MyClass	New	Next	Not
Nothing	Object	On	Option	Optional
Or	OrElse	Overrides	Private	Public
ReDim	Region	Resume	Return	Select
Shared	Static	Step	Stop	String
Structure	Sub	Then	Throw	To
True	Try	TypeOf	Unicode	Until
When	While	With	Xor	

LANGUAGE CHANGES FROM VISUAL BASIC 6

Better than Visual Basic 6, the previous version of Visual Basic, the Visual Basic .NET upgrade has many significant changes, which makes it a more powerful and cross-language oriented program. This section helps you understand these changes before attempting to upgrade a Visual Basic 6 project to Visual Basic .NET. To upgrade a project using the Upgrade Wizard, see the section "Using the Upgrade Wizard."

Variant

A special universal data type, the `Variant` data-type in Visual Basic 6 has the capability of holding data of any type. The variable morphs to store various data like numeric variables, strings, and even objects. `Variant` is also the default variable type in VB 6 if you do not specify a type for the variable. The `Object` variable type in VB 6 can store object references, but does not have the ability to store standard data types.

In VB .NET, the `Variant` type is no longer available. The common language runtime adopts the `Object` variable as the universal data type. Because VB .NET references simple variable types as objects, just like it does for other object data types, the `Object` variable type can now store any sort of data.

Integer and Long

In Visual Basic 6, the numeric data type `Integer` stores a 16-bit value, while the `Long` type stores 32-bit values. To provide support for larger numbers, VB .NET represents an `Integer` as a 32-bit value and the `Long` represents a 64-bit value. A new variable type, `Short`, represents 16-bit values.

Currency

In Visual Basic 6, the `Currency` data type stores a 64-bit number in integer format, but inserts a decimal point in the value at the fourth position. Also in VB 6, although you cannot declare a variable of type `Decimal`, the `Variant` type supports a `Decimal` type, which stores a 96-bit integer value with a moving decimal point.

Visual Basic .NET abandons the `Currency` type in favor of using only the `Decimal` data type. `Decimal` offers more accuracy and the CLR supports `Decimal` directly.

Date

In Visual Basic 6, the `Date` type stores as a `Double` floating-point variable that can manipulate dates. VB 6 lets you manipulate a variable of type `Date` as a `Double`.

Visual Basic .NET stores the `Date` type as a 64-bit integer, which improves speed of operations. But the new method of storing dates breaks the compatibility of working with `Date` variables as `Double` data types. The .NET Framework provides `ToOADate` and `FromOADate` methods to convert a date to and from a `Double` variable type.

Fixed-Length Strings

In Visual Basic 6, you can declare variables as a fixed length string by specifying the `String` type followed by a multiplication sign (*) and a length.

The Common Language Runtime (CLR) for Visual Basic .NET does not support fixed-length strings. A compatibility class enables you to create fixed length strings. You call the compatibility class `FixedLengthString` and you find it in the `Visual Basic.Compatibility` namespace.

Type

The `Type` statement in VB 6 declares a user-defined type.

Visual Basic .NET does not support the `Type` statement; instead, you use the `Structure` statement. You can learn about structures in Chapter 7.

Empty

Variants in Visual Basic 6 initialize to `Empty`, which automatically converts to zero when you use them in a numeric expression, or to an empty string when you use them in a string expression.

Visual Basic .NET initializes Object variables to `Nothing`, which also automatically converts to zero or an empty string, if necessary.

Null and Null Propagation

In Visual Basic 6, `Null` values are a subtype of the `Variant` variable, indicating that a variable contains no valid data. Also, in VB 6, if any part of an expression evaluates to `Null`, the `Null` value "propagates" through the expression and the entire expression becomes `Null`.

Visual Basic .NET does not support `Null` propagation and only supports `Null` variables as a variable type for ADO.NET. The CLR converts Variants containing `Null` values into a variable type `DBNull`. You can use the `IsDBNull` function to test for the type. No longer, in an expression involving string data, does an `Object` return `Null`, instead it returns an empty string value.

Local Variable Scope

In Visual Basic 6, you can use a variable from the line containing the declaration through to the end of the procedure.

Visual Basic .NET uses block scope for variables. This means you can access a local variable from the line containing the declaration to the end of the block in which it appears. So if you declare a variable inside a `Do Loop` block, you cannot access the variable when the loop ends.

Arrays

VB 6 allows you to define arrays with any lower and upper bounds. You can define the default lower bound in VB 6 using the `Option Base` statement.

In VB .NET, all arrays are zero-based; this means the first index of the array is always zero. You cannot set the lower bound of the array. For more information on declaring and using arrays, see Chapter 4.

ReDim

Visual Basic 6.0 distinguishes between fixed size and dynamic arrays. You declare fixed size arrays using the `Dim` statement; you define dynamic arrays using `Dim` with no bounds, and then size the array with `ReDim`.

In Visual Basic .NET, all arrays are dynamic, meaning you always use `Dim` to declare the initial array size and can change the size of the array later. This can cause upgraded VB 6 code to redundantly initialize the array twice.

Assignment

In Visual Basic 6, the `Set` statement assigns an object reference to a variable name. In VB .NET, because all variables are objects, the language only supports one form of assignment, the equal sign.

Calling Procedures

VB 6 provides two forms of procedure calls: using the `Call` statement, which requires you to enclose the arguments in parenthesis, and simply typing the name of the procedure without parentheses.

Visual Basic .NET requires parentheses for either method to improve conformity. Also, the default parameter passing method changes from `ByRef` in VB 6 to `ByVal` in Visual Basic .NET. This can create subtle bugs, so make sure you add `ByRef` keywords back where necessary when upgrading.

USING THE UPGRADE WIZARD

You can use the Project Upgrade Wizard to automatically convert Visual Basic 6.0 projects into fully native Visual Basic .NET applications. Because of the number of changes that VB .NET makes in the core language, Microsoft provides an upgrade wizard to assist in the porting of applications.

To invoke the Upgrade Wizard, open a Visual Basic 6 project using the standard Open Project dialog. The Upgrade Wizard takes a project, creates a new .NET project directory, and converts all of the files present in the project to new files that support Visual Basic .NET. The wizard does not change or overwrite the existing files in any way.

The Upgrade Wizard contains five steps. The first step provides a summary of the actions the wizard completes. Step 2 checks the project type of the Visual Basic 6 project and attempts to provide a match in the .NET Framework. The two options are EXE and DLL/custom control library.

The wizard should determine the appropriate type automatically. The wizard also provides a check box if you want to generate default interfaces for public classes. If your project provides a number of public COM objects, you should select this box. You can then select the directory to create the new VB .NET project and perform the conversion.

When the conversion completes, the VB .NET project opens. The Upgrade Wizard creates a file called _UpgradeReport.htm that contains upgrade issues for the various modules in the project. This report alerts you to sections of code that it can not convert or that need special attention. See the previous section, "Language Changes from Visual Basic 6" for a list of important changes that occur when you convert from Visual Basic 6 to Visual Basic .NET. In most cases, your project runs after the conversion, and you can test functionality to see if any problems appeared during the conversion.

USING THE UPGRADE WIZARD

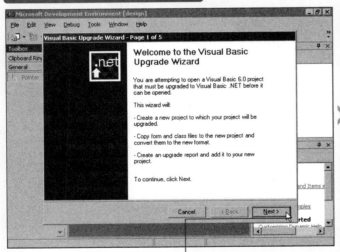

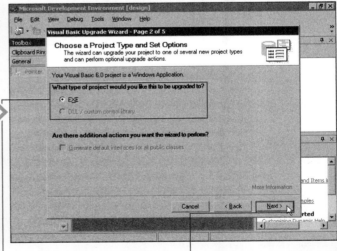

1 Open a VB 6 project file.

■ The Visual Basic Upgrade Wizard appears.

2 Click Next to skip the first screen of the wizard.

3 Verify that the wizard chose the appropriate application type in step 2.

4 Click Next.

Extra

To provide the compatibility functions, the .NET Framework includes the `Microsoft.VisualBasic.Compability` namespace when using the Upgrade Wizard. This namespace includes functions that exist in the Visual Basic 6 language. The .NET Framework duplicates much of the functions built into Visual Basic 6, making many functions in the language unnecessary. To make the upgrade process as simple as possible, these functions provide the same interfaces as VB 6 functions while remaining compliant with .NET managed code. For example, VB .NET does not include the ability to create control arrays. So for VB 6 projects to upgrade successfully, the compatibility library includes control arrays for each of the basic controls in the language. VB .NET also removes controls like the `FileListBox` and `DriveListBox` completely. The compatibility library provides these controls for use with upgraded projects. A number of removed functions like `SendKeys` also exist within this namespace.

You can use Visual Basic 6 to continue maintaining existing applications instead of upgrading. Both Visual Basic 6 and Visual Basic .NET can coexist on a single system. If you maintain a very large product that functions well in VB 6, you may want to leave your application in VB 6. You may find the upgrade process difficult due to the number of fundamental changes in the language.

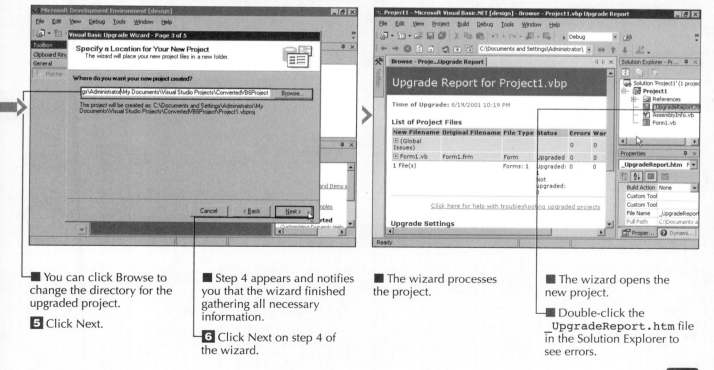

■ You can click Browse to change the directory for the upgraded project.

5 Click Next.

■ Step 4 appears and notifies you that the wizard finished gathering all necessary information.

6 Click Next on step 4 of the wizard.

■ The wizard processes the project.

■ The wizard opens the new project.

■ Double-click the `_UpgradeReport.htm` file in the Solution Explorer to see errors.

CREATE A PROJECT

A project contains one individual application or component. You must use a project to specify the files that make up your application, such as forms and classes. You place a project in VB .NET inside a solution. Even if the solution only holds a single project, you must have it present. When you create a new project, VB .NET creates the solution automatically.

When you create a new project in the Development Environment, it provides you with a dialog box where you select the type of application you want. On the left side of the dialog box, entries for the various programming languages and other project types appear. On the right side, the dialog lists the individual project templates. In this book, you focus mostly on the Windows Application, console application, and ASP.NET Web Application project types. A Windows Application uses Windows Forms to develop a graphical Windows application. The console

application generates a text-based Windows application, where you can attempt programming concepts without setting up and modifying Windows Forms controls. The ASP.NET Web application generates a Web Forms application.

The New Project dialog also asks where you want to store the project. VB .NET stores each project in its own folder to avoid naming problems. The name you give to the project functions as the name of the files VB .NET creates for the project. When you create the project, the components of the project load into the Solution Explorer. This is the main console to access the parts of your application. If you create a Windows Application project, you see a project with a single class called `Form1`, which is the main form of the application. A Console Application project creates a module file where you place code.

CREATE A PROJECT

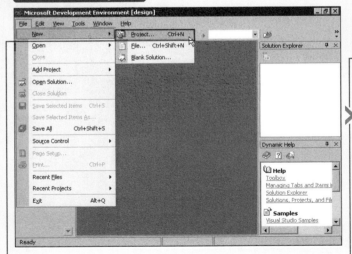

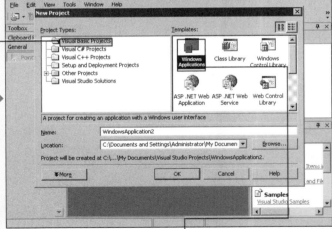

1 Open the Development Environment.

Note: See "Using the Development Studio" for more information.

2 Click File ➪ New ➪ Project.

■ If you have the Start Page open, you can click the New Project button. See the section "Using the Development Studio" for more on the Start Page.

■ The New Project dialog appears.

3 Click Visual Basic Projects from the Project Types.

4 Click the appropriate project template.

Extra

Each project in Visual Basic .NET has a file `AssemblyInfo.vb` and makes up a single *assembly*, the term the .NET Framework assigns to a single component in the system. You can use this file to define properties and information, which the compiler includes in your project. The file starts with an empty template and sets the various properties, which you can define for your assembly, to blank values. You can enter standard textual information for these properties, which include `AssemblyTitle`, `AssemblyDescription`, `AssemblyCompany`, `AssemblyProduct`, and others. The file also includes a GUID to make the project COM compatible and the version number of the project. The file is a .VB file you can open in the source editor by double-clicking its name in the Solution Explorer.

Example:
```
Imports System.Reflection
Imports System.Runtime.InteropServices

<Assembly: AssemblyTitle("Product.NET Main Application")>
<Assembly: AssemblyDescription("Main interface of the
    product.")>
<Assembly: AssemblyCompany("NETCompany")>
<Assembly: AssemblyProduct("Product.NET")>
<Assembly: AssemblyCopyright("(c) NET Company 2001")>
<Assembly: AssemblyTrademark("")>
<Assembly: CLSCompliant(True)>
<Assembly: Guid("F7DE8FE1-4F26-4D20-B60E-36D6C604C36C")>
<Assembly: AssemblyVersion("1.0.*")>
```

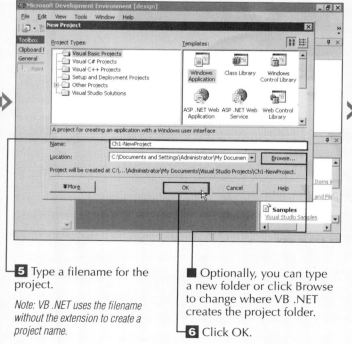

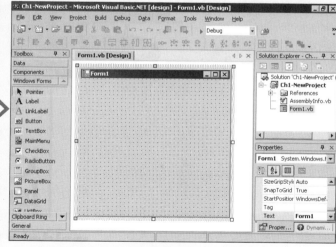

5 Type a filename for the project.

Note: VB .NET uses the filename without the extension to create a project name.

■ Optionally, you can type a new folder or click Browse to change where VB .NET creates the project folder.

6 Click OK.

■ VB .NET creates the project and opens its default resource.

WORK WITH PROJECT FILES

VB .NET provides a property page, which enables you to edit the properties of the project in the Solution Explorer.

A project file contains references to the other files inside your project. VB stores a variety of settings inside the project file. You can use the Development Environment to create a project, save it, and load it later through the use of your project file.

You must save your project files when you stop working, or when you make changes that cause you to update the files on your disk. The project saves the state of the Development Environment, and all of the files that make up the project. You can open a previously created project file at any time. If you open a project file while you have a solution with a different project loading into the Development Environment, the Open Project dialog presents you with two choices to open the project. The first option, Add to Solution, adds the

project you open into the current solution, creating a multi-project solution. The second choice, Close Solution, closes the previous solution, and opens the project in its own solution.

VB .NET provides a property page in the Solution Explorer, which enables you to edit the properties of the project. In the Common Properties section of the Property Page dialog box, the general subsection specifies the name of the assembly. It also provides the output type for the project, which provides options to alter the type of application the project generates. You can choose your startup object on this dialog and alter the root namespace. For more information on startup objects using Windows Forms, see Chapter 2. The Imports subsection enables you to define the various namespaces that globally import into your project. For more information on namespaces and the root namespace, see Chapter 8.

WORK WITH PROJECTS

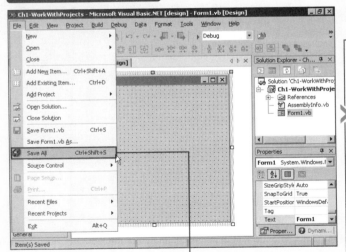

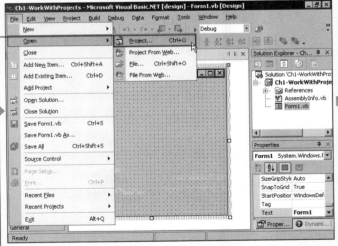

SAVE A PROJECT

1 Create a new project in the Development Studio.

Note: See "Create a Project" for more information.

2 Click File ➪ Save All to save the currently open project.

■ Alternately, you can press Ctrl+Shift+S to save your project.

OPEN A NEW PROJECT

3 Click File ➪ Open ➪ Project.

■ You can also press Ctrl+O to open a project.

Extra

You can right-click the Solution item in the Solution Explorer and click Properites. This opens the Project Property page, where you can set the various projects in your solution launch. You can use the ordering selection in the property page to ensure a component builds before the main application..

When you open a project, you can add it to the current solution via the radio buttons located beside the Open button of the Open Project dialog box. When you have multiple projects inside the same solution, each project still functions as its own project, creating a necessary EXE or DLL file. But if you have two applications that work together, and you want to develop both of them concurrently, you can easily manage them by adding them to the same solution. You can open multiple copies of the Development Studio to work with the different projects. The solution file maintains settings to start both applications, start just one of them, or start them in a particular order. You can right-click the Solution item in the Solution Explorer and click Properites. This opens the Project Property page, where you can set the various projects in your solution launch. You can use the ordering selection in the property page to ensure a component builds before the main application. You can load a Component project and a Windows Application project at the same time, and tell the environment to load the component first, followed by the application.

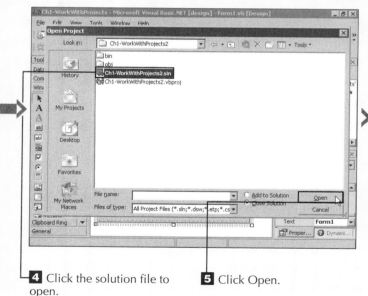

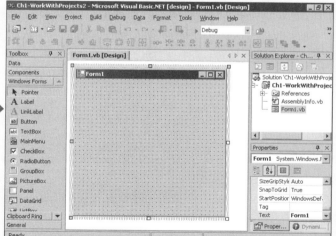

4 Click the solution file to open.

5 Click Open.

■ The Development Environment opens the project, closing other projects if necessary. The Solution Explorer reflects the change.

BUILD AND RUN A PROJECT

Because VB .NET creates EXE and DLL files, to test your work, VB must first build the created code and forms into a single file that your computer can run. In the case of Visual Basic, your computer can only understand the executable code you create with the assistance of the Common Language Runtime (CLR). The CLR provides the ability to work with the classes and other parts of your application and to interface with the .NET class frameworks. For more on the CLR, see the section "Understanding the Framework."

When VB builds code, the compiler creates code in the form of Microsoft Intermediate Language (MSIL). MSIL is a compiled format similar to traditional assembly code. It contains low-level instructions that move data in and out of registers, but it contains no dependencies on any particular operating system or hardware platform. The dependence on the CLR allows an EXE or DLL containing MSIL to deploy

on any target computer that supports the CLR. The CLR for the platform performs a final round of just-in-time (JIT) compilation to transform it into machine-specific assembly instructions.

When you build a project, VB .NET opens the Output tool window in the Development Environment. This window holds the text the compiler returns from the operation. If build errors occur, another tool window, called the Task List, appears with a list of errors the compiler finds. You can access an error and have the code editor load the appropriate line. You can then correct the error and build the project again. For more information on debugging projects, see Chapter 13.

At this point, you can start the project. If you invoke the start command with a project that you have not built since you made changes, the start command builds the project for you.

BUILD AND RUN A PROJECT

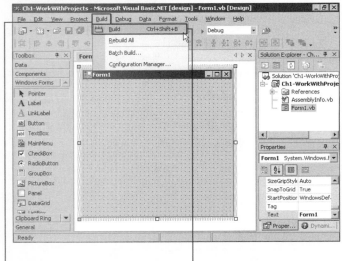

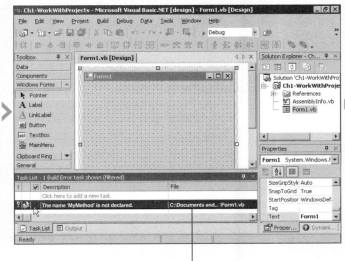

BUILD THE PROJECT

1 Click Build.

2 Click Build.

■ Alternately, you can access the build menu item by pressing Ctrl+Shift+B.

■ VB builds the project where the Output window shows the progress.

■ The Task window appears when the build completes and if errors exist.

■ You can double-click an error in the list to have the error appear in the code window.

Note: See Chapter 13 to correct errors.

Extra

You can receive a number of common errors when you work with the Visual Basic language. You can use the following list to decipher the meaning of some of these errors. For more help with error messages, press F1 with an error selected in the Task window.

ERROR MESSAGE	HOW TO CORRECT
The name 'x' is not declared.	The compiler cannot locate the variable or method name. Ensure that you declare the variable in question at the appropriate scope for the line of code to access it. Commonly, this error message displays because of a spelling error.
Expected an expression.	A line did not end appropriately. In some cases, this can cause a multitude of errors as VB .NET tries to find the end of line. Make sure open and close parentheses match and that you do not have an underscore on the last line of a multi-line command.
A value of type 'x' cannot be converted to 'x'	You assign a value to a variable that cannot accept it. This occurs often if you try to assign information to a control, for example, when you assign a string to a `Label` or `TextBox` control without specifying the Text property.

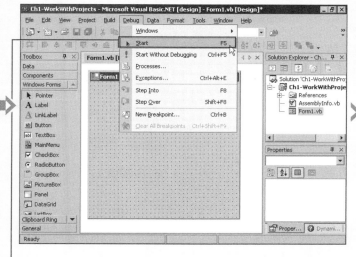

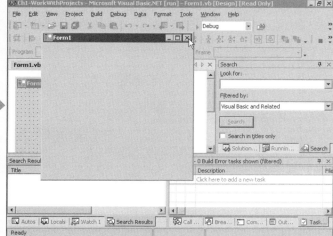

RUN A PROJECT

3 Click Debug ➪ Start.

■ Alternately, you can press F5 to access the Start function.

■ The project starts under the control of the .NET debugger.

■ Any run-time errors cause the debugger to stop execution of the program and to display an error message.

CREATE A WINDOWS APPLICATION

Windows Forms technology allows you to provide a powerful and unique visual interface. You can create world class Windows applications, which look and perform like other Windows applications, inside a powerful and easy-to-use graphical development environment.

Visual Basic .NET uses a project to store each individual application or component. To create a standard Windows application, you utilize the Windows Application project type. Your project holds all of the forms, classes, modules, and controls you create and makes them part of the application. For more information on the purpose of a project, see Chapter 1.

When you create a Windows Application project, VB .NET provides the main form for your application and gives it the name Form1. This form automatically loads when your application starts. To create new forms, and have the option to make them the default form for your application, see the section "Add a New Form."

The Development Environment provides a built-in visual form designer. This form designer enables you to change the properties of the form in the Property Window and use drag and drop to place components. For more information on where to find the Property Window or how to use the Development Environment, see page Chapter 1.

A Form is the main display element for a stand-alone application. You can create any window that you use on your computer in VB .NET using Form dialog boxes, toolbar windows, and main application windows. The section "An Introduction to Window Forms" includes a more detailed introduction to the abilities of a form.

CREATE A WINDOWS APPLICATION

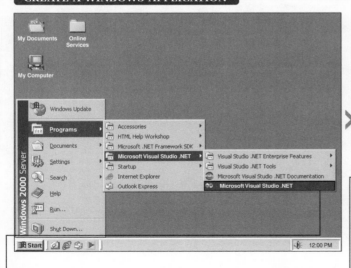

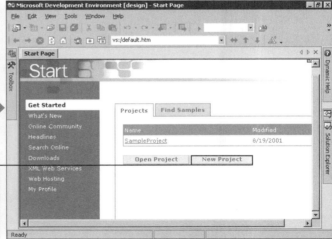

1 Click Start ➪ Program ➪ Microsoft Visual Studio .NET ➪ Microsoft Visual .NET to start the Visual Basic Development Environment.

■ To learn how to use the Development Environment, see Chapter 1.

■ The Start Page appears.

2 Click New Project.

■ If the Start Page does not appear when you load the Development Environment, you can create a new project by going to Help ➪ Show Start Page.

Extra

Many of the tasks in this chapter expect you to use the Property Window to make changes to the forms and controls. In some cases, you may find this window difficult to find with the large number of tool windows present at any time on the screen. You can access the Properties window by clicking the View menu and selecting Properties window from the menu or by pressing the F4 key.

You can use the Class View window to receive a representation of forms and other classes in your project instead of using the Solution Explorer window. The Class View window enables you to see the members, such as properties, methods, and events that make up all of the classes in the project, and jump directly to specific areas of code inside a module. By right-clicking a class inside the window, you can change view and sort options. For example, the Group by Type option enables you to show the members that make up the class in separate trees, splitting off private variables and public members. To show this window, go to the View menu and click Class View.

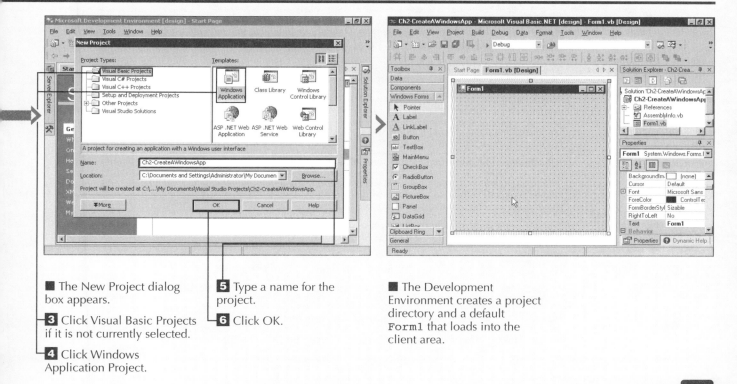

■ The New Project dialog box appears.

3 Click Visual Basic Projects if it is not currently selected.

4 Click Windows Application Project.

5 Type a name for the project.

6 Click OK.

■ The Development Environment creates a project directory and a default `Form1` that loads into the client area.

AN INTRODUCTION TO WINDOWS FORMS

You can use Windows Forms, a large technology encompassing a huge set of tools, to build powerful Windows applications quickly and easily. In this chapter, topics cover creating forms, manipulating forms, and adding controls to those forms.

To understand the capabilities of a form, see the summary of important Form members given below. A member refers to any part of a component in VB .NET available for your manipulation or viewing. Forms, controls, and classes all have a set of members such as properties, methods, and events that give them their ability to perform certain tasks. For more information on object-oriented terms, see Chapter 7.

A Form provides the backdrop where all of your application's abilities are accessible. Controls provide the functionality on the form, enabling the user to view, edit, manipulate, and explore your application. A control is anything that you place onto a form, like a button, or a list box, or a check box. To learn how to add controls to your form, see the "Add a Control" section.

The tables below do not include all of the abilities of a form, but touch on some of the abilities that you may find interesting or useful. Many members that are shown here are covered more fully throughout the chapter. For more information on setting a form's properties, see the section "Set a Property." For more information on responding to a form's events, see the section "Add an Event."

IMPORTANT FORM MEMBERS

PROPERTIES	DESCRIPTION
AcceptButton	Set this property to a Button control that automatically activates when the user presses Enter. The AcceptButton only activates If the current control uses the Enter key, like a multi-line text box, the current control uses the key press and the button does not receive the Click event.
AutoScale	Makes the form and its controls automatically resize to fit user font-size preferences. You may want to change this to False for proprietary interfaces not using standard controls.
AutoScroll	When True, AutoScroll adds scrollbars to the form when all of its constituent controls do not fit.
BackgroundImage	Loads an image into the form's background. The image tiles across the entire form. Supports a large number of formats, including BMP, GIF, JPEG, PNG, WMF, and others.
CancelButton	See the description of AcceptButton above, except CancelButton functions on the Esc key.
FormBorderStyle	Sets the border of the window. The default setting is Sized, which allows resizing. You use the FixedDialog setting to create a fixed window that looks like a dialog box. Fixed3D creates a fixed window with a sunken client area.
Location	This property determines the position of the window on the Desktop. Windows automatically corrects it depending on the position of the Taskbar. You need to set StartPosition to **Manual** for Location to work.
MaximizeBox	Determines whether the form displays a maximize button in the title bar.
MaximumSize	A Point object specifying the maximum width and height the form reaches. Beware: This is also in effect when you maximize the form.
Menu	Determines which MainMenu control actually provides the menu interface for the window.
MinimizeBox	Determines whether the form displays a minimize button in the title bar.

IMPORTANT FORM MEMBERS (CONT.)

PROPERTIES	DESCRIPTION
MinimumSize	A `Point` object specifying the minimum width and height the form reaches.
Opacity	The percentage of opacity the form has. For example, a 25% opacity level means the form blends a quarter of its contents with three-quarters of the underlying contents, making the form nearly invisible.
OwnedForms	A collection listing all of the forms this form owns.
Modal	Specifies if this form is modal. The property is read-only. You can use this to determine whether this form was invoked as a dialog box.
SizeGripStyle	Determines whether a sizing grip displays in the lower-right corner of the window. The default value is `Auto`. Available options are `Show` and `Hide`.
StartPosition	You use this to assist in placement of the form upon display. Default value is `WindowsDefaultLocation`. Options include `CenterScreen`, `CenterParent`, `Manual`, and `WindowsDefaultBounds`.
TopMost	Determines whether this form shows above all other forms in the application. Default is `False`.

METHODS	DESCRIPTION
Activate	Moves the form to the front of the application and makes it active.
Close	Hides the form.
DoDragDrop	Begins a drag and drop operation.
Show	Makes the form visible.
ShowDialog	Makes the form appear modally.
Update	Forces client area to redraw.

EVENTS	DESCRIPTION
Closed	Fires when the user closes the form or the `Close` method is called.
Closing	Fires as the user presses `Close` and allows the window to cancel the operation before the actual `Closed` event is called.
MouseEnter	Fires when the mouse enters the client area from outside.
MouseHover	Fires when the mouse is stationary for two seconds.
MouseLeave	Fires when the mouse leaves the client area.
MouseMove	Fires as the mouse moves around inside the client area.

ADD A CONTROL TO A FORM

You can use controls to provide the basic user interface to your program. A control is a special component designed to provide a visual interface on Windows Forms.

Standard controls you may see in applications include buttons, menus, toolbars, check boxes, radio buttons, and text boxes. You may not realize that the text on the form is actually a `Label` control, or the frame around a group of radio buttons is actually a `GroupBox` control. Many controls only provide layout and visual cues. See Chapter 3 for more information on these controls.

If the control is a hidden component and does not need form real estate, like the `Timer`, `MainMenu`, or `ErrorProvider` control, it loads into an area provided inside the form designer called the Component Tray. All of your hidden components appear here. You can still click them to edit their properties.

When you add a control to the form, it becomes selected automatically, and if you open the Property Window, the properties are shown for the selected control. For more information about modifying properties, see the section "Set a Property."

The controls that VB .NET provides are not the only controls you may use. The CD-ROM included with this book contains a variety of trial versions of components that you can add into your applications seamlessly. For more information on loading new components into your project and building your own controls, see Chapter 12.

You do not need to use controls to provide an interface. For example, in a game, you might choose to paint on the entire surface of the form, and therefore provide your own custom controls in the interface. See Chapter 5 for more information regarding graphics commands.

ADD A CONTROL TO A FORM

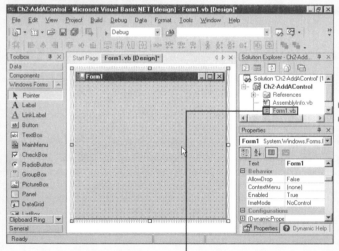

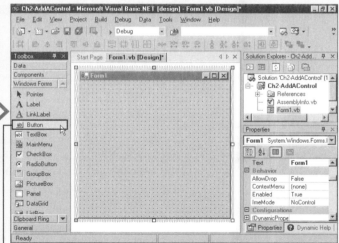

1 Create a new Windows Application project or open an existing one.

Note: For more information on creating a project, see the section "Create a Windows Application."

2 Double-click the form in the Solution Explorer to open it if necessary.

3 Click any control from the Toolbox.

Note: If you do not have the Toolbox opened, click View ⇨ Toolbox.

Apply It

Certain controls have the ability to contain other controls and are called *container controls*. Controls like `Panel`, `GroupBox`, and `TabControl` can all hold other controls inside their client space. Hidden components such as `Timer`, `MainMenu`, `ContentMenu`, and the common dialog box components do not load onto the form as an icon, as they did in previous versions of Visual Basic. Instead, they load into an area at the bottom of the Form Designer called the Component Tray. Clicking these entries enables you to edit their properties just like any other control.

You can create controls in code dynamically at runtime. This process is simple, and is actually the same process the IDE uses to create the controls you define in the Form Designer. Add this code to create a new list box control when a user clicks a button.

TYPE THIS:

```
Private Sub Button1_Click(ByVal sender As System.Object,_
    ByVal e As System.EventArgs) Handles Button1. Click
    Dim NewListBox As New ListBox()
    ' Define Left, Top
    NewListBox.Location = New Point(50, 50)
    ' Define Width, Height
    NewListBox.Size = New Size(200, 300)
    ' Edit the control before it becomes visible
    NewListBox.Items.Add("Sample item")

    Me.Controls.Add(NewListBox)
End Sub
```

RESULT:

When the button is pressed, a new list box is added to the form.

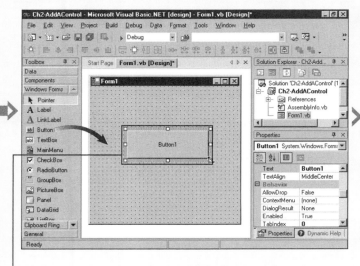

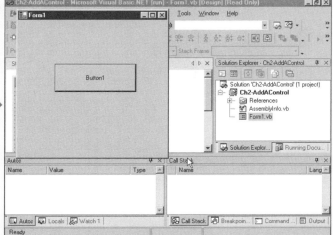

4 Add the control onto the form by clicking and holding the mouse button where you want the top-left corner to begin.

5 Release the mouse button at the bottom-right corner when you have achieved the proper size.

6 Press F5 to run your project.

■ The new control appears on the form.

SET A PROPERTY

P roperties provide the basis of a component's functionality, be it a form, dialog box, or control. You use properties to make a component look and function in a certain way. A property is actually an object-oriented programming (OOP) term: properties are used to describe a particular object.

For example, the most common property for visual components is the `Text` property. Earlier versions of Visual Basic had two separate properties, `Caption` and `Text`; `Caption` has been removed for standardization. By altering the `Text` property, you can change the *description* of the component. In the `Text` property of most controls, you can add an ampersand (&) before a particular letter to make the following letter function as the accessibility key for the control. For example, if the text of a control consists of Na&me, it appears as Name with an underscore under the letter *m*, and allows the user to press Alt+M to access the control.

You can alter a form or control's properties with two different methods. You can alter properties in code, or in the Forms

Designer using the Property Editor. When you alter properties in the Property Editor, the IDE automatically adds the code for the change you make into the `InitializeComponents` subroutine, which the form's `New` method calls. To learn more about `New` methods, see Chapter 7.

The Property Window splits properties into various categories. You can collapse these categories if you do not often use them. The first category, Accessibility, contains properties to make your program accessible to the handicapped, and you can learn more about it in Chapter 13.

Appearance contains properties such as `BackColor`, which changes the background color of the component. `Font` changes the default font the component uses to draw. You can use unique properties like `BackgroundImage` to load a picture into a form's background. For an introduction to the multitude of properties for a form, see the section "Introducing Windows Forms."

SET A PROPERTY

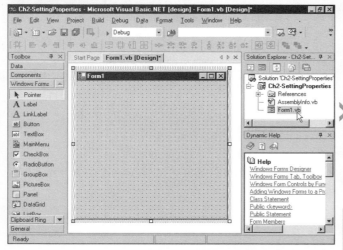

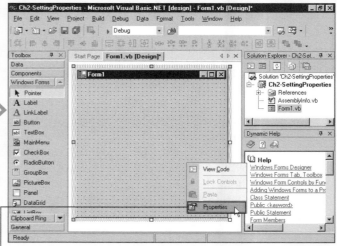

1 Create a new Windows Application Project or open an existing one.

2 Right-click the form or a control on the form and click Properties.

■ You can also press F4 to access the Property window.

Extra

Although not truly a property, one item listed out of convenience in the Visual Basic Property Editor is `Name`, which allows you to set the name of the component for the purpose of accessing the component in code without being forced to use assigned names like `Button1` or `Form1`. You cannot access `Name` from code.

A common notation to use when naming controls and variables is called Hungarian notation. This involves placing a three-character identifier in front of the descriptive name. For example, you might call a button that reads Cancel **btnCancel**. This enables you to easily read your code and see the type of component to which any given name refers.

By expanding the Windows Forms Designer Generated Code section, you can see how the IDE generates the components, properties, and so on. Be careful not to change this code, or the Form Designer may no longer function as expected.

You can select whether to display the properties in categories or alphabetically. The default is categorically in VB .NET. To do this, click the tool button on the properties window that has an A-Z with a downward arrow on it. Pressing the button adjacent to it changes the display order back to categorical.

Example:
```
Public Class Form1
    Inherits System.Windows.Forms.Form
+   Windows Forms Designer Generated Code
...
End Class
```

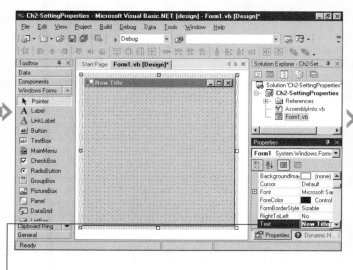

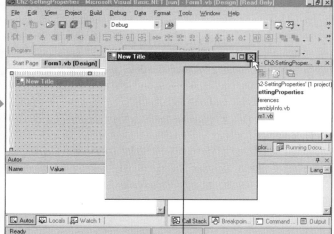

■ The Property window appears below the Solution Explorer.

3 Edit a property by clicking the property name in the Properties window.

4 Type or select the appropriate value and press Enter or click somewhere out of the edit area to save the change.

5 Press F5 to run your project.

■ VB .NET shows the form with any property changes you have made.

■ You can click the form's Close button (☒) to return to the IDE.

WRITE EVENT CODE

Y ou use event code to provide interaction between the software and the user. Properties provide the base of a form's ability. Events finalize this base by allowing components to interact. For example, if the user presses a key, Visual Basic .NET *fires* one or more events that a form, control, or class can capture and respond. Without events, your user sees a complete application with forms, controls, properties, and methods, but nothing can interact with the user.

The Code Editor provides a list of the available components on the form in the Class Name drop-down list located on the left side of the code window toolbar. To create an event handler for the form itself, select *(Base Class Events)*. The form also lists an Overrides section that you can use to override members of the form. For more information on overriding, see Chapter 8.

To provide an event handler for a control, you select the actual control name from the Class Name list. Upon selecting a control or the form's base class events, you can select from the full listing of possible events available to the form or control in the Event List drop-down list, located on the right side of the Code Editor toolbar.

Selecting an event from the list in the Code Editor causes the Visual Basic .NET IDE to create a procedure to hold your event code. Of the two arguments passed to an event procedure, the first is `sender`, which in most cases is the object where the event is defined. The second argument, far more useful, named `e`, contains all of the actual event information. For example, in a `Paint` event, which occurs when the form needs to redraw itself, `e` contains references to the `Graphics` object of the form, which is necessary to call graphics commands.

WRITE EVENT CODE

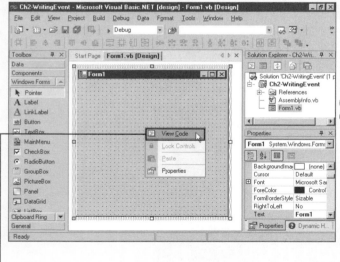

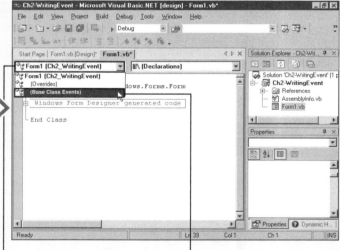

1 Open an existing form.

2 Right-click the form and click View Code.

■ You can also open the Code Editor by simply double clicking the form.

3 Click the class list.

4 Click (Base Class Events) to list form events.

■ Alternately, you can click a control's name to list that control's events.

Extra

The type of events you use can create more or less interaction, depending on what is necessary for your application. Small but useful interactions can include changing labels or colors in the control as the user moves their mouse around. Most visual controls provide MouseEnter, MouseLeave, and MouseHover events. These events fire when the mouse enters the control, leaves the control, and stays on top of the control for a few moments, respectively.

Not all events are in response to user interaction. All visual controls and the form itself have a Paint event. In this event, you provide code to draw directly onto the surface of the control. For example, you can draw a pattern in the background of a button. This event triggers anytime all or part of the control or form invalidates. Invalidation is when some part of the control or form needs to redraw. You can force a control or form to invalidate by using the Invalidate method of the component.

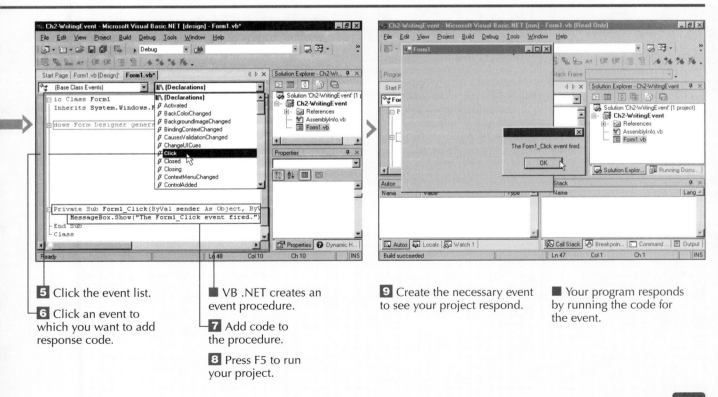

5 Click the event list.

6 Click an event to which you want to add response code.

■ VB .NET creates an event procedure.

7 Add code to the procedure.

8 Press F5 to run your project.

9 Create the necessary event to see your project respond.

■ Your program responds by running the code for the event.

RESIZE CONTROLS

You can give the main application window and dialog boxes the ability to change sizes based on a user's preference. In previous versions of Visual Basic, this involved writing a long and sometimes complex resize event handler. Now, however, each component in VB .NET provides properties to resize without requiring any code.

Each control contains two properties for resizing: Anchor and Dock. Anchor lets you select sides of the control you want to *anchor* to container borders. The Left and Top anchors hold the control at exactly the same relative location from the left or top of the form. The Right and Bottom anchors hold that side of the control to the same position relative to the right or bottom of the container.

For example, if you set the Anchor for a control to Left, Right, the control holds to the left side and stretch

proportionately out in the right directions when you resize the form. The top and bottom of the control, not anchored, move up and down as you resize the form to maintain a proportionate amount of space to both the top and bottom sides of the container.

The Dock control lets you *dock* a control to the left, right, top, or bottom edge of the form. For example, if you dock a control to the top of screen, the control maintains the assigned height, but automatically moves to the top of the screen and spreads the width of its container. You can also set Dock to Fill, and the control fills the entire client area.

The container form or control has a property DockPadding that lets you set the amount of space left around a docked control in each direction. By default, a control is added to the form with Anchor set to Left, Top.

RESIZE CONTROLS

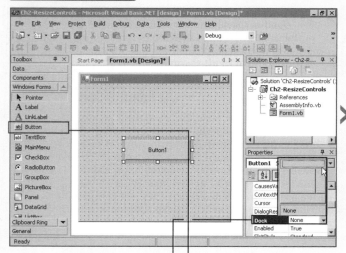
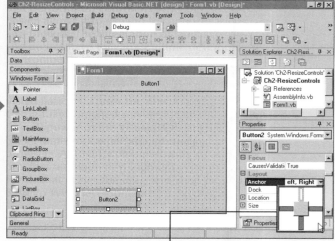

DOCK THE CONTROL

1 Create a new Windows Application project or open an existing one.

2 Open the form that you want a user to resize.

3 Add a control anywhere on the form.

■ The example uses button controls.

4 Change the control's Dock property.

Note: See the section "Add a Control to a Form" to add a control and "Set a Property" to edit a property.

■ In the example, Dock is set to Top. The control positions itself at the selected border.

ANCHOR THE CONTROL

5 Change the control's Anchor property.

■ In the example, another button was added with the Anchor property set to Bottom, Left, Right.

Extra

While automatic resizing using `Anchor` and `Dock` is very powerful, you may find that this does not meet your needs for a complex or custom-designed form. In this case, VB .NET provides a more sophisticated system. You can resize all of your controls by hand by using the `Resize` event. This event is called whenever you resize, maximize, minimize, or restore the form. Simply use the form's dimensions, which you can retrieve using the `Size.Width` and `Size.Height` members of the form. Then move and resize the controls accordingly. You can move a control by editing its `Location.Left` or `Location.Top` properties, or reassigning the entire `Point` structure by using `Location = New Point(Left, Top)`. Utilize `Size.Width` and `Size.Height` to resize the control, or use a `Size` structure like `Size = New Size(Width, Height)`. You can also use the manual resize event for some controls, and `Anchor` and `Dock` for others. Be careful when a user minimizes the form, or happens to make the form very small, because your calculated values may create negative values for width and heights and cause your program to have a run-time error.

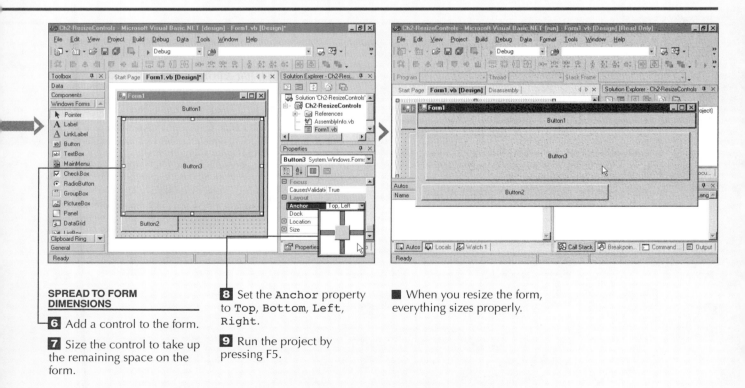

SPREAD TO FORM DIMENSIONS

6 Add a control to the form.

7 Size the control to take up the remaining space on the form.

8 Set the `Anchor` property to `Top`, `Bottom`, `Left`, `Right`.

9 Run the project by pressing F5.

■ When you resize the form, everything sizes properly.

ADD A MENU

You can use menus to provide a convenient way to access the main functionality of the form. Menu bars are a standard part of most Windows applications.

Simple utilities may not need them, but on the whole, menus provide an easy way for a user to learn and access the various functions in a hierarchical matter. Also, menus allow users to progress in a freely chosen order, rather than an order provided by other interfaces such as buttons or lists.

Visual Basic .NET adds simplicity to creating menus. Visual Basic 6.0 and earlier relied on an external dialog box called the Menu Editor. VB .NET integrates menu editing with the Windows Form Designer.

To create a menu, you access the Toolbox and select the `MainMenu` control, which adds a hidden `MainMenu` control

in the Component Tray, and adds a menu bar with a single empty menu title. You can add a caption to replace the placeholder menu title to create a menu title and an empty submenu. You can quickly create an entire menu system using this method.

You can assign access keys to menu items by placing an ampersand before the letter to use as the shortcut. For example, to make a file menu that a user can access by pressing Alt-F, set the `Text` to `&File`.

You can assign shortcuts to controls using the `Shortcut` property. You set the `ShowShortcut` property to `True` if you want to have the shortcut appear to the right of the menu item.

ADD A MENU

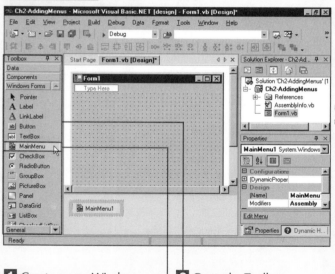

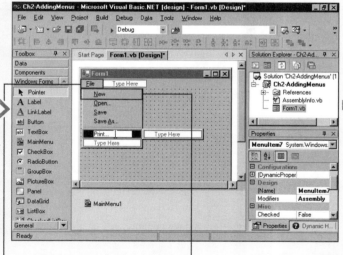

1 Create a new Windows Application project or open an existing one.

2 Open the Toolbox.

Note: If you do not have the Toolbox opened, click View ⇨ Toolbox.

3 Double-click the `MainMenu` control.

■ The `MainMenu` control appears in the Component Tray.

4 Click the first menu title item.

5 Type a title.

6 Press Enter to save it.

7 Add to the menu by typing items downwards.

■ You can type a dash to create a divider, or right-click the edit area and then click Insert Separator.

Extra

Each menu item has a number of properties you can individually modify. `MenuItem1.Visible = False` hides a menu item. `MenuItem1.Enabled = False` grays out menu items. You use these properties to dynamically change the menu based on the current state of the application. For example, for a File menu with the items New, Open, and Save, you can disable the Save item when your application has no changes by adding code to the File menu item's `Click` event.

You can create menu items dynamically in code as the program runs, by creating a new menu item using `Dim`, setting its properties, and then adding it to the parent menu of your choice.

Examples:
Example of dynamic menu changes:

```
Private changes As Boolean = False
Private Sub MenuItem1_Click(ByVal sender As _
    System.Object, ByVal e As _
    System.EventArgs) Handles MenuItem1.Click

    If changes Then
        FileSaveMenuItem.Enabled = True
    Else
        FileSaveMenuItem.Enabled = False
    End If
End Sub
```

Example of creating menu items dynamically:

```
Dim NewMenuItem As New MenuItem()
NewMenuItem.Text = "Text for new menu item"
NewMenuItem.Shortcut = _
    System.Windows.Forms.Shortcut.ShiftF1
MenuItem1.MenuItems.Add(NewMenuItem)
```

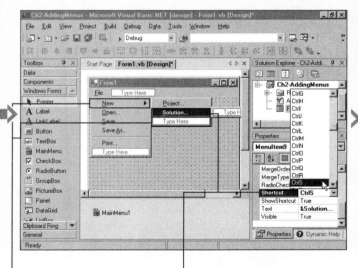

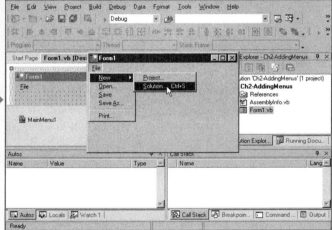

CREATE A SUB MENU

8 Click any `MenuItem`.

9 Click the placeholder to the right of the `MenuItem`.

10 Type a caption and press Enter.

SET A SHORTCUT

11 Click a `MenuItem`.

12 In the Property Window, select a new shortcut key press for the `Shortcut` property.

13 Press F5 to run the project.

■ Your project loads and a menu bar is provided across the top of the form.

Note: If you cannot see the access keys for menus when viewing the form, press and hold the Alt key to make them appear.

CREATE A CONTEXT-SENSITIVE MENU

You can use context sensitive menus to provide a list of options relevant to the specific area the user clicks. Context menus are sometimes referred to as "right-click menus" because you normally use the right mouse button to access them. Context-sensitive menus have existed since the introduction of Windows 95, and now context menus are a required feature to pass Microsoft's compatibility tests.

To add a context menu to a form, you add a new `ContextMenu` control and define the menu exactly like a standard menu. For more on creating menus, see the section "Add a Menu." There is no ability to name the menu title, because context menus appear from controls and not from the menu bar. Then use the `ContextMenu` property provided by all visual controls and the form itself, and pick the appropriate `ContextMenu` control to associate with it.

Only one `MainMenu` control should exist on a single form. That is not true with `ContextMenu` controls. An individual `ContextMenu` control should exist for most major visual components on the form.

To add and remove items from the context menu during program execution, you can manipulate the item collection provided by the `MenuItems` property of the context menu component. Declare an instance of a `MenuItem` object and then pass this object to the `MenuItems.Add` method as the only parameter. Also, if you want to duplicate the contents of a main menu inside a context menu, you can copy and paste during design-time, or you can add code at run-time to make a copy of a menu. Simply access the `MenuItem` from the main menu and call its `CloneMenu` method. Pass the new `MenuItem` object this method creates to the `Add` method of the `MenuItems` collection in the `ContextMenu` control.

CREATE A CONTEXT-SENSITIVE MENU

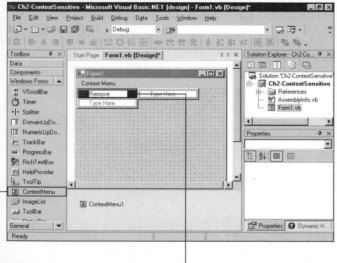

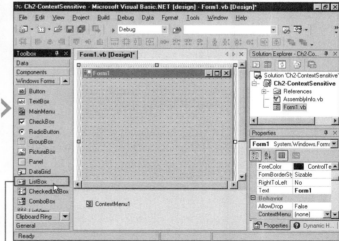

1 Open the default form in a new Windows Application project.

2 Double-click the **ContextMenu** control in the Toolbox.

3 Click the placeholder for the first menu item.

4 Type a caption for the menu item.

5 In the Toolbox, click the control to add that you want to assign the context menu.

Apply It

Context menus are an easy way to make your program more functional. Many users expect to see the functionality of an item when they right-click it. In most cases, you must place the same functionality located in the context-menu as buttons on the form or in the main menu. To do this poorly, you replicate the code in both a context menu item's click event and the button or main menu's click event.

It pays to make your main code sections in separate procedures instead of simply locating the code directly in events. This way, if you have a button on the form and a context menu with the same function, you can reuse the code. For this code to work, use the example presented below in the steps, and add a button to the form. For more information on handling events, see Chapter 2.

TYPE THIS:

```
Private Sub RemoveSelectedListItems()
If ListBox1.SelectedItem Is Nothing Then
MsgBox("Select an item to remove.")
Else
ListBox1.Items.Remove(ListBox1.SelectedItem)
End If
End Sub

Private Sub MenuItem1_Click(...)
   RemoveSelectedListItems()
End Sub

Private Sub Button1_Click(...)
   RemoveSelectedListItems()
End Sub
```

RESULT:

Both the button and the context menu function properly.

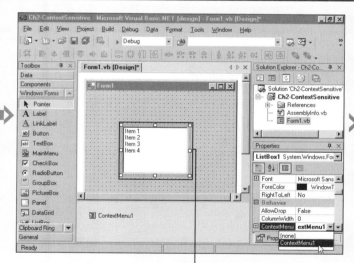

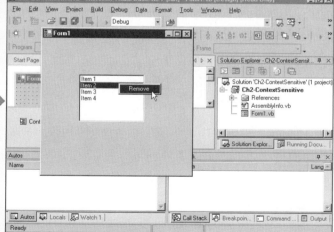

6 Add the control to the form.

■ The example adds a control to the form.

Note: To add controls to the form see the section "Add a Control to the Form."

7 Set the `ContextMenu` property of the `ListBox` to context menu you just created.

8 Press F5 to run your project.

9 Right-click your control to see your context menu appear.

■ The `ContextMenu` control provides the menu you create when you right-click the appropriate control.

ADD A NEW FORM

Additional forms are necessary to create pop-up windows, dialog boxes, and a variety of other functions in an application. You can create additional forms for your project by using the Add Form dialog box.

A VB .NET project consists of multiple files, including classes, forms, and modules. A project can work with an unlimited amount of each of these. You can use multiple forms to effectively break your program into more manageable sections for the user to navigate and understand. Include a single concept on a single form. For example, if your program has four core functions, do not attempt to represent them all on one form; instead make four forms.

In most cases, you use the standard `Form1` that VB .NET creates with the project as the main application window. You may need to add auxiliary windows. For example,

Microsoft Word has one main window and dozens of auxiliary windows to open and save files, modify options, and configure formatting. VB .NET represents each window in an application with a unique form.

Windows that provide options or allow opening and closing of files are called dialog boxes. You can create these windows in a VB .NET application. To create a dialog box see the section "Create a Dialog Box."

Another type of window that you can represent in VB .NET using a form is a toolbox. Many programs like Adobe Photoshop make use of floating windows to provide a set of tools, which a user can access in the main application window. You can create floating toolbox windows using owned forms. See the section "Add an Owned Form" for more information on creating your own owned form.

ADD A NEW FORM

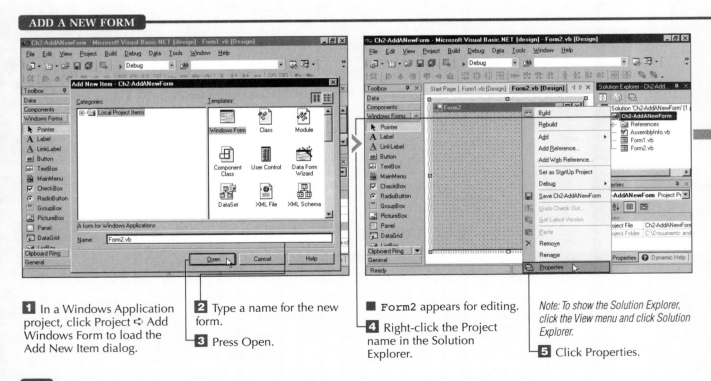

1 In a Windows Application project, click Project ➪ Add Windows Form to load the Add New Item dialog.

2 Type a name for the new form.

3 Press Open.

■ **Form2** appears for editing.

4 Right-click the Project name in the Solution Explorer.

5 Click Properties.

Note: To show the Solution Explorer, click the View menu and click Solution Explorer.

Extra

Although you can have any number of forms in a single project, only the default form appears automatically when you run the project. Different from previous versions of Visual Basic, you must create an instance variable of a form before showing it in VB. NET. Because the form that the Designer creates is nothing more than a class, you need to create an instance of the class. See Chapter 5 for more on creating classes.

Example:
```
Dim frm As New Form1
frm.Show()
```

You can alter the size of a form simply by selecting the form in the Form Designer and dragging the handles that appear. However, you cannot visually specify where you display the form.

By default, the StartPosition of the form is WindowsDefaultLocation. You can have the form start in the center of the screen by setting this property to CenterScreen. You can also place it precisely by setting StartPosition to Manual and filling the Location property's Point. A Point is comprised of an *x, y* location.

You limit the size the form can resize by using the MinimumSize and MaximumSize properties. Fill in the Point with a width and height and the user cannot resize the window out of these bounds, even though you limit maximizing to the MaximumSize property.

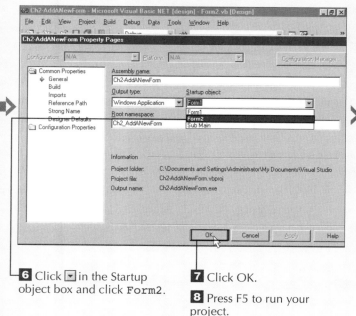

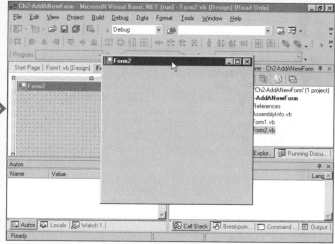

6 Click ▾ in the Startup object box and click Form2.

7 Click OK.

8 Press F5 to run your project.

■ The new form displays and the original form does not.

CREATE A DIALOG BOX

You can use dialog boxes to prompt the user for input. Dialog boxes do not disappear until the user provides the appropriate information or cancels out of the box.

A dialog box is a modal form because it restricts access to its parent form until the user closes the dialog box. Examples of dialog boxes include File Open, File Save, Print, and others.

To create a dialog box, you create a new form and provide a method to accept or cancel changes made. For more information on creating a form, see the section "Add a New Form." A dialog box should not use the entire screen, have menus, or include Minimize or Maximize buttons.

You make the form nonresizable by changing the `FormBorderStyle` property to `FixedDialog`. If you want to make your dialog box resizable, like the File Open/Save dialog boxes, leave the `FormBorderStyle` property alone, and set the `MinimumSize` and `MaximumSize` properties. Set `MaximizeBox` and `MinimizeBox` to `False` to remove the Maximize and Minimize buttons, respectively. Remove the form from the Windows Taskbar by changing `ShowInTaskBar` to `False`.

The `AcceptButton` and `CancelButton` properties allow you to select `Button` controls to act as default OK and Cancel buttons. Pressing **Enter** in the dialog box functions as the `AcceptButton` and **Esc** functions as the `CancelButton`.

To enable the dialog box's action buttons, set the `DialogResult` property on each `Button` to one of the available settings: `Abort`, `Cancel`, `Ignore`, `No`, `None`, `OK`, `Retry`, and `Yes`. The dialog box closes with the value of this property passed back to the parent. You can also set this property manually through code on the form at run-time, in which case, setting the property also makes the dialog box close immediately and pass back the `DialogResult`.

A parent form opens a dialog box by calling the dialog box's `ShowDialog` method. The form appears as a modal dialog box, and the `ShowDialog` method returns access to the parent form when a user closes the dialog box.

CREATE A DIALOG BOX

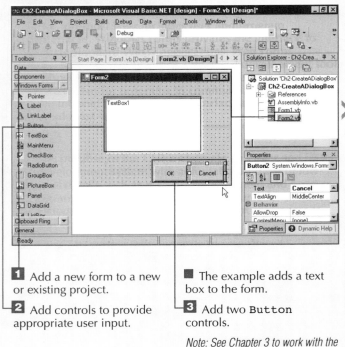

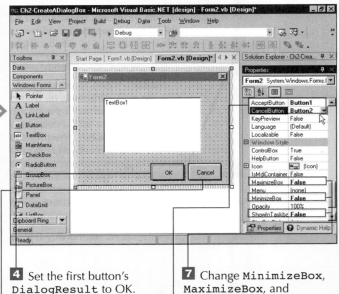

1 Add a new form to a new or existing project.

2 Add controls to provide appropriate user input.

■ The example adds a text box to the form.

3 Add two **Button** controls.

Note: See Chapter 3 to work with the button control.

4 Set the first button's `DialogResult` to OK.

5 Set the second button's `DialogResult` to `Cancel`.

6 Click the form to edit its properties.

7 Change `MinimizeBox`, `MaximizeBox`, and `ShowInTaskbar` all to `False`.

8 Change `AcceptButton` to the first button and `CancelButton` to the second button.

Extra

To access information entered on the form, you may want to add properties to the dialog box to enable the parent form to access information, or you can make the parent form access information in the dialog box's controls directly. For more information on adding properties, see Chapter 7.

Example:
```
Sub OpenDialog()
    Dim myDialog As New DialogForm2()
    Dim result As DialogResult

    result = myDialog.ShowDialog(Me)
    If result = DialogResult.OK Then
        Dim filename As String
        filename = myDialog.TextBox1.Text
        ' use the file name the user entered in the dialog.
    End If
End Sub
```

You can use property pages to display information without requiring immediate action from the user. By creating the property-page design, Microsoft chose to break many of the rules associated with dialog boxes. Property pages are non-modal, meaning they do make the user accept or cancel changes before continuing with the use of the application. Property pages often give information to the user on an object in the program. If you want to create a property-page dialog box, the standard convention is to use OK, Cancel, and Apply buttons. Also, you should show the property page using the Show method as opposed to the ShowDialog method to allow the user to work with the application when the property page is still open.

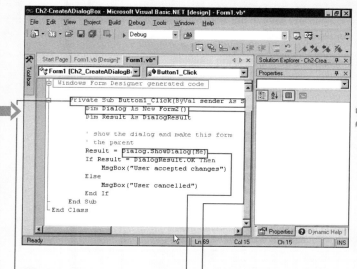

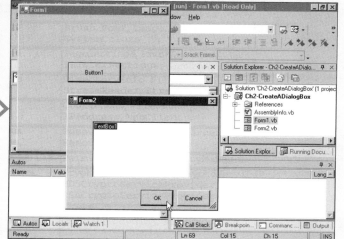

9 Open the event handler or method where you want the dialog to appear.

■ In the example, code is being added to **Button1_Click**.

Note: To add an event handler, see the section "Write Event Code."

10 Type the code necessary to create an instance of the form.

11 Type the name of the dialog variable followed by **.ShowDialog(Me)**.

12 Press F5 to run the project.

■ The main form appears.

■ Creating the necessary event causes your dialog box to appear, which you can close by pressing either of the two buttons.

USING MESSAGE BOXES

You can use a Message Box as a simple dialog box to present a message to a user. Message boxes provide simple interfaces to easily display information that does not require a custom designed form. Message Boxes require no visual setup and are invoked through the MessageBox class's Show method.

A simple Message Box presents a textual display of information with an OK button at the bottom. Configurations include adding Cancel buttons, using a Yes, No pair, an Abort, Retry, Ignore combination, and others. You cannot configure message boxes outside of the available button combinations. Do not use a Message Box for programming simplicity when the button combinations do not make sense for the prompt you display. For example, do not display "Would you like to save changes?" and then use OK and Cancel as button prompts: Yes and No make much more sense.

You can create a Message Box by using the code structure MessageBox.Show(Text, Caption, MessageBoxButtons, MessageBoxIcon, MessageBoxOptions). The MessageBoxButtons constants include AbortRetryIgnore, OK, OKCancel,

RetryCancel, YesNo, and YesNoCancel. To specify a constant from an enumerated type, use the type name and the constant, such as MessageBoxButtons.OK. The MessageBoxIcon constants include Asterisk, Error, Exclamation, Hand, Information, None, Question, Stop, and Warning. These icons are self-explanatory, and you use them in many common applications. Note that if the user has sound files set for Error, Question, and the other settings, these sounds play automatically.

The MessageBoxOptions enumeration lets you specify the default button. If the user presses Enter, the dialog box closes with the specified default button as the result. The enumeration includes only three constants, Button1, Button2, and Button3. If you want to ask a question, where the most likely answer is no, use MessageBoxButtons.YesNo, and MessageBoxOptions.Button2. Buttons are numbered in the order they are named in the button constant.

You can also display a message box by calling the simpler MsgBox command. Pass the message to display as the only parameter.

USING MESSAGE BOXES

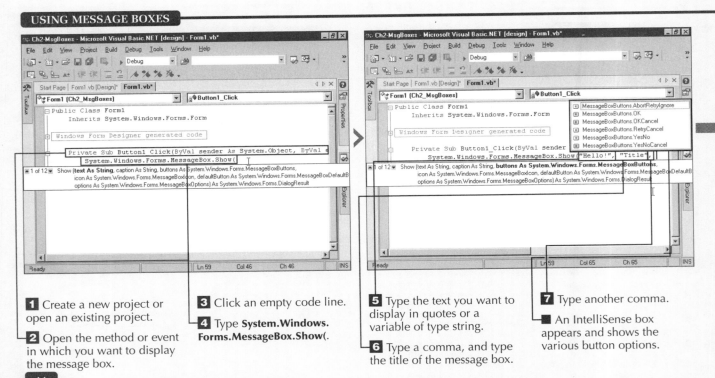

1 Create a new project or open an existing project.

2 Open the method or event in which you want to display the message box.

3 Click an empty code line.

4 Type **System.Windows. Forms.MessageBox.Show(**.

5 Type the text you want to display in quotes or a variable of type string.

6 Type a comma, and type the title of the message box.

7 Type another comma.

■ An IntelliSense box appears and shows the various button options.

Apply It

You can use a message box to ask the user a question and then respond to the user. The Show method returns a value corresponding to a DialogResult value. Each of the Message Box buttons have a corresponding DialogResult type you can use to determine which button the user presses: OK, Cancel, Yes, No, Retry, Ignore, Abort. To test the return value of the message box, use DialogResult.OK or one of the other constants. An If test can easily check for the user's response. For more information on using the If statement, see Chapter 4.

TYPE THIS:

```
Dim result As DialogResult
result = MessageBox.Show("Do you like strawberry ice cream?", _
        "Ice cream", MessageBoxButtons.YesNoCancel, MessageBoxIcon.Question)
If result = DialogResult.Yes Then
        MessageBox.Show("Me too!!")
Else
        If result = DialogResult.Cancel Then
                MessageBox.Show("You are no fun.")
        Else
                result = MessageBox.Show("Too bad. How about chocolate ice cream?", _
                        "Ice cream", MessageBoxButtons.YesNoCancel, _
                        MessageBoxIcon.Question)
                If result = DialogResult.No Then
                        MessageBox.Show("What do you like???")
                End If
        End If
End If
```

RESULT:

Do you like strawberry ice cream?

Me too!!

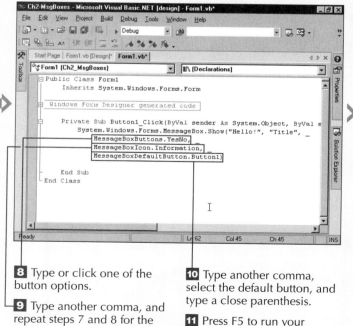

8 Type or click one of the button options.

9 Type another comma, and repeat steps 7 and 8 for the icon.

10 Type another comma, select the default button, and type a close parenthesis.

11 Press F5 to run your project.

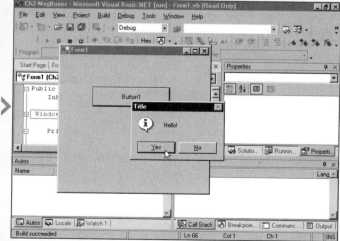

12 Invoke the necessary code to show your message box.

■ The message box appears and waits for the user to press a button.

ADD AN OWNED FORM

You can use owned forms to create floating windows that accompany a parent window. A single parent form can own any number of forms. Use owned forms to save space on the main program window while still allowing access to functionality. Owned forms also allow the user to move the floating windows around to customize their own environment.

You do not need to have owned forms inside a parent's boundaries, but an owned form always floats above its parent. If a user minimizes the parent form, then the owned forms disappears, and reappears when the user restores the parent. A good example of owned forms is the Visual Basic Development Studio itself. However, the docking abilities provided in the Development Studio are not part of the standard abilities provided by owned forms.

Owned forms are no different than any standard form. Creating a toolbox-style floating window requires a few

settings to make it appear like other applications. Set the `FormBorderStyle` equal to `FixedToolWindow` or `SizableToolWindow` to reduce the space the title bar wastes. Set `MaximizeBox` and `MinimizeBox` to `False`, and `ShowInTaskBar` to `False` so it does not appear to be a stand-alone application window.

To set up a form as an owned form, you can use two methods, depending on the easiest place for your application. You can set the child form to be owned; for example if `FormToolbar` needs to float above `FormMain`, set `FormToolbar.Owner = FormMain`. Or the parent form can take ownership of the child, for example `FormMain.AddOwnedForm(FormToolbar)`. You use the second method most often because in most cases the main application form creates the owned form and not the other way around.

ADD AN OWNED FORM

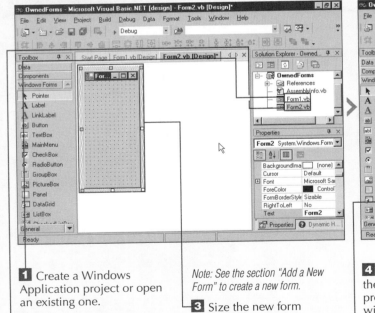

1 Create a Windows Application project or open an existing one.

2 Add a new form the project.

Note: See the section "Add a New Form" to create a new form.

3 Size the new form appropriately.

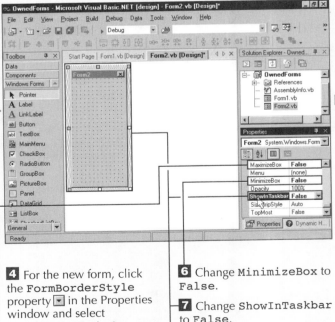

4 For the new form, click the `FormBorderStyle` property ▾ in the Properties window and select `SizableToolwindow`.

5 Double-click the `MaximizeBox` property to change it to `False`.

6 Change `MinimizeBox` to `False`.

7 Change `ShowInTaskBar` to `False`.

8 Load the original form and double-click it to enter the code editor.

Apply It

Often, you must make components that you place on an owned form perform an action on their parent window. For example, you need to make a button on the owned form that says Open do the same thing as a File, Open menu on the parent window. You must declare the code in the main window that provides the functionality — in the example, the code that provides the File Open dialog box, and opens the file — in its own subroutine. You make this routine Public so you can access it outside of the form. See Chapter 4 to learn more about methods.

TYPE THIS:

```
Public Class FormTollWindow

        Private Sub ButtonFIleOpen_Click(...)
                          Dim frm As FormMain = Me.Owner
                  Frm.FileOpenRoutine()
        End Sub
End Class

Public Class FormMain

    Public Sub FileOpenRoutine()

    End Sub

    Private Sub MenuFileOpen_Click(...)
        FileOpenRoutine()
    End Sub
End Class
```

RESULTS:

The Toolbox provides the same open function as the File ➪ Open menu item.

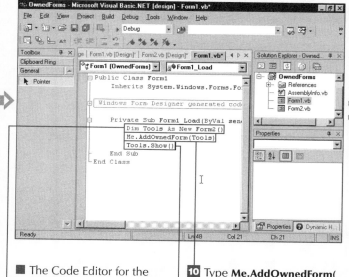

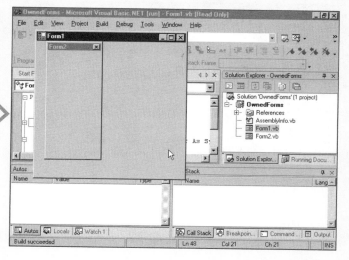

■ The Code Editor for the main form opens.

9 In the form load event, declare an instance of the owned form.

10 Type **Me.AddOwnedForm(** followed by the variable name of the owned form and a close parenthesis.

11 Type the variable name of the owned form followed by **.Show()**.

12 Press F5 to run the project

■ The owned form floats above its parent, disappears when a user minimizes the parent, and appears again when the user restores the parent.

ORDER TAB KEY MOVEMENT

You use the Tab key as a standard method to move around an application without the mouse. By default, Windows Forms assigns the movement in the order you added the controls to the form. Not many developers lay out the form perfectly the first time, so the `TabIndex` property allows you to edit the order of controls.

Users expect to begin typing at the top left side of the form. Normally, tabbing moves from either left to right or top to bottom. While you may find resetting all the tab indexes of all the controls tedious work, the Microsoft Windows Application guideline require it, and doing so makes an application more professional. Setting the tab order also makes your application more accessible for people performing data entry and for anyone accustomed to moving around their computer with the keyboard instead of forcing users to click each control before entering or changing data. Database and other applications that require

a significant quantity of data processing become significantly easier to use with an intelligent tab-order layout.

The simplest way to set the tab order is to completely design your form, moving around controls until you see a visual order become apparent. At this point, start at the top left corner of your application, and set the control's `TabIndex` property to zero. Then depending on what makes sense for your application, move to the next control in the proper direction and assign it `TabIndex = 1`. Continue until every control has a sensible tab order.

You can also remove a control from the tab order by setting the `TabStop` property of the control to `False`. The property is useful for labels and other controls that do not directly pertain to data input. By default, `TabStop` is `True` for every control on the form.

ORDER TAB KEY MOVEMENT

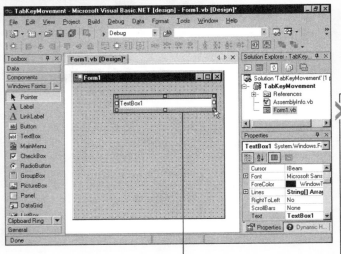

1 Create a new Windows Application project or open an existing one.

2 Add a control to the form.

3 Continue adding controls.

4 Position the controls into columns or rows.

5 Click the top, left component.

6 In the Properties window, type **0** (zero) into the `TabIndex` property.

Extra

You can use labels, frames, groups, and other visual cue components to enhance tab order just like input controls. For example, a label to the left of a control has `Text` equal to `Name:` and a text box is located directly to the right of it. You must add an access key to each label, so the label has the text `&Name:`. Then the user can press Alt+N. A label focuses on the control with the next tab index when you press its access key. It is important to set the `TabOrder` of the label, then the corresponding input control.

Both `GroupBox` and `Panel` contain other controls. You must set a container control's `TabIndex` to the number before the top-left control in the container. The title of a `GroupBox` acts like a label and passes focus to the first control inside the container. When numbering controls inside of a container, follow the same system as numbering the form. Start at the top-left of the container, and work your way through the entire container moving either right or down. You should not make the order pass out of the container and back into it later, as this may confuse the user.

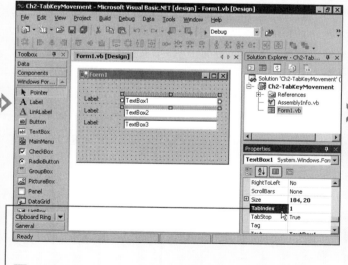

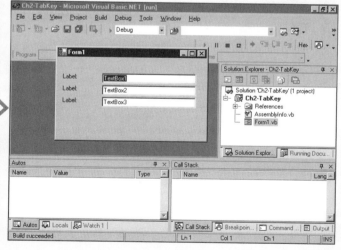

7 Click the next control (either to the right or below).

8 Set the `TabIndex` to the next highest index.

9 Repeat steps 7 and 8 until you set the `TabIndex` for all of the controls.

10 Press F5 to run the project.

11 Experiment using the Tab key to navigate your form.

■ The controls follow the order given with the `TabOrder` property.

USING BUTTONS

You can use buttons to provide simple user input in your application. A button represents a single action verb, such as accept, cancel, or go. This simplicity makes it effective in that most users understand the purpose of buttons.

You primarily use buttons on dialog boxes, and not normally on the main application screen. Instead of individual buttons, you may want to use a toolbar on the main window. See the section "Create a Toolbar" topic later in the chapter for more information.

The Button control has a variety of properties to change its appearance. The FlatStyle property allows you to create flat-style buttons. Flat buttons change color when a user moves over or clicks them, but have no three-dimensional effect. The Popup style makes the button appear flat. It takes on a raised three-dimensional appearance when the user moves the mouse over it,

and depresses when a user clicks it. The Standard style appears raised in all cases, and depressed when the user presses the mouse button.

You can load a background image into the button by setting the BackgroundImage property to a supported format. You place images in the foreground with the Image property. You can also load images from ImageList controls with the use of two properties, ImageList and ImageIndex. See the section "Work with ImageLists" for more information.

You use the ImageAlign to set the image alignment to the middle, edge, or corner of the button. You use the TextAlign property to align the Text in the same way.

To respond to the user pressing the button, you can create an event handler that responds to the Click event. For more information on creating event handlers, see the section "Add an Event."

USING BUTTONS

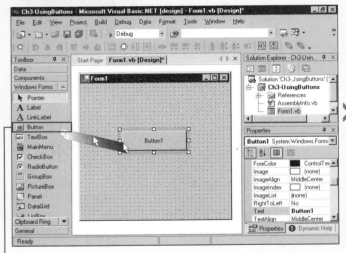

1 Create a new Windows Application project or add to an existing one.

2 In the Toolbox, click and drag the Button control to add it to the form.

Note: See Chapter 2 to learn about creating Windows Application projects, and adding a control to a form.

3 In the Properties window, set the **Text** property to change the button caption.

4 Change any necessary properties.

■ This example sets the FlatStyle to Popup.

■ The property changes take effect in the designer immediately.

Note: See Chapter 2 to set a property or create an event handler to respond to the Button's Click event.

USING LABEL CONTROLS

Labels provide information on the form to guide the user. You add a label control to provide an explanation of information the user needs to supply on the form or to explain information available on the form. A form often presents the user with various controls that contain data or lists of information, or blank controls waiting for user input, which make the labels necessary to describe the nature of the controls.

Try to make labels short, but descriptive. Most labels have a colon after the text to signify the label describes the control to the right or bottom of it. Refrain from placing labels to the right or below the control they describe.

Use the Text property to modify the text that label displays, and TextAlign allows you to align the text to the middle, side, or corner of the label. The AutoSize property, when set to True, automatically stretches the label's width to fit the text you place on it. This prevents the text from wrapping at the edge of the control.

The LinkLabel control expands on the capability of the Label control by providing an appearance of a hyperlink. By setting the LinkVisited property to True, you can cause the link to appear in the visited color. Just like a Web page, you can set this property and cause the link to appear visited after the user clicks the link.

For the LinkLabel control, the LinkArea property specifies a range of text you want to use as the hyperlink. By default, the entire text of the control is used. Set the Start property to the character position to start the hyperlink, and the Length, the number of characters that you want as part of the link. When you set the Start property, remember the first text position is zero. The control fires the LinkClicked event if the user clicks on the area of the control that is part of the link.

USING LABEL CONTROLS

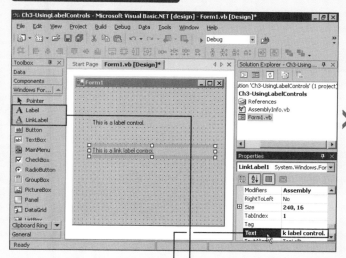

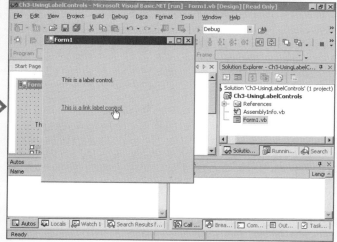

1 Create a new Windows Application project or open an existing one.

2 Click the Label or LinkLabel control in the Toolbox and add the control to the form.

3 In the Properties window, set the Text property of the control.

4 Press F5 to run your project.

■ The Label control provides textual information on the form.

■ For the LinkLabel control, you can handle the user clicking the link in the LinkClicked event.

Note: See Chapter 2 to add an event handler.

WORK WITH IMAGELISTS

You can use an ImageList control to store a large quantity of images without having to load them independently into controls and create a bloated executable. Many of the Windows Forms controls support directly loading from the ImageList control, and some controls, such as the ListView, TreeView, and ToolBar controls require the ImageList to provide their images.

An ImageList control is non-visual control, so when you load it onto a form, it appears in the Component Tray. The ImageList has a few requirements for the images you load into the control. All of the images must have the same dimensions. If the images are not the same size, the control resizes each image to the same dimension. You can change the overall dimension of the images using the ImageSize property, which is a Size structure. Specify the width using the Width property of the ImageSize structure and specify the height using the Height property.

The ImageList control also requires each of the images in the control, have the same color depth. The ColorDepth property specifies the color depth of all of the images. When you load images into the control at design-time, the control determines the color depth of the images automatically.

The Images property maintains the collection of images. The control represents each image file in the collection with an Image object. When you use the Visual Collection Editor to add images to the control at design-time, the editor allows you to browse for files to add to the collection. The actual representation of the image is stored inside your executable application, so you do not need to redistribute the individual image files with your application. Each image is given an index starting with zero, according to the order you add the images to the list.

WORK WITH IMAGELISTS

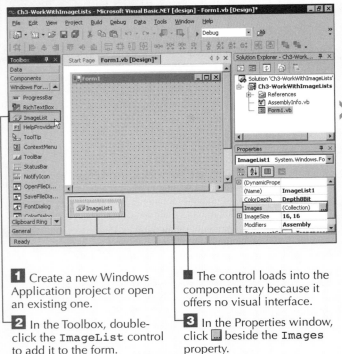

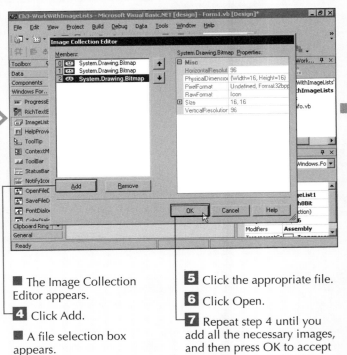

1 Create a new Windows Application project or open an existing one.

2 In the Toolbox, double-click the ImageList control to add it to the form.

■ The control loads into the component tray because it offers no visual interface.

3 In the Properties window, click ■ beside the Images property.

■ The Image Collection Editor appears.

4 Click Add.

■ A file selection box appears.

5 Click the appropriate file.

6 Click Open.

7 Repeat step 4 until you add all the necessary images, and then press OK to accept changes.

Extra

You can specify a transparency color for the images in the control. The default setting for the `TransparentColor` property is `Transparent`, meaning it reads the transparency color from the image file, if the file type supports transparency. Icon files (ICO) and Graphics Interchange format (GIF) support transparency. If you load a collection of Windows bitmap (BMP) files into the `ImageList` control, set the `TransparentColor` to the appropriate background color of the images.

You can add images to the `ImageList` control at run-time using the `Add` method of the Images collection. Supply an Image object as the only parameter to the method.

Example:

```
' Visual Basic
' Replace string with valid image file path:
Dim myImage As System.Drawing.Image = _
    Image.FromFile("c:\sample.gif")
ImageList1.Images.Add(myImage)
```

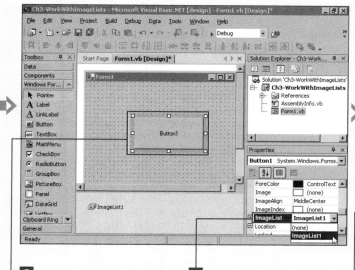

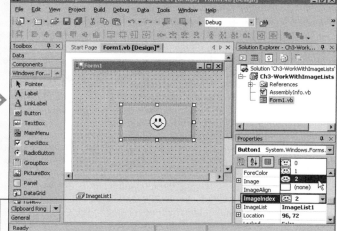

8 Add a control to display an image.

■ Controls such as the **Button** and **Label** control offer support for loading images from the **ImageList** control. The example adds a **Button** control.

9 In the Properties window, click the **ImageList** property ⊡ and select the **ImageList** control.

■ You can clear the **Text** property to make the button appear with only an image.

10 Click the **ImageIndex** ⊡ and select an image to display.

■ The **ImageList** provides the image to the control.

ALLOW TEXT ENTRY

Text input is a vital part of most programs. You use a text box to allow users to enter freeform information that you cannot represent by a list of options. Notepad is an example of the functionality the standard text box provides. Without using text boxes for users to enter information, you must provide a selected set of options using check boxes, radio buttons, and lists.

Text boxes support two basic modes: single-line, and multi-line, which you can toggle. A single line input box is normally limited to a certain number of characters by the MaxLength property, with the maximum available size being 32767, and the height fixed at font and system settings. The Text property controls the text displayed by the TextBox control, and updates as the user enters new information in the control. You can create a password field in a single-line text box by specifying a character in the PasswordChar property. The character you specify appears

instead of the actual information typed into the box. A normal value for the property is an asterisk (*).

You can make a multi-line text box can any size, and have unlimited text up to the available memory. Use the ScrollBars property to assign horizontal, vertical, or both scrollbars to the multi-line text box. The WordWrap property, which defaults to True, controls whether the box wraps text at the edge of the control. If WordWrap is False, the line can extend past the edge of the text box and the user must press Enter to move to a new line.

Using text boxes effectively requires significant testing. Because of the free-entry functionality present in a text box, users may type incorrect data, which requires the programmer to provide *validation* to check what the user enters. VB.NET has new validation abilities. You can learn about the ErrorProvider control in the section "Provide Error Messages."

ALLOW TEXT ENTRY

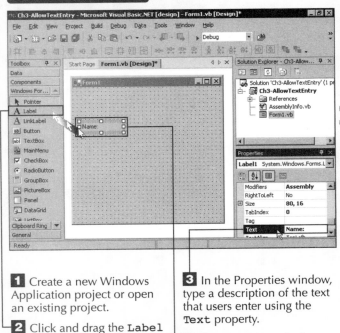

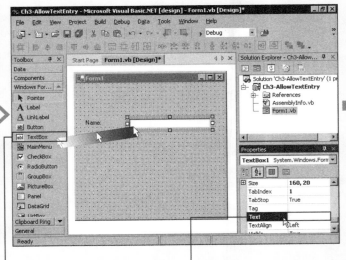

1 Create a new Windows Application project or open an existing project.

2 Click and drag the **Label** control from the Toolbox to add it to the form.

3 In the Properties window, type a description of the text that users enter using the **Text** property.

■ The text appears in the **Label** control on your form.

4 Click and drag the **TextBox** control in the Toolbox to add it to the form.

5 In the Properties window, remove the provided text by selecting the text and pressing the Delete key.

■ If desired, type your own default value in the **Text** property.

Apply It

In a multi-line `TextBox` control, the `Lines` property maintains an array of strings representing each line in the `TextBox` control. You can use this property to retrieve particular lines of information from the text box or to manipulate text in the control. The example below loads the contents of the property into a new array and displays each line in a `ListBox` control you must add to the form.

TYPE THIS:

```
Public Sub GetTextBoxContents()
    ' Create a string array and store the contents of the Lines property.
    Dim textLines() as String, line As String
    textLines = TextBox1.Lines

    For Each line In textLines
        ListBox1.Items.Add(line)
    Next
End Sub
```

RESULT:

This is line #1 in the text box.

This is line #2 in the text box.

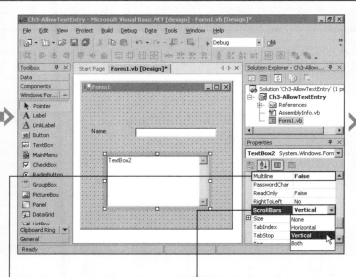

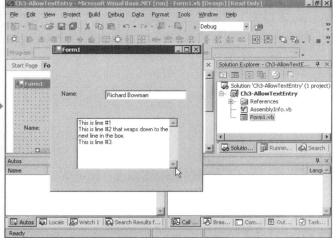

CREATE A MULTI-LINE TEXT BOX

6 With the **Text Box** control selected, double-click the Multi-line property to toggle it to **True** in the Property window.

7 Click the **ScrollBars** property's ▾ and select a constant for the scrollbar style you desire.

8 Press F5 to run your project.

■ The **TextBox** displays text and enables the user to edit the text in a standard way.

USING THE RICH TEXT CONTROL

Y ou can use the RichTextBox to enter rich data, such as formatted text, pictures, and OLE objects. An example of the rich text box in use is WordPad, a program included with Windows. You can create much of the functionality available in WordPad in your application.

The RichTextBox control stores the data inside the box in RTF format. Most applications can understand this format, so you can cut and paste rich text to and from applications such as Microsoft Word into this control during runtime. Similarly to the TextBox control, you can use the Text property to read or set the plain text of the box. The Rtf property returns the text with all of the formatting codes. When you set the AcceptsTab property to True, the user can enter a tab as text into a control. If the property is False, the focus shifts to the next control.

Scroll bars only show if the user types more than can fit in the boxes boundaries. The ScrollBars property allows you to set the control to None, Vertical, Horizontal, or Both scrollbars. The other settings for the property are FixedHorizontal, FixedVertical, and FixedBoth; they force the specified scrollbars to show.

Runtime properties play an important role in using the RichTextBox control's abilities. Formatting properties work for the selected text. Use the SelectionStart and SelectionLength properties to choose the starting point, and the length of the selection, respectively. If the user makes a selection, these properties update automatically. The first character in the box is index one for the RichTextBox control.

You can use the SelectedText and Selectedrtf properties to receive or set the text enclosed in the selection. You can also use the selection to change the format of the selected text. For example, the SelectionBullet property adds bullets to the selected lines of the control when set to True.

USING THE RICH TEXT CONTROL

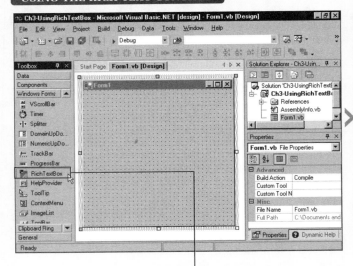

1 Create a new Windows Application project or open an existing one.

2 From the Toolbox, click and drag the **RichTextBox** control onto the form to the size you desire.

■ The control appears on the form.

3 Add a control for the user to alter the formatting of the rich text.

■ This example adds a **Button** control.

4 Double-click the control to alter the formatting.

Apply It

After the user specifies a selection, or you set a selection code, you can format the text by reassigning the text SelectionFont to a new Font class. SelectionColor allows you to reassign a color to the selected text. Set SelectedBullet = True to make the selected lines into bulleted items.

The SelectionIndent, SelectionRightIndent, and SelectionHangingIndent affect the paragraphs that have selected text inside them. These properties allow you to specify a pixel amount for the various indentation styles.

TYPE THIS:

```
Private Sub Button1_Click(ByVal sender As System.Object, _
ByValue As System.EventArgs) Handles Button1.Click

    ' Store the font for the selected text.
    Dim tempFont As System.Drawing.Font = RichTextBox1.SelectionFont
    ' Create FontStyle to contain the style for the current selection.
    Dim tempStyle As System.Drawing.FontStyle = _
    RichTextBox1.SelectionFont.Style

    ' Determine whether the current text selection is bold.
    If tempFont.Bold = True Then
        ' Create a new font based on the existing font for selection
        ' but use an exclusive or bitwise operator to remove the bold
        ' style.
        RichTextBox1.SelectionFont = New Font(tempFont.FontFamily, _
        tempFont.Size, tempStyle And Not FontStyle.Bold)
    Else
        ' Create a new font based on the existing font for selection
        ' but use an exclusive or bitwise operator to remove the bold
        ' style.
        RichTextBox1.SelectionFont = New Font(tempFont.FontFamily, _
        tempFont.Size, tempStyle Or FontStyle.Bold)
    End If
End Sub
```

RESULT:

Font switches between bold and normal styles.

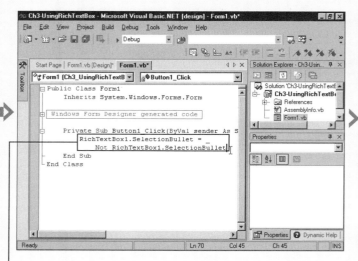

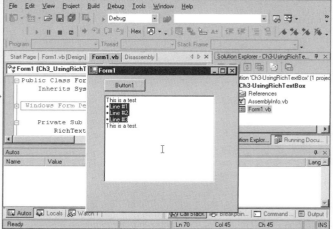

■ The default event for the control loads in the code editor.

5 Type the appropriate code to alter the selection.

■ In this example, the selected text toggles between bulleted and standard text.

6 Run the project by pressing F5.

■ The rich text box allows editing.

■ You can see formatting changes by completing the necessary action to run the event or method code.

PROVIDE OPTION CONTROLS

You can use the `Check Box` and `Radio Button` controls to provide a selection of choices that the user can click to activate. The major difference between these controls is that radio buttons are exclusive in a set and check boxes are not. When users select one radio button, they cannot select the others in the same container, but they can check an unlimited number of check boxes at the same time.

Edit the `Text` property of either control to change the caption. `FlatStyle` allows you to set the controls to look flat, look raised when you move the mouse over them, or look like a standard control. `Appearance` changes the appearance of both controls into a button, which is pressed down when a user checks it.

The `Checked` property toggles whether the control is checked. If you set `Checked = True` for a radio button, it automatically unchecks any other radio button control. When the user checks the control, the `CheckedChanged` event of the control fires.

You can align the check box and the option button independently of the text using the `CheckAlign` property. You can align the caption text using the `TextAlign` property. Both alignment properties support the full range of alignment, from corners to sides to the middle.

You can place images on the control. Use the `Image` property to load an image, and you can align it using the `ImageAlign` property. An `ImageList` control can also hold the images, along with using the `ImageList` and `ImageIndex` properties of the `CheckBox` and `RadioButton` controls.

To create multiple groups of radio buttons that you do not have connected on a form, you must place the radio buttons inside container controls. The `GroupBox` is the most readily used because it allows you to assign a label to the grouping. See the section "Frame Controls" for more information.

PROVIDE OPTION CONTROLS

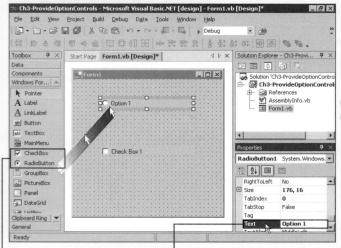

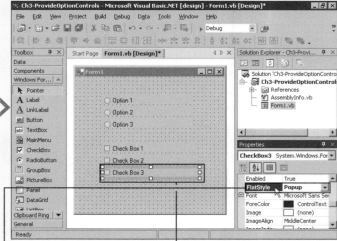

1 In a Windows Application project, click and drag a `RadioButton` or `CheckBox` control to the form.

■ You can separate groups of radio buttons and check boxes using frames.

Note: See the section "Using Frame Controls" for more information.

2 In the Properties window, type a caption for the control into the `Text` property.

3 Change any desired formatting properties.

Note: See Chapter 2 to set a property.

4 Add multiple buttons or boxes to fit your needs by repeating steps 1 through 3.

5 Double-click one of the controls to handle the `CheckedChanged` event.

Extra

In previous versions of Visual Basic, you can create control arrays, where multiple controls had the same name and an associated index to distinguish them. Because this functionality no longer exists in VB .NET, you must assign separate names to each check box and radio button. With the separate names, you can no longer loop through the controls in code. However, you can create an array and load the controls manually into it. While this requires some extra code, you can easily access the controls when processing their results with this method. To do this, first place an array declaration in the base of the `Form` class, directly after the class declaration and `Inherits` statement. Type **Private CheckBoxArray(9) As CheckBox**, modifying the name of the array and the number of indices as needed. An array starts at zero, so declare the array as the number of controls - 1. Then in the `Form_Load` event, load the checkboxes into the array. The `DoneButton_Click` event holds the processing of the check boxes.

Example:
```
Form_Load:
CheckBoxArray(0) = CheckBox1
CheckBoxArray(1) = CheckBox2
...
CheckBoxArray(9) = CheckBox10


DoneButton_Click:
Dim check As CheckBox
For Each check In CheckBoxArray
    If check.Checked Then
        MessageBox.Show(check.Text)
    End If
Next
```

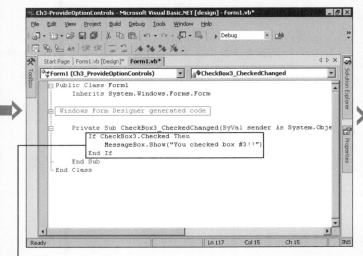

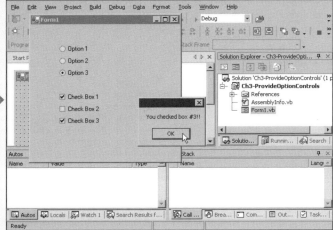

6 Type code to respond to the **CheckedChanged** event of the particular option control.

■ To retrieve the check state of the control, type the name of the control followed by **.Checked**.

7 Press F5 to run the project.

■ You can select an option from the radio button list and check various check boxes.

FRAME CONTROLS

You can create a frame around other controls and visually separate them from the rest of the form using a GroupBox. For example, a user may better understand the function of a list of check boxes, radio buttons, buttons, or any other control if you locate them inside a GroupBox control. The group box draws a border around itself with a label header at the top of the frame. You can change the header displayed using the Text property.

A GroupBox control is a container control, meaning it can hold other controls inside it. Think of it as a form inside the main form. If you add controls to the box, and then move the box, the controls you place inside move with it. If you use the Dock and Anchor properties to resize controls inside the group box, they resize independently inside the GroupBox without regard to the form shape. To use the Dock and Anchor properties, see Chapter 2.

Group boxes typically contain a logical group of RadioButton controls. For example, if you have two lists of options where the user needs to select one response in each, you must place each set of controls inside its own GroupBox control. VB .NET does not allow you any other way to separate RadioButton controls into groups except by placing them in container controls. For more information on the RadioButton control, see the section "Provide Option Controls."

The BackgroundImage property allows you to place a picture in the background of the GroupBox. Note that placing a background image in the group box can make the controls the box contains hard to see and can distract the user.

FRAME CONTROLS

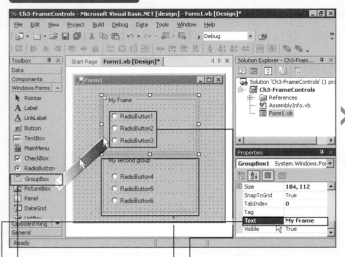

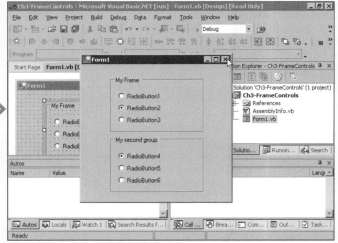

1 In a Windows Application project, click and drag the **GroupBox** control from the Toolbox to the form.

2 In the Properties window, set the **Text** property to alter the heading of the frame.

3 Click and drag controls from the Toolbox to the inside of the **GroupBox**.

■ This example shows radio buttons inside each **GroupBox**.

4 Repeat steps 1 through 3 to add multiple groups to the form.

5 Press F5 to run your application.

■ The controls inside the group boxes respond separately. For example, radio button controls act as separate groups.

WORK WITH PANELS

You can use the `Panel` control to provide an area to hold other controls. The `Panel` control, like the `GroupBox` control, acts as a container, which allows you to group controls, such as radio buttons. Because the `Panel` control's default state is borderless and indistinguishable from the form, you can use it when you do not want a visual framing around your controls. See the section, "Frame Controls" for more on the `GroupBox`.

You can add a frame to a `Panel` control by setting the `BorderStyle` property to `FixedSingle` or `Fixed3D`. `FixedSingle` creates a single pixel black border around the control, while `Fixed3D` creates a two pixel sunken edge.

You can set `AutoScroll` to `True` to allow the `Panel` to create scrollbars if a user resizes the panel smaller than the right or bottom-most controls. The `AutoScrollMargin` regulates the distance that you place controls from the right

or bottom edge before a scrollbar appears. This allows you to create scrolling frames inside your application window that scroll independently of the main form. Keep in mind that scrolling is a bad design technique that you should minimize unless necessary. A more effective option is to make the controls inside the panel resize as necessary based on the available space.

The `Panel` aids in creating a very flexible layout environment and, thus, allows you to create complex interfaces with the `Dock` and `Anchor` properties. See Chapter 2 for information on these properties. You can dock the `Panel` control to a side of the form, or anchor it in a certain way. Doing so allows the controls inside the box to resize independently by docking and anchoring to the client space of the `Panel`. You can also use the scrolling functionality of the `Panel` to make the controls stay at the same spot and allow the `Panel` to scroll the area.

WORK WITH PANELS

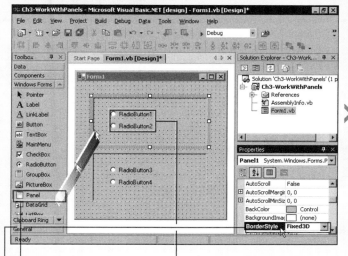

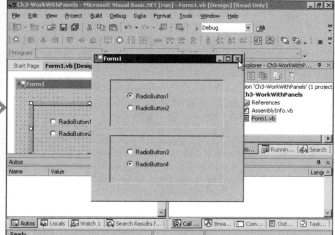

1 In a Windows Application project, click and drag the `Panel` control from the Toolbox to the form.

■ If desired, you can change the `BorderStyle` property.

Note: To set a property, see Chapter 2.

2 Click and drag controls from the Toolbox to inside the `Panel`.

3 Repeat steps 1 through 3 as desired.

4 Press F5 to see your application run.

■ Each `Panel` control holds its constituent controls and enables them to function as separate groups.

■ In this example, the `BorderStyle` is set to `Fixed3D` and the panels contain radio buttons.

LIST ITEMS

List controls allow you to display long lists of information in a smaller space on screen. You can add list controls to the your form to allow the user to make a selection from this list or just to provide information to the user. You should use list controls whenever you have a long or varying set of data from which the user needs to choose. For example, you can use list controls to display a listing of files in a directory, or display a list of products from your company.

VB .NET provides three list controls: the `ListBox`, `CheckedListBox`, and `ComboBox`. A `ListBox` allows the users to select single or multiple items from the list. A `CheckedListBox` places a check box beside each item in the list, allowing users to check multiple items. A `ComboBox` allows the list to drop down and provides the user the ability to enter a new item or select an existing item via the keyboard.

VB .NET stores list items in the `Items` collection. Design-time editing of this collection allows you to predefine list items, or you can use the code `ListControl.Items`.

`Add("item text")` to add an item during runtime. Set the `Sorted` property to `True` if you want the controls to sort your items alphabetically.

For `ListBox` and `CheckedListBox` controls, you can add horizontal scrollbars by setting `HorizontalScrollbar` to `True`. For the `ComboBox` control, specify the width of the drop-down list by setting `DropDownWidth`. You can use these properties to show data that is wider than the width of your control. `SelectionMode` has three settings. One allows the user to select a single item. `MultipleSimple` allows the user to toggle item selections by clicking an item. `MultiExtended`, on a click, selects the item and unselects any other items, and you must hold down Ctrl to pick another item, or Shift to select a range of items.

The `ComboBox` also has three specific modes, specified in the `DropDownStyle` property. `Simple` creates a list box with a textbox at the top, allowing users to make new entries. `DropDown` allows a user to type a value or select an item in the box. `DropDownList` displays a list and only lets the user select items.

LIST ITEMS

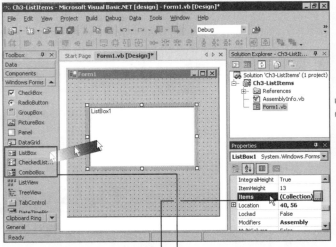

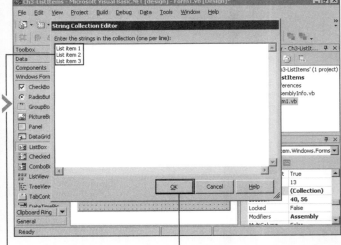

1 Create a new Windows Application project or open an existing one.

2 Click and drag the `ListBox`, `CheckedListBox`, or `ComboBox` control to the form.

3 In the Properties window, click ▦ beside the `Items` property.

■ The String Collection Editor appears.

4 Type separate items for the list control on separate lines.

5 Click OK to load the items into the list.

■ Alternately, you can add items at design-time rather than at runtime.

Apply It

You can use the `Items` property of any of the list controls in this section to add and remove items at runtime, as well as determine the items in the list the user selects. For a single selection list box or a combo box, you can retrieve the selected item by using the `SelectedItem` property. For multiple-selection list boxes, you need to loop through the `SelectedItems` collection. For the `CheckedListBox`, you can loop through the `CheckedItems` collection. You can place the sample code that follows in a Button's event procedure. The code runs through a `CheckedListBox` and adds all of the items that a user checked in a `ListBox`.

Example:

```
Private Sub Button1_Click(ByVal sender As System.Object, ByVal e As _
    System.EventArgs) Handles Button1.Click

    ' Clear the result check box
    ListBox1.Items.Clear()

    ' Run through checked items in CheckBoxList1
    Dim item As String
    For Each item In CheckedListBox1.CheckedItems()
        ' Add the item to the receiving list box
        ListBox1.Items.Add(item)
    Next
End Sub
```

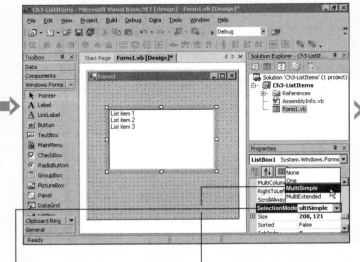

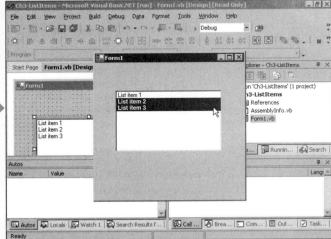

6 For the **ComboBox** control, click the **DropDownStyle** property; for the **ListBox** control, click the **SelectionMode** property.

■ If desired, click ▾ and select a new value.

7 Run your project by pressing F5.

■ VB .NET creates the list box or combo box and allows interactions with it.

SELECT NUMERIC DATA

You can use the `TrackBar` control to allow users to select numbers or other ordered data. The `TrackBar` control provides a slider that you can display from left to right, or top to bottom.

The `TrackBar` provides two settings for the `Orientation` property. `Horizontal` makes the control slide left and right. `Vertical` orientation makes the control slide up and down. Once you place it on a form, the control does not change height in horizontal mode or width in vertical mode.

The `Minimum` property determines the smallest value of the slider that the user can select by moving the slider to the left or top position. The `Maximum` property determines the largest value of the slider that the user can select at the right or bottom position of the bar. You can set the `Value` property at design-time or in code to position the slider. When the user changes the slider, the `Value` property updates as well.

On the control display, the slide bar draws into a point that points towards a set of tick marks. A tick is a little dash on the control that indicates the values of the slider. The `TickFrequency` property determines how many ticks the control displays. For example, if the `TrackBar` ranges from 0 to 10, and `TickFrequency` = 1, the track bar contains eleven ticks, one for each value. For a `TickFrequency` of two, the ticks skip every other value. The `TickStyle` property allows you to place the ticks on the `BottomRight` — bottom for a horizontal bar, right for a vertical bar — `TopLeft`, `Both`, or `None`.

The `Scroll` event fires when the user moves the slider with the mouse or keyboard. The `Value` property updates to the new position of the slider before the event fires so you can display the number or make appropriate changes based on the slider position in the event.

SELECT NUMERIC DATA

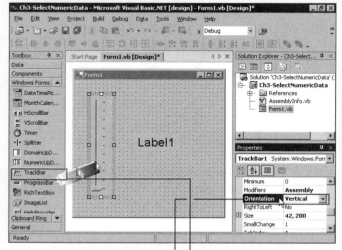

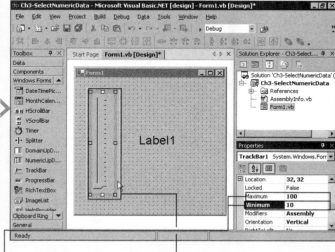

1 In a Windows Application project, add a control to respond to the value of the slider.

■ The example adds a `Label` control.

2 Click and drag the `TrackBar` control from the Toolbox to the form.

3 In the Properties window, double-click the `Orientation` property to switch between the two values.

■ In this example, the orientation is vertical.

4 Type an integer value for the `Minimum` property.

5 Type an integer value for the `Maximum` property.

6 Edit any other properties.

Note: See Chapter 2 to edit a property.

7 Double-click the control to add code for the `Scroll` event.

Extra

You can use the events available to the `TrackBar` control to make mouse scrolling an effective method of scrolling through values of the control. If the user moves the slider using a mouse wheel, the control does not raise the `Scroll` event. Instead, the control raises the `MouseWheel` event. You can call the `Scroll` event from the `MouseWheel` event to perform the same functionality.

Example:
```
Private Sub TrackBar1_Scroll(ByVal sender As _
      System.Object, ByVal e As _
      System.EventArgs) Handles TrackBar1.Scroll
   Label1.Text = TrackBar1.Value.ToString()
End Sub
Private Sub TrackBar1_MouseWheel(ByVal sender As _
      Object, ByVal e As _
      System.Windows.Forms.MouseEventArgs) _
      Handles TrackBar1.MouseWheel
   TrackBar1_Scroll(sender, e)
End Sub
```

You can manipulate properties to allow the user to move easily through the range of values. The `SmallChange` property specifies the smallest increment the slider moves. You use this to decide what values the slider moves to when the user drags it. For example, a value of two only allows the user to select every other number when moving the tracker. The `LargeChange` property determines how much the slider moves when the user clicks on the bar or uses the page up and page down keys to the sides of the slider.

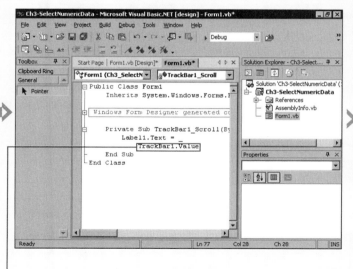

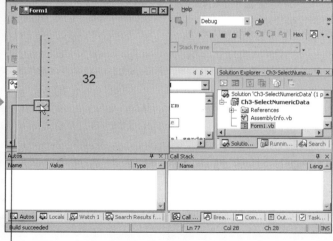

■ The Code Editor appears.

8 To retrieve the TrackBar value on the form, type the name of the control followed by **.Value**.

9 Press F5 to run your program.

■ The user can move the bar around as necessary.

CREATE TIMED EVENTS

You can use the Timer control to run code at defined intervals. The Timer control works in the background, raising events in your form at specified intervals. You can use the Timer control's event to perform background processing in increments of time without interrupting the user.

The Interval property specifies the time before an event fires. Interval is an integer number that specifies times in milliseconds. The default is 100, which means 100/1000 of a second, or 10 times a second. For example, you can specify one second as 1000, and a minute as 60000. Intervals smaller than 50 are not reliable on most machines and may fire irregularly.

The Enabled property determines if the control actively fires events. The default is False. You can set this property to True at design-time if you want the control to start firing events based on the Interval immediately after the form loads.

To start the control as your program runs, use the Start method. To stop the timer, use the Stop method. If the event has already fired, it runs until complete, even if you execute a Stop.

The event where you place your timer code is called Tick. You place any code in here that needs to run every timer count.

If your code does not finish before the next time interval, another Tick event loads, creating a large stack of the event waiting, which in most cases leads to undesirable results, and if it happens for an extended period, may cause the program to crash or your computer to run out of memory. Make sure your Interval is long enough to allow the code inside of the event to complete.

CREATE TIMED EVENTS

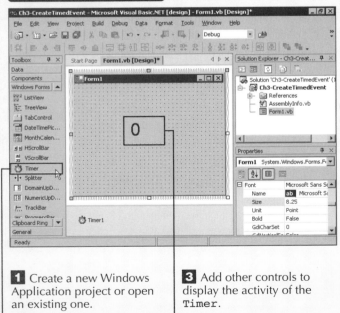

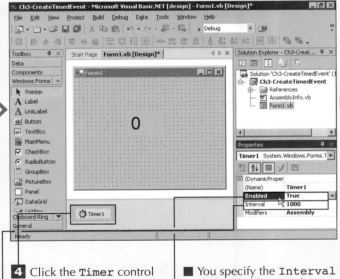

1 Create a new Windows Application project or open an existing one.

2 In the Toolbox, double-click the **Timer** control to add it to the form.

3 Add other controls to display the activity of the **Timer**.

■ The example adds a **Label** control to the form.

4 Click the **Timer** control in the Component Tray to edit its properties.

5 In the Property Window, type a value representing the speed at which you want events to fire in the **Interval** property.

■ You specify the **Interval** property in milliseconds.

6 Double-click the **Enabled** property to toggle it to **True**.

7 Double-click the **Timer** control in the Component Tray.

Extra You must develop your application carefully for the `Timer` control to function properly. The Timer control does not operate in a separate thread, meaning it can only function if your application is idle. If your application is running a calculation or intensive loop of operations and you want the Timer control to function at the same time, you must call the `DoEvents` method of the `Application` object. This method allows other queued events and operations to occur like the `Timer` control's `Tick` event and UI redraws. Keep in mind that when you call `DoEvents`, events such as mouse clicks fire, so you must make sure that the user does not attempt to start an action that is already in process again.

Example:
```
Do
    ' do lots of processing
    ' ...


    ' let the application do any necessary queued
actions
    Application.DoEvents()
Loop Until done
```

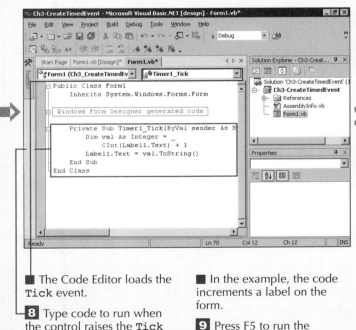

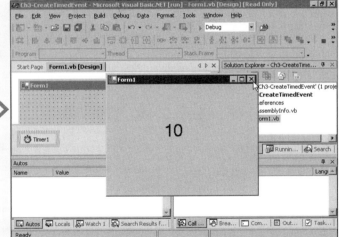

■ The Code Editor loads the **Tick** event.

8 Type code to run when the control raises the **Tick** event.

■ In the example, the code increments a label on the form.

9 Press F5 to run the project.

■ The **Timer** raises the event as specified in the **Interval** property.

PROVIDE DATE SELECTION

You can use the `MonthCalendar` and `DateTimePicker` controls to provide simple date selection. The `MonthCalendar` control provides a full monthly calendar with month scrolling, and the ability to select a range of dates. The `DateTimePicker` is a date or time display with a drop-down `MonthCalendar` control for date selection.

The `MonthCalendar` control provides a great deal of flexibility. You can alter the number of months shown by changing the `CalendarDimensions` structure's `Width` and `Height` properties. For example, if you set the width to six and the height to two, the control displays twelve months on screen at once.

The `MinDate` and `MaxDate` properties allow you to set the range from which the user can select. These properties allow you to limit the months the user can browse through using the control.

The `MaxSelectionCount` determines the maximum range of days that a user can select at once. For example, setting

this property to seven allows the user to select up to seven days on the calendar. The `SelectionRange` property provides the selected range of dates. The `SelectionRange` property returns a class that contains `Start` and `End` properties that allow you to set or retrieve the currently selected range of dates. To access the selected beginning date, use `MonthCalendar1.SelectionRange.Start`. The control also supports two shortcut properties, `SelectionStart` and `SelectionEnd`, which provide the same function.

The `DateTimePicker` control provides many of the same properties to set and return the selection of the user. With the `DateTimePicker` control, the display shows the date selected with a down arrow that the user can click to display a `MonthCalender` to select a single date. The `MinDate` and `MaxDate` properties function like the `MonthCalendar` control explained above. You can retrieve or set the selected date using the `Value` property.

PROVIDE DATE SELECTION

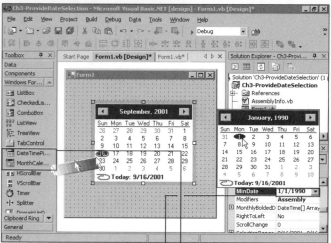

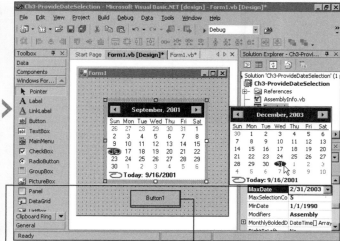

1 Create a new Windows Application project or open an existing project.

2 Click and drag either the **DateTimePicker** or **MonthCalendar** control from the Toolbox to the form.

3 Click the **MinDate** property's ■ and click the minimum date the user can select.

4 Repeat step 3 to modify the **MaxDate** property.

5 Edit any other necessary properties.

6 Add a control to use the value the user selects.

Note: See Chapter 2 to set properties and controls.

7 Double-click the control to edit its default event.

Extra

The ShowToday property allows you to enable or disable the label at the bottom of the calendar that shows today's date. The ShowTodayCircle enables or disables the display of a red circle from today's date both at the bottom and in the calendar.

You can set the DateTimePicker control to allow display and allow the entry of a time by changing Format to Time. You must set the ShowUpDown property to True to use the DateTimePicker control as a time editor.

Three properties allow you to store dates to show as bolded in the calendar. The BoldedDates property stores an array of DateTime variables that bold when shown on the calendar. Add a BoldedDate by calling the AddBoldedDate method and passing a DateTime class. The MonthlyBoldedDates array uses the day given in each stored DateTime, but display every month on the calendar. You can add a monthly date using the AddMonthlyBoldedDate method. AnnuallyBoldedDates use the month and day specified in each DateTime, and display on that day every year. You add an annual bolded date using the AddAnnuallyBoldedDate method.

Example:
```
Dim Birthday As DateTime = New DateTime(2001, 8, 23)
Dim Deadline As DateTime = New DateTime(2001, 10, 25)
MonthCalendar1.AddAnnuallyBoldedDate(Birthday)
MonthCalendar1.AddBoldedDate(Deadline)
```

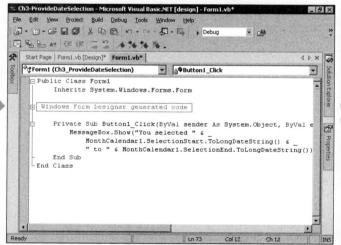

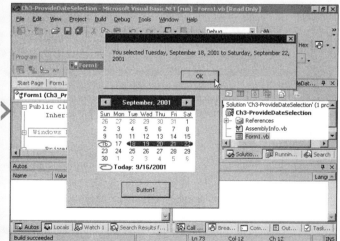

■ The Code Editor window appears.

8 To access the selected date, type the name of the date control followed by a period.

9 For a DateTimePicker, type **Value**; for a MonthCalendar, type **SectionStart** or **SectionEnd**.

■ In the example, the **Button1_Click** event displays a message box containing the selected date range.

10 Run the project by pressing F5

■ The date control interacts with the user and the returns the appropriate selection.

EXPLORE LIST VIEWS

You may have some instances where you must display more data than you can easily fit in a simple `ListBox` control. You use the `ListView` control to provide a list of data with multiple columns and with different view modes. The Windows Explorer uses the `ListView` control to provide file listings.

A `ListView` provides four views that you can set with the `View` property: `LargeIcon`, `Details`, `SmallIcon`, and `List`. The `LargeIcon` view shows a full-size icon with the associated text shown below the icon. The `SmallIcon` view shows a small icon with the text to the right of the icon. The `Details` view shows a small icon and a single item per line with a definable set of columns describing the item.

You can attach a large and a small icon to each item. You must create a single `ImageList` control to hold the icons for both of these types. When you add an item to the list, you can assign the index for the icon the item displays. VB .NET provides a `LargeImageList` and

`SmallImageList` property to link the corresponding `ImageList` controls. For more information about the `ImageList` control, see the section "Work with ImageLists."

VB .NET stores items in the list in the `Items` collection. Each item consists of a caption you assign using the `Text` property and an assigned icon, chosen with the `ImageIndex` property. At design-time, you can modify the item list using a visual editor.

You define columns, which you see in detailed view, using the `Columns` collection. `Details` view requires you to define at least one column. The `SubItems` collection of each `ListViewItem` in the list stores the settings for the information to display about an item in the various columns.

When you select an item, the `ListView_SelectedIndexChanged` event fires. You can retrieve a collection of the selected items using the `SelectedItems` collection.

EXPLORE LIST VIEWS

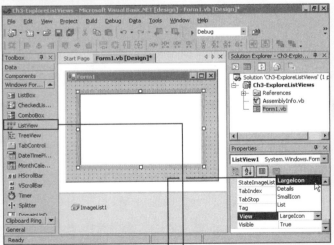

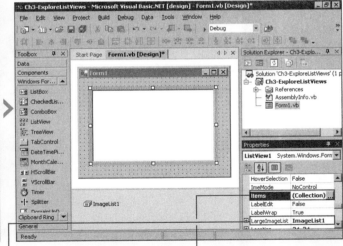

1 In a Windows Application project, add an `ImageList` control to the form and add images to it as appropriate.

Note: See the section "Work with ImageLists" to add an `ImageList` control.

2 In the Toolbox, click and drag the `ListView` control to add it to the form.

3 In the Properties window, select the appropriate view.

■ The example uses the `LargeIcon` view.

4 Click ▾ in `LargeImageList` or `SmallImageList` and select `ImageList`.

■ If you use the large icon view, set the `LargeImageList` property; otherwise set the `SmallImageList` property.

5 In the Properties window, click ▦ beside the `Items` property.

■ The ListViewItem Collection Editor appears.

Extra

The `ListViewItem` class stores the information of a single item in a `ListView`. Because you can access this class, you can create a new `ListViewItem` and then add it to the `ListView` control. Using this method allows the flexibility of setting the properties of the `ListViewItem` before adding it to the control.

Example:
```
Dim newItem As New System.Windows.Forms.ListViewItem
newItem.Text = "sample item"
newItem.BackColor = System.Drawing.Color.Red
newItem.ForeColor = System.Drawing.Color.White
ListView1.Items.Add(newItem)
```

You can remove an item by locating the `ListViewItem` that you want to remove. Once you have a reference to a `ListViewItem`, you can call its `Remove` method to delete it from the `ListView`. To remove the items the user has selected, loop through the `SelectedItems` collection and remove each of them.

Example:
```
Dim item As System.Windows.Forms.ListViewItem
For Each item In ListView1.SelectedItems
    item.Remove
Next
```

6 Click Add to add a list item.

7 Click the `Text` property and type the appropriate text for the item.

8 Click the `ImageIndex` property ▪ and select an image for the item.

9 Repeat steps 6 through 8 as necessary.

10 Click OK.

11 Press F5 to run the project.

■ The `ListView` shows the items created during design-time editing.

EXPLORE TREE VIEWS

You can use `TreeView` controls to provide a tree-like display of hierarchal information. Any data that has a root source with various subcategories is well suited to the capabilities of the `TreeView` control. The Windows Explorer uses a tree view to display the hierarchy of the directory system.

With the `TreeView` control, you can use an `ImageList` control to assign pictures to items of the tree. You assign the `ImageList` control you create to the `ImageList` property. The `ImageIndex` property sets the image for all of the items in the `TreeView`. The image you select using the `SelectedImageIndex` property is used in its place for a selected item. You cannot individually assign pictures to the items in a `TreeView` as you can with a `ListView` control.

The `TreeView` control provides a number of properties to control its interface. If you enable `ShowLines`, the control draws lines from parent items to all of its children. `ShowPlusMinus` displays plus and minus signs beside items with children, which the user can click to expand and collapse a node. Set `Sorted` to `True` and VB .NET sorts each individual tree and subtree alphabetically. The `HotTracking` property makes the control draw the text caption, like a hyperlink, when a user places the mouse pointer over it.

The `Nodes` collection contains the list of top-level nodes in the tree. Then, each top-level `TreeNode` contains a `Nodes` collection of all of its children, and so on. You can use the `Add` method to insert a node to a tree. The `AddRange` method creates an entire tree, deleting current items. You can use `Clear` to delete an entire tree, while `Remove` can delete a single node.

EXPLORE TREE VIEWS

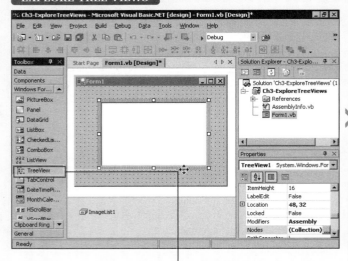

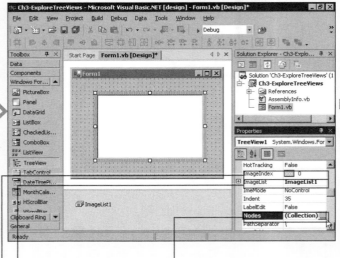

1 Create a new Windows Application project or open an existing one.

2 Set up an `ImageList` control that contains an image for unselected nodes and an image for selected node items.

Note: See the section "Work with ImageList" to add an image list control.

3 In the Toolbox, click the **TreeView** control and add the control to the form.

4 Click the **ImageList** property ▼ and select the **ImageList** control.

5 Click the **ImageIndex** property ▼ and select the default image for the items in the control.

■ Optionally, set the **SelectedImageIndex** property using the same method.

6 In the Properties window, click ⬚ beside the **Nodes** property.

■ The TreeNode Editor appears.

Extra

You have the ability to create an entire node with children using the `TreeNode` class. Using this method allows you to set all of the properties of a `Node` before adding it to the control. Building a `TreeNode` also allows you to build an entire set of nodes and children before adding to the `TreeView`. This method is extremely useful when the program is already running, because adding the entire tree at the same time is much faster than adding items individually to the tree.

Example:
```
Dim newNode As New System.Windows.Forms.TreeNode()
Dim newChildNode As New _
  System.Windows.Forms.TreeNode()
newNode.Text = "Sample item"
newChildNode.Text = "Sample child node"
newNode.Nodes.Add(newChildNode)
TreeView1.Nodes.Add(newNode)
```

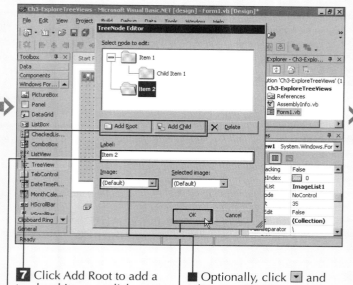

7 Click Add Root to add a top-level item, or click an existing item and click Add Child to add an item as a child.

8 Type a label for the node.

■ Optionally, click 🔽 and select a custom image for the item.

9 Repeat steps 7 through 8 to add the necessary items.

10 Click OK when done.

11 Press F5 to run the project.

■ The `TreeView` shows the items and allows a user to close and open subtrees.

CREATE A TOOLBAR

You can use toolbars to provide buttons on a form, typically at the top, to access the most common features. The `Toolbar` control provides the functionality to create a basic toolbar with two styles, set by the `Appearance` property: `Normal`, or `Flat`. While `Normal` is the default setting, most toolbars in modern applications use the `Flat` style.

The `Toolbar` control, part of the `ListView` and `TreeView` family, requires an `ImageList` to retrieve images for the toolbar buttons. You can attach an `ImageList` control using the `ImageList` property.

Each button is contained in the `Buttons` collection. A single button has a `Text` property, an `ImageIndex` property to select the appropriate image from the `ImageList`, `ToolTipText` to display a tool tip for a button, and a `Style` property. The `PushButton` style is a standard toolbar button that the user can click. `ToggleButton` is a button that stays down when pressed

until pressed again. `Seperator` is a divider, and the user cannot click it.

The `DropDownButton` style creates a button that has an associated drop-down menu. The `DropDownMenu` property allows you to assign a `ContextMenu` control to the property. For more information on Context Menu controls, see Chapter 2.

The `TextAlign` property allows you to place the text `Underneath` the icon, or to the `Right` of the icon.

To make the buttons on the toolbar functional, use the `Toolbar_ButtonClick` event. The event variable, e, returns a reference to the button that a user clicks. For a toggle button, you can check to see if the button was toggled into a pressed state by accessing the `Pressed` property like `e.Button.Pushed`. A drop-down button should provide a default action on a click. When the user clicks the drop-down button, this event is not fired.

CREATE A TOOLBAR

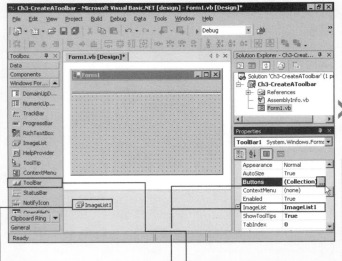

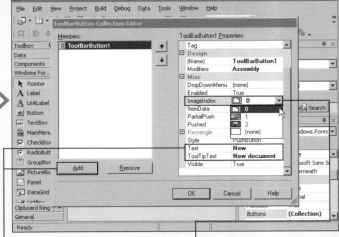

1 In a Windows Application project, add and set up an `ImageList` control to hold toolbar images.

Note: See the section "Work with ImageLists" for more information.

2 Double-click the `Toolbar` control to add it.

3 Click the `ImageList` property ⬇ and select the `ImageList` control.

4 Click the `Buttons` property ⬜.

■ The Toolbar Collection Editor appears.

5 Click Add.

6 Type a label for the button into the `Text` property box and a description into the `ToolTipText` property box.

7 Click the `ImageIndex` property ⬇ and select the appropriate image for the tool button.

■ You do not need to fill the `Text` property if you assign an image to the button.

Apply It

You can customize the VB .NET ToolBar control using a context menu. The code below loads the toolbar buttons into the menu and allows the user to toggle each one's visibility. You can use the code with any toolbar, as long as each button has a caption set with the Text property. Add a ContextMenu control to the form and set the Toolbar's ContextMenu property to this control.

TYPE THIS:

```
Private Sub Form1_Load(ByVal sender As System.Object, ByVal e As _
    System.EventArgs) Handles MyBase.Load

    Dim button As ToolBarButton, menuItem As MenuItem
    ' loop through all toolbar buttons
    For Each button In ToolBar1.Buttons
        ' add a menu item for each toolbar button
        menuItem = ContextMenu1.MenuItems.Add(button.Text, _
        AddressOf MyMenuClick)
        ' if button is visible, check menu.
        menuItem.Checked = button.Visible
    Next
End Sub

Private Sub MyMenuClick(ByVal sender As Object, ByVal e As System.EventArgs)
    ' get menu item from sender object
    Dim menuItem As MenuItem = CType(sender, MenuItem)
    ' find toolbar button based on menu item
    Dim button As ToolBarButton = ToolBar1.Buttons(menuItem.Index())

    button.Visible = Not button.Visible
    menuItem.Checked = Not menuItem.Checked
End Sub
```

RESULT:

A context menu for the toolbar that allows the user to selectively show and hide toolbar buttons.

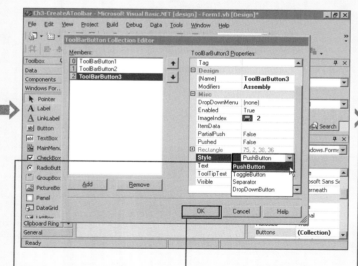

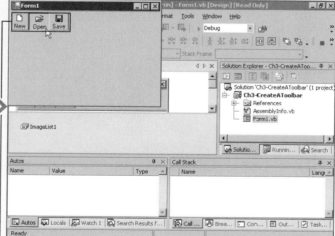

8 Click the Style property's ▼ and then click the appropriate style.

■ The default, PushButton, is a standard toolbar button. You can use the Separator type to create a blank space between buttons.

■ You can repeat steps 5 through 8 as necessary.

9 Click OK when done.

10 Press F5 to run your project.

■ The Toolbar appears and allows you to press buttons.

■ To make the buttons functional, you can handle the ButtonClick event.

Note: See Chapter 2 to handle events.

PROVIDE STATUS INFORMATION

Y̲ou can provide status and help information on the form, typically at the bottom with the StatusBar control. The status bar also places an easy resize grip in the right-hand corner for easier resizing. StatusBar controls easily broadcast information to a user working in the main application space without interfering with them.

The StatusBar control has two modes: simple mode and paneled mode. The simple mode allows you to simply set the Text property and provide a single line of information on the status bar.

To enable paneled mode, you set ShowPanels to True. In this mode, you define custom ranges of space called panels. Each panel is a sized area into which you can load textual information. VB .NET defines panels in the Panels collection.

Each Panel in the Panels collection has a number of properties. Text allows you to set or retrieve text into the panel. Alignment lets you control left, center, or right-align the contents of the panel. BorderStyle controls the

panel's edges. The default is Sunken, but other options include Raised and None. You can load an icon into the panel by using the Icon property. The Toolbar does not scale the icon, so the icon needs a 16x16 version.

AutoSize, when set to Content, allows the panel to resize itself to its contents. If this is not True, the Width property defines the width of the panel. When the panel has AutoSize set, you can define the minimum width it reaches using the MinWidth property.

So in ShowPanels = False mode, you can update the status bar at any time by setting StatusBar.Text equal to a text string. In ShowPanels mode, you need to update the different panels individually by setting StatusBarPanel.Text equal to a text string.

The StatusBar notifies you to clicks using the Click event for default status bars, or the PanelClick click for paneled bars.

PROVIDE STATUS INFORMATION

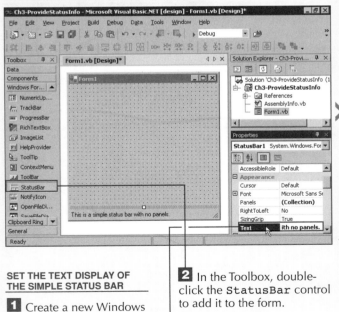

SET THE TEXT DISPLAY OF THE SIMPLE STATUS BAR

1 Create a new Windows Application project or open an existing one.

2 In the Toolbox, double-click the StatusBar control to add it to the form.

3 In the Properties window, set the Text property.

CREATING A PANELLED STATUS BAR

4 Set the ShowPanels property in the Properties window to True.

Note: See Chapter 2 to learn about setting properties.

5 Click the Panels property.

6 Click ▦.

Apply It

You can create a progress meter that updates inside a single panel of your status bar. To create custom panels, set the panel's `Style` to `OwnerDraw`. When this is set, the `StatusBar` control fires the `DrawItem` event every time you need to redraw the panel. If you want to manually redraw the panel, you can use the `Invalidate` method. In the example below, place the `percentDone` declaration at the top of the form code. Add a button to the form and set one panel's `Style = OwnerDraw`. When you press the button, the progress meter fills by 5 percent.

TYPE THIS:

```
Private percentDone As Integer

Private Sub StatusBar1_DrawItem(ByVal sender As Object, ByVal sbdevent _
    As System.Windows.Forms.StatusBarDrawItemEventArgs) _
    Handles StatusBar1.DrawItem
    Dim g As Graphics = sbdevent.Graphics
    Dim b As Brush = New SolidBrush(SystemColors.Highlight)
    Dim rect As Rectangle = sbdevent.Bounds
    rect.Width = CInt(CSng(percentDone) / 100 * rect.Width)
    g.FillRectangle(b, rect)
End Sub

Private Sub Button1_Click(ByVal sender As System.Object, ByVal e As _
    System.EventArgs) Handles Button1.Click
    percentDone = percentDone + 5
    StatusBar1.Invalidate()
End Sub
```

RESULT:

The progress bar panel fills when a user repeatedly clicks the button.

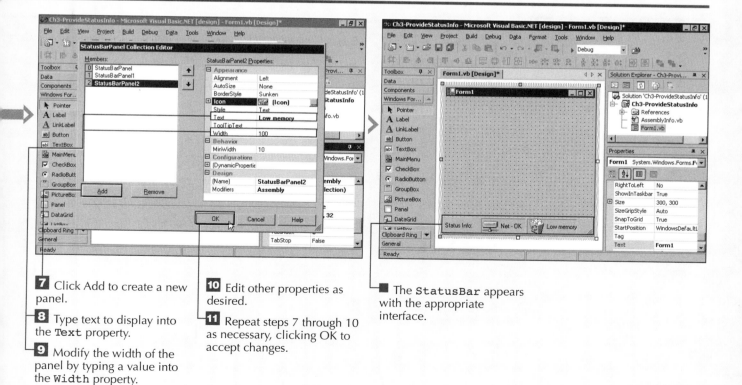

7 Click Add to create a new panel.

8 Type text to display into the **Text** property.

9 Modify the width of the panel by typing a value into the **Width** property.

10 Edit other properties as desired.

11 Repeat steps 7 through 10 as necessary, clicking OK to accept changes.

■ The **StatusBar** appears with the appropriate interface.

CREATE A TAB INTERFACE

You can create a tabbed interface to allow the user access to several screens of controls. A *tabbed interface* allows a single form to contain multiple screens of information, designated by named tabs, between which the user can switch. The TabControl control provides a fully functioning container control, much like a Panel control, but allows you to create multiple screens in the same client space. For more on the Panel control, see the section "Work With Panels."

The TabPages collection contains the list of tabs present. Each tab has an independent Text property, a BackgroundImage property to assign a picture, and a ToolTipText property. By setting the AutoScroll property to True, tabs provide scrollbars, as necessary, to let users scroll through the controls the tab contains.

By setting the ImageList property of the TabControl to a valid ImageList, you can assign images using the ImageIndex property of each tab to place on the left of the text.

The Padding structure allows you to add space around the text in the tab. Padding.X defines the amount of space to the left and right, while Padding.Y defines space to the top of the bottom of the tab. The HotTrack property makes the text label change colors when the user moves the mouse pointer over it.

The Appearance property allows three different modes. Normal displays standard tabs. Buttons displays a toggle button at the top of the control. FlatButtons exhibits a toolbar as well as a toggle. Alignment lets you move the tabs to various sides, with Top being the default, and Bottom, Right, and Left aligning tabs bottom, right and left.

When the user clicks a tab header, the control automatically switches to that tab. The control notifies you of the click using the TabControl_Click event. Each TabPage provides the standard abilities of a container, meaning controls contained in the page can use Dock and Anchor to resize within the tab page. For more information on resizing controls, see Chapter 2.

CREATE A TAB INTERFACE

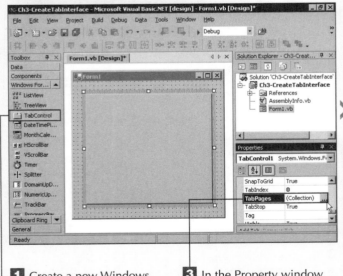

1 Create a new Windows Application project or open an existing one.

2 In the Toolbox, click and drag the TabControl to add it to the form.

3 In the Property window, click ▦ for the TabPages property.

4 Click Add.

5 Type the name of the tab beside the Text property.

6 Change any other necessary properties.

Note: To edit a property, see Chapter 2.

7 Repeat steps 4 through 6 to add tabs as necessary, clicking OK to the accept changes when done.

Extra

Be careful when using the `TabControl` on resizing windows. By default the `Multiline` property is set, which means that if the tabs do not fit on the row when a user sizes down the form, they move to two rows, making the client space smaller to accommodate the tabs. You can use the properties of the `TabControl` to make sure when the tab pages resize, the contents of the control remain visible. If you do not plan for resizing, this may cause controls on the client area to appear clipped at the bottom. To avoid this problem, set `Multiline` to `False`. In this case, VB .NET adds a scroll arrow to allow the user to see tabs that do not fit. You can provide resize settings to the controls on the tab pages. See Chapter 2 for more information on using `Dock` and `Anchor` to provide automatic resizing. You can also add scrollbars to the client area of the tab page. Set `AutoScroll = True` to allow scrollbars to appear if the tab area becomes too small to fit the controls on the tab page. Keep in mind that scrollbars often make using the program more difficult because users cannot see all of the information on screen at once.

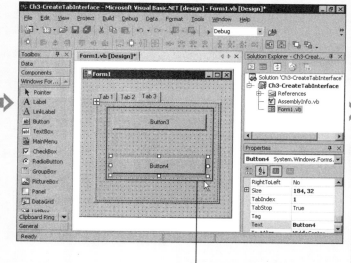

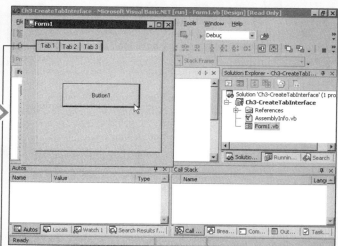

■ The tabs appear and you can move between them at design time.

8 Add any necessary controls to each tab page.

9 Press F5 to run your project.

■ The **TabControl** allows movement between its tabs.

PROVIDE ERROR MESSAGES

You can use the `ErrorProvider` control to alert a user to a data entry error by displaying an unobtrusive small error icon. The `ErrorProvider` control allows you to show an error message related to a control without bringing up a message box that stops the user's flow of information entry. The `ErrorProvider` provides three properties to all of the controls on a form that allow you to monitor the controls for errors. The properties the provider adds to controls are `Error`, `IconAlignment`, and `IconPadding`. Typically, you use the `ErrorProvider` with text box controls because they provide a free-flow information entry area that can easily contain errors.

The `Error` on ErrorProvider property allows you to set an error message to appear for the control. Placing a string into this property makes an error icon appear beside the control. When the user moves the mouse over the icon, a tool tip pops up with the error text specified in the

property. In most cases, you do not want to set the error at design-time and instead want the error icon to appear dynamically when an error occurs.

The `SetError` method allows you to set the error message for a control at runtime. Its first argument is the control where the error exists, and the second is the error text, for example, `SetError(TextBox1, "Error Message")`. You use this method when doing validation on a control.

Controls on the form provide a `Validating` event that each control raises after the user moves to another control. This event allows you to check the value of the control for errors. If you find an error with a selection, set the error text using the `SetError` method. If the user fixes the error, clear the message by calling the method with a blank string for the error message.

PROVIDE ERROR MESSAGES

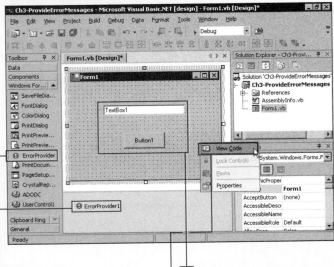

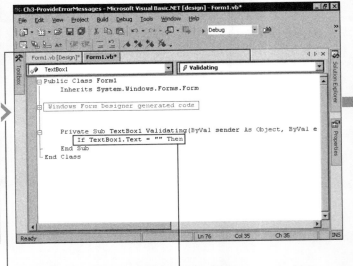

1 Create a new Windows Application project or open an existing one.

2 In the Toolbox, double-click the `ErrorProvider` control.

■ The control appears in the component tray.

3 Add an input control to the form and another control to move the focus so validation occurs.

■ The example adds a **TextBox** control and a **Button** control on the form.

4 Right-click the form and click View Code.

■ The Code Editor appears.

5 In the class list, select the input control you added.

6 In the event list, select the **Validating** event.

■ VB .NET creates the event handler.

7 Type code to check for an input error.

Extra

You can specify the `IconAlignment` property the `ErrorProvider` control adds to each control to customize the location of the error icon on the form. The `IconPadding` on `ErrorProvider` property allows you to set the number of pixels between the control and the icon. Remember to be careful of the spacing you set. You should not add so much spacing it is hard to distinguish which icon relates to which input control. A useful feature of this property is to make all of your error icons line up in a column running down the screen beside the controls, even if the controls are not all of the same length.

Some properties are available in the `ErrorProvider` control itself that allow you to control the appearance of the icon that appears beside the input controls. The `Icon` property allows you to change the error icon you display. You can assign any icon file to this property. You can also set the `BlinkStyle` property to manipulate the blinking properties of the icon. You can set the property to `AlwaysBlink`, which makes the icon blink until the user corrects the error message, `NeverBlink` to ensure the error icon never blinks, or the default, `BlinkIfDifferentError`, which blinks only if the error message changes.

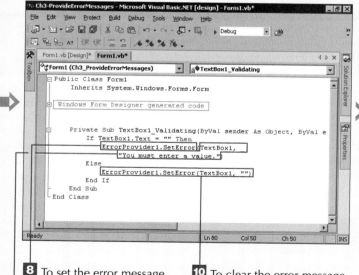

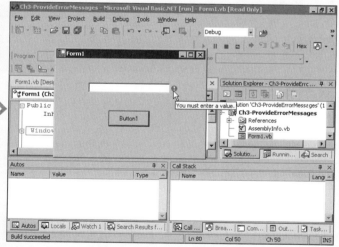

8 To set the error message, type the name of the **ErrorProvider** control followed by **.SetError()**.

9 Inside the parentheses, specify the input control followed by a comma and the error message in quotes.

10 To clear the error message, follow steps 8 and 9 but enter a blank error message.

11 Press F5 to run the project.

■ An alert icon appears beside the control when validation fails and your text appears when a user holds the mouse over it.

CREATE A CONSOLE APPLICATION

Console applications provide the most basic Visual Basic .NET program; they display textual information in a console. An example of a console window is the Command Prompt application. You can create console applications to provide a simple way to test and develop code without the additional effort necessary for visual form development. The Console object gives all the necessary methods to output information to the user and read information from the user, taking the place of forms and controls. See Chapter 2 for more information on Windows Forms applications.

The System.Console object provides the functionality to access the console. Unlike a Windows Forms-based application, a console application does not require a class and simply loads from a default module with a Sub Main procedure.

You use the Console Application project template to create a new application. Code execution always begins in the Sub

Main module, but you can create supplementary classes and modules to support the application. Chapter 7 contains more information about classes.

To write a line of text to the console, use the WriteLine method of the Console object. For example, WriteLine("Test") writes Test to the console and moves to the next line. If you want to output text without moving to the next line, use the Write method. Pass a string of text enclosed in quotes or pass a variable to either of these methods to output the information. For more information on passing parameters to methods, see the section "Pass Information Through a Method."

To read a single character from the input stream, use the Read method. The Read method returns the character value as an Integer. To read in a line of information, use the ReadLine method. The ReadLine method returns a String variable. For more information on creating a string variable to hold the result, see the section "Create a String."

CREATE A CONSOLE APPLICATION

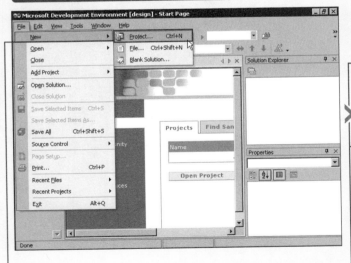

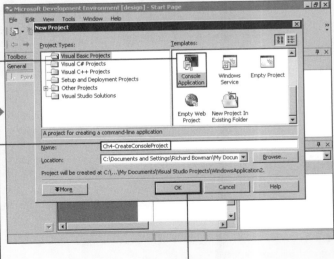

1 Click File ➡ New ➡ Project.

■ The New Project dialog box appears.

2 Click Console Application from the templates list.

3 Type a name for the project.

4 Click OK to create the project.

■ The project opens a default module and declares a Sub Main procedure.

Extra

You can use the `Console` object to perform *asynchronous* reading and writing in a console application. This means you can run a block of code in an application without stopping for input. You can then check the input buffer at your leisure. To start an asynchronous read, use the `Console.OpenStandardInput` method. VB .NET provides a method `BeginRead` that sets up the buffer to store the characters. In the code below, the `Sub Main` procedure enters an infinite loop where it never polls for input, but simply checks a buffer variable set up in the `BeginRead` method.

Example:

```
Module Module1
        Private b(10) As Byte
        Sub Main()
                Console.OpenStandardInput.BeginRead(b, 0, 10, AddressOf OnRead, Nothing)
                Do
                        ' TODO: Do important calculations here without stopping for input.
                        If Not (b(0) = "") Then Console.Write(b)
                Loop
        End Sub
        Sub OnRead(ByVal e As IAsyncResult)
                Dim count As Integer = Console.OpenStandardInput.EndRead(e)
                Console.OpenStandardInput.BeginRead(b, 0, 10, AddressOf OnRead, Nothing)
        End Sub
End Module
```

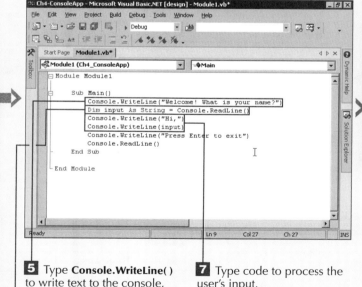

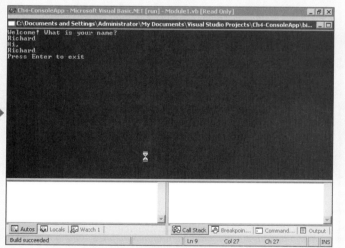

5 Type **Console.WriteLine( )** to write text to the console, placing the variable or text to display within the parentheses.

6 Type **Dim input As String = Console.ReadLine( )**, replacing `input` with the variable name.

7 Type code to process the user's input.

Note: To declare variables, see the section "Declare a Variable." To process string variables, see "Work with Strings."

8 Press F5 to run the application.

■ The application reads and writes data to and from a console window.

ADD A METHOD

A *method* enables you to split up parts of a module or class into various subroutines, as well as create a block of code associated with a subroutine name. You can use methods to call a block of code from other methods inside the class or module. Depending on its *scope*, you can access the method outside of its module or class. For more information on the scope of a method, see the section "Declare a Variable."

When a block of code calls a method, the execution of that code block stops and your method begins. When VB .NET reaches the end of the code in your method, execution passes back to the code block that calls it and proceeds. However, any code you place in a separate method cannot access data from the code block that invokes it. You use arguments to give a list of required information. For more information on arguments, see the section "Pass Information Through Methods."

To create a new method inside an existing code module, you have two options. If the code does not need to pass information back to the code that calls it, you can use the Sub keyword. If the routine needs to return a value to the code that calls it, use the Function keyword. For a method defined as a Function, you must designate the return type for the Function using the As keyword along with a variable type after the parameter list. For more information on returning values, see the section "Pass Information Through Methods."

To call a method that you create in the same module or class, place the name of the method on a line of its own and follow it by a set of parentheses. If the method requires arguments, enclose the values to pass to the method inside the parentheses. You separate multiple arguments with commas.

ADD A METHOD

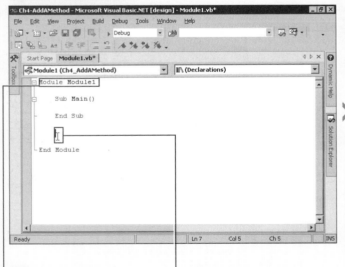

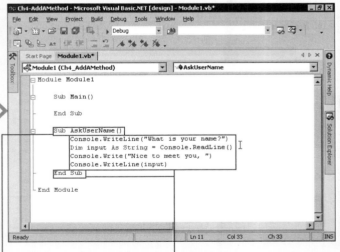

1 Create a new Console Application or open any existing project.

Note: See the section "Create a Console Application" for details.

2 Open the class or module to which you want to add a method in the Code Editor.

■ You can right-click a module or form in the Solution Explorer and click View Code to open a module.

3 Click a blank line outside of any other methods.

4 Type **Sub AskUserName()**, replacing **AskUserName** with the name of the method.

■ You can type the **Function** keyword instead of **Sub** to create a method that returns parameters.

5 Press Enter.

■ Visual Basic creates the **End Sub** keyword.

6 Type the code for your method between the **Sub** and **End Sub**.

You can create a loop of code where a `Do` or `For` loop does not provide adequate functionality. In this case, you can use *recursion* to have a method call itself a number of times. Recursion can be difficult to properly code, and you can easily lock up your program. When writing recursive methods, remember to provide an exit. You must allow the recursion to stop in all cases. For this to occur, you must have variables outside of the scope of the function.

TYPE THIS:

```
Module Module1
    Private counter As Integer

    Sub Main()
        counter = 10
        RecursiveFunction()
    End Sub

    Sub RecursiveFunction()
        Console.WriteLine(counter)
        counter = counter - 1
        If counter > 0 Then RecursiveFunction()
    End Sub
End Module
```

RESULT:

```
10
9
...
2
1
```

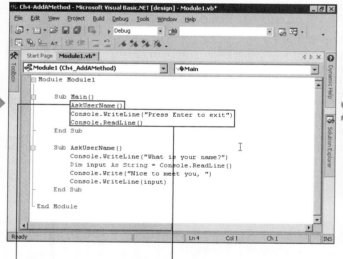

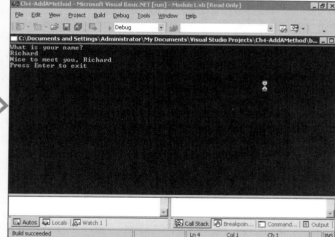

7 In the code that calls the method, type **AskUserName()** on a new line, replacing `AskUserName` with the name of the method.

■ If you call a method that requires a set of arguments, specify values for the necessary arguments inside the parentheses.

8 Add other method code.

9 Press F5 to run your application.

■ The existing method calls your newly created method and your method runs its code and returns.

DECLARE A VARIABLE

You can employ a variable to store a piece of information in memory that your program can use as it runs. For example, you may want to store the fact that the user's age is 31. To store this information, you tell VB .NET to reserve a space in memory to store a certain type of information. You then assign the memory area a name so that the program can reference it.

To declare a variable, the act of telling the compiler to reserve memory, you specify the kind of data that you require the variable to store. A variable can only store one type of data such as a number, date, or string of text. To store the aforementioned example age, or any other small positive or negative whole number, you use the `Short` data type. You can learn about the various data types in the section "Using Variable Data Types."

To create a variable, you must assign the variable a particular type, as well as a name for your identification

purposes. The name of a variable can include any letter (uppercase or lowercase), numbers, and underscores (_). You cannot use a number as the first character of the variable name, and if you start the variable name with an underscore, you must follow it with another valid character.

You use the `Dim` command to declare a variable. After `Dim` you place the variable name you want to create. After the variable name, type **As** and the variable type. Type **=** after the definition to assign a default value to the variable, as in the example, `Dim userAge As Integer = 31`.

The location you define a variable determines where VB .NET allows access to it. You can refer to this as the *scope* of the variable. Placing the variable declaration at the top of a method lets you access it while the method runs and delete it when the method exits.

DECLARE A VARIABLE

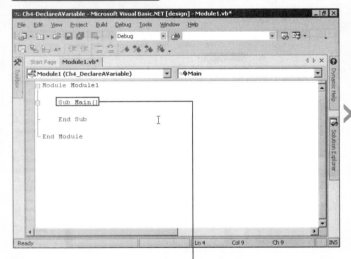

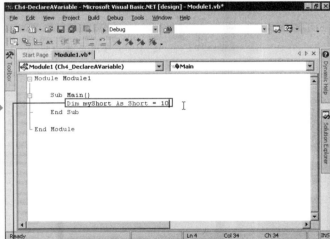

1 Create a new project or open an existing one.

Note: See Chapter 1 for more on creating new projects.

2 Place the insertion point on a blank line beneath the method in which you want to declare a variable.

■ In this example, the `Main` procedure of a console application acts as the method.

3 Type **Dim myShort As Short = 10**, replacing `myShort` with the variable name, and `10` with the number to assign to `myShort`.

■ The example creates a short integer variable.

Note: See the next section, "Using Variable Data Types," for more variable types.

Extra

VB .NET uses variable scope to determine where you can use a variable name depending on where you define it. If a programming language did not use scoping, all of the variables you declare take up a significant quantity of memory. The scope of a variable defines where a variable is active and when VB .NET removes the variable from memory because you can no longer access it.

When you declare a variable inside a method, you cannot access the variable outside of that method. For example, you cannot declare a variable inside a method, then access the variable when you call another. If you declare a variable inside a block statement, like an If block or a Do loop, you can only access the variable inside the block. Unlike Visual Basic 6 and earlier versions, code following the block inside the same method cannot access the variable. To make a variable accessible to all of the methods of a class, you can define member variables. See Chapter 7 for more information. You can also create global variables in VB .NET using shared member variables. See Chapter 8 for more information.

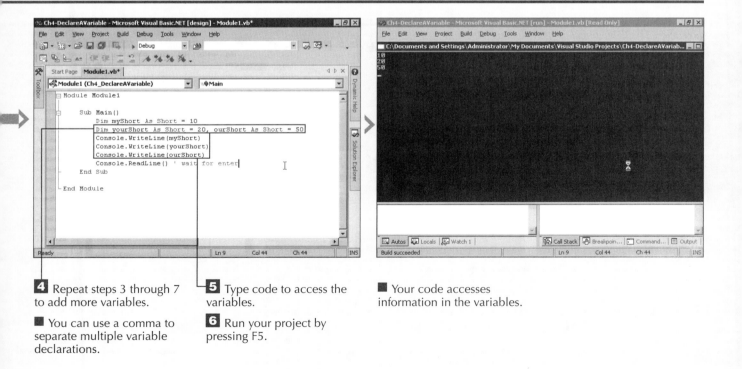

4 Repeat steps 3 through 7 to add more variables.

■ You can use a comma to separate multiple variable declarations.

5 Type code to access the variables.

6 Run your project by pressing F5.

■ Your code accesses information in the variables.

USING VARIABLE DATA TYPES

When you assign a type to a variable in VB .NET, you essentially specify what particular kind of data a variable can store. For example, you may need to store a number to use in your program. To do so you create a variable capable of storing the number. If you store text later, you cannot use the same variable. You must declare a variable that stores text.

Ten different basic variable types allow the storage of a variety of data. Many of the types, such as Short, Integer, and Long, represent the same type of data, only in different sizes. For example, Short can only store a whole number value from -32768 to 32767. An Integer expands that range to about -2 billion to 2 billion. Long extends that range to +/- 9 quintillion (9×10^{18}).

Using the largest available variable can adversely affect how fast your program runs. Use a variable size, therefore, that holds your data but is no larger than necessary.

Variable types cannot change as a program runs. If you store a number into a Short variable type, you cannot use the variable to store other types of data, such as an Integer. When you assign data of a different type to a variable, VB .NET converts the data if possible and assigns the converted value to the variable.

Programmers call the process of converting variables from type to type *casting*. Casting is done automatically when necessary in VB .NET, unless you have defined Option Strict as True in the project preferences. Casting can cause loss of information. For example, if you convert a Single, which stores decimal point numbers, such as 12.24, into a Short, VB .NET chops the value to 12 because a Short lacks the ability to work with decimals.

USING VARIABLE DATA TYPES

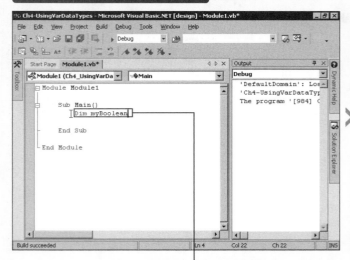

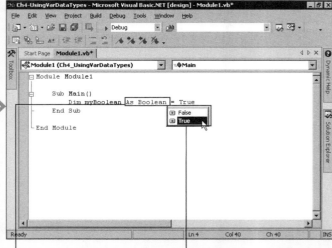

1 Create a new project or open an existing one.

2 Open the method in which you want to declare a variable.

3 Type **Dim MyBoolean** to declare a variable, replacing MyBoolean with the variable name you want to create.

4 Type **As Boolean**, replacing Boolean with the variable type you want to create.

■ You can assign a value by typing an equal sign and the appropriate value.

■ The IntelliSense window appears. You can type the appropriate code or click the entry in the list.

Extra

The following table lists the basic data types available in the
Visual Basic .NET language along with information on the amount
of memory each type uses and the values the variable can hold.

TYPE	STORAGE SIZE	VALUE RANGE
Boolean	2 bytes	True or False
Byte	1 byte	0 to 255 (unsigned)
Char	2 bytes	0 to 65535 (unsigned)
Date	8 bytes	January 1, 1 CE to December 31, 9999
Decimal	16 bytes	+/-79,228,162,514,264,337,593,543,950,335 with no decimal point; +/-7.9228162514264337593543950335 with 28 places to the right of the decimal; smallest non-zero number is +/-0.0000000000000000000000000001
Double	8 bytes	1.79769313486231E308 to -4.94065645841247E-324 for negative values; 4.94065645841247E-324 to 1.79769313486232E308 for positive values
Integer	4 bytes	-2,147,483,648 to 2,147,483,647
Long	8 bytes	-9,223,372,036,854,775,808 to 9,223,372,036,854,775,807
Short	2 bytes	-32,768 to 32,767
Single	4 bytes	-3.4028235E38 to -1.401298E-45 for negative values; 1.401298E-45 to 3.4028235E38 for positive values

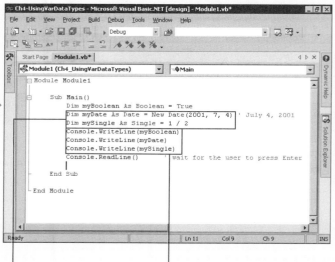

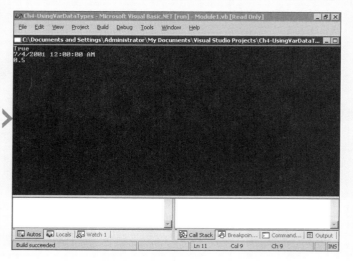

5 Type any other necessary
variables.

■ You can type a comma to
start the declaration of a new
variable on the same line.

6 Type code to use the
variables.

*Note: See the section "Create a
Console Application" to use variables
for input and output. See the next
section, "Work with Operators," to
compare and manipulate variables.*

7 Press F5 to run your
project.

■ The variables store data
and the output statements
use the various types.

WORK WITH OPERATORS

You can use operators to assign, compare, and manipulate the data that variables contain. For example, you use the assignment operator (=), the most common operator, to assign values to variables, as in the code, x = 8, which assigns the numeric value eight to the variable x.

You can also use the equal sign as an operator in an equality test. For example, suppose the variable x = 8. You use a Boolean variable y to store a test like y = (x = 8). Because x is equal to eight, the test is true, and you set y to True. Other comparisons include inequality (<>), less than (<), greater than (>), less than or equal (<=), and greater than or equal (>=).

Arithmetic operators include addition (+), subtraction (–), multiplication (*), and division (/). Integer division (\) and modulus arithmetic (mod) are also available.

Logical operators enable you to perform logic testing on Boolean variables with the four standard operations being: And, Or, Not, and Xor. For example, suppose you have three Boolean variables, x, y, and z. In the code x = y Or z, if either y or z is True, you set x to True.

Using the combination of available operators, you can create very complex expressions. For example, x = (20 * (y + z)) ^ (8 / 21) * 5 + z is a valid expression that uses variables y and z to compute an answer that VB .NET stores in x.

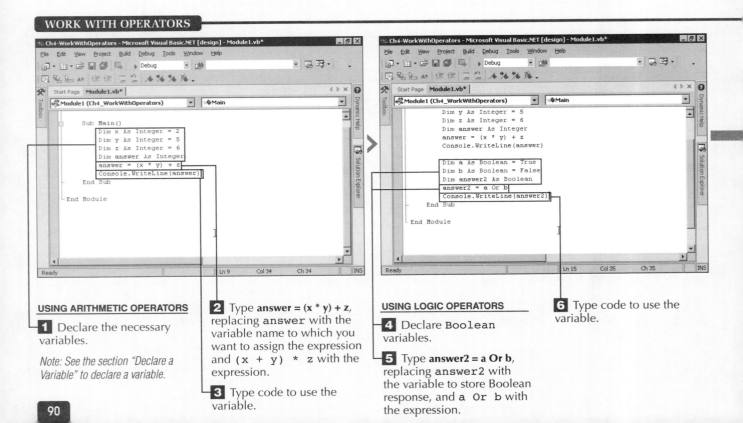

WORK WITH OPERATORS

USING ARITHMETIC OPERATORS

1 Declare the necessary variables.

Note: See the section "Declare a Variable" to declare a variable.

2 Type **answer = (x * y) + z**, replacing answer with the variable name to which you want to assign the expression and **(x + y) * z** with the expression.

3 Type code to use the variable.

USING LOGIC OPERATORS

4 Declare Boolean variables.

5 Type **answer2 = a Or b**, replacing answer2 with the variable to store Boolean response, and a Or b with the expression.

6 Type code to use the variable.

Extra

When several operations occur in an expression, VB .NET evaluates the expression in a predetermined order called *operator precedence*. Understanding operator precedence helps you determine how VB .NET processes a line of code containing many operators. When expressions contain operators from more than one category, arithmetic operators evaluate first, comparison operators evaluate next, and logical operators evaluate last. Comparison operators all have equal precedence and evaluate in order, from left to right, in the order they appear. The table below shows arithmetic, concatenation and logical operators in the order VB .NET evaluates them from top to bottom.

ARITHMETIC/CONCATENATION	COMPARISON	LOGICAL/BITWISE
Exponentiation (^)	Equality (=)	`Not`
Negation (−)	Inequality (<>)	`And, AndAlso`
Multiplication and division (*, /)	Less than (<)	`Or, OrElse, Xor`
Integer division (\)	Greater than (>)	`Xor`
Modulus arithmetic (Mod)	Less than or equal to (<=)	
Addition and subtraction (+, −),		
String concatenation (+)	Greater than or equal to (>=)	
String concatenation (&)	`Like, Is, TypeOf...Is`	

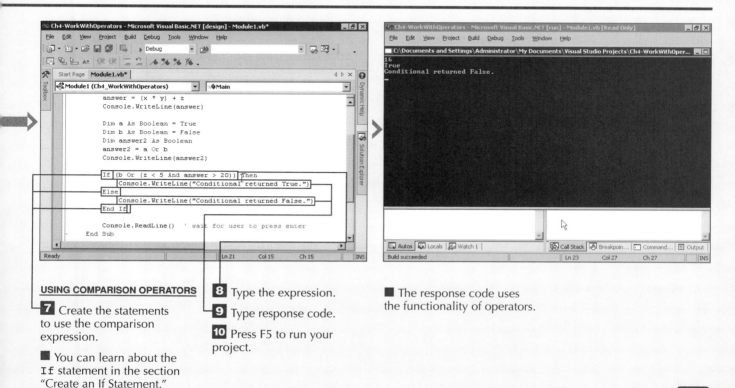

USING COMPARISON OPERATORS

7 Create the statements to use the comparison expression.

■ You can learn about the `If` statement in the section "Create an If Statement."

8 Type the expression.

9 Type response code.

10 Press F5 to run your project.

■ The response code uses the functionality of operators.

CREATE A STRING

You can use *strings* to contain a set of character data. Almost limitless in length, strings store any characters, including letters, numbers, and special characters such as $, #, or @.

You declare a string like any other variable, using the Dim statement typing String after the As modifier. For more information on declaring variables, see the section "Declare a Variable."

Use double-quotes to enclose textual data that you want VB .NET to store in a string. For example, the code Dim s As String = "Sample text" stores data in the string when you declare it.

You can alter the contents of a string at any time during run-time execution by using the assignment operator (=). For example, myString = "test" stores the value test into a string variable named myString. To include a double-quote in a string, you place two of them directly

beside each other. You combine strings together using the string concatenation operator (&). For example, combinedString = string1 & string2.

The Substring method extracts specified sections of a string. You pass the method the index of the character with which you want it to begin, and the number of characters to extract. It returns a new string containing a section of the original screen. The index of characters begins with zero (0), meaning the first character in the string is index 0.

Because a string simply contains a long list of individual characters, you can use the Chars property to extract a single character. The Char data type stores an individual character. For example, myString.Chars(3) returns the fourth character of the string myString in a Char variable. The first character is 0 for the Chars property. You can convert an entire string to an array of Char variables using the ToCharArray method of a string.

CREATE A STRING

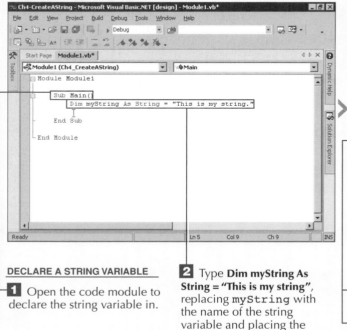

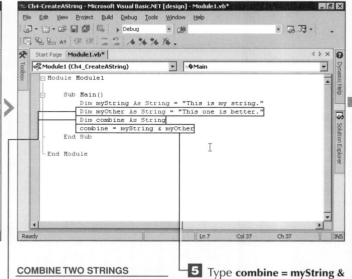

DECLARE A STRING VARIABLE

1 Open the code module to declare the string variable in.

2 Type **Dim myString As String = "This is my string"**, replacing myString with the name of the string variable and placing the value of the string inside of the quotes.

COMBINE TWO STRINGS

3 Repeat step 2 to create another string.

4 Type **Dim combine As String**, replacing combine with the name of the variable to declare another string with no default value.

5 Type **combine = myString & myOther**, replacing combine with the name of the string created in step 4, myString with the first string's name, and myOther with the second string's name.

Extra

You can easily convert numeric data to strings and strings back to numbers. For example, if you expect a user to type a number into a `TextBox` control, you know `Text` property returns a string with the contents of the number. You can convert the text into a number before processing. The `CType` function lets you convert any type of variable to another variable type. Pass the `CType` function to the variable, and provide the type to which you want to convert the variable. Although convenient to use because it accepts any sort of conversion, `CType` does not allow VB .NET to preprocess the conversion in the compiling process, and makes `CType` run very slow. Instead, VB .NET provides conversion function to every basic type. The `CStr(var)` function converts numeric, dates, and other simple data types into a string. `CInt(var)` converts a string or decimal number into an integer type. `CDate(var)` can take a string and convert it to a date according to locale preferences. You can search the VB .NET help system for "Type Conversion Functions" for a complete overview.

Example:
```
Dim myNumber As Integer = CType(TextBox1.Text, Integer)
myNumber = CInt(TextBox2.Text)
Dim myString As String = CStr(myNumber)
```

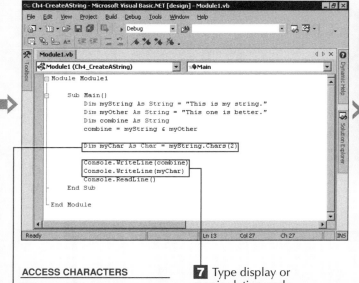

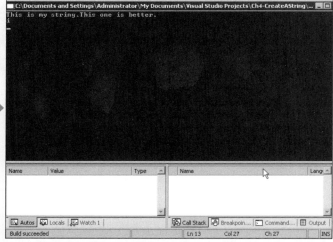

ACCESS CHARACTERS

6 Type **Dim myChar As Char = myString.Chars(2)**, replacing `myChar` with a string variable's name, and **2** with a character index.

7 Type display or manipulation code

8 Press F5 to run the project.

■ You see a string variable function and display its contents.

WORK WITH STRINGS

Visual Basic .NET contains a number of methods that you can use to manipulate string data. You use these commands to perform actions such as cutting the string into pieces, retrieving the length of the string, and searching for sub-strings.

The Length method of a String class lets you determine the length of a string. Length takes no parameters and returns an Integer representing the number of characters in the string, including spaces and any other special characters.

PadLeft takes the content of its string and uses spaces to right-align the string to the length you specify as the parameter to the method. For example, if x = "dog" and you call x.PadLeft(5), the method returns two spaces in front of the word. PadRight has the same function, adding spaces to the right of the word.

You can use the Insert method to insert a string at a particular location. The format of the method is Insert(startPosition, stringToInsert). For example, if a = "John is a boy" and b = "bad", then a.Insert(10, b) returns "John is a bad boy". You can use Remove to remove a known length of characters from the string. The format of the method is Remove(startPosition, length). In the preceding example, assuming the Insert command saves to string c, c.Remove(10, 4) removes the substring.

ToUpper and ToLower convert the string to uppercase and lowercase strings, respectively. They take no parameters.

The methods available in the String class do not alter the string the class represents; instead, each method returns a new string. For example, to save the lowercase string returned by ToLower back into the string where you call the method, you can use this line: a = a.ToLower().

WORK WITH STRINGS

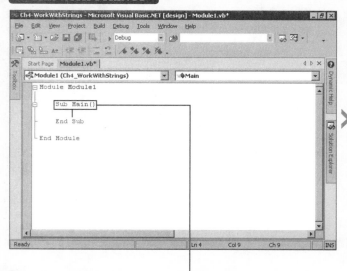

1 Create a new project or open an existing one.

2 Open the code module where you want the string manipulation to occur.

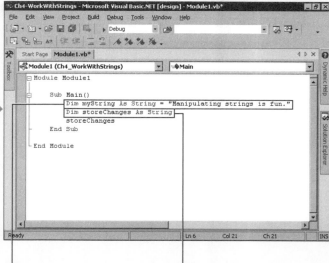

3 Declare a string and set its contents.

Note: For more information on strings, see the section "Create a String."

4 Declare a string to use for storage of the manipulated string.

Apply It

The Join and Split method, part of the String class, enable you to concatenate an array of strings or break them up, respectively. You can use these methods to easily store a set of information in a single string and break it apart when necessary. For more information on creating and using arrays, see "Create an Array" later in this chapter. To combine an array of strings, pass the String.Join method the string to use as a separator and a string array. You place a separator between each adjacent item in the array. A common string to use is a comma followed by a space. To combine a set of words into a sentence, simply use a space as the separator. The Split function breaks apart a string and returns a string array. Pass the Split function a string followed by a separator. If you do not pass a separator, Split uses a space.

TYPE THIS:

```
Dim words() As String = {"The", "car", "is", "going", "fast."}
Dim sentence As String

sentence = String.Join(" ", words)
Console.WriteLine(sentence)

Dim splitSentence() As String = Split(sentence, " ")
Dim word As String
For Each word In splitSentence
    Console.Write(word & "/")
Next
```

RESULT:

The car is going fast.

The/car/is/going/fast./

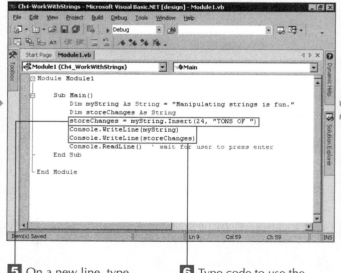

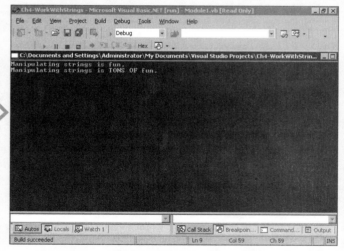

5 On a new line, type **storeChanges = myString.Insert (24, "TONS OF ")**, replacing **myString** with the name of the string you want to manipulate, **Insert** with the manipulation method, and **24, "TONS OF "** with the appropriate arguments.

6 Type code to use the manipulated string.

7 Press F5 to run your project.

■ The **String** class alters the string data and your program uses the changes.

PASS INFORMATION THROUGH A METHOD

Many methods need external data to function and must have the abilities to send data back to the caller. You can use *arguments* to create a conduit to pass any type of variable through to a method. *Return values* let you pass back a variable to the code that called the method.

To define a list of arguments a method accepts, you enclose the list of variable names inside the parentheses after the method's name. When you specify the argument, you place the ByVal or ByRef keyword in front of the variable name for the argument, and specify a variable type for the argument using the As keyword after the argument. Specify ByVal to pass the value of the variable, and specify ByRef to pass the memory location of the original variable. VB .NET automatically adds ByVal if you do specify the argument passing method.

List multiple arguments by separating them with commas. You use the variable names you assign in the argument list

as local variables of the method, so you must use different names than you use for local variables in the method.

To return values to code calling a method, use the Function keyword to define the method instead of Sub. When using the Function keyword, you must specify the type of variable or object that the function returns. For more information on creating and calling methods, see the section "Add a Method."

To set the information to return, you use the Return keyword. After the keyword, place the return variable or object. Make sure the variable matches the type you specify in the method header.

For a method that returns a value, use the method as a variable name inside other code, or assign it to a variable, for example test = TestNumber(number).

PASS INFORMATION THROUGH A METHOD

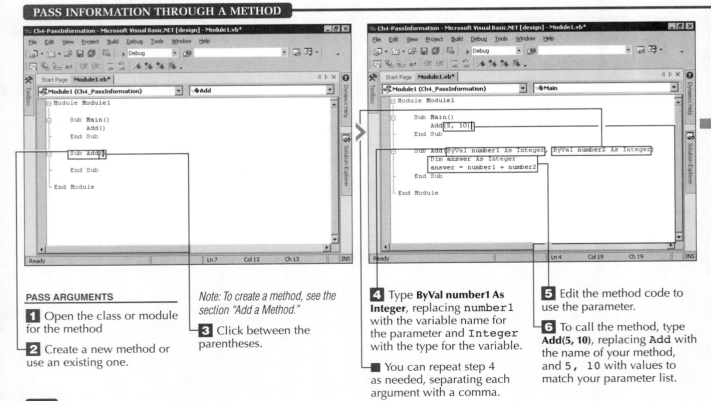

PASS ARGUMENTS

1 Open the class or module for the method

2 Create a new method or use an existing one.

Note: To create a method, see the section "Add a Method."

3 Click between the parentheses.

4 Type **ByVal number1 As Integer**, replacing number1 with the variable name for the parameter and Integer with the type for the variable.

■ You can repeat step 4 as needed, separating each argument with a comma.

5 Edit the method code to use the parameter.

6 To call the method, type **Add(5, 10)**, replacing **Add** with the name of your method, and **5, 10** with values to match your parameter list.

Apply It

You can use the `ByVal` and `ByRef` keywords to manipulate how VB .NET passes information to your method. The keyword `ByVal` stands for *by value*, and means that VB .NET creates a copy of the data passed into the method for the method to use. The `ByRef` keyword stands for *by reference*, and means that VB .NET sends the actual location in memory of the variable passed into the method. Because you work with the original variable when you use the `ByRef` keyword, VB .NET maintains changes you make to the value when the method exits.

TYPE THIS:

```
Sub AddNumber(ByRef number1 As Integer, ByVal number2 As Integer)
    ' make number1 ByRef so you can change the value
    number1 += number2
End Sub

Sub Main()
    Dim x As Integer = 10, y as Integer = 15
    Console.WriteLine("The value of x is : " & CStr(x))
    AddNumber(x, y)
    Console.WriteLine("The value of x is : " & CStr(x))
    Console.ReadLine()
End Sub
```

RESULT:

```
The value of x is: 10
The value of x is: 25
```

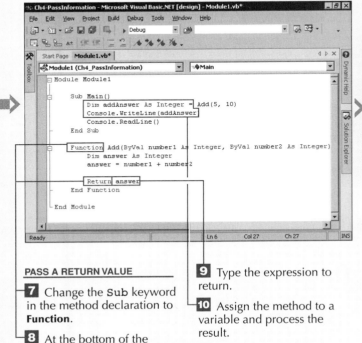

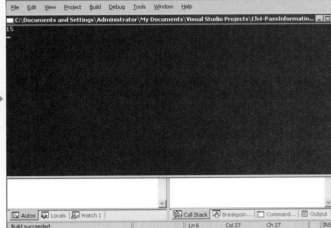

PASS A RETURN VALUE

7 Change the `Sub` keyword in the method declaration to **Function**.

8 At the bottom of the method code, type the keyword **Return**.

9 Type the expression to return.

10 Assign the method to a variable and process the result.

11 Press F5 to run the project.

■ The method passes data back and forth to the code that calls it.

USING THE IF STATEMENT

You can use conditional statements when you run different code based on specific conditions. The most frequently used conditional block relies on the If statement.

For example, if you want to display a message based on a calculation that determines the temperature, you can qualify anything over 80 degrees as hot, and any other temperature as too cold. This calls for a test of the temperature value to determine into which range it falls.

The If statement tests a conditional statement you provide, and runs a block of code if it is True. If the statement is False, VB .NET skips over the block of If code. For more information on forming conditional statements, see "Work with Operators."

The format for an If statement is If expression Then. You can place code to execute if the conditional statement

is true on the same line. If you have more that you need to execute, you can start the code on the next line and enclose the statements with an End If statement.

In the case you want to provide code when the condition is False, you can insert an Else statement between the If...Then and End If statements. If the condition is False, the code jumps to the code located between the Else and the End If instead of the code directly after the If.

To make your code easier to understand, you can line up the If, Else, and End If statements with the rest of the code in your method. You can then indent the blocks of code inside the statements. This capability enables you to identify blocks of code easily. The Development Studio provides the smart tab feature, which automatically indents your code, and the environment enables this option by default.

USING THE IF STATEMENT

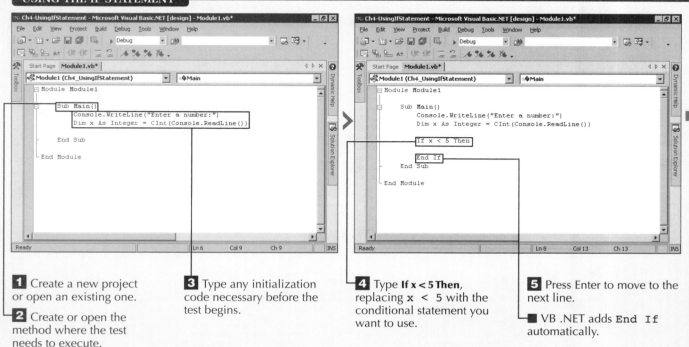

■1 Create a new project or open an existing one.

■2 Create or open the method where the test needs to execute.

■3 Type any initialization code necessary before the test begins.

■4 Type **If x < 5 Then**, replacing **x < 5** with the conditional statement you want to use.

■5 Press Enter to move to the next line.

■ VB .NET adds **End If** automatically.

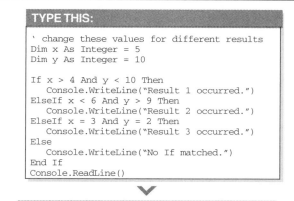

Apply It

You may need to test a significant amount of different conditions at a time. Using the `If...Else...End If` structure, you can create a large quantity of code because you must place `If` blocks inside other `If` blocks. You use the `ElseIf` statement to create more advanced `If` blocks. You must place `ElseIf` inside of an `If` and any condition after an `ElseIf` statement followed by a `Then`. The code runs if the condition is `True` until it reaches an `ElseIf`, `Else`, or `End If`. You can place the following code in a Console Application in `Sub Main`.

TYPE THIS:

```
' change these values for different results
Dim x As Integer = 5
Dim y As Integer = 10

If x > 4 And y < 10 Then
    Console.WriteLine("Result 1 occurred.")
ElseIf x < 6 And y > 9 Then
    Console.WriteLine("Result 2 occurred.")
ElseIf x = 3 And y = 2 Then
    Console.WriteLine("Result 3 occurred.")
Else
    Console.WriteLine("No If matched.")
End If
Console.ReadLine()
```

RESULT:

Result 2 occurred.

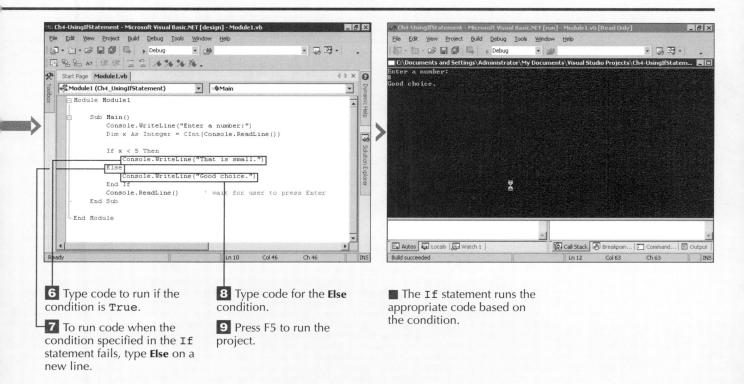

6 Type code to run if the condition is `True`.

7 To run code when the condition specified in the `If` statement fails, type **Else** on a new line.

8 Type code for the **Else** condition.

9 Press F5 to run the project.

■ The `If` statement runs the appropriate code based on the condition.

USING THE SELECT CASE STATEMENT

You can use the `Select Case` statement to check a single variable for a variety of possible conditions. For example, if you want to display a message that depends on a number entered by the user, you can create a large number of `If` statements for the different possibilities. For more information on `If` statements, see the section "Using the If Statement." The `Select Case` statement compares any simple data type including strings.

To build a `Select` block, use `Select Case` followed by the variable to evaluate. For example, if you have an integer `myNumber`, you can test its value with `Select Case myNumber`. The `End Select` statement closes the block of code. Inside of the block, use the `Case` statement to run a conditional test on the variable. To test for equality, place the value you want to compare to the variable in the `Select Case` directly after the `Case` statement. For

example, using the example `myNumber` from above, the line `Case 2` tests `myNumber = 2`. If the condition is `True`, the code directly after the `Case` statement run until the compiler reaches either another `Case` statement or an `End Select` statement.

To test for conditions other than equality, such as less than, greater than, less than or equal to, or greater than or equal to, you use the `Is` keyword after the `Case` statement. For example, `Case Is < 5` runs if the integer value is less than five.

You use the `To` keyword to create range conditions. For example, if you want the `Case` to run if the integer is between 5 and 10, use `Case 5 To 10`. You must place the lower bound of range on the left side of the `To` and the higher bound on the right.

USING THE SELECT CASE STATEMENT

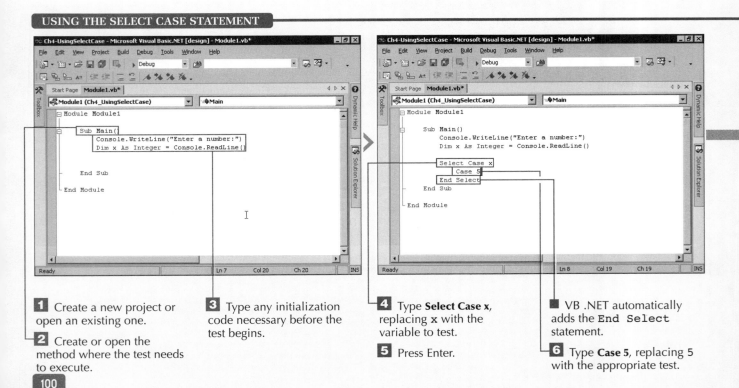

1 Create a new project or open an existing one.

2 Create or open the method where the test needs to execute.

3 Type any initialization code necessary before the test begins.

4 Type **Select Case x**, replacing **x** with the variable to test.

5 Press Enter.

■ VB .NET automatically adds the **End Select** statement.

6 Type **Case 5**, replacing 5 with the appropriate test.

Extra

When VB .NET finds a `Case` that matches the value of the variable in the `Select`, the `Case` block runs and then jumps outside of the `Select Case...End Select` block. If two `Case` statements match the tested variable, only the first runs. You can use this to your advantage when making a set of `Case` statements. For example, if the first test is `Case Is <= 5`, you do not need to check in the following case statements for values five or below.

You can write complex cases by separating tests by commas. The `Case Else` statement provides a catchall for a value that does not meet any of the `Case` statements available. You make a `Case Else` the last `Case` before the `End Select` statement.

Example:
```
Select Case myNumber
    Case 1 To 4, 8, 16, Is > 32
        ...
    Case Is < 1, 5 To 7, 9 To 15
        ...
End Select
```

Example:
```
Select Case myString
    Case Is <= "E"
        ...
    Case "F" To "H"
        ...
    Case Else
        ...
End Select
```

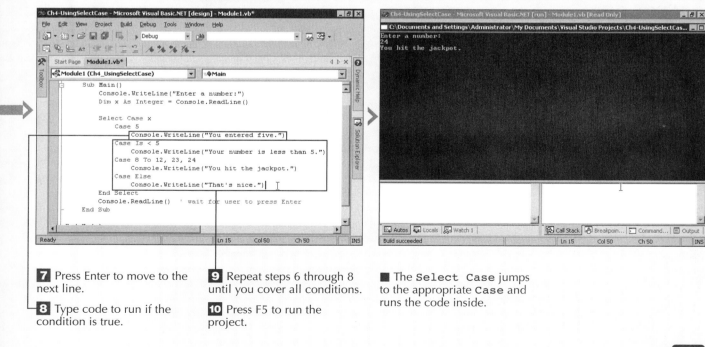

7 Press Enter to move to the next line.

8 Type code to run if the condition is true.

9 Repeat steps 6 through 8 until you cover all conditions.

10 Press F5 to run the project.

■ The `Select Case` jumps to the appropriate `Case` and runs the code inside.

USING FOR LOOPS

You can use a `For` loop to run a block of code a specified number of times. For example, you may want to output a set of available font sizes to a `ListBox` control. Instead of doing this manually, you use a `For` loop to increment through the specified range.

To create a `For` loop, specify `For` and follow it with a counter variable. This variable stores the current value of the loop as it runs. Place an equal sign and follow it by a range of numbers using the `To` keyword. For example, to loop from 1 to 10, you type the line **For x = 1 To 10**. You can only use the integer variable types `Short`, `Integer`, and `Long` for the counter variable, and you must declare the variable in the method before using it as the counter.

By default, a `For` loop increments by positive ones. You can place the `Step` keyword after the range indication,

determining by what number the `For` loop should count. For example, `For x = 1 to 9 Step 2` starts at one and increments two at a time until it reaches nine.

You place the necessary code inside of the loop and close it with a `Next` statement. At the point of the `Next` statement, VB .NET determines whether it needs to loop again because the counter has not reached the end state, or exit the loop and run the line of code after the `Next` statement.

You can use the `Exit For` statement to break out of a `For` loop before it completes. You may find this useful if an error occurs during the looping process. Keep in mind that using this command makes your program harder to understand and harder to debug.

USING FOR LOOPS

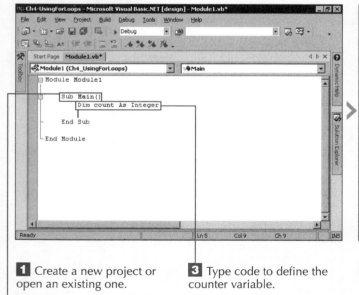

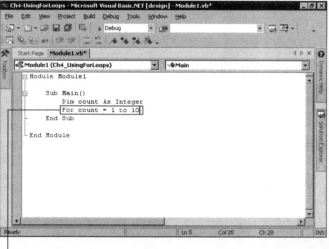

1 Create a new project or open an existing one.

2 Create or open the method where you want the loop to execute.

3 Type code to define the counter variable.

4 Type **For count = 1 to 10**, replacing **count** with the name of the counter variable, 1 with the start point for the counter, and 10 with the end point for the counter.

5 Press Enter.

Apply It

You can create a loop that decrements from a larger number to a smaller number, like a countdown. You do this by providing the For command with a negative Step value.

TYPE THIS:

```
Dim counter As Short
For counter = 10 To 1 Step -1
    Console.Write(CStr(counter) & "..")
Next
Console.WriteLine("BOOM!")
Console.ReadLine()
```

RESULT:

```
10..9..8..7..6..5..4..3..2..1..BOOM!
```

You can nest For loops inside of each other to create a sort of two-dimensional counter. You can use nested For loops to fill a grid.

TYPE THIS:

```
Dim counterX, counterY As Short
For counterY = 10 To 14
    For counterX = 0 To 9
        System.Console.Write(counterX + counterY)
    Next
    System.Console.Write(_
    Microsoft.VisualBasic.ControlChars.CrLf)
Next
Console.ReadLine()
```

RESULT:

```
10111213141516171819
11121314151617181920
12131415161718192021
13141516171819202122
14151617181920212223
```

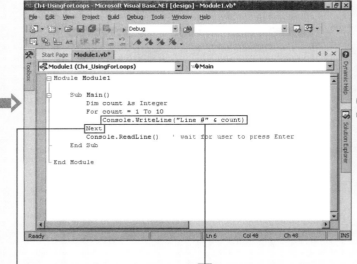

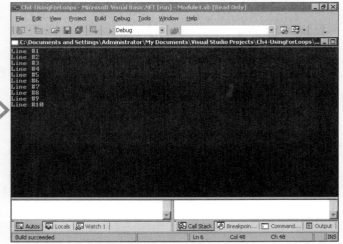

■ VB .NET creates the **Next** statement automatically.

6 Type the code that you want to run as the counter increments.

7 Run your project by pressing F5.

■ The result of the loop displays in the sample console application.

USING DO LOOPS

You can use a Do loop to run a block of code repeatedly and test a conditional statement you specify for a change to stop the loop. The Do statement lets you create powerful loops that can check a variety of criteria before exiting.

You end the Do loop with the Loop statement. The Do statement does not function without the aid of one of two keywords: Until and While. These keywords specify the type of conditional checking the loop uses. For more information on creating conditional expressions, see the section "Work with Operators."

A Do Until loop runs until the condition you specify after the Until becomes true. VB .NET runs the Do While loop

until the given condition becomes False. If the condition for an Until loop is True or the condition for a While loop is False before the loop begins, VB .NET completely skips the block of code inside the loop. You must declare any variables used in the condition before the loop begins.

Whatever code you place inside, the Do...Loop runs until the condition causes the loop to stop, so you must base the condition on one or more variables that change inside the loop. Otherwise the loop runs indefinitely and your program appears to stop functioning to the user. Known as an infinite loop, this situation is hard to debug. As you write your code make sure that the loop can exit in every case.

USING DO LOOPS

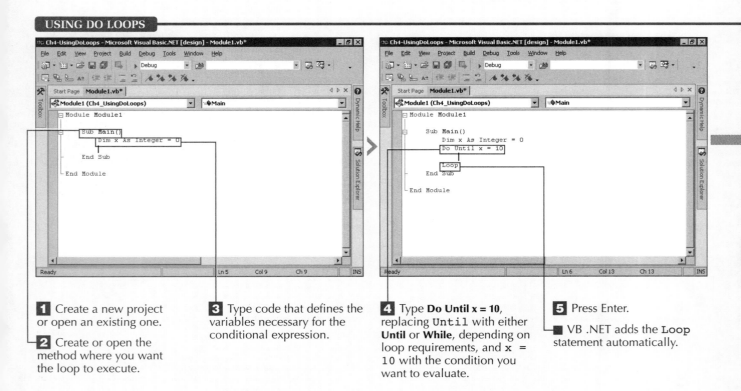

■1 Create a new project or open an existing one.

■2 Create or open the method where you want the loop to execute.

■3 Type code that defines the variables necessary for the conditional expression.

■4 Type **Do Until x = 10**, replacing Until with either **Until** or **While**, depending on loop requirements, and **x = 10** with the condition you want to evaluate.

■5 Press Enter.

■ VB .NET adds the Loop statement automatically.

In some cases, the code you place in the loop needs to run at least once even if the conditional expression evaluates to `False`. You can place the condition at the end of the loop to force the loop to run once even if the condition is not true. Place the conditional statement at the end of the loop by using the `Do...Loop Until` or `Do... Loop While` syntax. When you specify the condition at the end of the loop, VB .NET runs the code inside the loop before evaluating the condition, enabling the code inside the loop to run without the condition evaluating to `True`.

TYPE THIS:

```
Dim counter As Integer = 0
Do
    Console.WriteLine("This is line " & CStr(counter))
    counter += 1
Loop While counter < 0
Console.ReadLine()
```

RESULT:

This is line 0

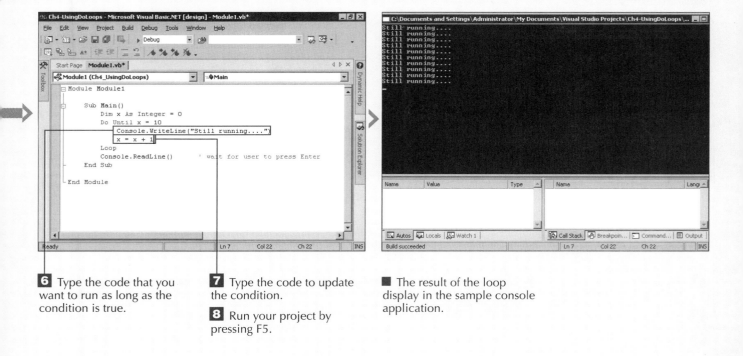

6 Type the code that you want to run as long as the condition is true.

7 Type the code to update the condition.

8 Run your project by pressing F5.

■ The result of the loop display in the sample console application.

CREATE AN ARRAY

Y ou can use an array to store a number of items, all of which are the same variable type. Think of an array as a shopping list. It holds a list of information. For example, you can use an array of 24 integers to hold the temperature at the beginning of every hour.

To create an array, define a variable and place the maximum index of the array enclosed in parentheses after the variable name. Arrays are zero-based, meaning the first index of the array is zero, so for the example above, you want to declare an array with maximum index 23.

You can use an array item just like any other regular variable of that type. To read or write an array item, use the variable name followed by the index in parentheses.

An array with one index is called a *single-dimension array*. You can also create multidimensional arrays that consist of multiple indexes. For example, a two-dimensional array can

represent a table or grid of values. To add dimensions, simply place a comma after the previous maximum index declaration. For example, `Dim hourlyTempForWeek(23, 6) As Integer` to store an item for each hour of a week.

You can assign contents to the entire array when declaring by equating it to a list of values separated by commas enclosed in braces ({}). When assigning values to the array during declaration, do not specify the size of the array. VB .NET automatically assigns the size based on the list.

If you want to assign values to the array later, a `For` loop can easily loop through the entire array and assign the necessary values. For more information on using `For` loops, see the section "Using For Loops."

CREATE AN ARRAY

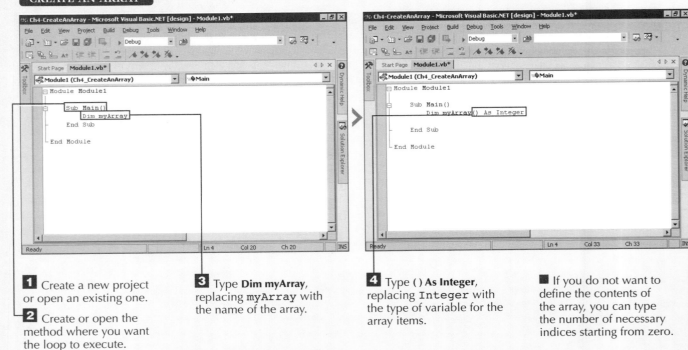

1 Create a new project or open an existing one.

2 Create or open the method where you want the loop to execute.

3 Type **Dim myArray**, replacing **myArray** with the name of the array.

4 Type **( ) As Integer**, replacing **Integer** with the type of variable for the array items.

■ If you do not want to define the contents of the array, you can type the number of necessary indices starting from zero.

Apply it

You can redefine an array to increase its size after you previously declare it with `Dim`. The `ReDim` command tells Visual Basic .NET to resize an array. Follow the statement with the array name and in parentheses the new maximum indexes. You cannot add more dimensions using the `ReDim` command. `ReDim` does clear the contents of the entire array however. To preserve the contents of the array when you resize it, place the `Preserve` keyword after `ReDim`. When using a `Preserve`, only the right-most index can change.

TYPE THIS:

```
Dim myArray(5) As Integer
Dim x As Integer
For x = 0 to 5
    myArray(x) = x
Next
Console.WriteLine(myArray(5))

ReDim Preserve myArray(10)
For x = 6 To 10
    myArray(x) = x * 2
Next
Console.WriteLine(myArray(5))
Console.WriteLine(myArray(10))
Console.ReadLine()
```

RESULT:

5

5

20

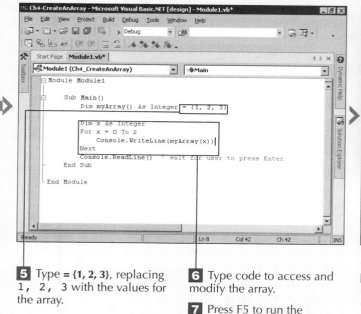

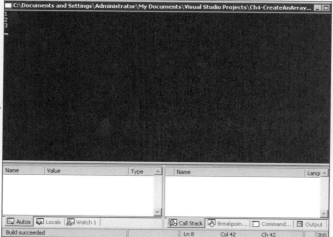

5 Type **= {1, 2, 3}**, replacing 1, 2, 3 with the values for the array.

6 Type code to access and modify the array.

7 Press F5 to run the project.

■ The array initializes and allows you to access and change items in the array.

■ In this example, the array contents print out to the console.

WORK WITH ARRAYS

Visual Basic .NET contains a number of functions for manipulating arrays. You can use these functions to sort the array, remove items, and determine the size of the array.

The LBound and UBound functions provide the index of the lower- and upper-most position of the array. Pass the array as the only parameter to either of these functions to return an integer specifying the bound. You use LBound for compatibility with Visual Basic 6 and earlier versions, but an array in VB .NET always begins with index 0, LBound always returns 0. UBound returns the last index of the array. For example, if you make the array declaration Dim myArray(5) As Integer, UBound(myArray) returns 5. You can use this in methods where you have a parameter in an array, but you do not know its size. For example, For x = 0 To UBound(myArray) loops through any array with the name myArray.

The Array object exposes a Sort method. Pass an array to Sort for a standard alphanumeric sort, for example, Array.Sort(myArray). The method sorts the items in the array and saves them back into the same array. The Sort method only supports one-dimensional arrays.

The Array object also exposes a BinarySeach method. BinarySearch locates an individual item in the array. Pass the array and the key to find to locate as the two arguments to the method. For example, Array.BinarySearch(myArray, "John"). You must ensure that the key value you pass to the method is the same type as the objects in the array, meaning if you define the array as an array of Date variables, you must pass a Date variable as the key value. The method returns an integer that specifies the index of the item. A value of less than zero means the item does not exist in the array.

WORK WITH ARRAYS

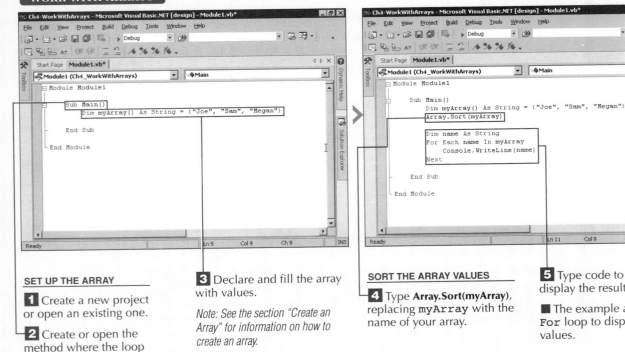

SET UP THE ARRAY

1 Create a new project or open an existing one.

2 Create or open the method where the loop needs to execute.

3 Declare and fill the array with values.

Note: See the section "Create an Array" for information on how to create an array.

SORT THE ARRAY VALUES

4 Type **Array.Sort(myArray)**, replacing **myArray** with the name of your array.

5 Type code to work with or display the results.

■ The example above uses a **For** loop to display all of the values.

Apply It

Often, you need to sort a column of data while keeping another column of data properly in line with it. For example, if you have two arrays, one with last names and one with first names, you need to sort based on last name while keeping the first names together with the last names. The `Sort` method provides an alternative set of parameters to do this. Pass the array to sort followed by the second array, and `Sort` sorts the first array. `Sort` reorders the secondary array as it sorts.

TYPE THIS:

```
Dim firstName() As String = {"John", "Sally", "Chris"}
Dim lastName() As String = {"Normal", "Peck", "Cross"}
Dim x As Integer

For x = 0 To 2                    ' display the initial arrays
    Console.WriteLine(lastName(x) & ", " & firstName(x))
Next

Array.Sort(lastName, firstName)   ' sort the two arrays based on last names

For x = 0 To 2                    ' display the results
    Console.WriteLine(lastName(x) & ", " & firstName(x))
Next

Console.ReadLine()
```

RESULT:

```
Normal, John
Peck, Sally
Cross, Chris

Cross, Chris
Normal, John
Peck, Sally
```

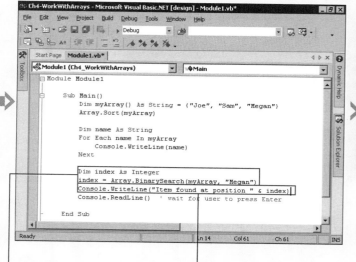

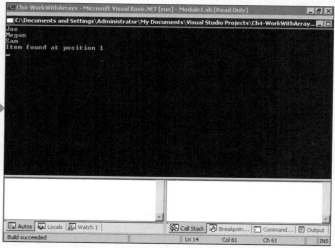

FIND A VALUE IN THE ARRAY

6 Type **index = Array.BinarySearch(myArray, "Megan")**, replacing `index` with an integer variable name, `myArray` with the name of your array, and **"Megan"** with the key string.

7 Type code to work or display the results.

■ The example above prints the index of the located item.

8 Press F5 to run your project.

■ The **Array** object modifies and searches your array.

USING A FILE STREAM

Most applications provide the ability to save and load users' files. Other applications use files to store configuration data. You can read or modify existing files and create new files using the `FileStream` class. The `FileStream` class does not provide the necessary functions to support reading and writing the contents of the file. You must use separate reader and writer classes to access the `FileStream`. To read from a file stream, see the section "Read from a File Stream," and to write to a file stream, refer to the section "Write to a File Stream."

To set up the file stream, you must create a new instance of the `FileStream` class by placing the `New` keyword in the declaration line. When you use `New`, VB .NET calls a constructor in the class to set it up. For more information on instantiating classes and using constructors, see Chapter 7.

One of the constructors available to you requires the name of the file you want to open or create, the file mode, the file

access level, and the file sharing mode:
`FileStream(path, mode, access, share)`. The `FileMode` constant determines how the stream opens or creates the file. The `FileAccess` constant determines read or write access to the file. The `FileShare` constant determines if other processes can read or write to the file when this process opens it. When you call the constructor, the file opens, or VB .NET creates the necessary file in the file system. Use the `Close` method to close the stream when you finish with the file.

To specify the `FileShare` constant, use a constant from the `FileShare` enumeration: `None`, `Read`, `ReadWrite`, and `Write`. If you specify `None`, no other program can access the file you open at the same time. `Read` enables them to read from the file while you use it, `Write` enables other programs to write to the file, and `ReadWrite` lets other files have full access.

USING A FILE STREAM

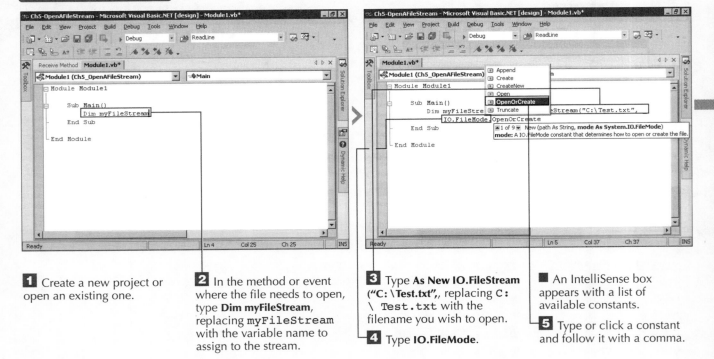

1 Create a new project or open an existing one.

2 In the method or event where the file needs to open, type **Dim myFileStream**, replacing myFileStream with the variable name to assign to the stream.

3 Type **As New IO.FileStream ("C: \Test.txt",**, replacing C: \ Test.txt with the filename you wish to open.

4 Type **IO.FileMode**.

■ An IntelliSense box appears with a list of available constants.

5 Type or click a constant and follow it with a comma.

Extra

You can use the `FileMode` and `FileAccess` enumerations to specify how the stream opens the file.

FILEMODE ENUMERATION:	
NAME	**DESCRIPTION**
`Append`	Opens the file if it exists and seeks to the end of the file, or creates a new file. Only works in conjunction with `FileAccess.Write`.
`Create`	Specifies that the operating system Creates a new file. Overwrites the file if it exists.
`CreateNew`	Specifies that the operating system creates a new file. If the file exists, an error occurs. Creates a new file. An error occurs if the file exists.
`Open`	Specifies that the operating system opens an existing file.
`OpenOrCreate`	Specifies that the operating system opens a file if it exists; otherwise creates a new file.
`Truncate`	Specifies that the operating system opens an existing file and clear its contents.

FILEACCESS ENUMERATION:	
NAME	**DESCRIPTION**
`Read`	Opens the file for reading. Allows you to read data from the file. Combine with `Write` for read/write access.
`ReadWrite`	Opens the file for reading and writing. Allows you to read and write data from the file.
`Write`	Opens the file for writing. Allows you to write data to the file.

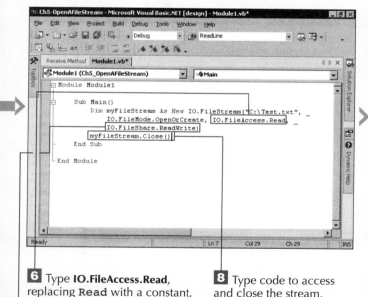

6 Type **IO.FileAccess.Read**, replacing **Read** with a constant, which you type or click.

7 Type **IO.FileShare.ReadWrite)**, replacing **ReadWrite** with a constant, which you type or select.

8 Type code to access and close the stream.

9 Press F5 to run your project.

■ The **FileStream** opens or creates the specified file.

READ FROM A STREAM

A *stream* provides a conduit to access many different types of data with the same set of methods and properties. For example, the `FileStream` class enables you to access data in files and the `NetworkStream` class lets you access data from a network socket. You can use a stream reader to retrieve information from any sort of stream.

The simplest reader, `StreamReader`, works with textual information and you can use it to read information from a text file.

To declare a new instance of the class, place `New` in front of the class name and pass the constructor of the `StreamReader` class an instance of a file stream. For more information on instantiating classes, see Chapter 7.

After creating the reader, call the `Read` method to retrieve one character out of the stream. `Read` returns the next

available character from the stream as an `Integer` and moves the current position to the next character. It returns negative one if no more characters remain in the buffer. Use the `ReadLine` method to read a line out of the text file, return it as a `String`, and advance the current position to the next line. The `ReadToEnd` method retrieves all of the data from the current position to the end of the stream and returns it as a `String`.

The `Peek` method extracts the character at the current position but does not consume it or advance to the next character position. Like `Read`, the `Peek` method returns a negative one if the stream contains no more data. You can use `Peek` to determine if you have reached the end of the file without reading any data out of it. Always use the `Close` method after you finish reading from the file to release any resources.

READ FROM A STREAM

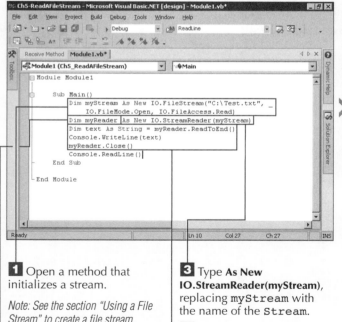

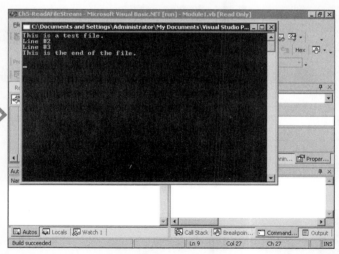

1 Open a method that initializes a stream.

Note: See the section "Using a File Stream" to create a file stream.

2 Type **Dim myReader**, replacing myReader with the variable name for the reader.

3 Type **As New IO.StreamReader(myStream)**, replacing myStream with the name of the Stream.

4 Type code to read from the file.

5 Press F5 to run the project.

■ The stream reader processes the text in the file.

WRITE TO A STREAM

A stream works in two directions, streaming information in and out of your program. You can use a stream writer to output information to a data source. You can use a stream writer to write to a file stream that you open with write access, or write data over a socket connection on a network.

A simple stream writer, the StreamWriter class, provides support for writing textual data. To declare a StreamWriter, use the Dim statement. To declare a new instance of the class, place New in front of the class name and for the most basic constructor, pass the StreamWriter class an instance of a file stream. Chapter 7 provides detailed information on instantiating classes and using constructors.

After you initialize a StreamWriter, the Write method writes a Char, Char array, or a String to the stream but does not move to the next line. The variable passes in as the

only parameter. For more information on strings, see Chapter 4. The WriteLine method performs the same action but automatically adds a new line to the file stream.

When you call the Write or WriteLine method, the stream updates in memory only. The Flush method writes any new data you store in the stream to the file. You can write a large amount of information to the stream and flush it to disk in one step. Doing a single large write to disk is more efficient because memory transfers data much faster than disks. If the data needs to move to the disk immediately after calling Write or WriteLine, set StreamWriter.AutoFlush = True.

The Close method closes the writer's connection to the file and removes any resources from memory related to the writing. Unwritten data automatically flushes to the file before the StreamWriter closes.

WRITE TO A STREAM

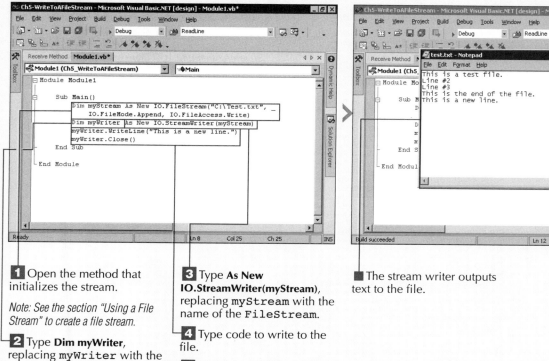

1 Open the method that initializes the stream.

Note: See the section "Using a File Stream" to create a file stream.

2 Type **Dim myWriter**, replacing myWriter with the variable name for the reader.

3 Type **As New IO.StreamWriter(myStream)**, replacing myStream with the name of the FileStream.

4 Type code to write to the file.

5 Press F5 to run the project.

■ The stream writer outputs text to the file.

WATCH FOR FILE SYSTEM CHANGES

The Windows Explorer immediately updates whenever a file saves onto disk. The Windows subsystem allows programs to request notification when certain directories update. You can receive events using the `FileSystemWatcher` class when file system changes occur on a particular drive or directory.

You can create an instance of the `FileSystemWatcher` class or you can add the `FileSystemWatcher` to a Windows Form from the Component category of the Toolbox. This topic assumes you use the Windows Form component because of the simplicity it adds through the visual interface.

The `Path` property specifies what drive or directory the component monitors for changes. Set `IncludeSubdirectories` to include any directories under the specified `Path`. The `EnableRaisingEvents` property enables or disables the component's notification events.

The component provides four events that fire when file system changes occur: `Changed`, `Created`, `Deleted`, and `Renamed`. For more information on events in Windows Forms, see Chapter 2.

The `Changed` event fires when an attribute of a file changes such as the file size, last modified date, and last viewed date. You alter the `NotifyFilter` property to set conditions for when the `Changed` event fires. For example, set `NotifyFilter` to `LastWrite` to have a component fire only when an application writes to a file.

The `Created` event fires when a new file or directory appears in the file system. The `Deleted` event fires when the user removes a file or directory from the file system, and the `Renamed` event fires when a file or directory name changes.

Each of the events passes a `FileSystemEventArgs` object as variable `e` to your event handler. The object includes a property `Name` that specifies the name of the file or directory of the change relative to the specified `Path`. The property `FullName` returns the entire path. For the `Renamed` event, the property `OldFullName` specifies the previous name of the file.

WATCH FOR FILE SYSTEM CHANGES

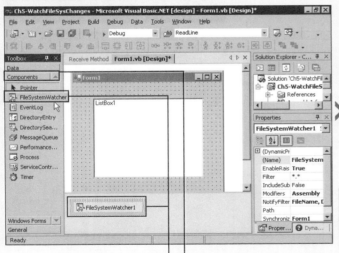

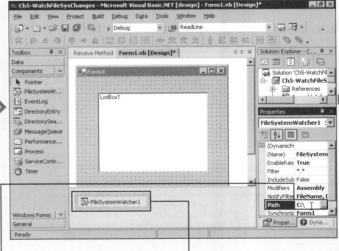

1 Create a new Windows Application project or open an existing one.

■ This example loads a **ListBox** control onto the form to display the output.

2 In the Toolbox, click the Components category.

3 Double-click the **FileSystemWatcher** component.

■ The component loads into the form's component tray.

4 In the Properties window, type the path to watch in the **Path** property.

5 Set any other necessary properties.

6 Double-click the **FileSystemWatcher** in the component tray.

Extra

You can use a few rules to make sure your FileSystemWatcher performs properly. The FileSystemWatcher watches disks as long as you do not switch or remove them. If network problems occur for a remote drive, the component may no longer respond to changes. The FileSystemWatcher does not function with CDs or DVDs, because the drive content is static. FileSystemWatcher only works on Windows 2000 and Windows NT 4.0. Remote machines must have one of these platforms installed for the component to function properly. However, you cannot watch a remote Windows NT 4.0 computer from a Windows NT 4.0 computer.

You can alter the buffer size of the FileSystemWatcher depending on the size of the file system. The system notifies the component of changes through a buffer. If many changes occur in a short time, the buffer can overflow, causing the component to lose track of changes in the directory. The InternalBufferSize property lets you alter the amount of memory used by the control. Increasing the size of the buffer can cause significant reduction in computer speed, so increase the buffer as little as possible. To avoid buffer overflows, use the NotifyFilter, and IncludeSubdirectories properties to filter out unwanted notifications.

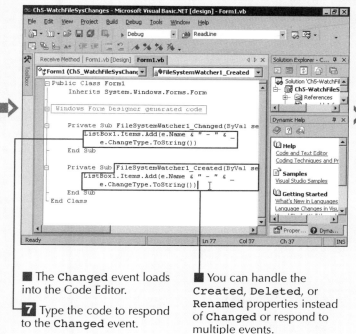

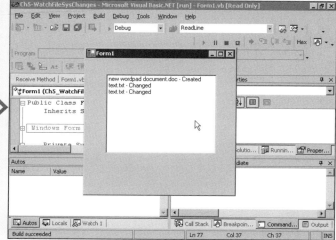

■ The Changed event loads into the Code Editor.

7 Type the code to respond to the Changed event.

■ You can handle the Created, Deleted, or Renamed properties instead of Changed or respond to multiple events.

Note: For more information on working with events, see Chapter 3.

8 Press F5 to run your project.

■ The FileSystemWatcher records changes made in the Path.

ACCESS FILE INFORMATION

You can use the `FileInfo` class of the `IO` namespace to move through files and directories, delete and move files, and modify attributes.

To link the `FileInfo` class to a file, create an instance of the class using the `New` keyword. The constructor accepts one parameter, the path and filename you want to access. After creating the instance of class, you can begin to access properties.

The `DirectoryName` property returns the full path of the file. If you want to access properties of that directory, the `Directory` property provides access to the `DirectoryInfo` object. For more information on `DirectoryInfo`, see the section "Access Directory Information."

The `Extension` property returns the extension of the file, the three- or four-character extension following the final period in the filename. The `Name` property specifies the

name of the file with no path. `FullName` returns the entire path including the filename. The `Length` property returns a `Long` and specifies the number of bytes in the file. The `Attribute` property enables you to retrieve or change the attributes of the file.

The `CreationTime` property enables you to retrieve or change the creation date and time of the file using a `DateTime` variable. The `LastAccessTime` property enables you to retrieve or change the most recent access of the file. The `LastWriteTime` property enables you to retrieve or change recent write to the file.

The `Delete` method removes the file from the file system permanently, and requires no parameters. `CopyTo` copies the file to a new location. Pass a string as the argument with the path of the new location. You can provide the path to copy to, or a new filename for the copy. `MoveTo` performs the same action except the method copies the file to the new location and removes the original.

ACCESS FILE INFORMATION

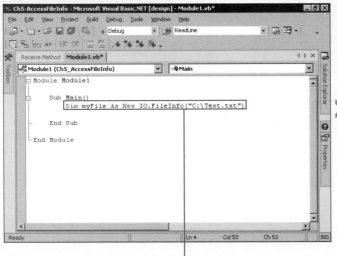

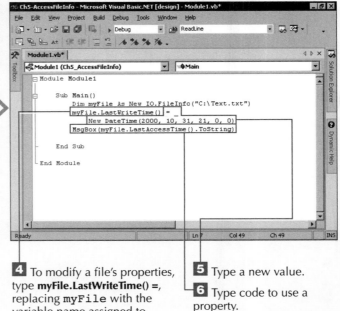

1 Create a new project or open an existing one.

2 Open the method or event where the file functions need to occur.

3 Type **Dim myFile As New IO.FileInfo("C:\Text.txt")**, replacing `myFile` with the variable name and `C:\Text.txt` with the full path to the file.

4 To modify a file's properties, type **myFile.LastWriteTime() =**, replacing `myFile` with the variable name assigned to the `FileInfo` class, and `LastWriteTime` with a property.

5 Type a new value.

6 Type code to use a property.

Extra

The `Attributes` property consists of a bit-wise combination of constants from the `FileAttributes` enumeration. You can use the `Attributes` property to test a file for particular attributes. To test a file, use the `And` operator combined with a constant. To set the attributes for a file, combine multiple attributes with the `Or` operator and assign the value to the `Attributes` property. A table of the most important constants in `FileAttributes` appears here. See Visual Basic .NET help for the full list.

FILEATTRIBUTE CONSTANTS:	
NAME	**DESCRIPTION**
`Archive`	Applications use this attribute to mark files for backup or removal.
`Directory`	A folder or directory.
`Hidden`	Ordinary directory listings do not list this file.
`Normal`	The file is normal and has no other attributes set.
`ReadOnly`	You cannot write to this file.
`System`	The file is part of the operating system.

Example:
```
Dim file As New IO.FileInfo("c:\test.txt")
' assign attributes
file.Attributes = IO.FileAttributes.Hidden Or IO.FileAttributes.Archive
Dim test As Boolean
' check attributes
test = file.Attributes And IO.FileAttributes.Hidden
```

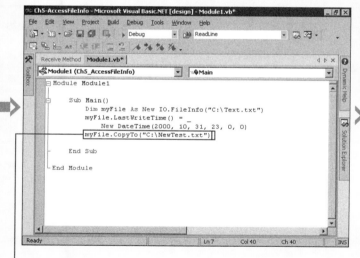

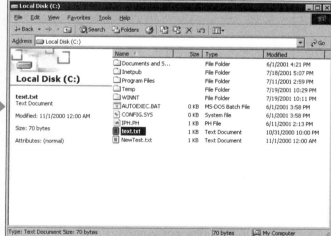

7 To perform an action on the file, type **myFile.CopyTo ("C:\NewTest.txt")**, replacing `myFile` with the variable name assigned to the FileInfo class, and "`C:\NewTest.txt`" with the destination for the `CopyTo`.

■ Alternatively, you can replace `CopyTo` in step 7 with `Delete` or `MoveTo`.

8 Press F5 to run your project.

■ The `FileInfo` class modifies file properties, accesses file properties, and uses methods to perform disk operations.

ACCESS DIRECTORY INFORMATION

Directories listings help the user to store documents in a hierarchal, logical manner. You can view and modify disk directory structures using the `DirectoryInfo` class.

The `IO` namespace contains the `DirectoryInfo` class. You declare a variable to hold the class using the `Dim` statement. To create an instance of a class, use the `New` statement. The constructor needs only one argument, the name of the directory, to load into the `DirectoryInfo` class. For more information on instantiating classes and using constructors, see Chapter 7.

The `Name` property retrieves and sets the name of the directory and `FullName` returns the entire path including the drive letter. You can return the parent directory with the `Parent` property, which returns a `DirectoryInfo` class. The `Root` property returns the bottom-most directory in the specified path. For example, if you have the directory

on the local computer, `Root` returns the root drive directory as a `DirectoryInfo`.

You can use the `GetDirectories` method to return an array of `DirectoryInfo` classes representing this directory's subdirectories. The `GetFiles` method returns an array of `FileInfo` classes that represent the files in the directory. Both methods have optional parameters to specify a search pattern to filter directories or files. For example `GetFiles("*.txt")` returns only files with a txt extension. For more information on arrays, see Chapter 4.

The `CreateSubdirectory` method creates a subdirectory relative to the directory loaded into the `DirectoryInfo`. Pass the subdirectory path in as the only parameter. Use the `MoveTo` method to move the entire directory and all of its contents to another location. Pass the new location in as the single parameter. The `Delete` method deletes the entire directory and all of its content.

ACCESS DIRECTORY INFORMATION

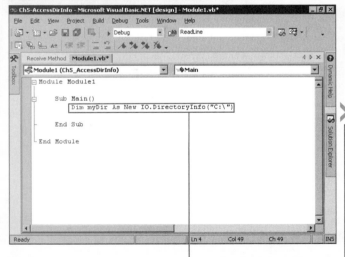

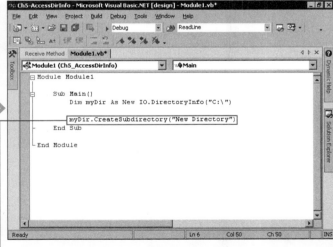

1 Create a new application or open an existing one.

2 In the method or event, type **Dim myDir As New IO.DirectoryInfo("C:\")**, replacing **myDir** with the variable name, and **C:** with the path to load into the class.

3 Type code to access any necessary properties or methods.

■ The example creates a new subdirectory.

Apply It

Using a recursive method, you can build entire directory trees using the `DirectoryInfo` component. In fact, you can use this recursive algorithm to fill a `TreeView` control and build an Explorer-like program. This example assumes you add a `TreeView` control named `TreeView1` to the form. To learn more about adding a `TreeView` control to a form. See Chapter 3 to add controls to the form.

TYPE THIS:

```
Private Sub Form1_Load(...)
        BuildNode("My C Drive", "C:\", TreeView1.Nodes)
End Sub

Sub BuildNode(ByVal Name As String, ByVal FullPath As String, _
ByVal nodes As TreeNodeCollection)
        Dim directory As New IO.DirectoryInfo(FullPath)
        Dim newNode As TreeNode,  subDir As IO.DirectoryInfo
newNode = nodes.Add(Name)
        Try
                        For Each subDir In directory.GetDirectories()
                                BuildNode(subDir.Name, subDir.FullName, newNode.Nodes)
                        Next
        Catch                           ' an error occurred. Add a response here.
        End Try
End Sub
```

RESULT:

```
- My C Drive
    + Document and Settings
    + Inetpub
    - Program Files
        + Accessories
        + Common Files
  Temp
    + WinNT
```

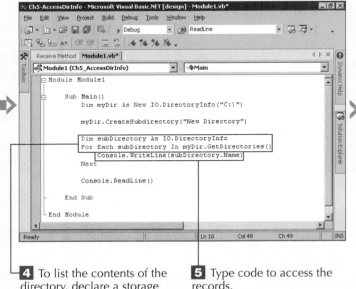

4 To list the contents of the directory, declare a storage variable and create a loop to access the contents of the directory.

■ The example declares a **subDirectory** variable and creates a **For Each** loop.

5 Type code to access the records.

6 Press F5 to run the project.

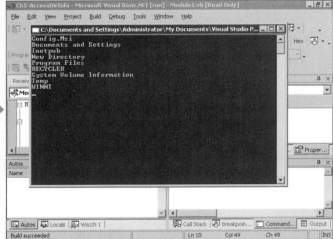

■ The `DirectoryInfo` class responds with file and directory listings, and by manipulating the underlying directory structure.

PROVIDE A FILE DIALOG BOX

You use the File Open and Save dialog boxes every day to work with applications. In most cases, these dialog boxes enable a user to move between applications and understand how to load and save documents in the same method. The `OpenFileDialog` and `SaveFileDialog` controls enable you to use common dialog boxes for users to select files in your application.

Both of these dialog boxes are available as Windows Form controls in the Toolbox. The control appears in the Component Tray when loaded and allows you to edit properties concerning its appearance.

The `Filter` property specifies the file types that the dialog box displays. You can specify the list of supported file formats here so users know which files they can select. The `Filter` property contains a description followed by the format to filter separated by pipe characters (|). You can add multiple filters by placing a pipe character between them. If your application supports opening the text file format, you need to add an entry to the `Filter` property

to allow the user to see only text files for selection. For example, the `Filter` may look like `"Text files (*.txt)|*.txt|All files (*.*)|*.*"`. You can specify the default filter using the `FilterIndex` property with the first filter index 1.

The `InitialDirectory` specifies the directory the dialog box loads when it appears. `ValidateNames` insures the user does not enter invalid characters.

The `DefaultExt` property specifies an extension to add to files automatically when the user does not enter one. You must set `AddExtention` to `True` for this to occur.

To show either file dialog box, call the `ShowDialog` method. The method does not accept a parameter, but it returns a `DialogResult` specifying the user's selection of OK or Cancel. For more information on dialog boxes and `DialogResult`, see Chapter 3.

The `FileName` property contains the full path of the file the user selects.

PROVIDE A FILE DIALOG BOX

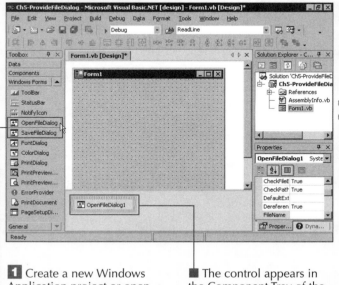

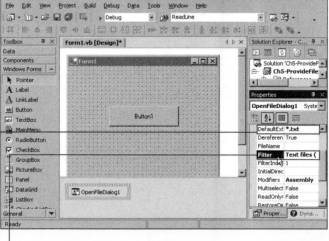

1 Create a new Windows Application project or open an existing one.

2 In the Toolbox, double-click either the `OpenFileDialog` or `SaveFileDialog` control.

■ The control appears in the Component Tray of the current form.

3 In the Property Window, type a file filter string in the `Filter` property.

4 Edit any necessary properties.

■ The example above sets `DefaultExt = "txt"`.

Note: See Chapter 2 for information about editing a property value.

Apply it

You can enable your users to select multiple files to open with `OpenFileDialog` when you set the `MultiSelect` property to `True`. When the dialog closes, the `FileName` property normally contains the file the user selected. For multiple selections, the `FileNames` array fills with the selected files.

TYPE THIS:

```
Private Sub Button1_Click(ByVal sender As System.Object, ByVal e As _
    System.EventArgs) Handles Button1.Click

    ' declare a variable to hold the result
    Dim result As DialogResult
    result = OpenFileDialog1.ShowDialog()
    ' only process the file list if the user hit the Ok button
    If result = DialogResult.OK Then
        ' use a For Each loop to move through the array
        Dim fileName As String
        For Each fileName In OpenFileDialog1.FileNames()
            ListBox1.Items.Add(fileName)
        Next
    End If
End Sub
```

RESULT:

```
C:\My Documents\Sample1.txt
C:\My Documents\Sample2.doc
C:\My Documents\Sample3.xls
```

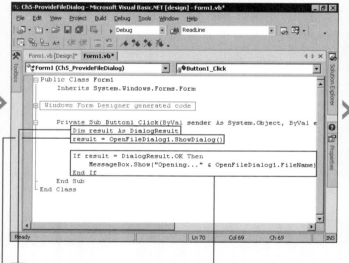

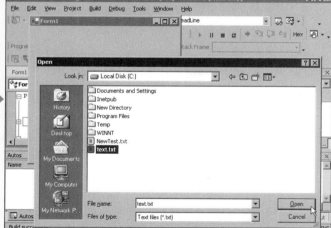

5 In the method or event where the dialog box needs to appear, declare a variable to hold the dialog box result.

6 Type **result = OpenFileDialog1. ShowDialog()**, replacing `result` with the variable name, and `OpenFileDialog1` with the name of the control.

7 Type code to respond to the dialog box.

8 Press F5 to run the project.

■ The file dialog box appears and allows file selection.

121

USING THE PRINTDOCUMENT CONTROL

Users expect solid printing abilities in any application. The computer monitor does not provide the resolution to make reading completely comfortable. You can use the `PrintDocument` control to provide the foundation of a printing system in your Windows Forms application.

VB .NET integrates all printing facilities into a combined system that works together. A `PrintDocument` provides you with a surface to draw contents onto the pages of your document. The `PrintDocument` control appears in the Toolbox under Windows Forms.

To begin printing the document, you call the object's `Print` method. Because of the integration, a variety of dialog boxes work with the `PrintDocument` control. See the section "Using the Printer Dialog" to provide a `PrintDialog` control to present printer options to the user. A Page Setup dialog box lets the user set up margins and page sizes; for details, see the section "Using the Page Setup Dialog."

When it receives a print command, the `PrintDocument` fires the `BeginPrint` event. This lets you perform initialization. For more information on events, see Chapter 2. After `BeginPrint` completes, the `PrintPage` event fires. You then draw the page onto the `Graphics` object provided by the event argument e. For more information on graphics, see Chapter 6. The event's argument also provides a `MarginBounds` rectangle, which gives you the prescribed boundaries to print within. The `e.PageSettings` provides a list of all the settings the `PrintDocument` uses to process the print job.

When you finish drawing a page, you must determine if your application needs to print another page. Set `e.HasMorePages` equal to `True` if you need to print another page and `False` otherwise. If you set `HasMorePages` to `True`, the event fires again. The current number of the event expects you to print is not available. You need to use module level variables to store information about previously printed pages.

USING THE PRINTDOCUMENT CONTROL

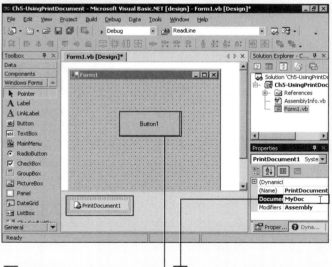

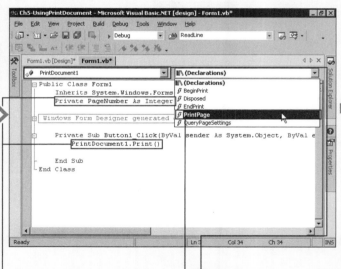

1 In a form of a Windows Application project, double-click the **PrintDocument** control in the Toolbox.

2 In the Properties window, type a name for the document in the **DocumentName** property.

3 Double-click the control you want the user to press to begin printing.

■ The default event of the control appears in the Code Editor.

4 Type **PrintDocument1.Print()**, replacing **PrintDocument** with the name of the control.

5 In the module level, declare necessary storage variables.

6 Click the **PrintDocument** control from the component list.

7 Click the **PrintPage** event from the event list.

Apply It

You can create a simple text file printer using a combination of the `PrintDocument` and `Stream` commands. For this code to work, you need a `Button` named `Button1` and a `PrintDocument` named `PrintDoc`.

TYPE THIS:

```
Private printFont As New Font ("Arial", 10),  streamToPrint As IO.StreamReader

Private Sub Button1_Click(ByVal sender As Object, ByVal e As EventArgs)
        streamToPrint = New IO.StreamReader("C:\My Documents\MyFile.txt")
        PrintDoc.Print()
End Sub

Private Sub PrintDoc_PrintPage(ByVal sender As Object, ByVal e As _
    System.Drawing.Printing.PrintPageEventArgs)
        Dim linesPerPage As Single =
            e.MarginBounds.Height / printFont.GetHeight(e.Graphics)
        Dim line As String = Nothing, count As Integer, yPos As Single = 0
        For count = 0 To  linesPerPage - 1            ' print each line of file.
                line = streamToPrint.ReadLine()
                If line Is Nothing Then Exit For      ' no more lines in file

                yPos = e.MarginBounds.Top + count * printFont.GetHeight(e.Graphics)
                e.Graphics.DrawString(line, printFont, Brushes.Black, _
                    e.MarginBounds.Left, yPos, New StringFormat())    ' output line of text
        Next
        If Not (line Is Nothing) Then e.HasMorePages = True             'print another page?
End Sub
```

RESULT:

The text file prints to the default printer.

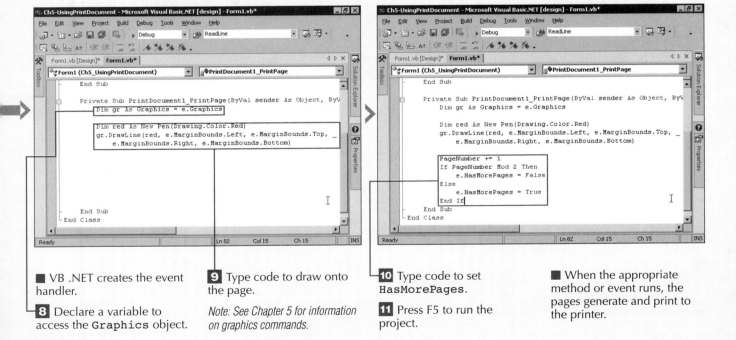

■ VB .NET creates the event handler.

8 Declare a variable to access the `Graphics` object.

9 Type code to draw onto the page.

Note: See Chapter 5 for information on graphics commands.

10 Type code to set `HasMorePages`.

11 Press F5 to run the project.

■ When the appropriate method or event runs, the pages generate and print to the printer.

USING THE PRINTER DIALOG BOX

Before an application prints, it often presents a Printer selection dialog box to let the user select which printer to use and any printer driver options, such as draft mode. You can add the Print dialog box to your application using the `PrintDialog` control.

The `PrintDialog` control is available in the Windows Form section of the Toolbox. A required property for the function of the `PrintDialog` control is `Document`. You must set this property to a valid `Document` provided by a `PrintDocument` control.

Other than the `Document` property, you can edit properties to determine what functions to make available to the user. `AllowPrintToFile` enables or disables the "Print To File" checkbox. If `AllowPrintToFile` is `True` and the user checks the box, the `PrintToFile` property is set to `True`. `AllowSelection` enables or disables the range selector boxes, which enable the user to print only a particular range of pages. `AllowSomePages` enables or disables the box where the user can enter a selection of pages either

individually or by range. If you enable these properties, the `PrintDocument` control manages the correct pages to print.

To make the dialog box appear, invoke the `ShowDialog` method with no arguments. The method returns a `DialogResult` specifying either OK or Cancel. For more information on `DialogResult`, see Chapter 3. If the user clicks OK, the `PrinterDialog` sets the dialog box settings to the `PrinterSettings` of the `PrintDocument` component. If you call the `ShowDialog` method and the user does not have any defined printers, a message appears notifying the user how to add a printer and the `DialogResult` returns Cancel. You can use the `Reset` method to clear any previous settings the user has made and reset the dialog box to defaults.

The example uses a `Button` control to activate the Print dialog box. You can use a variety of controls such as a toolbar or menu as well.

USING THE PRINTER DIALOG BOX

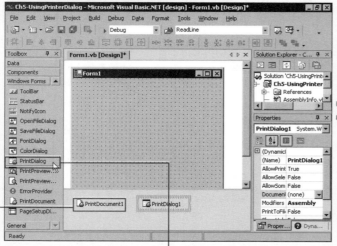

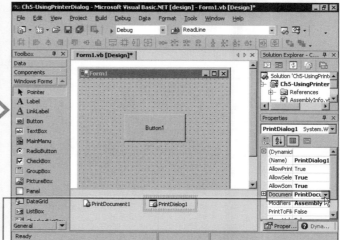

1 Open a form in a Windows Application project.

2 Add and configure a `PrintDocument` component on the form.

Note: See the section "Using the PrintDocument Control" to add a **PrintDocument** *to the form.*

3 In the Toolbox, double-click the **PrintDialog** control to add it to the form.

■ The control appears in the Component Tray.

4 In the Properties window, click the **Document** ▾ and select **PrintDocument** control.

■ You can optionally set other properties and toggle preference properties like **AllowSelection** by double-clicking the property name.

5 Open the method or event where the Printer dialog box needs to appear.

Extra

The `PrinterSettings` object of the `PrintDocument` component provides a number of properties that set up how the document prints, and what features the selected printer supports. You can use the `PrinterSettings.PrintRange` property to determine the print range the user selected. The property contains one of the values available in the `PrintRange` enumeration: `AllPages`, if the user selects to print all of the pages in your application's document, `Selection`, to print only the information the user previously selected in the application, or `SomePages`. If the value is `SomePages`, the user entered a range they want your application to print. You can access this range using the `FromPage` and `ToPage` properties of the `PrinterSettings` object. A number of properties return information about the printer the user selects. The `SupportsColor` property returns `True` if the printer supports color printing, and `False` if it does not. The `PaperSizes` property maintains a collection of the paper sizes the printer supports, and `PaperSources` maintains a collection of the print trays available for the printer. For a full list of the properties available in the `PrinterSettings` object, you can search Visual Basic .NET Help by typing **PrinterSettings members**.

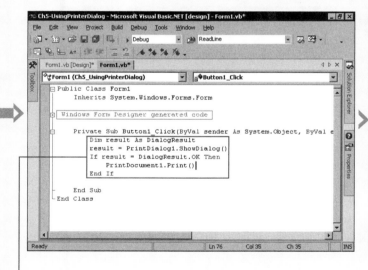

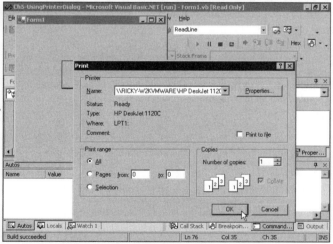

6 Type code to show the dialog box and respond to it.

■ You can type **PrintDialog1.ShowDialog()** to show the dialog box, replacing `PrintDialog1` with the name of the component.

■ The Print dialog box appears and allows printer selection and editing of various properties.

USING THE PAGE SETUP DIALOG BOX

The Page Setup dialog box lets the user select paper sizes and page orientation using a standard interface. You can use the `PageSetupDialog` control to add this dialog box to your application. The control automatically modifies the settings of a `PrintDocument` control. For more information on using the `PrintDocument` control, see "Using the PrintDocument Control."

You find the `PageSetupDialog` control in the Windows Form section of the Toolbox. A required property for the function of the `PageSetupDialog` control is `Document`. You must set this property to a valid `PrintDocument` control.

The `PageSetupDialog` control provides properties to control its appearance and enable or disable functionality for the user. `AllowMargins` enables the margin-editing section of the dialog box. If enabled, `MinMargins` is a `Margin` object and allows you to enter the `Left`, `Right`, `Top`, and `Bottom` minimum margins the user can enter. `AllowOrientation` allows the user to switch between portrait and landscape orientations. `AllowPaper` enables

or disables paper selection. `AllowPrinter` shows or hides the Printer button, which allows editing of the printer's settings. `ShowNetwork` shows or hides the Network button on the secondary printer dialog. `ShowHelp` determines if the Help button is present.

To make the dialog box appear, invoke the `ShowDialog` method with no arguments. The method returns a `DialogResult` specifying either OK or Cancel. For more information on `DialogResult`, see Chapter 2. If the user clicks OK, the dialog box loads the `PageSettings` and `PrinterSettings` given by user to the `PrintDocument` assigned to the control. This creates a totally automated printing system. Note that if you call the `ShowDialog` method and the user does not define a printer, a run-time error occurs. See Chapter 12 for more information on how to trap errors.

The example uses a `Button` control to activate the Page Setup dialog box. You can use a variety of controls such as a toolbar or menu as well.

USING THE PAGE SETUP DIALOG BOX

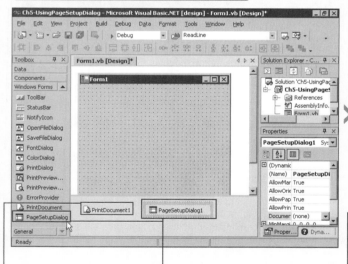

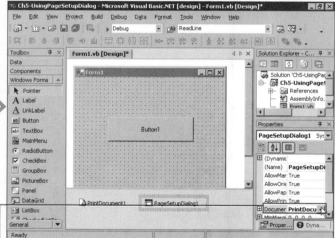

1 Open a form in a Windows Application project.

2 Add and configure a `PrintDocument` control on the form.

Note: See "Using the PrintDocument Control" to add a `PrintDocument` to the form.

3 In the Toolbox, double-click the `PageSetupDialog` control to add the control to the form.

■ The control appears in the component tray.

4 In the Properties window, click the `Document` ▼ and select `PrintDocument` control.

■ You can optionally set other properties. Toggle preference properties like `AllowPaper` by double-clicking the property name.

5 Open the method or event where the Page Setup dialog box needs to appear.

Extra

You can edit printer settings to certain requirements. Even if you provide the user with selections, you may want to check those settings. Note, you cannot make the changes while in the `PrintPage` event because the `PrintDocument` component has already built a page for you. Instead, use the `BeginPage` event. The `DefaultPageSettings` and `PrinterSettings` properties provide the settings that affect printing and page layout.

PAGESETTINGS PROPERTIES

PROPERTY	DESCRIPTION
Bounds	A `Rectangle` object that retrieves the bounds of the page, given the page orientation.
Color	A `Boolean` value that retrieves or sets whether the page prints in color.
Landscape	A `Boolean` value that determines whether the page prints in landscape or portrait orientation.
Margins	A `Margins` object that retrieves or sets the margins for the page. Use the `MarginBounds` of the `PrintPage` event argument to specify the dimensions of the printable area.
PaperSize	Retrieves or sets a `PaperSize` object indicating the paper size for the page.
PaperSource	Retrieves or sets a `PaperSource` object indicating the page's paper source (for example, the printer's upper tray).
PrinterResolution	Retrieves or sets the printer resolution for the page.
PrinterSettings	Retrieves or sets the printer settings associated with the page.

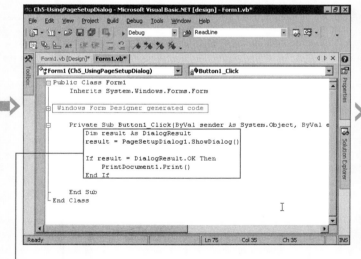

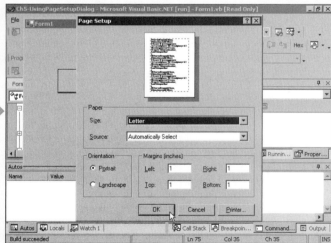

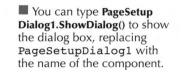

6 Add code to show the dialog box and respond to it.

■ You can type **PageSetup Dialog1.ShowDialog()** to show the dialog box, replacing `PageSetupDialog1` with the name of the component.

■ The Page Setup dialog box appears and allows editing of various properties.

CREATE A PRINT PREVIEW

Many modern applications enable the user to preview his or her print job before choosing to print it. You can add this powerful feature to your application using the `PrintPreviewDialog`. This control takes all the pages printed by a `PrintDocument` control and maps them onto a virtual onscreen page. The `PrintPreviewDialog` control also provides an easy to use and familiar dialog box with a toolbar of display options and a panel to show the page or pages in the print job.

To use the control, you need to set the `Document` property to a valid `PrintDocument` control. When the print preview control displays, the dialog box calls the `PrintDocument` control to output the pages, which in turn calls your page output event handler. Instead of the pages outputting to the printer, the pages store in memory for the Print Preview dialog box to display. See the section "Using the `PrintDocument` Control" for more information on the `PrintDocument` control.

The `PrintPreviewDialog` control only makes one property available: `UseAntiAlias`. Set the property to `True` to have the control draw the page on screen using anti-alias to smooth the appearance of lines, shapes, and text. Keep in mind that anti-aliasing is an intensive process that may slow some older systems. If your application needs to run well on older machines, you may want to leave this property disabled.

To make the Print Preview dialog box appear, call the `Show` or `ShowDialog` method. See Chapter 2 to learn about the differences between `Show` and `ShowDialog` methods.

When the dialog appears, it shows a toolbar with a Print button, a Zoom button, and Column/Row selections. The control provides all the interaction with the user for the display interface. When the user clicks the Print button, the dialog calls the `Print` method of the `PrintDocument` control assigned to the `PrintPreviewDialog`.

CREATE A PRINT PREVIEW

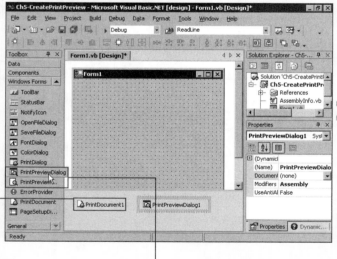

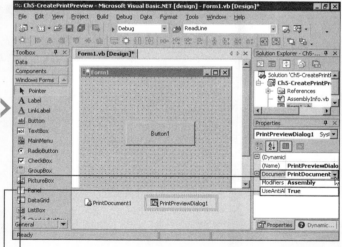

1 Open a form in a Windows Application project.

2 Add and configure a `PrintDocument` control on the form.

Note: See the section "Using the PrintDocument Control" to add a `PrintDocument` to the form.

3 In the Toolbox, double-click the `PrintPreviewDialog` control to add it to the form.

■ The control appears in the Component Tray.

4 Click the `Document` ▾ in the Properties window and select `PrintDocument` control.

■ To cause the `PrintPreview Dialog` control to anti-alias the pages, double-click the `UseAntiAlias` property to toggle it to `True`.

5 Add a control to the form to make the dialog box appear and double-click the control to edit its default event handler.

Extra

While the `PrintPreviewDialog` control enables you to create a quick and easy Print preview window with a single line of code, you may want to customize your program more extensively. You can use the `PrintPreviewControl` to add the print preview pane directly to a form of your own. The `PrintPreviewDialog` control uses the `PrintPreviewControl` to provide the view in the dialog box, so they appear exactly the same. If you use the `PrintPreviewControl`, you must provide your own interaction with the user by setting the control properties. The `Zoom` property controls the zoom of the display. The property accepts a `Double` value, with 1.0 being full-size, or 100%. To make the page appear half-size, use the value 0.5. The `Columns` property determines the number of pages to display horizontally. The `Rows` property determines the number of pages to display vertically. For example, Print previews in many applications let you switch the view to display two pages side by side, or a 3 x 2 configuration of six pages. To make the control automatically size the pages to fit in the available space of the control when you alter properties such as `Columns` or `Rows`, set the `AutoZoom` property of the `PrintPreviewControl` to `True`.

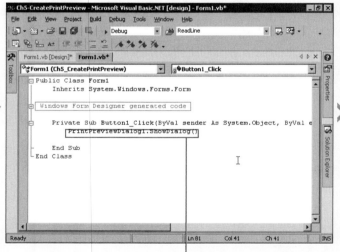

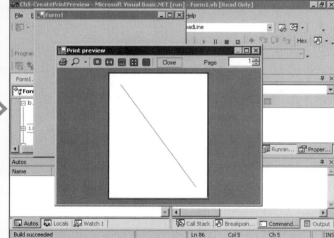

■ The Code Editor appears.

6 Type **PrintPreviewDialog1. ShowDialog()**, replacing `PrintPreviewDialog` with the name of the control.

7 Press F5 to run the project.

■ The `PrintPreviewDialog` or `PrintPreviewControl` appears and allows you to view the document.

■ The example above uses the same `PrintPage` event handler for the `PrintDocument` as in the section "Using the PrintDocument Control."

DOWNLOAD FROM A WEB SERVER

Networking, clients, servers, and the Internet are fast becoming an important feature for every application to support effectively. You can use the `WebClient` class to connect to an HTTP:// or HTTPS:// server to download and upload data. This class provides a high-level interface for accessing network sockets by working off other classes.

`WebRequest` and `WebResponse`, made to send and receive data from a server, form the basis of `WebClient`, and you can use them directly instead of `WebClient` to perform more powerful tasks. The `System.Net` namespace provides all of these classes. See the Visual Basic .NET help system for more information.

To begin using a `WebClient`, declare a new variable and place `As New Net.WebClient()` for the type declaration. The `New` keyword tells VB .NET to create a new instance of the class in memory and assign it the variable

name you give. For more information on instantiating classes and using constructors, see Chapter 7.

After creating the `WebClient`, multiple methods enable you to chose the appropriate method for accessing the server. The `OpenRead` method expects one parameter, the URL to download, and returns a `Stream`. This method enables you to load the data from the server directly into your program as a string, or manipulate the data in any way a `Stream` allows. For more information on reading from a `Stream`, see the section "Read from a Stream."

The `DownloadData` method accepts a URL as its parameter and returns a `Byte` array with the contents of the server request. The `DownloadFile` method accepts two parameters, the URL to download, and the file into which you save the download. This method saves the entire contents of the URL request directly to the file. The method returns nothing.

DOWNLOAD FROM A WEB SERVER

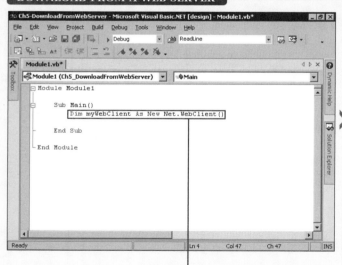

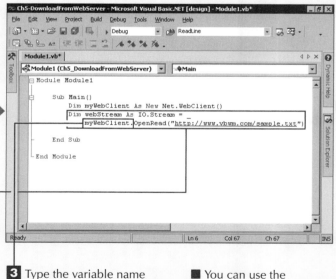

1 Create a new project or open an existing one.

2 In the method or event to download a file, type **Dim myWebClient As New Net.WebClient()**, replacing `myWebClient` with the variable name.

3 Type the variable name assigned to the `WebClient`.

4 Type **.OpenRead(url)**, replacing `OpenRead` with the download method to use and `url` with the appropriate parameters to the method.

■ You can use the `DownloadData` or `DownloadFile` methods instead of `OpenRead`.

Extra

Some Web sites require users to fill out a form before they can access a particular web page. To make your application upload form information to the server for a particular page, use the `UploadValues` method. This method accepts a URL as the first parameter, and a `NameValueCollection` class as the second. The class holds a list of form values. Create a new instance of the class and use the `Add` method to specify the name and value pairs to pass to the URL.

Example:
```
Dim loginForm As New Net.WebClient()
Dim loginFormElements As New _
System.Collections.Specialized.NameValueCollec
tion()
loginFormElements.Add("UserID", "rbowman")
loginForm.UploadValues("http://www.sample.com/
login.asp", _
loginFormElements)
```

Servers can lock resources on a Web site and force the browser to request a username and password. If your program needs access to a restricted directory, use the `Credentials` property of the `WebClient`. To do so, you must first create a new instance of the `CredentialCache` class in which to store the credentials. `CredentialCache` can hold any number of Web sites' credentials, and the `WebClient` selects the right one when necessary.

Example:
```
Dim restrictedPage As New Net.WebClient()
Dim myCache As New Net.CredentialCache()
Dim credential As New _
Net.NetworkCredential("myUser", "myPass")
myCache.Add(New
Uri("http://www.sample.com/restricted/"), _
"Basic", credential)
restrictedPage.Credentials = myCache
```

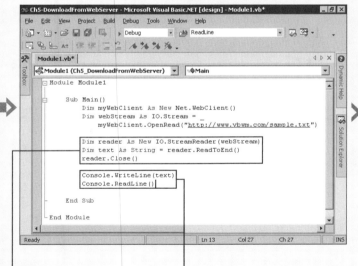

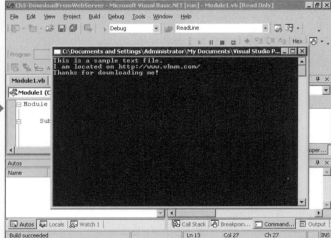

5 Type code to retrieve the data into a useable variable.

■ The `OpenRead` method returns a stream you can read.

Note: See the section "Read from a Stream" to retrieve data from a stream.

6 Type code to display or use the results.

7 Press F5 to run the project.

■ The `WebClient` retrieves the file from the Internet-based server.

MAKE A CONNECTION TO A SERVER

Although most transactions of data in your application may transfer over HTTP protocols, in some cases you need to connect to servers that do not run HTTP protocols. In this case, you cannot use the `WebClient` class explained in the section "Download from a Web Server." You can, however, use the `TcpClient` class to create a connection to any sort of server. Because of the flexibility of the `TcpClient` class, you may find code to support the class harder to write. If you want to create a client/server pair of applications, see the next section, "Accept Incoming Connections," for more information.

To create a connection to a server, declare a new instance of the `TcpClient` class. For more information on declaring instances of classes and using constructors, see Chapter 7. If you want the object to open the connection immediately, pass the server to which you want to connect as the first

argument to the constructor, and follow it with the port number. Leave the constructor empty to connect later. Use the `Connect` method to connect at a later time. The `Connect` method accepts the same two arguments. Use the `Close` method to close the connection.

To send and receive data, the `TcpClient` provides a `GetStream` method. The method returns a `NetworkStream` object. You can use this stream to read and write to the network socket. To use the stream the method returns, assign the stream to a variable of type `Stream`, defined in the `System.IO` namespace. You can then use this variable to create stream readers and writers to send and receive information over the network socket. For more information on reading or writing from a stream, see the sections "Read from a Stream" or "Write to a Stream."

MAKE A CONNECTION TO A SERVER

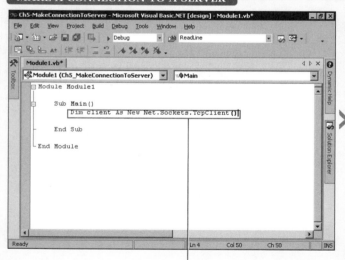

1 Create a new project or open an existing one.

2 In the method or event where the connection needs to occur, type **Dim client As New Net.Sockets.TcpClient()**, replacing `client` with the variable name.

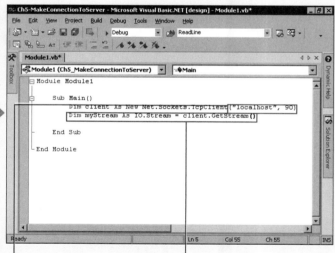

3 Inside of the parentheses, type **"localhost", 90**, replacing **"localhost"** with the server and **90** with the port number.

4 Type **Dim myStream As IO.Stream = client.GetStream** (), replacing `myStream` with the variable name to store the `Stream`, and `client` with the variable name of the `TcpClient`.

Extra

You can use a set of properties available in the `TcpClient` class to ensure that a connection remains open. The `LingerState` property represents an instance of the `LingerOption` class. Linger time is the time the connection stays open after you call the `Close` method. You can enable the `LingerState` option to make sure your application acts like a proper client and does not disconnect in the middle of a transfer. If `LingerState.Enabled` is `True`, data continues to send over the network with a timeout of `LingerState.LingerTime`, in seconds. After your data is sent or the timeout expires, the connection closes gracefully. If the `TcpClient` object finds no data in the send queue, the socket closes immediately.

Example:
```
myClient.LingerState.LingerTime = 2
myClient.LingerState.Enabled = True
```

The `TcpClient` class buffers information as it comes across a connection until you process it. You can control the buffering of the control using a set of properties. The `ReceiveBufferSize` and `SendBufferSize` properties control the size in bytes of the two respective buffers. `ReceiveTimeout` and `SendTimeout` control the amount of time the class waits for a server response in milliseconds. Set `NoDelay` to `True` to make the connection delay, if the buffers fill, so you do not lose data.

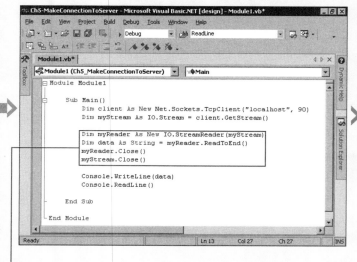

5 Read and write as appropriate to the stream.

Note: See the section "Read a Stream" to read from the stream, or "Write to a Stream" to write to the stream.

6 Press F5 to run the project.

■ The **TcpClient** connects to the server and exchanges data.

■ The example shows the output of connecting to the server shown in the section "Accept Incoming Connections."

ACCEPT INCOMING CONNECTIONS

Many packages and even hardware devices provide network connections and a Web server you can connect to configure the package. Then a user can modify a setting in an application wherever their location. You can create a server by accepting incoming TCP/IP connections with the `TcpListener` class. Part of the `System.Net.Socket` namespace, this class relies heavily on the `Socket` class. See the section "Make a Connection to a Server" to learn how you use `Socket` to make outgoing connections.

Create a `TcpListener` class by declaring a `New` instance of the class. Pass the port you want to listen on as the single parameter to the constructor of the class. For more information on creating class instances and using constructors, see Chapter 7.

To attach the listener to the port, call the `Start` method. At this point the class activates the port and awaits connections. To respond to a connection, call the `AcceptSocket`

method. Calling this method blocks your program until a connection occurs, so you can place code to respond to the connection directly after it. The `AcceptSocket` method returns a `Socket` which you need to maintain a reference for reading and writing to the stream.

Once you have the `Socket`, you can freely write information to it as long as the client stays connected. To write to a socket, use the `Send` method. The first parameter of the `Send` method is the `Byte` array to send. You can optionally follow this with the length of the data and a `SocketFlags` constant. In most cases, you can safely pass a zero for `SocketFlags`. To learn more search **Visual Basic .NET Help** for `SocketFlags`.

After writing data to the socket, make sure to close it using the `Socket.Close()` method. Then you can wait for another connection by invoking the `AcceptSocket` method again. Disable the `TcpListener` by calling the `Stop` method.

ACCEPT INCOMING CONNECTIONS

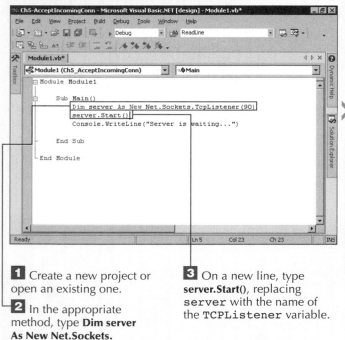

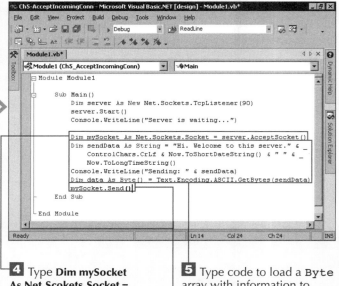

1 Create a new project or open an existing one.

2 In the appropriate method, type **Dim server As New Net.Sockets. TcpListener(90)**, replacing `server` with the variable name and `90` with the port.

3 On a new line, type **server.Start()**, replacing `server` with the name of the `TCPListener` variable.

4 Type **Dim mySocket As Net.Scokets.Socket = server.AcceptSocket()**, replacing `mySocket` with the variable name to create a socket and `server` with the name of the `TCPListener` variable.

5 Type code to load a `Byte` array with information to send the client.

6 Type **mySocket.Send()**, replacing `mySocket` with the variable name of the socket.

Extra

You can use the `TcpListener` class to build full-featured applications. For example, the basic function of a Web server is to wait for connections on port 80, to process the request string the browser sends to the server, and to write content back over the socket. You can retrieve information sent by the client using the `Receive` method of the `Socket` object. For the parameter to the `Receive` method, pass a `Byte` array to use as the buffer. The method returns the actual number of bytes it loads into the buffer. Call the method multiple times in sequence until all of the data loads. To convert a byte array into a string, use the `Text.Encoding.ASCII.GetString` method. The example loads information until it receives a new line control character in the text.

Example

```
Dim server As New Net.Sockets.TcpListener(90)
server.Start()
Dim mySocket As Net.Sockets.Socket = _
    server.AcceptSocket()
Dim buffer(100) As Byte, data As _
    String = "", size As Integer = 0
Do Until InStr(headers, ControlChars.CrLf) > 0
    size = sock.Receive(buffer)
    data += Text.Encoding.ASCII.GetString(buffer)
Loop
mySocket.Close()
Server.Stop()
Console.WriteLine("Received a character return.")
Console.ReadLine()
```

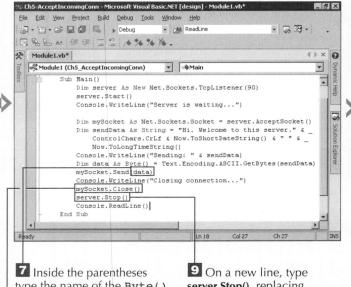

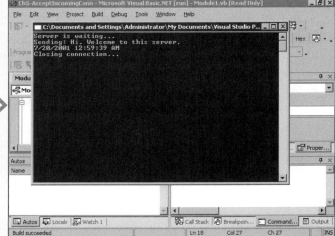

7 Inside the parentheses type the name of the `Byte()` variable.

8 On a new line, type **mySocket.Close()**, replacing `mySocket` with the name of the variable.

9 On a new line, type **server.Stop()**, replacing **server** with the name of the **TCPListener**.

10 Press F5 to run your project.

■ The server loads and waits for a connection.

Note: See the section "Make a Connection to a Server" to create a client program.

ADD A PICTURE TO A FORM

Many Windows applications use pictures to make a window more attractive and easier to understand. You can add a picture to a Windows Form with the PictureBox control.

The PictureBox control appears in the Windows Forms section of the Toolbox. After adding it to the form, you can assign a single picture file to its Image property. Use the SizeMode property to determine how the control draws the image. Normal makes the PictureBox draw the image in its actual size at the top, left corner of the control. For SizeMode equal to StretchImage, the control stretches the image to fill the entire control space. AutoSize makes the control size to the actual image size. When you set SizeMode to AutoSize, you can no longer resize the control. CenterImage draws the image at actual size in the center of the control.

The PictureBox control also allows you to place a border around the edge. Set BorderStyle to FixedSingle to

draw a one-pixel black border. Use Fixed3D to draw a more traditional 3D sunken border around the control. None removes the borders completely. You can also load another image into the control using the standard control property BackgroundImage. Because VB .NET does not allow you to align the foreground image like many other controls, you may not find this property useful. You can use BackgroundImage to draw a frame around an image with SizeMode set to CenterImage.

You can use standard control events with the PictureBox, like Click, MouseDown, MouseMove, and others to respond to actions of the user. Use the Paint event to draw onto the control. If you need to create an interactive picture control, a Button control allows you to use an image and provide interactive cues. For more information on the Button control, see Chapter 3.

ADD A PICTURE TO A FORM

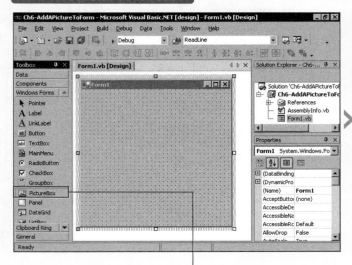

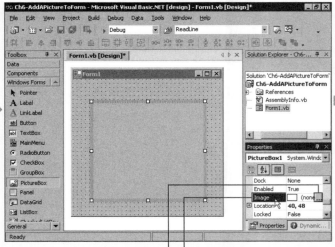

1 Create a new Windows Application project or open an existing project and create or open the form to load onto the control.

2 In the Toolbox, click the **PictureBox** control.

3 Drag the control to the form.

■ The control appears on the form.

4 Edit any necessary properties.

Note: See Chapter 3 to edit properties.

5 In the Properties Window, click the **Image** property.

6 Click the link button (⬜).

Extra

When you load an image into a `PictureBox` control, it saves the image into the executable, which can balloon in size unnecessarily in an application where a variety of forms may include the same image. To prevent this, you can use a resource file to store only a single copy of the file in the executable. You can then load the appropriate resource image into the `PictureBox` control in the `Form_Load` procedure. The `ResourceManager` class contains the necessary functions to access a resource file. For more information on creating a resource file and loading resources into it, search Visual Basic .NET help for Resource Editors. Once you connect to a resource file, use a line similar to the one below to read the image out and load it into a `PictureBox`.

Example:
```
PictureBox1.Image =
  CType(ResourceManager.GetObject("flag"),_
  System.Drawing.Image)
```

The `PictureBox` control accepts drawing commands like the `Form` and many other controls. This means the tasks later in the chapter explaining the `Graphics` object work using a `PictureBox` as well. Just place the code from a `Form_Paint` routine into a `PictureBox_Paint` routine. The `PictureBox` contains all the same drawing methods and properties.

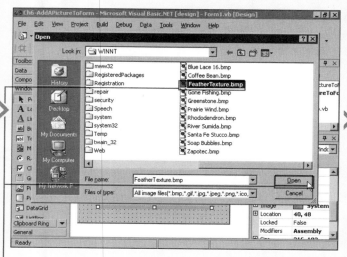

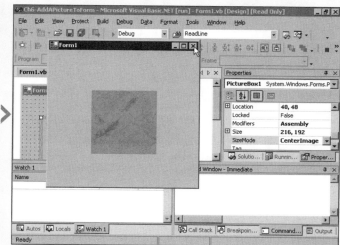

■ The Open dialog box appears.

7 Click an image file from disk.

8 Click Open to load the image into the control.

■ The example sets `SizeMode` to `CenterImage`.

9 Press F5 to run the project.

■ The `PictureBox` control displays the picture file appropriately.

137

USING THE COLOR DIALOG BOX

When editing colors in an application or simply changing the colors on your desktop, the color common dialog box supplies the standard method of selecting a color. You can use the `ColorDialog` control in your application to provide color selection abilities to your user.

The Toolbox locates the `ColorDialog` control in the Windows Forms section. When you place the control onto a form, it loads into the Component Tray of the form because it is a hidden control.

The most important property for a color dialog box is the `Color` property because it controls the color you display in the box. When the user clicks OK, this property stores the selection. If the user presses Cancel, the control does not alter the property value.

The `AllowFullOpen` property enables or disables the custom color section of the dialog where the full color box

is available. By setting `FullOpen` to `True`, the custom color area appears automatically when the dialog box opens. The `SolidColorOnly` property determines whether the dialog selects only solid colors. This only affects 256 color or less displays, which must blend multiple colors. This blending creates a dotted appearance and makes text reading difficult. If you plan to have small to normal size text over the area where the selected color is in use, set `SolidColorOnly` to `False`. The `CustomColors` property stores an array of the stored custom colors.

Like other dialogs, use the `ShowDialog` method of the control to make the dialog box appear. The method returns a `DialogResult` variable indicating either OK or Cancel, depending on the button the user clicks. See Chapter 3 for more information on dialog boxes and `DialogResult` constants.

USING THE COLOR DIALOG BOX

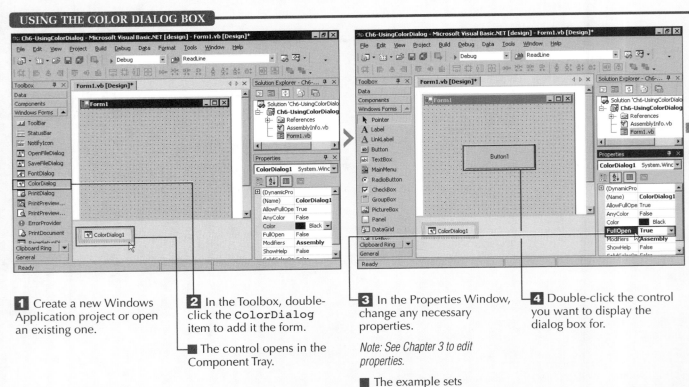

1 Create a new Windows Application project or open an existing one.

2 In the Toolbox, double-click the `ColorDialog` item to add it the form.

■ The control opens in the Component Tray.

3 In the Properties Window, change any necessary properties.

Note: See Chapter 3 to edit properties.

■ The example sets `FullOpen` to `True`.

4 Double-click the control you want to display the dialog box for.

Extra

You can use the `CustomColors` property to both provide your own set of colors to the user or to store the user's own selection of colors. The variable type of the property is an integer array. You can use a `For Each` loop to run through the list and store the user's settings.

Example:
```
ListBox1.Items.Clear()
Dim myColor As Integer
For Each myColor In ColorDialog1.CustomColors
    ListBox1.Items.Add(myColor)
Next
```

To store an entire set of new values into the `CustomColors` array, create a new array of size fifteen. Fill the sixteen values (0 to 15) and assign the array to the property.

Example:
```
Dim counter As Integer
Dim red As Integer = 100
Dim newColors(15) As Integer
For counter = 0 To 15
    newColors(counter) = red
    red = red + 10
Next
ColorDialog1.CustomColors = newColors
```

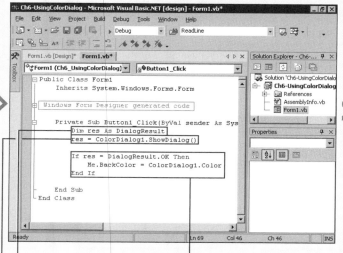

5 In the method where you want the dialog to appear, declare a variable to store the `DialogResult`.

6 Type **res = ColorDialog1. ShowDialog()**, replacing **res** with the variable name and **ColorDialog1** with the control name.

7 Type code to process the result of the dialog using the `Color` property to retrieve the selected color.

8 Press F5 to run the project.

■ The color dialog allows color selection and upon the user selecting a color, your application responds by using their color choice.

UNDERSTANDING THE GRAPHICS OBJECT

Using controls and forms creates simple interfaces. But for some applications, you may want to draw custom art onto a form or control. To do so, you can use the Graphics object that forms and controls provide.

Use the Paint event of a component to draw onto the component's surface. When a control needs to redraw because a window overlaps it, the Paint event fires when the control redraws itself. The Paint event provides the Graphics object in the event arguments. In most cases, this means you access the object using e.Graphics.

The DpiX and DpiY properties return the number of dots, or resolution, per inch available on the device represented by the Graphics object.

The VisibleClipBounds property returns a RectangleF structure that specifies the visible region of the control available for drawing. This class contains Left, Top, Width,

and Height properties. The Graphics object's Clip property allows you to set a Region of the control where pixels can appear. When graphic methods attempt to draw out of the clip region, only the section inside of the region draws. Retrieve the current Clip region as RectangleF using the ClipBounds property.

A number of properties combine to specify the total quality of the image drawn. The CompositingMode property specifies how pixels draw into the Graphics object. It provides two constants: SourceCopy to overwrite background pixels, and SourceOver to combine with background pixels. Set CompositingMode to SourceOver to create a more realistic blend when overlapping translucent objects. SmoothingMode determines the quality of antialiasing you use when drawing curves and diagonals. TextRenderingHint sets the antialiasing mode for text. InterpolationMode determines how VB .NET calculates intermediate values between two endpoints.

PAINT EVENT

By default, a Paint event invalidates the area that changes. For example, if the user makes the form larger, VB .NET allows only the part of the form that did not exist prior to repaint. This means if your code relies on the size of the form and resizes graphics as the form resizes, VB .NET does not redraw the entire surface.

Also when a Panel or other scrolling container scrolls, only the invisible part of the control invalidates. For a form or control that resizes, you can place the name of the object followed by .Invalidate() to invalidate the entire contents and draw on the entire surface.

POINT OBJECT

The Point object specifies a set of two pixel values that make up a particular coordinate on screen. To create a new instance of the Pen object, pass the x coordinate followed by the y coordinate. The properties X and Y store the values you specify.

Example:
```
' define a point that represents
' the (100, 100) position.
Dim pt As New Drawing.Point(100, 100)
```

SIZE OBJECT

The Size object represents the size of a particular object. To create an instance of the Size object, pass the width and height to the constructor. The properties Width and Height store the vaues that you specify.

Example:
```
' define a size of 200 pixels across
' and 100 pixels in height.
Dim sz As New Size(200, 100)
```

RECTANGLE OBJECT

The `Rectangle` object specifies a set of four coordinates to define the size of a rectangle. Many of the graphics primitives throughout the chapter use the `Rectangle` object. To create a new instance of a `Rectangle` object, pass the left (*x*) coordinate, the top (*y*) coordinate, and the width and height. The properties `Left`, `Top`, `Width`, and `Height` store each of the values that you specify.

```
Example:
' define a rectangle that starts at
' position (100, 100), is 200 pixels
' across, and 50 high.
Dim rect As New Drawing.Rectangle(100, 100, 200, 50)
```

COLORS

The `Graphics` object works with colors in the ARGB format. A value of 0-255 represents transparency (alpha-blending), and a range of 0-255 for each of the red, green, and blue values combine to create the full set of 32-bit colors. To create a custom color, call the `Color.FromArgb` method and either specify the combined ARGB integer or separate each of the four values by commas. The function uses the color given or generates the appropriate combined number and returns a `Color` object.

VB makes a large variety of colors available to you by name in the `Drawing.Color` object. Colors range from `AliceBlue` to `YellowGreen`. Below is a partial list of the available colors in the `Color` object. For the complete list, search VB .NET help by typing **Color members**.

SAMPLE SYSTEM.DRAWING.COLOR MEMBERS

AliceBlue	AntiqueWhite	Aqua	Beige
Black	Blue	BlueViolet	Brown
CadetBlue	Chartreuse	Chocolate	Coral
CornflowerBlue	Crimson	Cyan	ForestGreen
Fuchsia	GhostWhite	Gold	Goldenrod
Gray	Green	GreenYellow	Honeydew
Indigo	Ivory	Khaki	Lavender
Lime	LimeGreen	Linen	Magenta
Maroon	MidnightBlue	Navy	OldLace
Olive	Orange	OrangeRed	Orchid
Peru	Pink	Plum	PowderBlue
Purple	Red	RoyalBlue	Salmon
SandyBrown	SeaGreen	Sienna	Silver
SkyBlue	SlateBlue	SlateGray	Snow
SpringGreen	SteelBlue	Tan	Teal
Thistle	Transparent	Turquoise	Violet
White	WhiteSmoke	Yellow	YellowGreen

CREATE A BRUSH

You use a `Brush` class to tell VB .NET how to fill an area. Each of the filled primitives, such as filled rectangles, requires you use a `Brush` to specify how to fill the area. To produce a `Brush` for use in VB .NET, create an instance of type `Brush` using the `New` operator. VB provides a number of `Brush` classes depending on the style you need. Each brush has a particular size. If the shape to fill is larger than the brush, the brush tiles to fill the entire space.

The `System.Drawing` namespace holds both the `SolidBrush` and `TextureBrush` classes. The `SolidBrush` paints an area in a single color. Pass the color to use for the brush as the only parameter. Because these brushes are a solid color, the brush is only 1 x 1 in size.

The `System.Drawing.Drawing2D` namespace contains a number of more complex brushes. The `HatchBrush`

creates a brush based on a pattern. Windows provides a collection of 2-bit hatch patterns. VB .NET provides constants for each of these patterns in the `HatchStyle` enumeration, ranging from `BackwardDiagonal` to `ZigZag`. To create the brush, declare an instance of the `HatchBrush` class and pass the constructor the pattern to use, followed by the foreground color as the second parameter, and the background color as the third parameter.

`LinearGraidentBrush` fills in a steady range from one color to another, at any angle. For the constructor, pass an instance of a `Rectangle` class filled with the size of the gradient brush to create. The next parameter specifies the start color and the third parameter specifies the end color. See the section "Understanding the Graphics Object" to specify a color. The last parameter is the angle in degrees of the gradient. An angle of zero creates a horizontal gradient, and an angle of 90 creates a vertical gradient.

CREATE A BRUSH

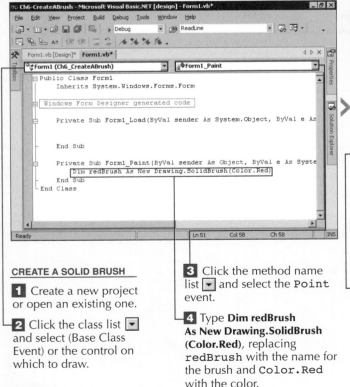

CREATE A SOLID BRUSH

1 Create a new project or open an existing one.

2 Click the class list ▼ and select (Base Class Event) or the control on which to draw.

3 Click the method name list ▼ and select the `Point` event.

4 Type **Dim redBrush As New Drawing.SolidBrush (Color.Red)**, replacing `redBrush` with the name for the brush and `Color.Red` with the color.

CREATE A HATCH BRUSH

5 Type **Dim confettiBrush As New Drawing2D.HatchBrush()**, replacing `confettiBrush` with the name for the brush.

6 Inside the parentheses, type the hatch pattern to use followed by the foreground and background colors, all separated by commas.

Extra

If you need a simple solid-color brush, you may find it time-consuming to constantly create custom brush objects. However, you can use a pre-created brush to save you the trouble of creating a new instance of a `SolidBrush` class. The `System.Drawing.Brushes` class provides a set of brushes for each color in the standard color list. See the section "Using the Graphics Object" for a list of common color choices.

Example:
```
Dim myPlum As Drawing.SolidBrush =
    Drawing.Brushes.Plum
```

In Windows, the user sets a variety of colors in their Desktop preferences, and all Windows applications respond in the same way. You may want to draw onto the form, but you need to follow the Windows colors the user selects. You can use the `SystemBrushes` class to fill an area in a particular system color. The `SystemBrushes` class is part of the `System.Drawing` namespace. For example, `SystemBrushes.Desktop` returns a brush in the color of the current user's desktop. You can also retrieve the individual color values that each brush relies on using the `SystemColors` class. You can type **SystemBrushes members** in Help to search for a full list of the available system colors.

Example:
```
Dim myControlColor As
    Drawing.SolidBrush =
    Drawing.SystemBrushes.Control
```

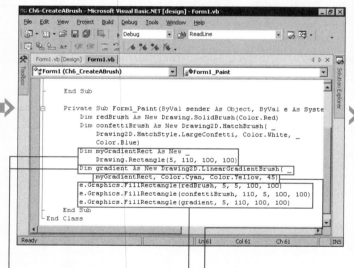

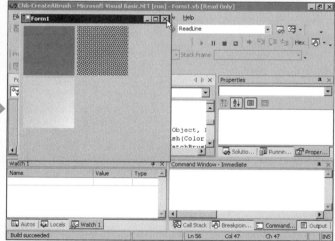

CREATE A LINEAR GRADIENT

7 Declare a `Rectangle` object.

Note: See the section "Using Your Graphics Object" to create a Rectangle.

8 Type **Dim gradient As New Drawing2D.LinearGradientBrush** (), replacing `LinearGradient` with the name for the brush.

9 In parentheses, type the `Rectangle` name, the start and end color, and the angle of rotation separated by commas.

10 Type the code to use the brushes.

11 Press F5 to run the project.

■ The brush draws into the area to fill, tiling if necessary.

143

CREATE A PEN

You use a Pen to tell VB .NET the style, color, and thickness of a line to draw for the various primitives. For example, a variety of outlined primitives use a Pen, like rectangles, ellipses, and curves. A Pen specifies details for VB .NET to know how to draw these shapes. Use a Brush to fill a primitive object or the inside of a Pen. For more information on the Brush object, see the section "Create a Brush."

To produce a single color pen, create a new instance of the Pen class using the Dim command and the New operator. VB .NET stores the Pen class in the System.Drawing namespace. For more information on instantiating classes, see Chapter 7. For the most basic constructor of the Pen, pass a color as the single parameter. The second constructor expects a color for the first parameter and the line width as the second parameter. See the section "Using the Graphics Object" for more information on specifying a color.

To create a Pen object based on a Brush, create a new instance of the Pen class and provide the Brush as the first argument. To specify the width of the pen, use the alternate constructor that expects a Brush and a line width passed in as a Single.

After you create a Pen instance, a number of properties allow editing the appearance. The StartCap and EndCap properties expect a constant from the LineCap enumeration. The properties specify the type of end caps to put on a pen. A primitive without ends, for example, a rectangle or ellipse, ignores the values. Instead, the LineJoin property specifies how to connect corners of lines and expects a value from the LineJoin enumeration. To create different styles of dashed lines, set the DashStyle. The DashCap property specifies a DashCap enumerated value that represents the style to use for dashes.

CREATE A PEN

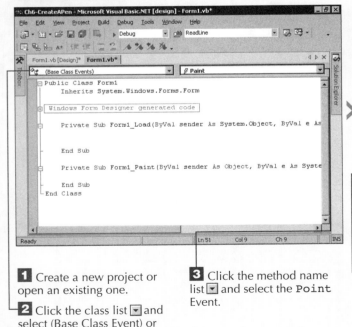

1 Create a new project or open an existing one.

2 Click the class list ▼ and select (Base Class Event) or the control on which to draw.

3 Click the method name list ▼ and select the Point Event.

4 Type **Dim redPen As New Drawing.Pen(Color.Red)**, replacing **redPen** with the variable name and **Color.Red** with the type of the color to use.

■ The example uses the Color class to provide a supplied color Red.

Extra

You can use the `LineCap`, `DashCap`, and `LineJoin` constants to specify how a pen draws.

DRAWING.DRAWING2D.LINECAP ENUMERATION

MEMBER	DESCRIPTION
AncorMask	A mask used to check a line cap
ArrowAnchor	Arrow-shaped anchor cap
Custom	A custom line cap
DiamondAnchor	Diamond anchor cap
Flat	Flat line cap
NoAnchor	No anchor
Round	Round line cap
RoundAnchor	Round anchor cap
Square	Square line cap
SquareAnchor	Square anchor line cap
Triangle	Triangular line cap

DRAWING.DRAWING2D.DASHCAP ENUMERATION

MEMBER	DESCRIPTION
Flat	Squares off ends of each dash
Round	Rounds off ends of each dash
Triangle	Points ends of each dash

DRAWING.DRAWING2D.LINEJOIN ENUMERATION

MEMBER	DESCRIPTION
Bevel	Beveled join
Miter	Angled miter join
MiterClipped	Clipped miter join
Round	Smooth, rounded join

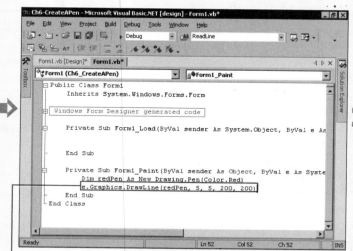

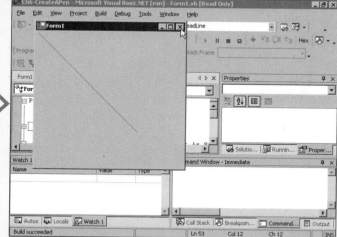

5 Type **e.Graphics.DrawLine (redPen, 5, 5, 200, 200)**, replacing `DrawLine` with the Graphics method to use the pen, `redPen` with the variable name of the Pen object, and `5, 5, 200, 200` with the appropriate parameters.

Note: See the section "Draw Simple Primitives" to draw a primitive.

6 Press F5 to run your project.

■ The graphics method runs and draws using the selected color.

DRAW BITMAPS AND IMAGES

You can add images to a form in conjunction with drawing commands. The `PictureBox` control provides a simple way to load an image onto the form, but you cannot draw around the `PictureBox`, unless you contain all of the drawing inside. You can use commands from the `System.Drawing` namespace to draw images onto the form without using a control.

Two classes provide the ability to work with bitmapped images. You more commonly use the `Bitmap` class to load a raster image from a file, create an instance of a `Bitmap` class and pass the filename as the parameter to the `Bitmap` constructor. The class stores the pixel data and properties of the image.

Only a few of the many method calls available for `DrawImage` appear in the introduction. See Visual Basic .NET help for a complete list. The simplest constructor expects an `Image` and a `Point`, which specifies the

position for the top, left corner of the image. By providing an array of three `Point` classes that form a parallelogram, `DrawImage` skews the image to fit the shape. By passing a `Rectangle` as the second parameter, `DrawImage` scales the image to fit the dimensions of the rectangle starting from the top, left corner of the rectangle.

You can use `TextureBrush` to paint an image onto a shape. This allows you to create an image that has shaped edges, and lets you place the image inside an ellipse or more advanced shapes. The first parameter of the available constructors accepts an `Image` or `Bitmap` class. For the simplest constructor, you only need this parameter. Another constructor of the `TextureBrush` class expects a `Rectangle` as the second parameter that specifies the section of the image to use as the brush. The width and height of the rectangle determine the size of the brush.

DRAW BITMAPS AND IMAGES

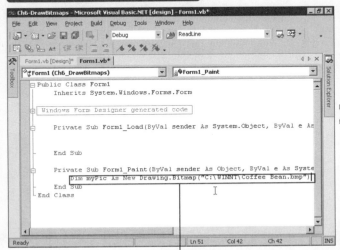

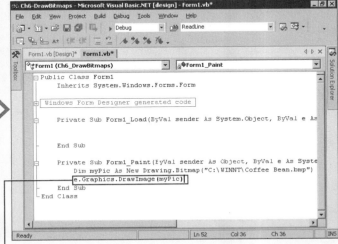

1 Create a new Windows Application or open an existing one.

2 Open the method or event where the image needs to draw.

3 Type **Dim myPic As New Drawing.Bitmap("C:\WINNT\ Coffee Bean.bmp")**, replacing `myPic` with the name for the image variable and `"C\WINNT\ Coffee Bean.bmp"` with the path to a supported raster image file.

4 On a new line, type **e.Graphics.DrawImage (myPic)**, replacing `e.Graphics` with the name of the `Graphics` object and `myPic` with the variable name of the `Bitmap` object.

Extra

You use a *metafile,* a format designed to hold a list of vector commands, to make up an image. You can use a metafile image in a variety of sizes and have the image maintain its detail. Unlike raster files, metafiles, which have the extension `.wmf`, do not contain any information about individual pixels, only information about lines and curves, shapes, and fill patterns. Pass a new instance of the `Metafile` class a WMF file and use it with the standard drawing commands to draw it onto the form. Using `DrawImage`, you can draw the metafile in any size necessary because metafiles have the ability to scale to any size. You can create metafiles in most Windows drawing applications like Adobe Illustrator and CorelDRAW.

The `Icon` class allows you to load icon files. Create a new instance of the `Icon` class and pass an icon file as the parameter. Use the `DrawIcon` method of the `Graphics` object to draw the icon. Pass the `Icon` object as the first parameter, followed by two points specifying the location to draw it. Visual Studio .NET provides many icons in the `Common` directory.

Example:
```
Dim myIcon As New System.Drawing.Icon("C:\Explorer.ico")
e.Graphics.DrawIcon(myIcon, 100, 100)
```

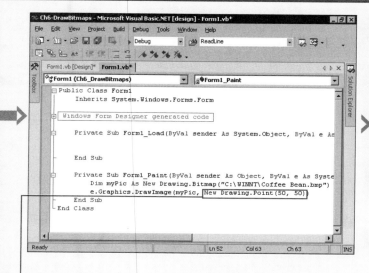

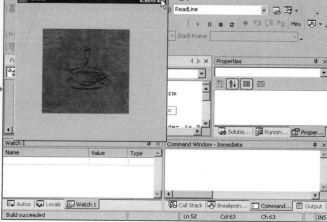

5 Type a comma and follow it with **New Drawing.Point(50,50)**, replacing **50,50** with the coordinates to draw the image.

6 Press F5 to run your project.

■ The image draws onto the form.

DRAW SIMPLE PRIMITIVES

In many cases, you need to draw borders and boxes around items in a Windows Application. You can use a variety of primitives in your Windows Forms application to add aesthetics to parts of the form.

A number of commands draw outlined objects such as lines, rectangles, and ellipses. For these commands to work, you need to create a Pen. To create a Pen object, see the section "Create a Pen."

The DrawLine method draws a line onto the graphics region. The first parameter the method expects is a Pen. After the first parameter, you give the method two Point structures, the first specifying the starting (x, y) coordinates, and the second specifying the end (x, y) coordinates. Instead of the two Point objects, you can also pass four integers or four singles in the form x1, y1, x2, y2. The DrawRectangle expects a Pen for the first argument, and

a Rectangle object for the second argument. Instead of the Rectangle, you can provide four integers or singles after the Pen parameter. DrawEllipse draws an ellipse to fill a rectangular space and expects the same arguments as DrawRectangle. For more information on using Point and Rectangle objects, see the section "Using the Graphics Object."

DrawLines creates a connected set of line segments. When you pass a Pen as the first parameter with an array of Point objects as the second argument, the method starts at the point and connects each point together in sequence. DrawRectangles draws a series of rectangles with a single Pen. Pass the Pen as the first argument and an array of Rectangle objects as the second parameter. DrawPolygon draws a polygon based on a set of points. It automatically connects the first point and last point. Pass a Pen and an array of Point objects for the parameters.

DRAW SIMPLE PRIMITIVES

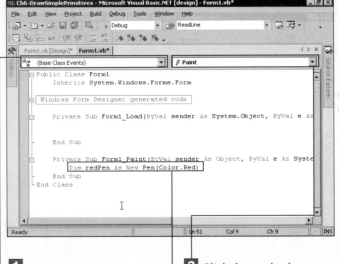

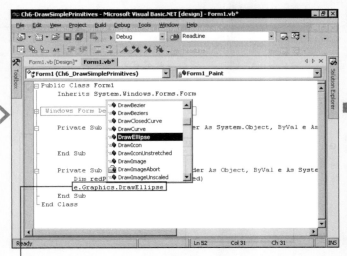

1 Create or open a Windows Application project and double-click a form you want to paint.

2 Click the class list ▾ and select (Base Class Events) or the control on which to draw.

3 Click the method name list ▾ and select the **Paint** event.

■ The Code Editor creates the event handler.

4 Declare a new instance of a **Pen** class.

Note: To declare a Pen, see the section "Create a Pen."

5 Type **e.Graphics.DrawEllipse** replacing **DrawEllipse** with the method name to draw.

Extra

You can create filled regions using the `Graphics` object, which contains a set of methods to draw filled primitives. You can use these commands to create a primitive just like the drawing commands like `DrawLine` and `DrawEllipse`, except instead of drawing an outline, these commands fill the region. Each of these methods accepts the same parameters as their outlined counterparts, except you switch the `Pen` parameter to a `Brush`. To create a `Brush`, see the section "Create a Brush." `FillRectangle` fills a rectangular space with the supplied brush. `FillEllipse` fills an elliptical area. `FillRectangles` fills a series of rectangles. `FillPolygon` fills a polygon area based on a set of points. If you want to draw a filled region with a border, use a combination of the two commands. Draw the filled primitive first and then pass the same set of sizes and parameters to the outlined primitive. Calling the methods in the other order can cause the fill to overwrite the pen.

Example:

```
Dim rect As New Drawing.Rectangle(50, 50, 200, 100)
Dim redBrush As Drawing.SolidBrush = _
    System.Drawing.Brushes.Red
e.Graphics.FillEllipse(redBrush, rect)
```

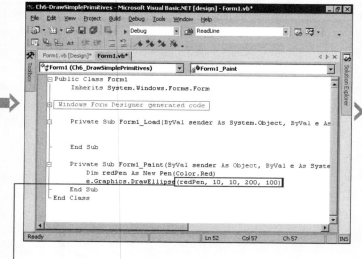

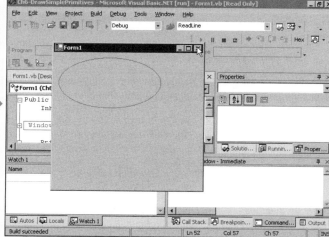

6 Type appropriate parameters inside parentheses.

7 Press F5 to run your project.

■ The form draws the primitive.

DRAW A CURVE

VB .NET provides a set of functions to draw curves, complex line forms that use advanced algorithms to draw given only a few reference points. You can use simple graphics primitive commands to create a variety of curved lines and shapes.

The DrawArc method is the simplest curve command because it draws a portion of an ellipse. You pass the method a Pen as the first parameter. For the next parameters, you pass either a Rectangle containing the size of the ellipse for the entire ellipse, or four integers or singles holding the dimensions of the ellipse. Following these parameters, you specify the start angle, and then the sweep angle, both in degrees. The angles measure clockwise from the x-axis. The DrawPie and FillPie methods draw a pie wedge just like an arc, except two lines draw to the center of the ellipse. Because FillPie creates a filled region, pass it a Brush instead of a Pen as the first argument.

The DrawCurve method draws a curve through a specified array of points. The first parameter for the DrawCurve constructor is the Pen you use to draw the curve. The second parameter is an array of the Point class, which specifies the points through which you draw the curve. Another constructor takes the same two arguments plus the tension to draw the curve as the third parameter. A tension of zero creates a straight line.

DrawClosedCurve draws a curve with a line connecting the first and last point in the curve. The basic constructor requests only a Pen and Point(), for example DrawCurve. Another constructor takes those two arguments plus the tension as the third argument and a constant from the FillMode enumeration for the fourth. The FillMode determines which part of the curve encloses the section. FillClosedCurve fills the enclosed space of the curve. You pass a Brush as the first argument rather than a Pen.

DRAW A CURVE

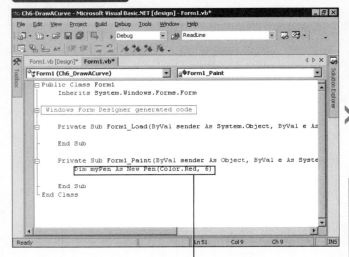

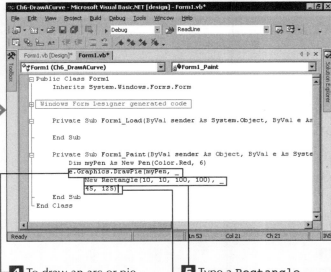

1 Create a new Windows Application project or open an existing project.

2 Open the Paint event where the curve needs to draw.

3 Declare a Pen to draw the curve.

■ To use the fill routines, you can also declare a Brush.

Note: To create a Pen, see the section "Create a Pen." To create a Brush, see the section "Create a Brush."

4 To draw an arc or pie, type **e.Graphics.DrawPie (myPen)**, replacing DrawPie with either DrawPie or DrawArc and myPen with the name of the Pen object.

5 Type a Rectangle object representing the size.

6 Type a comma and follow it with the start and sweep angles.

Extra

You can create different fill patterns for objects with complex shapes, such as curves, using the `FillMode` enumeration. You have two options for `FillMode`: `Winding`, and the default, `Alternate`. `Alternate` moves across the curve and alternates between filling and not filling as it hits lines of the curve. `Winding` uses the direction of the curve to determine whether to fill it. Generally, the default `Alternate` does an effective job, but you may try `Winding` when `Alternate` does not give the appropriate results.

You can use `Bezier` curves, a more advanced cubic curve, to specify more exact coordinates of curvature. Most professional drawing applications work with `Bezier` curves instead of the simpler cardinal spline curves used by `DrawCurve`. To draw a `Bezier` curve, you use the `DrawBezier` method, which only draws one curve defined by four points. The method requires a `Pen` object, which you follow with four `Point` objects for its parameters. The first and last `Point` objects make up the curve's endpoints. The two middle `Point` objects make up the two control points that create the desired curvature. When the curve draws, it pulls the curve out to the control points.

Example:
```
e.Graphics.DrawBezier(Drawing.Pens.Red, _
    New Point(100, 100), New Point(150, 150), _
    New Point(150, 200), New Point(100, 250))
```

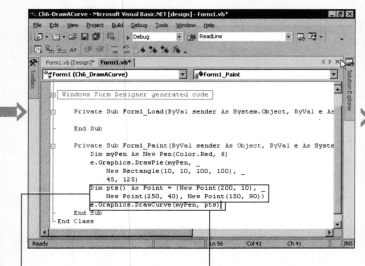

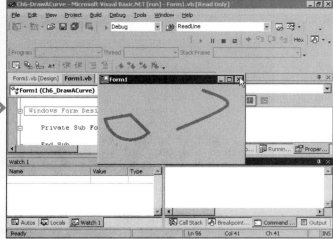

7 To draw a curve, declare an array of `Point` objects that the curve passes through.

8 Type **e.Graphics. DrawCurve (myPen, pts)**, replacing **DrawCurve** with either **DrawCurve** or **DrawClosedCurve** and **myPen** with the name of the **Pen** object and **pts** with the name of the **Point** array.

9 Press F5 to run your project.

■ The curve draws onto the graphics container.

DRAW TEXT

Most applications use text to title, label, and explain functions on a form. In some cases, a `Label` control can provide the appearance necessary. For advanced text rendering, you can use the text drawing routines that VB .NET includes in the `Graphics` object. For more information on the `Label` control, see Chapter 3. Using the `Graphics` system, you can apply a `Brush` to your text to create text filled with a gradient, a bitmapped texture, or a hatch pattern.

The standard method of rendering text with the `Graphics` object is the `DrawString` method. In each available overloaded method call, the first parameter contains the `String` to print. `DrawString` expects a `Font` object as the second parameter and a `Brush` object as the third parameter. For the fourth parameter, you pass a `Point` object specifying the top, left point to draw the text. The simplest constructor requires these four parameters. Optionally for the fifth parameter, you can pass a `StringFormat` object to designate how the text styles.

Chapter 4 contains more detailed information on the `String` variable type.

To provide the font to pass to `DrawString`, create a new instance of the `System.Drawing.Font` class. Depending on the data you want to provide to the Font constructor, you can pass either a `FontFamily` object, or a `String` to select a font family, such as Arial or Times New Roman. The second parameter is the size of the font in points. Optionally for the third parameter, specify the font style using the `FontStyle` enumeration.

The `Graphics` object exposes a method called `MeasureString`. Use this method to determine the width and height of a string you want to draw. Pass the `String` and `Font` as the two parameters to the method. `MeasureString` returns a `SizeF` structure, contained in the `System.Drawing` namespace. The `Width` and `Height` properties of the `SizeF` contain the appropriate values.

DRAW TEXT

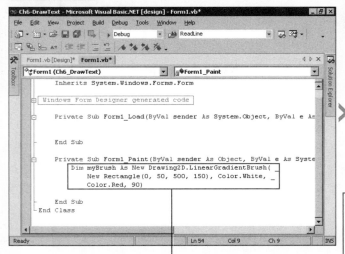

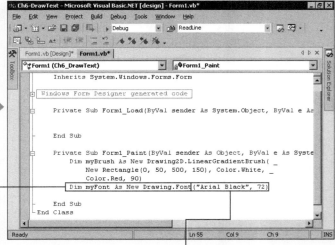

1 Create a new Windows Application project or open an existing project and the form with which to work.

2 Open the `Paint` event where the primitive needs to draw.

■ The example above shows the `Form1_Paint` event open.

3 Declare a `Brush` object to draw the text.

Note: To create a `Brush`, see the section "Create a Brush."

4 Type **Dim myFont As New Drawing.Font()**, replacing `myFont` with the name for the `Font` variable.

5 Inside the parentheses, type **"Arial Black", 72**, replacing `Arial Black` with the font face to use and 72 with the size of the font.

Extra

You can use the `FontStyle` enumeration to provide options for the style of font to draw. For example, you can print in bold italics font. To do this, you can combine the constants with the `Or` operator.

MEMBER	DESCRIPTION
Bold	Bold text
Italic	Italic text
Regular	Normal text
Strikeout	Text with a line through the middle
Underline	Underlined text

Example:
```
Dim arial As New Font("Arial", 16, _
    FontStyle.Bold Or FontStyle.Italic)
Dim red As Brush = Brushes.Red
e.Graphics.DrawString( _
    "Bold Italic Arial Font", arial, _
    red, 10, 10)
```

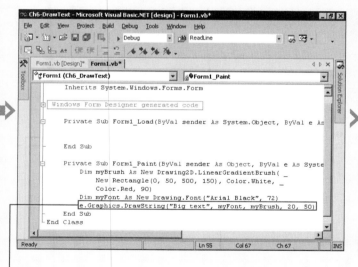

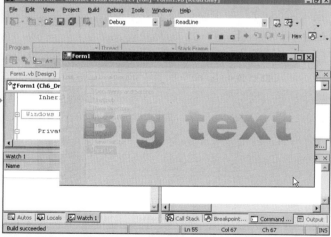

6 On a new line, type **e.Graphics.DrawString("Big text", myFont, myBrush, 20, 50)**, replacing `Big text` with the string to print or a string variable, **myFont** with the name of the **Font** variable, **myBrush** with the name of the **Brush** variable, and **20, 50** with the coordinates to draw the text.

7 Press F5 to run your project.

■ The text renders onto the appropriate graphics container.

CREATE A PATH

Because simple primitives may not provide the desired appearance for your application, you can combine multiple primitives into a single object with a single fill. You use the `GraphicsPath` object to create a complex object from a number of primitives. The `GraphicsPath` can also represent multiple figures, completely separate in space. A figure consists of an open or closed shape.

To create a `GraphicsPath`, declare a new instance of a `GraphicsPath` class with no entries passed to the constructor as parameters. The class is part of the `System.Drawing.Drawing2D` namespace. However, you may find creating the path through the constructor difficult. For more information on declaring new instances of classes and using constructors, see Chapter 7.

To begin building an individual figure, call the `StartFigure` method with no parameters. The `AddLine` method adds a line to the figure. `AddCurve` adds a curve to the figure. You can replicate all of the `Draw` methods

throughout this chapter, such as `DrawEllipse` and `DrawPie`, with the prefix `Add` instead of `Draw`. The methods accept all the same parameters with the exception of the `Pen` parameter, which you leave out completely. To create a functioning path, the last point of a previous primitive and the first point of the following primitive must match. For more information on primitive drawing methods, see the section "Draw a Primitive."

If you want to close the figure before starting a new one, call the `CloseFigure` method. Call `StartFigure` again to start a new figure without closing the current one. Use the `CloseAllFigures` method with no parameters to close any open figures previously created.

To draw the path onscreen, call `DrawPath` with a Pen as the first argument and the `GraphicsPath` as the second argument. You can fill the interior areas of a path using `FillPath`. Pass a `Brush` as the first parameter and the `GraphicsPath` as the second.

CREATE A PATH

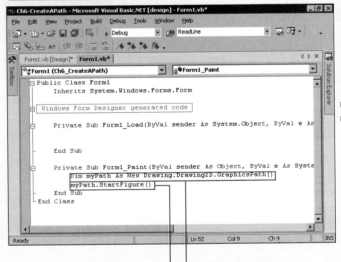

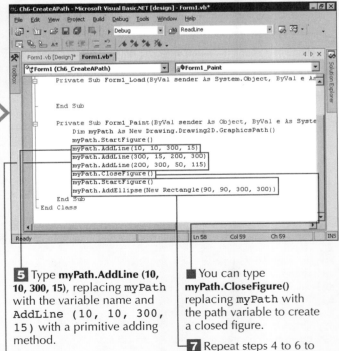

1 Create a new Windows Application project or open an existing project.

2 Open the `Paint` event where the primitive needs to draw.

3 Type **Dim myPath As New Drawing.Drawing2D. GraphicsPath()**, replacing `myPath` with the variable name for the path.

4 Type **myPath.StartFigure()**, replacing `myPath` with the path's variable name.

5 Type **myPath.AddLine (10, 10, 300, 15)**, replacing `myPath` with the variable name and `AddLine (10, 10, 300, 15)` with a primitive adding method.

6 Repeat step 5 until the figure is complete.

■ You can type **myPath.CloseFigure()** replacing `myPath` with the path variable to create a closed figure.

7 Repeat steps 4 to 6 to create the necessary figures.

Extra

You can use the `Warp` method of the `GraphicsPath` object to warp objects. Pass a rectangle specifying the bounds of the path and an array of points making up a parallelogram into which you warp the rectangle. If you specify three points, the parallelogram adds the points and makes the lower-right point automatically. The command then warps all of the points in the path to fit the shape.

Example:
```
Dim myPath As New Drawing2D.GraphicsPath()
Dim srcRect As New RectangleF(0, 0, 100, 200)
myPath.AddRectangle(srcRect)

e.Graphics.DrawPath(Pens.Black, myPath)

Dim point1 = New PointF(200, 200)
Dim point2 = New PointF(400, 250)
Dim point3 = New PointF(220, 400)
Dim destPoints() As PointF = {point1, point2, point3}

myPath.Warp(destPoints, srcRect)
e.Graphics.DrawPath(Drawing.Pens.Red, myPath)
```

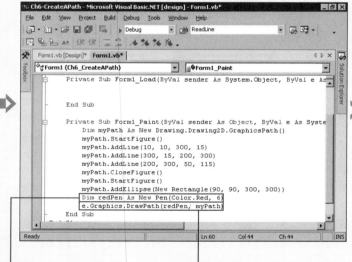

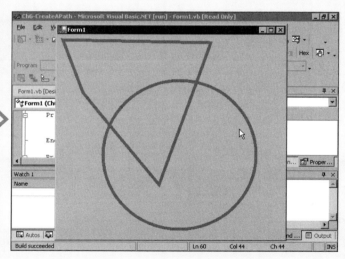

8 Declare a `Pen` to draw the path.

9 Type **e.Graphics.DrawPath (redPen, myPath)**, replacing `e.Graphics` with the name of the Graphics object, **redPen** with the name of the Pen, and **myPath** with the name of the GraphicsPath.

10 Press F5 to run the project.

■ The `GraphicsPath` draws onto the drawing region.

USING REGIONS

Windows GDI+ enables you to create complex areas of space defined as a *region*. A region consists of any number of rectangles and paths that build a contained area of space. The `Region` class that VB .NET provides represents a region. Windows uses a region to determine the shape of a window. For more information on creating a shaped window, see the section "Create a Shaped Window."

To create a region, declare a new instance of the `Region` class using `Dim` combined with the `New` operator. The class is part of the `System.Drawing` namespace. To create a simple rectangular region, pass the constructor a `Rectangle` object. To create a more complex region, you create a `GraphicsPath` object and pass it to the `Region` constructor. For more information on creating a `GraphicsPath`, see the section "Create a Path."

The real power of regions comes from their ability to combine. Each of the two methods below expects a

`GraphicsPath`, `Rectangle`, or another `Region`. `Union` takes the object from the argument and adds the object's space to the current region. `Intersect` takes the object from the argument and leaves only the part of the current region where both objects exist. `Complement` updates the current region to the portion of the specified object that does not intersect with the object. `Exclude` updates the current region to the portion of its interior that does not intersect with the specified object. `Xor` updates the current region with the union minus the intersection of itself with the object.

To draw a region, the `Graphics` object provides a `FillRegion` method. This method accepts a `Brush` as the first parameter and a `Region` as the second parameter. To use a `Region` you create as a `Clip` region in a `Graphics` object, and set the `Graphics.Clip` property equal to the `Region`.

USING REGIONS

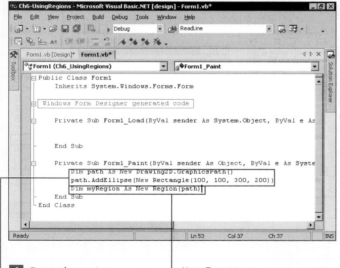

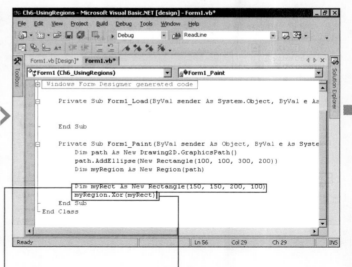

1 Open the `Paint` event where the primitive needs to draw.

2 Create a `GraphicsPath` object specifying a closed path.

Note: To create a `GraphicsPath`, see the section "Create a Path."

3 Type **Dim myRegion As New Region(path)**, replacing **myRegion** with the name for the `Region` and **path** with the name of the `GraphicsPath`.

4 To combine regions, declare and initialize a new `GraphicsPath` or `Rectangle` object.

5 Type **myRegion.Xor (myRect)**, replacing **myRegion** with the name of the `Region`, `Xor` with one of the combination methods, and **myRect** with the name of the new object.

Extra

Although the coordinates of a `Region` are fixed, you can move the `Region` around when drawing it using its `Translate` method. Pass a set of integers or singles to the method that specifies the movement in the horizontal and vertical direction, respectively. The `GetBounds` property returns a `RectangleF` object that represents the smallest rectangle the `Region` fits within.

Example:

```
myRegion.Translate(100, 100)
e.Graphics.FillRegion(myBrush, myRegion)
Dim rect As RectangleF = myRegion.GetBounds(e.Graphics)
e.Graphics.DrawRectangle(Drawing.Pens.Red, rect.X, rect.Y,_
    rect.Width, rect.Height)
```

A `RegionData` object stores the information necessary to recreate a particular `Region` object. The `RegionData` object uses an array or characters as a representation to store the region. A `Region` object's `GetRegionData` method returns a `RegionData` object that represents it. One of the constructors available for the `Region` class accepts a `RegionData` class. The example shows one `Region` object replicated into a new `Region` using the `RegionData` object.

Example:

```
Dim myRegionData As Drawing2D.RegionData = myRegion.GetRegionData()
Dim myNewRegion As New Region(myRegionData)
```

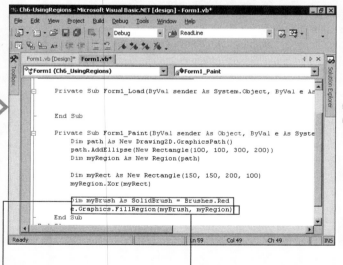

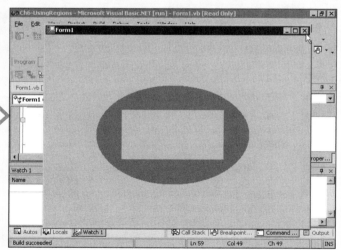

6 To draw the region, create a `Brush` object.

Note: To create a Brush, see the section "Create a Brush."

7 Type **e.Graphics.FillRegion (myBrush, myRegion)**, replacing **myBrush** with the name of your brush.

8 Press F5 to run your project.

■ The region accepts a range of space, combines new space, and draws to the screen.

CREATE A SHAPED WINDOW

Many utilities like media players create a custom shaped window to resemble a real-life object. You can use a Region to define a shape for a window.

To define a Region object, see the section "Using Regions." Defining a Region for a window is somewhat different than creating a drawing region or even a clip region. A Region object does not require you to make the shape a single enclosed object. Remember that the user still needs to use the window, so make the Region fairly simple.

To shape your form, set the Form.Region property equal to the Region. While resizable forms support a Region, you must use a nonresizing Form and place the Region loading code in Form_Load. If you choose to create a resizable shaped window, place code based on the form's Size in both Form_Load and Form_Resize.

When the Region lies over the form, Windows uses the intersection of the actual form and the Region object to draw the same parts of the form that exist there. That means, if the region includes the top of the window, a title bar still draws. The code that draws the title bar does not support regions, so the caption of the window, the icon, and the buttons remain in the same corners as if you had set no region, and cut just like the rest of the Form. If your shape cuts off part of the title bar, you can hide the title bar by setting FormBorderStyle to None.

To close the window without using the form's close button, simply use a button or other control and the form's Close method. To minimize the window, set the WindowState property to FormWindowState.Minimized.

CREATE A SHAPED WINDOW

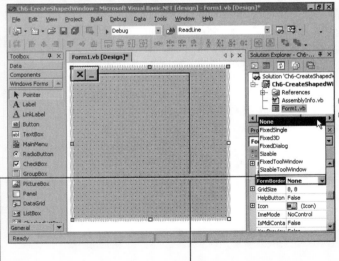

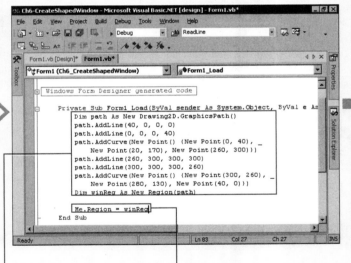

1 Create a new Windows Application project or open an existing project and the form to work with.

2 In the Property Window, click the **FormBorderStyle** ▾ and then click a new value.

3 Add controls to allow the user to minimize and close the form.

Note: To add controls, see Chapter 2.

4 Double-click the form.

■ The **Form1_Load** event handler opens.

5 Create a **Region** object for the window.

Note: To create a Region object, see the section "Using Regions."

6 Type **Me.Region = winReg**, replacing **winReg** with the name of the **Region** object.

When you create a shaped window, you often cut off the title bar or remove it explicitly. With the example code, which uses the Windows Application Programming Interface (API) to access the underlying Windows system's functions, a user can move the window by clicking anywhere on the shaped form. You can change the constant for `SendMessage` to a specified constant to resize the window without using the edges of the window. You can also move the code from the `Form1_MouseDown` to the mouse down event of controls on the form.

TYPE THIS:

```
Private Declare Function ReleaseCapture Lib "user32" () As Long
Private Declare Function SendMessage Lib "user32" Alias "SendMessageA" _
      (ByVal hwnd As IntPtr, ByVal wMsg As Integer, ByVal wParam As _
      Integer, ByVal lParam As Integer) As Integer
Const WM_NCLBUTTONDOWN = &HA1, HTCAPTION = 2, HTLEFT = 10
Const HTTOPRIGHT = 14, HTRIGHT = 11,HTTOP = 12, HTTOPLEFT = 13
Const HTBOTTOM = 15, HTBOTTOMLEFT = 16, HTBOTTOMRIGHT = 17
Private Sub Form1_MouseDown(ByVal sender As Object, ByVal e _
      As System.Windows.Forms.MouseEventArgs) Handles MyBase.MouseDown
      ReleaseCapture()
      SendMessage(Me.Handle, WM_NCLBUTTONDOWN, HTCAPTION, 0)
End Sub
```

RESULT:

The user can drag the window around by clicking anywhere on its surface.

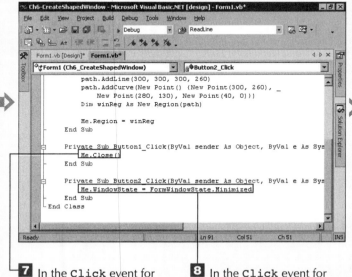

7 In the `Click` event for the Close button, type **Me.Close()**.

8 In the `Click` event for the Minimize button, type **Me.WindowState = FormWindowState.Minimized**.

9 Press F5 to run your project.

■ The window shapes to the `Region` and allows you to close and minimize the window without using the standard buttons.

CREATE A CLASS

When using Visual Basic .NET, you work with dozens of classes to perform even the simplest operation. VB .NET uses classes to split its massive number of functions into smaller blocks for you to use. You can create your own classes to enclose a set of functionality for reuse and ease of programming. When you create a class, it allows you to forget the implementation details of the class and focus on using the abilities of the class you create. Designing code for a class is more difficult then placing all of your code in large modules and forms, but makes your code much easier to read, debug, extend, and reuse.

VB .NET declares classes using the `Class...End Class` structure. Before the `Class` keyword, you specify the instancing of the class using `Public`, `Private`, or the other available options. The name for the class goes after the `Class` keyword. The name of a class follows standard

variable-naming techniques. The body code of the class resides between the `Class` and `End Class` statements. Code inside the block specifies methods, properties, and events of the class.

Two options enable you to specify details for inheritance. Place `MustInherit` in front of the `Class` keyword to not allow VB .NET to make instances of the class and only allow other classes use of this class as their base. The `NotInheritable` keyword is the opposite and does not allow you to specify this class as a base class. For more information on inheritance, see Chapter 8.

By default, VB .NET places each class in a separate file. You can place multiple classes inside each file if you want, which is especially useful for a set of classes that work together.

CREATE A CLASS

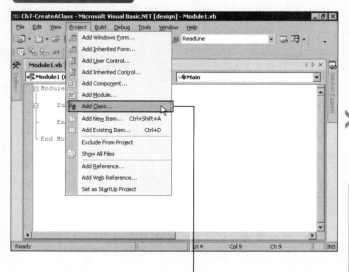

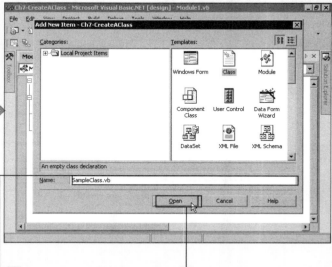

1 Create a new application or open an existing one.

2 Click Project ➪ Add Class.

3 Type a filename for the new class.

4 Click Open.

Extra

You can use accessibility operators to specify how classes and members of classes work in relation to other parts of the project. When you declare a class, you specify an accessibility operator to define how the rest of your project and even outside applications can access the class.

Each member inside a class has a particular accessibility as well. The two main operators are `Public` and `Private`. Other operators exist to work with inheritance and other advanced topics. See Chapter 8 for more information.

ACCESSIBILITY OPERATORS

`Public`	Public accessibility allows you to access the element from anywhere within the same project and from other projects that reference the project. Public members of classes are available to any user who creates an instance of the class.
`Private`	Private accessibility allows access only from within the same module, class, or structure where you declare the element. You cannot access members of a class you declare as `Private` outside of the class, but can use it inside the class.

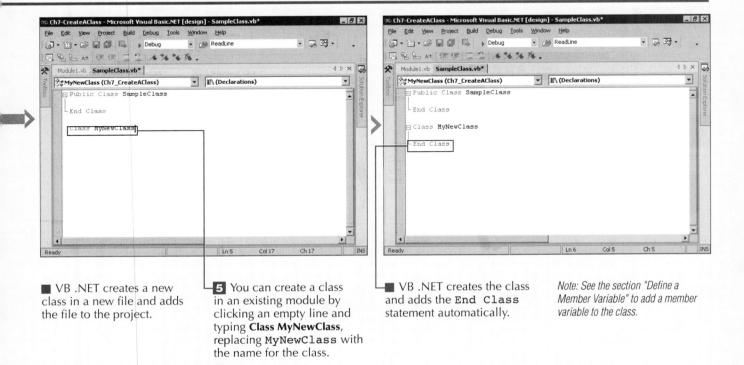

■ VB .NET creates a new class in a new file and adds the file to the project.

5 You can create a class in an existing module by clicking an empty line and typing **Class MyNewClass**, replacing `MyNewClass` with the name for the class.

6 Press Enter.

■ VB .NET creates the class and adds the **End Class** statement automatically.

Note: See the section "Define a Member Variable" to add a member variable to the class.

DEFINE A MEMBER VARIABLE

You can use a member variable as a field or a data storage mechanism. Everything you add to a class is a *member* including a property, method, or event. A member variable provides the simplest member to any class: the ability for the class to store data.

To create a field users of the class can access, just declare a variable using the `Public` statement instead of `Dim`. This declares a variable in the class, but because you declare the variable public, anyone who creates an object of this class can access the variable as well, loading and setting the value. This makes the member variable not only store data, but also enable outside users of the class to manipulate the value. The problem with making the variable public is that you cannot monitor the values that the outside user gives to the member variable.

To make a variable only available inside the class, you can create a member variable for its most common use — a

private data field. You create a private data field by placing the `Private` statement on a line and follow it with a variable name and the `As` type specification. You can use private variables to store property values. You provide public access to properties with the `Property` blocks. See the section "Define a Property" for more information on creating a property.

The reason to create a private member variable with a public `Property` block is so the class can check values it receives, raise errors when necessary, or edit the data appropriately. For example, if you have a property called `Counter` with valid values from one to ten, creating a public member variable enables the user to set a value much larger than the correct range. Instead, the private member variable only stores values that make sense to the rest of the class.

DEFINE A MEMBER VARIABLE

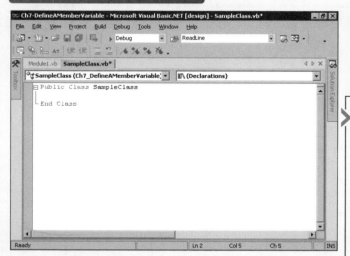

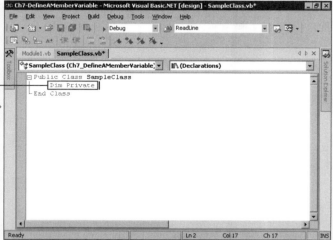

1 Create a new class or open an existing one.

Note: See the section "Create a Class" to create a class.

2 Click in an empty line in the class, but outside of all methods and properties.

3 Type an accessibility keyword, such as **Public** or **Private**.

Note: See the section "Create a Class" for information on accessibility operators.

Extra

To avoid defining all of the possible variables the class needs as member variables, a common mistake of new programmers, you should always remember the scope for which you need a certain piece of data. If you have a method that does a calculation and returns the result, do not store the result in member level variables. Instead, create variables in the method to use as temporary variables. When the method exits, VB .NET can release the memory these variables use. Every member-level variable you create must remain in memory for the entire time the class stays in memory. If you create an unnecessary amount of member variables, you can create a very inefficient application.

Although creating a public member variable generates a quick and easy property for a class, the design ideas of a class inherently foster reuse and reliability of the internal workings of the class. A public member variable can create a number of problems that are hard to debug. You can ensure the class performs reliably if you define the criteria of a property value by using a `Property` block.

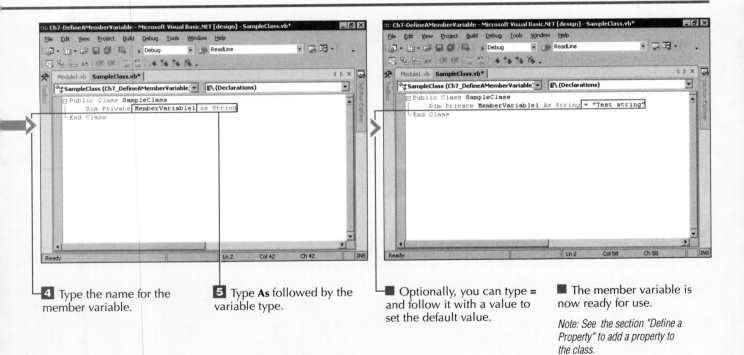

4 Type the name for the member variable.

5 Type **As** followed by the variable type.

■ Optionally, you can type **=** and follow it with a value to set the default value.

■ The member variable is now ready for use.

Note: See the section "Define a Property" to add a property to the class.

DEFINE A PROPERTY

In classes you use, such as forms and controls, *properties* enable you to specify the details that make up the characteristics of that component. Most classes and components require information to operate and adapt to different functions. You can define properties to let the user of your class specify how your class should perform and which data it uses to perform operations.

To define a property in VB .NET, use the `Property...End Property` statement block. After the `Property` keyword, specify the name of the property. Property names follow standard variable-naming techniques. Following the name of the property, you specify an argument list in parentheses. You only define an argument list if the property allows the user to edit a particular index of a list of data. For simple properties, you do not need to specify any arguments. Following the argument list, you specify the variable type of the property using the `As` keyword.

Inside of the block, the `Get...End Get` and `Set...End Set` blocks provide separate blocks of code for when the user of the class retrieves the property and when the user sets the value of the property. A `Set` block always receives a parameter `Value` that is of the same type as the property. This variable contains the value the user assigned to the property.

Normal code for a property revolves around a private member variable. For more information on member variables, see the section "Define a Member Variable." In most cases, a property functions as a public access point to a variable the class needs to operate. The class stores the value of this variable in a private variable, and provides the opportunity to change this value through the property, where it can perform error checking and validation. The `Set` code assigns `Value` to a private member variable, and `Get` uses the `Return` function to return the member variable.

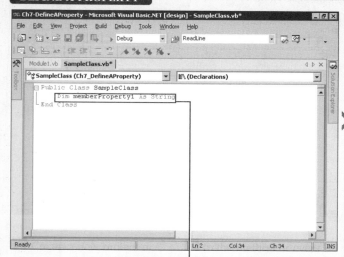

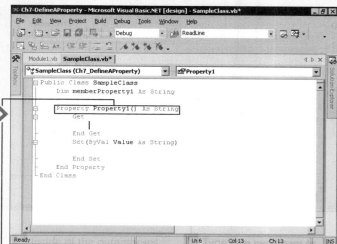

1 Create a new class or open an existing one.

Note: See the section "Create a Class" to create a class.

2 Declare a private member variable to hold the property value.

Note: See the section "Define a Member Variable" to create a member variable.

3 On an empty line inside the **Class** block, type **Property Property1() As String**, replacing `Property1()` with the name of the property and `String` with the property type.

■ If you need parameters for the property, type them after the name inside parentheses.

4 Press Enter.

Extra

You use the argument list of a property to access data values of a list or array the class stores. You can also make a property with an argument the default property of the class. If the property is the default, you can access it by typing the name of the class, followed directly by the index in parentheses without specifying the property name.

Example:
```
Private myData(10) As String
Default Public Property Data(ByVal Index As Integer) As String
    Get
        If Index >=0 And Index <= 10 Then Return myData(Index)
    End Get
    Set(ByVal Value As String)
        If Index >=0 And Index <= 10 Then myData(Index) = Value
    End Set
End Property
```

You can create properties that only support reading their value or only support writing to the property using the `ReadOnly` and `WriteOnly` keywords before the `Property` keyword.

Example:
```
Public ReadOnly Property ReadMe()
    Get
        Return myData
    End Get
End Property
Public WriteOnly Property WriteToMe()
    Set(ByVal Value)
        myData = Value
    End Set
End Property
```

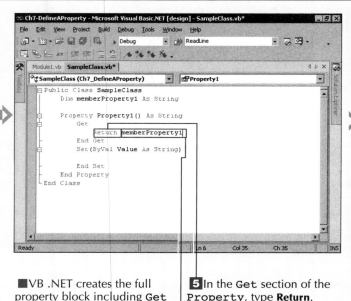

■VB .NET creates the full property block including `Get` and `Set` blocks.

5 In the `Get` section of the `Property`, type **Return**.

6 Type the private member variable name.

7 In the `Set` section of the `Property`, type an `If` statement to validate the `Value` variable.

8 Type the name of the private member variable.

9 Type **= Value**.

■The property is complete.

Note: See "Using an Existing Class" for more on properties in your custom class.

CREATE A CONSTRUCTOR OR DESTRUCTOR

Y ou can use a *constructor* to load initial values into private variables, set initial property values, and load necessary data. Constructors enable the user of the class to initialize the class with proper values without having to individually set a long list of properties. Also, in many cases, a class needs to know a particular setting and cannot alter this setting later in execution, so it requires this information at the time of construction. You can use a *destructor* to destroy class and component references the class holds during execution.

A constructor is actually a method with the name New. VB .NET automatically calls this method when the class initializes using the New keyword. You must create the constructor using the Sub...End Sub block because a constructor cannot return a value. For the parameter list, specify the values the user must set for the class to function.

One set of parameters is rarely convenient for every possible use of your class. You may need to specify different data for different situations where you use the class. You can create

multiple versions of the constructor to accept different sets of input parameters. You can create multiple versions of New without explicitly overloading the constructor like VB .NET requires you to do for other methods. You use overloading to define multiple instances of the same method. To overload the constructor, simply create multiple New methods with different parameter lists. For more information on overloading any method, see chapter 8.

You create a destructor in VB .NET with the Finalize method of the class. In classes that do not create objects, you do not need a destructor. You need a destructor when the class holds references to objects. For example, if you create an instance of a class and save it as a member variable for use during the execution of the class, you can set the variable equal to Nothing in the Finalize event so VB .NET can delete the object from memory. You can also use destructors to perform other cleanup for your class, such as closing network and file connections. To create a destructor, you must specify the keywords Protected and Overrides before the Sub statement. You can learn more about these keywords in Chapter 8.

CREATE A CONSTRUCTOR OR DESTRUCTOR

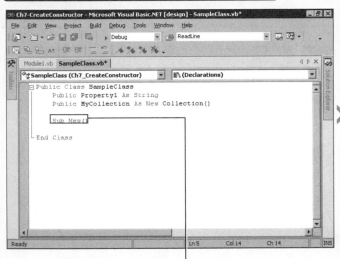

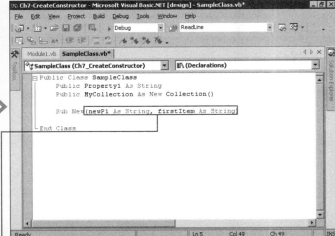

CREATE A CONSTRUCTOR

1 Create a new class or open an existing one.

Note: To create a class, see the section "Create a Class."

2 In an empty line outside of all methods in the class, type **Sub New()**.

3 Inside the parentheses, type any required construction parameters.

4 At the end of the line, press Enter.

Extra

VB.NET uses garbage collection to remove objects from memory at an arbitrary time later when the program is idle. You can implement a `Dispose` method to allow the user of your class to clear the memory it uses immediately instead of waiting for the destructor to run. You use a `Dispose` method for classes dealing with finite resources like files or streams. The example uses the `disposed` variable to determine if `Dispose` is called more than once. Your `Dispose` method should allow for this as well.

Example:

```
Public Class Class1: Implements IDisposable
    Private myFile As  New IO.FileStream("C:\test.txt", IO.FileMode.OpenOrCreate)
    Private disposed As Boolean = False
    Public Sub Dispose() Implements IDisposable.Dispose        ' allow disposal
        If Not disposed Then myFile.Close(): disposed = true
        GC.SuppressFinalize(Me)   ' don't run destructor since we already cleaned up
    End Sub
End Class
Public Class Class2
    Dim UseClass1 As New UseClass1()
    Sub Method1()
        ...                        ' use the instance of the class you create
        UseClass1.Dispose()        ' dispose the class to clean it up immediately
    End Sub
End Class
```

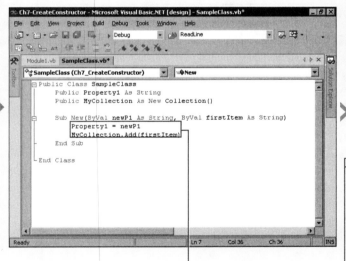

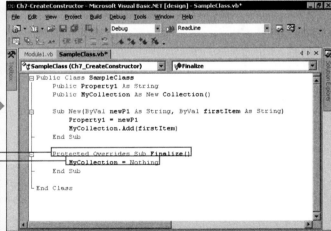

■ The **End Sub** statement appears automatically.

5 Type the necessary construction code.

CREATE A DESTRUCTOR

6 Outside of any methods, type **Protected Overrides Sub Finalize()**.

7 Press Enter.

8 Inside the block, type code to remove any references.

■ An instance of your class can now be customized using the constructor.

Note: See the section "Using an Existing Class" to use your class.

167

CREATE AN EVENT

Events perform the final component necessary to create a fully functioning class module. Think of an event as a response from an object. For example, imagine yourself bouncing or throwing a ball; you consider those things actions and represent them with methods in a class. Eventually the ball you throw hits the ground, making a change in direction to which the owner of the ball must respond. You can use events to pass back information on the status of an operation, the completion of an event, a notification of a change, or for a variety of other reasons.

To add an event to a class, use the Event statement. You place this statement in the declaration section of the class; you must locate the statement outside of any method and property blocks. In most cases, you should declare the event using the Public accessibility keyword before the Event statement so outside users of the class can respond to the event.

After the Event statement, you specify the name of the event and follow it with the argument list that returns to the owner of the class instance. You do not place a list of data here, only a list of variable names followed by the As keyword and the type of data. Separate multiple entries with commas, just like when you write a method declaration. The Event statement does not form a block of code; it is just a statement to tell VB .NET that your class fires a particular event.

When the event needs to fire, call the RaiseEvent statement from inside the class. After the RaiseEvent statement, specify the name of the event you declared and all of the values to send through the parameter list of the event in parentheses.

CREATE AN EVENT

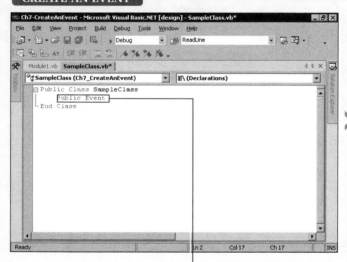

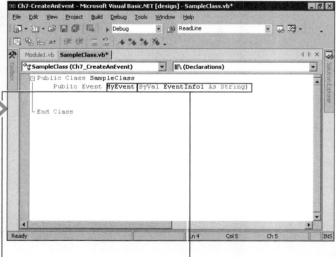

1 Create a new class or open an existing one.

Note: To create a class, see the section "Create a Class."

2 On an empty line outside of all methods in the class, type an accessibility parameter followed by **Event**.

■ You can insert the Public keyword to specify that any code using the class can respond to its events.

3 Type the name of the event and follow it with parentheses.

4 Type the parameters for the event inside the parentheses.

Apply It

You can fire an event that reports the percentage of the task that is complete. You can also allow the event handler to send information back to your class. The form using the class can have a Cancel button whose handler code tells the method to stop when the event fires. A parameter with the `ByRef` keyword, which allows VB .NET to pass changes to the variable back when a routine finishes, make this possible.

TYPE THIS:

```vb
Class LongTimeClass
    Event PercentDone(ByVal Percent As Integer, ByRef Cancel As Boolean)
    Sub DoWork()
        Dim done as Boolean, cancel As Boolean, percent As Integer
        Do Until done Or cancel     ' do work in loop until done or user cancels
            RaiseEvent PercentDone(percent, cancel)    ' send new percentage
        Loop
    End Sub
End Class
Class Form1
    Inherit System.Windows.Form
    Private WithEvents workerClass As New LongTimeClass
    Private CancelWork As Boolean = False
    Private Sub CancelButton_Click(...)
        CancelWork = True  ' user wants to cancel. tell class when event fires.
    End Sub
    Private Sub PercentDoneChanged(ByVal Percent As Integer, _
        ByRef Cancel As Boolean) Handles workerClass.PercentDone
        Application.DoEvents()       ' you must update percentage bar here
        If CancelWork Then Cancel = True    ' cancel the work activity
    End Sub
End Class
```

RESULT:

The class method cancels work when a user presses the Cancel button.

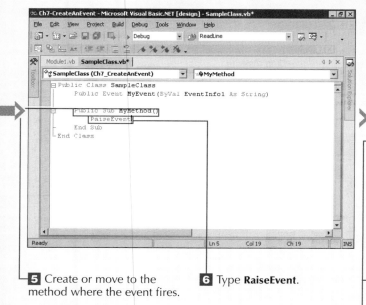

5 Create or move to the method where the event fires.

Note: To define a method, see Chapter 4.

6 Type **RaiseEvent**.

7 Type the name of the event you previously declared and follow it with parentheses.

8 Type the values required by the parameter definitions and enclose them in parentheses.

■ The method raises the event when a user of your class calls it.

Note: See the section "Using an Existing Class" for information on handling the event.

169

USING AN EXISTING CLASS

After you define a class, you can use it throughout your project just like you use classes that VB .NET provides. To create a class, see the section "Create a Class." A class by itself only defines the properties, methods, and events. To use the class, you must create a new instance of the class. An instance of a class is an *object* that lets you call and manipulate the members that the class defines. You can create any number of separate objects from the same class. Each object is a separate entity with its own data, and each object uses the code you specify in the class to work with its data.

To declare a variable to hold an instance of a class, you specify the name of the class. To actually create an instance of the class, you must use the New keyword. You assign a new instance of the class to the variable when you declare it by placing the New keyword after the As keyword. When

you specify the New keyword, VB .NET assigns an object with its own data to the variable you can then manipulate.

To access a property of the object you create, specify the variable name of the object and the name of the property. You can only access the properties that the class makes available to you. To call a method in your class, use the variable name again with the name of the method. You place the arguments for the method inside parentheses.

To handle events raised by your class, you must declare the object variable for the class in the declaration section of the class or module. To respond to events, place WithEvents before the variable name in the declaration.

The example in this section assumes you create a class and add members to the class. See the previous topics in the chapter to learn how to create a class.

USING AN EXISTING CLASS

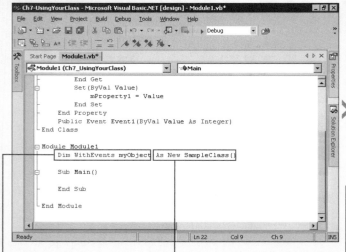

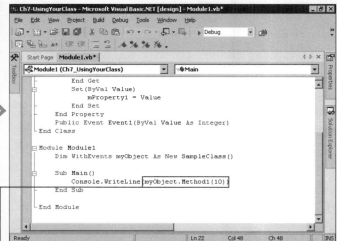

1 In the class or module where you need to use your class, outside of all methods blocks, type Dim followed by a variable name.

Note: To create a class, see the section "Create a Class."

■ If you need to respond to events, type **WithEvents** after Dim. You can replace Dim with a particular accessibility keyword.

2 Type As New SampleClass( ), replacing SampleClass( ) with the name of your class.

3 To call a member of your class, type **myObject.Method1(10)**, replacing **myObject** with the object variable name, **Method1** with the method to call, and **10** with the appropriate parameters for the method.

Apply It

If you name a member variable the same thing as a local variable, you can still access the member-level variable by specifying the Me in front of the variable separated with a period. You can run the following example in a Console Application project.

TYPE THIS:

```
Class Class1
    Public Variable1 As String = "Module Level variable"
    Public Sub Method1()
        Dim Variable1 As String = "Method1 variable"
        Console.WriteLine(Variable1)
        Console.WriteLine(Me.Variable1)
    End Sub
End Class
Module Module1
    Sub Main()
        Dim varTest As New Class1()
        varTest.Method1()
        Console.ReadLine()
    End Sub
End Module
```

RESULT:

Method1 Variable

Module Level variable

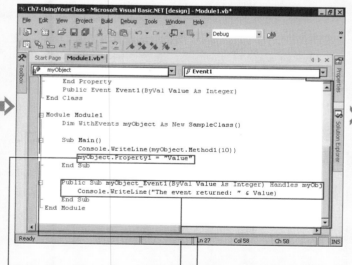

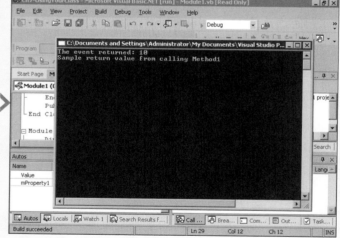

4 To assign a value to a property, type myObject.Property1 = "Value", replacing myObject with the object variable, Property1 with the property name, and "Value" with an appropriate value or variable to assign.

5 To respond to an event, select your object variable.

6 In the event list, click an event to handle.

7 Type response code for the event.

8 Press F5 to run the project.

■ You create an object from your class and use the methods, properties, and events that you define.

DEFINE AN INTERFACE

Each class in an object-oriented programming language contains two parts: the interface and the implementation. The *interface* defines the methods, events, and properties available to users of the class. The *implementation* makes up the rest of the class including the code behind the methods, properties, and private variables. In most cases, you create these two parts together. VB enables you to create a separate interface you can then define later with a class. This gives you the ability to create multiple classes that function off the same set of methods and properties with different underlying implementations.

For example, you can define an interface TwoNumbers for working with two numbers. A class AddTwoNumbers can implement the interface to add the two numbers, and MultiplyTwoNumbers can implement the interface to multiply the two numbers. This enables the user of the class to work with a variable defined as TwoNumbers with both of the two classes working interchangeably.

Use the Interface...End Interface block to define an interface. The block appears outside of any other class or module. VB defines an interface as Public unless otherwise specified. For an explanation of available accessibility keywords, see "Create a Class."

Inside the block, define a property with the Property statement. After the Property keyword, VB expects the name for the property, parameters enclosed in parentheses, and the variable following the As keyword.

Define public methods using Function or Sub keywords and the name of the method. You can specify the parameters that the class must use to implement the method and the return type for a Function method. To define events, use the Event statement and follow it with the event name and parameters.

DEFINE AN INTERFACE

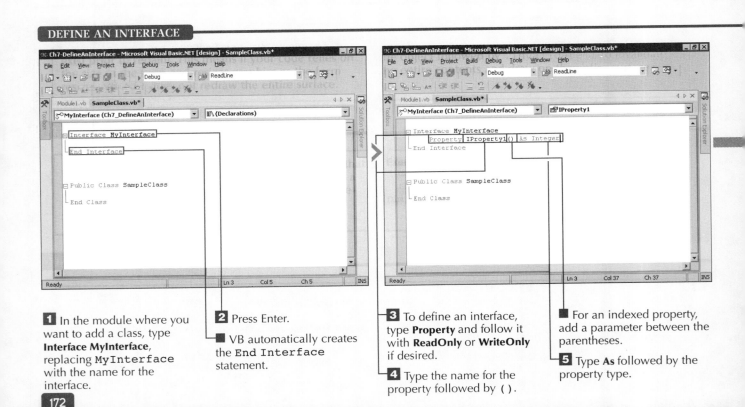

1 In the module where you want to add a class, type **Interface MyInterface**, replacing MyInterface with the name for the interface.

2 Press Enter.

■ VB automatically creates the End Interface statement.

3 To define an interface, type **Property** and follow it with **ReadOnly** or **WriteOnly** if desired.

4 Type the name for the property followed by ( ).

■ For an indexed property, add a parameter between the parentheses.

5 Type **As** followed by the property type.

Extra

You can define an interface and then use the `Inherits` statement in another interface to import the defined members to the new interface. For more on inheritance, see Chapter 8.

Example:
```
Interface Automobile
    ReadOnly Property NumberOfWheels() As Integer
End Interface
Interface Truck
    Inherits Automobile
    ReadOnly Property TowingAbility() As Integer
End Interface
Class MyBigRig
    Implements Truck
    ReadOnly Property NumberOfWheels() As Integer Implements Truck.NumberOfWheels
        Get
            Return 18
        End Get
    End Property
    ReadOnly Property PossibleTrailerWght() As Integer Implements Truck.TowingAbility
        Get
            Return 60000
        End Get
    End Property
End Class
```

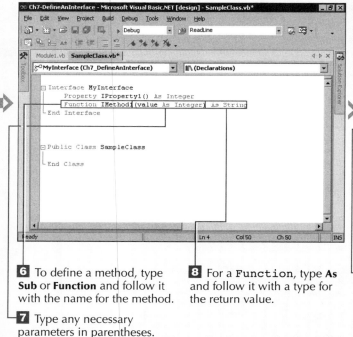

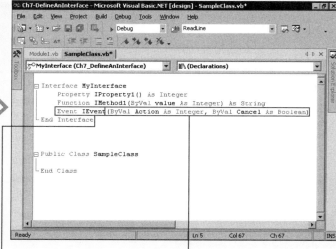

6 To define a method, type **Sub** or **Function** and follow it with the name for the method.

7 Type any necessary parameters in parentheses.

8 For a `Function`, type **As** and follow it with a type for the return value.

9 To define an event, type **Event** and follow it with the name of the event.

10 Type necessary parameters for the implemented event to return inside parentheses.

■ The interface is complete. You can now create a class to implement the interface.

Note: See the section "Implement an Interface" to implement your interface.

IMPLEMENT AN INTERFACE

After you define an interface, you can use it to build classes. Each class must implement all of the methods, properties, and events specified in the interface. Any number of classes can build off of a single interface. To define an interface, see the section "Define an Interface."

To create the class based on the interface, create a standard class block using `Class...End Class`. For more information on creating classes, see the section "Create a Class." The class name need not relate to the name of the interface and cannot have the same name as the interface. On the first line inside the class block, specify the interface you want to implement using the `Implements` statement. Follow the keyword with the name of the interface.

You must implement each method, property, and event that resides in the interface. You do not have to make the names

you use for each class member the same as the interface names. To define the interface that you implement with a particular `Property`, `Method`, or `Event` statement, use the `Implements` keyword at the end of the line, past any declarations or type specifications. After the keyword, you specify the interface member you implement with the class member.

In most cases, you want to make the implemented name of the member the same as the interface name so you can create multiple classes that work interchangeably. You can define a variable with the `Interface` name as the type and then assign an instance of a class that implements that interface to the variable. This lets you work with classes that have different underlying functions, but because they export the same interface, VB .NET lets you work with them in one variable type.

IMPLEMENT AN INTERFACE

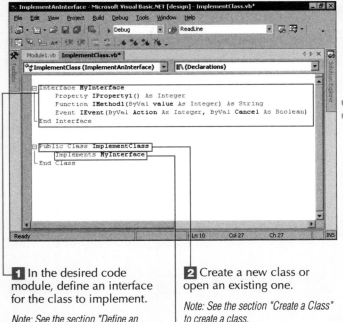

1 In the desired code module, define an interface for the class to implement.

Note: See the section "Define an Interface" to define an interface.

2 Create a new class or open an existing one.

Note: See the section "Create a Class" to create a class.

3 Inside the class block, type **Implements** followed by the interface name.

4 To implement a method of the interface, define the method using **Sub** or **Function**.

5 At the end of the line, type **Implements MyInterface.I Method1**, replacing `MyInterface` with the interface name and `IMethod1` with the name of the interface method you implement.

6 Type the appropriate method code.

Note: See the section "Define a Method" to properly set up a method.

Extra

You can use a class to implement multiple interfaces. To do so, place multiple `Implements` keywords at the beginning of the class block making sure to implement all of the members from all of the interfaces. You can use one member in the class to implement multiple members of the interfaces. After typing the method or property declaration, place multiple members from the interfaces after the `Implements` keyword separated by commas. You can implement multiple members when you have two similar interfaces or where two interfaces provide the same methods. You can simply write the code once in the class and implement both of the interface methods.

Example:

```
Interface Animal
    Sub Eat()
    Property Age() As Integer
End Interface
Interface Plant
    Sub GetNutrients()
    Property Age() As Integer
End Interface
Class VenusFlyTrap
    Implements Animal, Plant
    Sub EatInsects() Implements_
        Animal.Eat, Plant.GetNutrients
        ...
    End Sub
    Property Age() As Integer Implements_
        Animal.Age, Plant.Age
        ...
    End Property
End Class
```

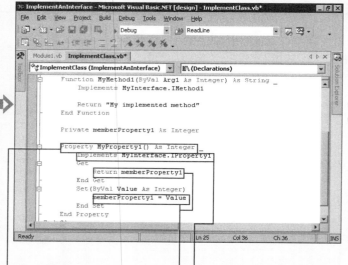

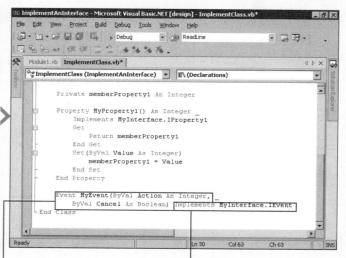

7 To implement a method, type **Property MyProperty1() As Integer**, replacing `MyProperty1` with the name for the property and `Integer` with the same for the property as the interface.

8 At the end of the line, type **Implements MyInterface.IProperty1**, replacing `MyInterface` with the interface name and `IProperty1` with the interface property.

9 Type appropriate code for the `Property`.

10 To implement an event, type **Event MyEvent**, replacing `MyEvent` with the name for the event, and inside the parentheses, type the list of parameters the interface defines.

11 At the end of the line, type **Implements MyInterface.IEvent**, replacing `MyInterface` with the interface and `IEvent` with the event name.

Note: See the section "Using an Existing Class" to use your implemented class.

USING STRUCTURES

A *structure* is a simplified class. Structures distinguish themselves from classes by primarily functioning as a data storage mechanism rather than a representation of an object. Structures support properties, methods, and events just like classes. If you need to pass a large amount of data between methods, you can create a structure to contain the data and pass the single structure variable instead.

You define a structure in VB .NET using the `Structure...End Structure` block. Inside the block, place only variable declarations or procedures types `Function`, `Property`, or `Sub`. You can declare a variable using `Public` to make it function like a property, or declare it `Private` and use it for storage of a public property. `Property` declarations follow the syntax of a class. For more information on member variables, see the section "Define a Member Variable," and for properties, see Chapter 4.

`Function` and `Sub` statements form methods exactly like they do for classes. For more information on creating a method, see the section "Define a Method." You can define events in the structure that you raise in methods of the structure. See the section "Create an Event" to create an event.

A structure works like a data type, meaning you create an instance of the structure without using the `New` keyword. In VB .NET, this makes it a value-variable instead of a reference-variable, because the variable you create holds the corresponding `Structure`, while a class variable holds a reference to a class you declare using the `New` keyword. Simply declare a structure like any other variable. See Chapter 4 to declare a variable. Use the name of the `Structure` as the variable type name. When you define a variable based on a `Structure`, you can access its members just like a class.

USING STRUCTURES

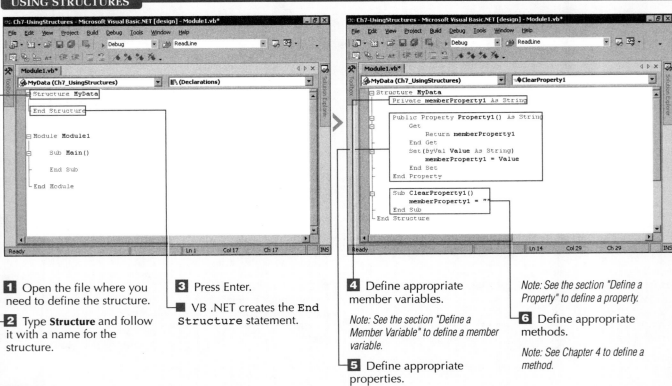

1 Open the file where you need to define the structure.

2 Type **Structure** and follow it with a name for the structure.

3 Press Enter.

■ VB .NET creates the **End Structure** statement.

4 Define appropriate member variables.

Note: See the section "Define a Member Variable" to define a member variable.

5 Define appropriate properties.

Note: See the section "Define a Property" to define a property.

6 Define appropriate methods.

Note: See Chapter 4 to define a method.

Extra

Structures have a few very specific rules that set them apart from classes. You can use these rules to decide whether a class or a structure is most appropriate for your data. The default accessibility of data members in structures if you declare them with the `Dim` statement is public. The default accessibility in classes and modules is private. Unlike the declarations of data members of classes, the declarations of data members of a structure cannot set the values of a variable during declaration. Data type definitions also cannot include the `New` keyword, or initial sizes for arrays. Normally, methods use structures to return a large quantity of data, so the class sets the values before passing it.

Inheritance is a way for classes to build off of one another. If you want to inherit the data type that you create with a structure, use a class instead. Structures cannot inherit from any other type, and other structures or classes cannot inherit from them. All structures are implicitly `NotInheritable`. For more information on inheritance, see Chapter 8. Structures can implement an interface. See the section "Implement an Interface" earlier in this chapter for more information on interfaces.

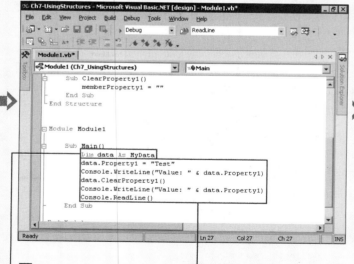

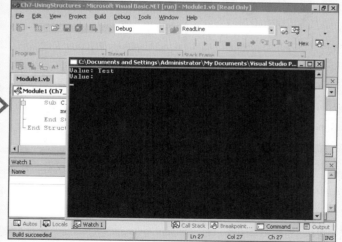

7 In the class or module where you want to use the structure, declare a variable using the name of the structure as the variable type.

Note: See Chapter 4 to define a variable.

8 Access the structure elements in a method or event by typing the variable name of the structure and following it with a period and the name of the member.

9 Press F5 to run your project.

■ The structure holds and returns data appropriately.

USING COLLECTIONS

Collections are built-in classes provided by Visual Basic .NET that store a list of items. This description sounds much like an *array,* but the `Collection` class provides a much more powerful storage mechanism. You can use a collection to store any type of data, including simple variable types, arrays, classes, and objects. The `Collection` class's ability to resize dynamically at runtime creates a powerful yet memory efficient storage mechanism. For a `Collection`, the list is one-based, meaning the first item is index one.

To create a collection, declare a new instance of the `Collection` class. Add items to the `Collection` using the `Add` method. Pass the variable or object to add to the collection as the first parameter. Optionally, pass a key as the second parameter. A *key value* is a string you use to identify the object you add. Although you do not have to specify a key, doing so makes finding objects you add to the

collection much easier. You must make the key values unique for each object.

The third and fourth parameters of the `Add` method enable you to specify the key or index of an existing item in the collection to place the new object. The new object adds before the item you specify for the third argument, or adds after the item you specify for the fourth argument. You cannot specify both. If you specify neither, the new object adds to the end of the list.

The `Item` property returns an item based on the index or the key. Pass either of these values to the `Item` method to return the appropriate item. You can use a `For Each...Next` loop to quickly iterate through the entire collection. For more information on `For` loops, see Chapter 4.

USING COLLECTIONS

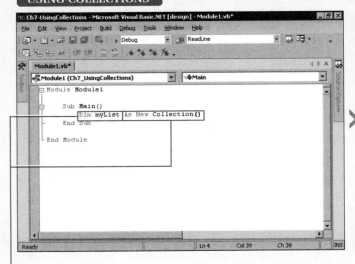

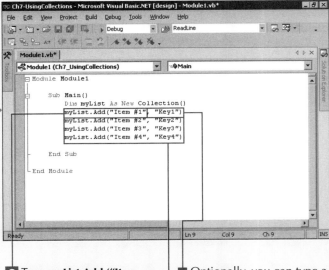

CREATE A COLLECTION

■1 In the module, method, or event to define the collection, type **Dim** and follow it with a variable name.

■2 Type **As New Collection()** to define the new instance.

■ If you declared the collection as a member of the class or module, move to a method or event handler to enter code to use the collection.

■3 Type **myList.Add ("Item #1")**, replacing **myList** with the instance name of the `Collection`, and "Item #1" with the object to add to the `Collection`.

■ Optionally, you can type a comma and a string defining the key for the object.

■4 Repeat step 3 to add the necessary items.

Extra

Keep in mind that the flexibility of the `Collection` means it uses significantly more memory than an array. If you need to store a primarily unchanging and fixed-size set of data, the array provides much better performance. See Chapter 4 for more information on creating arrays.

The `Item` property is the default member of the class. You can retrieve an item just by placing parentheses after the variable name of the collection with the key value or index inside. To remove a single item, you use the `Remove` method. This method accepts the index or key of the item to remove. The `Count` method returns the number of items in the collection.

Example of the default property:
```
value = myCollection("myKey")
```

Example of removing an item:
```
myCollection.Remove("myKey")
myCollection.Remove(1)
```

Example of the using Count:
```
MessageBox.Show("The number of items in the collection is " & myCollection.Count())
```

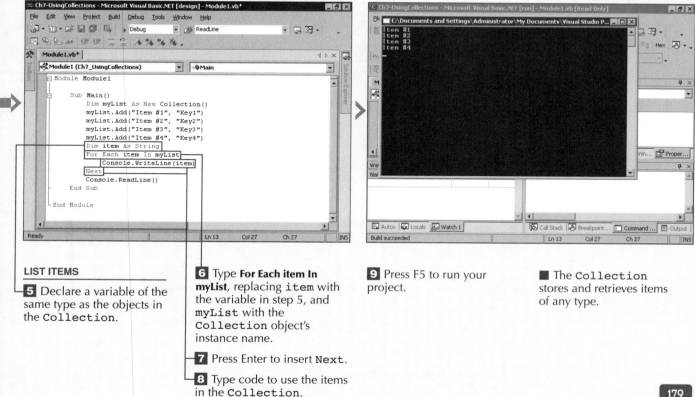

LIST ITEMS

5 Declare a variable of the same type as the objects in the `Collection`.

6 Type **For Each item In myList**, replacing **item** with the variable in step 5, and **myList** with the `Collection` object's instance name.

7 Press Enter to insert **Next**.

8 Type code to use the items in the `Collection`.

9 Press F5 to run your project.

■ The `Collection` stores and retrieves items of any type.

OVERLOAD A METHOD

Often a class you create needs to offer methods that accept various types of data. Most methods in the .NET Framework offer a number of different methods with the same name, letting you choose the method that provides the proper arguments for your usage. You can overload a method to provide different sets of arguments to a method of the same name. For example, a method may need to accept either an integer value or a floating-point value. You can provide an overridden method `Add` that accepts two `Integer` variables and returns an `Integer` value, and another overridden method `Add` that accepts two `Single` variables and returns a `Single`.

To create multiple methods with the same name, you use the `Overloads` keyword. You place this keyword following any accessibility keyword but before the `Sub` or `Function` keyword of the method declaration. You must place this keyword on every different instance of the method that

uses the same name. You cannot create two versions of the method with the same parameter list. Creating two methods with the same parameters fails because VB .NET does not know which method to call. To make valid overloaded methods, you can provide different numbers of arguments for each method, or provide the same number of arguments as long as you make one of the arguments a different type.

If you declare the method as a `Function`, you can also change the return type of the overloaded method. The same rules apply, meaning you must still specify different argument sets when the return types differ. You can also create an overloaded method as a `Sub` statement, returning no parameters, and another overloaded method as a `Function` statement, enabling you to return information only when necessary for the method.

OVERLOAD A METHOD

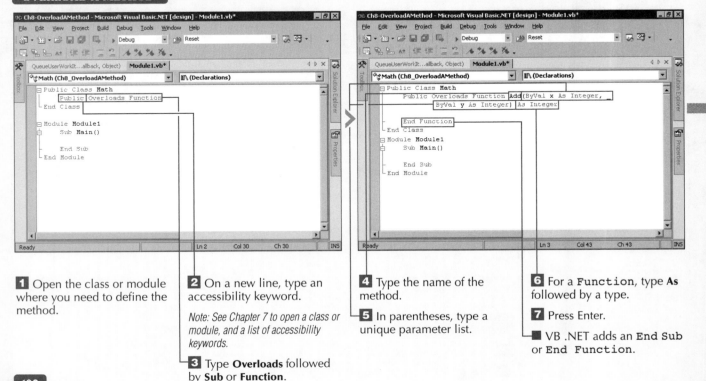

1 Open the class or module where you need to define the method.

2 On a new line, type an accessibility keyword.

Note: See Chapter 7 to open a class or module, and a list of accessibility keywords.

3 Type **Overloads** followed by **Sub** or **Function**.

4 Type the name of the method.

5 In parentheses, type a unique parameter list.

6 For a **Function**, type **As** followed by a type.

7 Press Enter.

■ VB .NET adds an **End Sub** or **End Function**.

Extra

You can change the accessibility of overloaded methods, making one method `Public` and another `Private`, or use other supported accessibility keywords. This functionality enables you to create a more complex private version of the method that the public versions can use to perform the work.

TYPE THIS:

```
Public Class Class1
Public Overloads Function Add(n1 As Integer, n2 As Integer) As Integer
        Dim array As Integer() = {n1, n2}
        Return Add(array)
End Sub
Public Overloads Function Add(n1 As Integer, n2 As Integer, n3 As Integer) As Integer
        Dim array As Integer() = {n1, n2, n3}
        Return Add(array)
End Sub
Protected Overloads Function Add(numArray As Integer()) As Integer
        Dim number As Integer, sum As Integer = 0
        For Each number In numArray
           sum += number
        Next
        Return sum
End Sub
End Class
...
Private Sub Button1_Click(...) Handles Button1.Click
        Dim myClass As New Class1
        MessageBox.Show(myCls.Add(10, 20) & " " & myCls1.Add(20, 30, 40))
End Sub
```

RESULT:

30 90

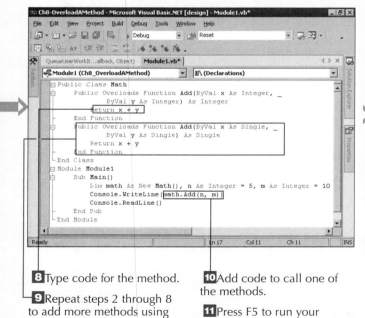

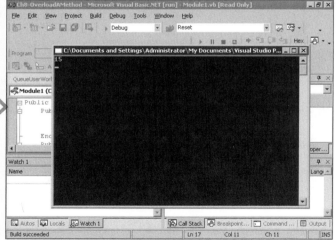

8 Type code for the method.

9 Repeat steps 2 through 8 to add more methods using the same name.

10 Add code to call one of the methods.

11 Press F5 to run your project.

■ VB .NET calls the correct overloaded method for the specified parameters.

INHERIT FROM AN EXISTING CLASS

Just like a person often inherits traits of their parents, a class can inherit the traits of another class. To understand when to use class inheritance, think of the phrase "is a type of." For example, begin with the word mammal. A variety of animals inherit traits from mammals, such as cats and dogs. A cat is a type of mammal. A dog is a type of mammal as well.

After you create a base class, you define an inherited class with the `Inherits` statement. Place the keyword `Inherits` on a blank line at the top of a class followed by the name of the base class. Visual Basic .NET does not support multiple-inheritance, which means you can only inherit from one base class. You can, however, implement multiple interfaces. See Chapter 5 for more information on interfaces.

Public members of a base class become public members of the inherited class, meaning a user of the class can access

the base class members as if the inherited class contains them. Although it cannot access the base class's private members, the inherited class can access protected members of the base class when users of the class cannot.

You can override a method from the base class if the base class specifies the `Overridable` keyword in the declaration of a method. You override a base class's method by declaring a method of the same name in the inherited class with the `Overrides` keyword placed at the beginning of the line.

VB .NET only calls the lastest descendant method in a set of classes. For example, assume the base class defines a method `Calculate` and an inherited class overrides the method. If you declare a variable in the type of the base class and assign an instance of the inherited class to the variable, VB .NET calls the inherited class's method.

INHERIT FROM AN EXISTING CLASS

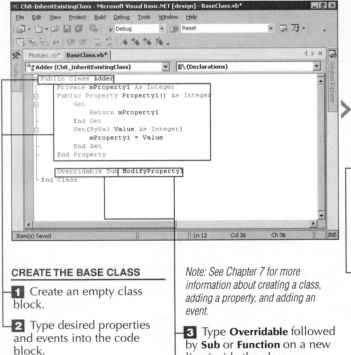

CREATE THE BASE CLASS

1 Create an empty class block.

2 Type desired properties and events into the code block.

Note: See Chapter 7 for more information about creating a class, adding a property, and adding an event.

3 Type **Overridable** followed by **Sub** or **Function** on a new line inside the class.

4 Type a method name.

5 Type parameters in parentheses and a return type if the method is a **Function**.

6 Press Enter.

7 Add code to the method.

■ You can repeat steps 3 through 5 to create more base methods.

Extra

When you override a method in the base class, you may want to access the underlying base method. This is especially useful if the code the base class contains needs to run in addition to the code you add in the overridden method. You can still access the base class's method by using the `MyBase` keyword. This keyword contains a reference to the original base class, enabling you to run any method available in the base class even if you override it.

Example
```
Public Class BaseClass
    Public Overridable Sub Method1()

    End Sub
End Class
Public Class InheritedClass : Inherits BaseClass
    Public Overrides Sub Method1()
        MyBase.Method1()
    End Sub
End Class
```

Be careful when you make a method call using a class that you may later inherit. Because of Visual Basic .NET's bottom-most method of accessing overloaded methods, you may have a method in the base call a method in the inherited class. But if a class inherits from this class, the inherited class may overload the method, changing its functionality. You can make a method not support overriding by using the `NotOverridable` keyword. You can make sure a base class always calls its own method by using the `MyClass` object. This object maintains a reference to the class without using the bottom-most technique to determine the method to call.

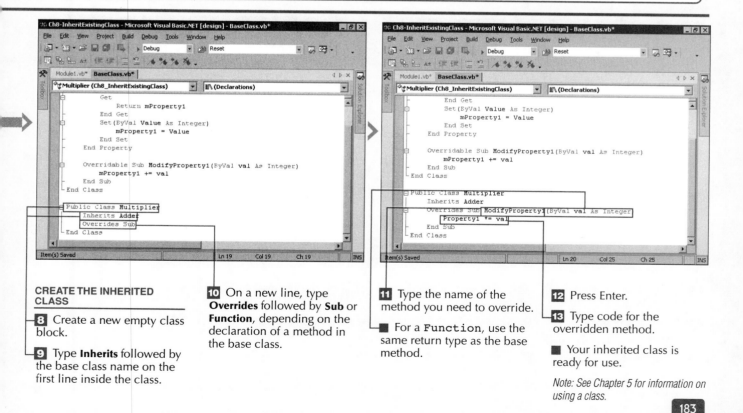

CREATE THE INHERITED CLASS

8 Create a new empty class block.

9 Type **Inherits** followed by the base class name on the first line inside the class.

10 On a new line, type **Overrides** followed by **Sub** or **Function**, depending on the declaration of a method in the base class.

11 Type the name of the method you need to override.

■ For a **Function**, use the same return type as the base method.

12 Press Enter.

13 Type code for the overridden method.

■ Your inherited class is ready for use.

Note: See Chapter 5 for information on using a class.

CREATE A SHARED METHOD

Because some methods need to function more like global procedures throughout a project, you may want to call methods inside classes without first creating an instance of the class. For example, if you create a class of mathematic routines, you do not want to declare a new instance of your class every time you need to perform a simple routine. Or, if you declare a class `File` and want to expose a method called `Open`, you can let the user call `Open`, which opens the file and then actually returns an instance of the `File` class without first having to create an instance of the `File` class. You can use shared methods to let a module invoke a method in a class without first creating an instance of the class.

To create a shared method, you use the `Shared` keyword in front of the `Sub` or `Function` keyword in the declaration

of the method. When you place the keyword in front of the method, you can still use it as a normal method if you create a class instance. But you can also access the method by placing the name of the class, not a variable name of an instance of the class, in any other method that can access the class followed by a period and the name of the method.

When VB .NET runs the code, it runs the shared method just like a method in a code module. The method has no attachment to the class when run as a shared method, and therefore cannot access member variables or other class members inside the class. A shared method can only access a shared variable or shared event. For more information on shared member variables, see "Create a Shared Variable." See "Using Delegate and AddressOf" for information on the `AddressOf` statement.

CREATE A SHARED METHOD

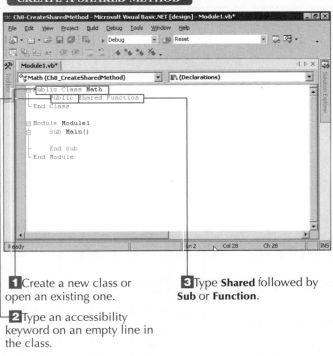

1 Create a new class or open an existing one.

2 Type an accessibility keyword on an empty line in the class.

3 Type **Shared** followed by **Sub** or **Function**.

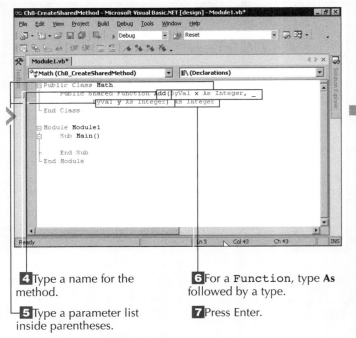

4 Type a name for the method.

5 Type a parameter list inside parentheses.

6 For a **Function**, type **As** followed by a type.

7 Press Enter.

Extra

When you create a shared method, which can only access other shared members, it does not run in the memory space of a class instance. You can fire an event from a shared method using shared events. To create a shared event, use the `Shared` keyword before the `Event` keyword when defining the event. In the class or module to handle the event, you use the `AddHandler` command to set up the method to handle the event. You can use this command for standard events as well as to dynamically handle events of a component. For the first parameter, specify the event. In the case of a shared event, type the class name, following it with a period and the name of the event. For a standard event, specify the instance variable name followed by a period and the event name. For the second parameter, type `AddressOf` followed by a method in the class or module to handle the event.

Example:
```
Public Class Class1
    Public Shared Event Event1()
    Public Shared Sub Method1()
        RaiseEvent Event1()
    End Sub
End Class
Public Class Class2
    Sub RunMethod()
        AddHandler Class1.Event1,_
            AddressOf HandleEvent
        Class1.Method1()
    End Sub
    Sub HandleEvent()
    ...
    End Sub
End Class
```

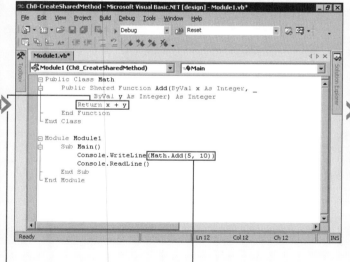

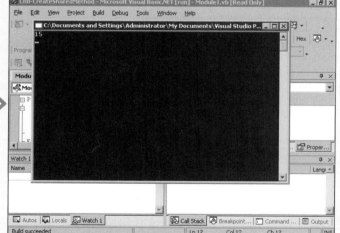

■ VB .NET creates the End Sub or **End Function** statement.

8 Type code for the shared method.

9 In the location that you need to use the method, type **Math.Add (5, 10)**, replacing `Math` with the class name of the shared method, and **5, 10** with any necessary parameters.

10 Press F5 to run your project.

■ The shared method runs its code without the class being initialized.

CREATE A SHARED VARIABLE

A global variable is a variable that any part of your application can access, meaning all parts of your application access a single instance of created data when the program initializes. In many programming languages, such as Visual Basic 6 and C++, you declare global variables outside of all class modules to alert the language to declare the variable globally. VB .NET provides an improved version of global variables called shared variables, which you place inside a class, but which still allow you to access a single instance of data throughout your application. Declaring shared variables inside of classes allows you to create more readable code that maintains the modularity of classes with the flexibility of globally available data.

You declare a shared variable inside a class much like a standard member variable. Unlike a standard member variable, the application can access the shared variable without creating an instance of the class. Also, even if no instances of the class exist, the variable remains in memory and never loses its value. For example, say your program has a counter class. Normally, you create an instance of the counter class and make sure not to lose the reference to it

throughout your program's operation. Using a shared variable, you can instatiate the class when necessary to update the counter, but the shared member variable keeps the value of the counter at all times.

You create a shared member variable by placing the Shared keyword before the variable name, but after the Dim or accessibility keyword. When you declare a shared variable Public, you can read or modify the variable from any module that has access to the class. To access the shared variable outside of the class, you use the name of the class, following it with a period and the name of the variable. You can also access the variable normally using an instance of the class. To access members of a class, see Chapter 5.

As with standard private member variables, you cannot access shared member variables you declare Private outside of the class. The variable stores value in memory across instances of the class. The value does not reset when you create a new instance of the class. This means if one instance of the class changes the variable, all other instances of the class work with the same new value. See Chapter 5 to learn more about member accessibility.

CREATE A SHARED VARIABLE

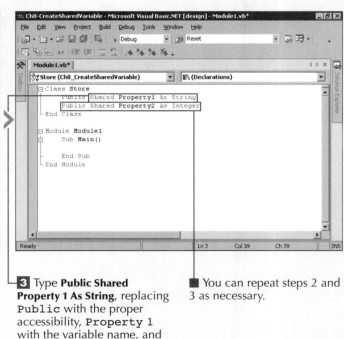

1 Create a new class or open an existing one.

2 Type an accessibility keyword such as **Public** or **Private** on an empty line inside the class outside of methods and events.

3 Type **Public Shared Property 1 As String**, replacing Public with the proper accessibility, Property 1 with the variable name, and String with the variable type.

■ You can repeat steps 2 and 3 as necessary.

Extra

Shared variables that you declare in your classes sometime initialize during program execution. VB .NET does not specify a single point to execute them, only that they initialize before you create an instance of the class or access a shared variable. VB .NET guarantees they only initialize once. You can create shared constructors to initialize the values of the shared variables. A shared constructor does not support any parameters, because VB .NET calls it directly. Declare a new constructor and place `Shared` before the `Sub New` statement. You can only initialize shared variables in this constructor.

TYPE THIS:	RESULT:

``
Public Class Class1
    Public Shared Variable1 As Integer
    Shared Sub New()
        Variable1 = 5
    End Sub
End Class
Public Class Form1
    Inherits System.Windows.Forms.Form
    Sub Form_Load(...) Handles MyBase.Load
        MsgBox(Class1.Variable1)
    End Sub
End Class
``
	5

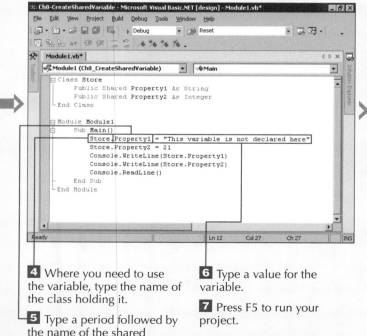

4 Where you need to use the variable, type the name of the class holding it.

5 Type a period followed by the name of the shared variable to access.

6 Type a value for the variable.

7 Press F5 to run your project.

■ The shared variable holds the value without an instance of the class existing.

USING DELEGATE AND ADDRESSOF

VB .NET provides delegates to allow code in a class to call methods defined outside of the class. This enables you to implement different code based on the reason you call the class's method. You can place the method in any part of the application that you want the class to use. In the class, you define the necessary parameters and return types that the function needs to accept. Then, you pass the class the outside method. The class can use this method to perform an operation. For example, if you needed to load data from various datasets in a class but you want to leave the actual implementation of reading the data out of the class, you can use a delegate so that the owner of the class provides the appropriate function to read the data.

To set up the delegate, you must first define the expectations the class has for the method. In the class

module, you use a `Sub` or `Function` line with the keyword `Delegate` in front. You define no code for the method and you do not add an `End Sub` or `End Function` command. This enables VB .NET to accept an outside function and to make sure it works with the class. In a method of the class, you create a parameter to accept the function. You make the type name for the parameter the same as the name of the delegate method header you declare.

Now you can call the method with an instance of the class you create. First, you must define a method that accepts the same parameters and returns the same type the delegate declaration expects. Then, you can pass your method using the `AddressOf` keyword. Place this keyword followed by the name of the method you declare as the parameter you pass to the class's method.

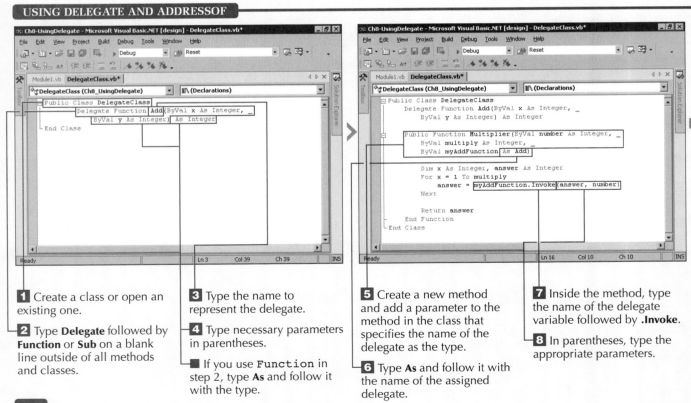

USING DELEGATE AND ADDRESSOF

■1 Create a class or open an existing one.

■2 Type **Delegate** followed by **Function** or **Sub** on a blank line outside of all methods and classes.

■3 Type the name to represent the delegate.

■4 Type necessary parameters in parentheses.

■ If you use **Function** in step 2, type **As** and follow it with the type.

■5 Create a new method and add a parameter to the method in the class that specifies the name of the delegate as the type.

■6 Type **As** and follow it with the name of the assigned delegate.

■7 Inside the method, type the name of the delegate variable followed by **.Invoke**.

■8 In parentheses, type the appropriate parameters.

Extra

The `Delegate` class supports an unlimited number of separate methods. You can use delegates to call more than one method with the `Invoke` method. Use the `Combine` method of the delegate you define to pass two functions, or pass an entire array.

TYPE THIS:

```
Public Delegate Sub StatusDel(status As String)
Public Class BigCalculationClass
        Public Sub MyMethod(ByVal sendInfo As StatusDel)
sendInfo.Invoke("Status info here")
        End Sub
End Class
Public Class Form1
        Public Sub Simple1(status As String)
                        MsgBox("Method1: " & status)
        End Sub
        Public Sub Simple2(status As String)
                        MsgBox("Method2: " & status)
        End Sub
        Public Sub Form1_Load() Handles MyBase.Load
                        Dim d As StatusDel =
                        StatusDel.Combine(New
                                StatusDel(AddressOf   Simple1),  New
                                StatusDel (AddressOf _
                                Simple2)), work As New
                                  BigCalculationClass()
                        work.MyMethod(d)
        End Sub
End Class
```

RESULT:

Method1: Status info here

Method2: Status info here

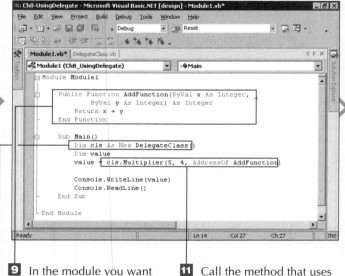

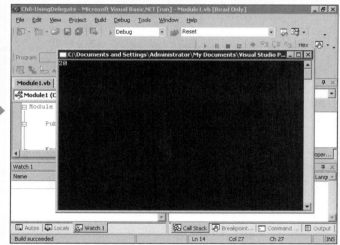

9 In the module you want to use the class, declare a new method exactly like the delegate you created in step 2.

10 Declare an instance of the class in a separate method.

11 Call the method that uses the delegate.

■ For the parameter you created in step 5 that expects the delegate, type **AddressOf** and the name of the new method you define in step 9.

12 Press F5 to run your project.

■ The delegate calls the method in the other class.

USING NAMESPACES

Namespaces provide a naming scheme for classes, components, and applications that helps to organize the enormous number of classes that make up an application. You use namespaces without being aware of them because all code in .NET exists within namespaces. The largest namespace in the .NET Framework is `System`. This namespace contains a number of other namespaces, like `Drawing`, which provides classes for drawing, and `IO`, which provides classes for file and socket input and output.

The normal method of accessing a class, direct addressing, involves you typing the full namespace when you use the class name. For example, to create a `Pen` for drawing, you declare a variable using the full name `System.Drawing.Pen`. Although distinctive and easy to read, this name requires you to type a lot of characters when working with code.

To save yourself time, you can use the `Imports` keyword to access components inside a particular namespace without specifying the namespace each time you use a class the namespace contains. You place the `Imports` statement at the top of a code module, above all modules and classes. The namespace to import follows the keyword. You can separate multiple namespaces on a single line using commas, and you can add as many `Imports` statements as necessary. Then, for any of your classes or modules inside the code module, you can access classes the namespace contains without specifying the namespace. For example, if you import the `System.Drawing` namespace, you can create a `Pen` using `Dim var As Pen`.

Importing a number of namespaces into a code module can create conflicts of class names. If two classes have the same name in different imported namespaces, you need to specify enough of the namespace to distinguish the two classes.

USING NAMESPACES

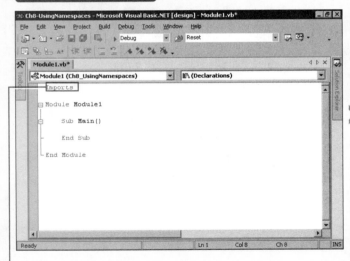

1 Type **Imports** at the top of a code module on an empty line, outside of all modules and classes.

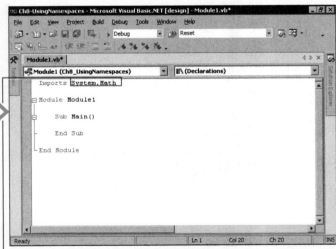

2 Type the name of a namespace to import.

3 Repeat steps 1 and 2 to import the necessary namespaces.

Extra

Although the namespaces provided by the .NET Framework appear as a single entity, many of the large namespaces exist within distinct separate DLLs. For example, the `System.Data` namespace resides in the `System.Data.dll` and the `System.Windows.Forms` namespace resides within `System.Windows.Forms.dll`. If you cannot access a particular namespace within a project, you need to reference the appropriate DLL. See Chapter 12 for more information on adding a reference to a DLL to a project.

You can use the `Imports` keyword to shorten the name of a particular namespace. This saves you from typing a full namespace without creating ambiguity for classes of the same names. You can specify an alias name using the `Imports` keyword followed by an equal sign and the name of the namespace.

Example:
```
Imports winfrm = System.Windows.Forms
Public Class Class1
      Sub Method1()
                          Dim btn As winfrm.Button

      End Sub
End Class
```

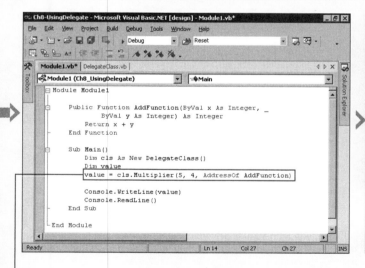

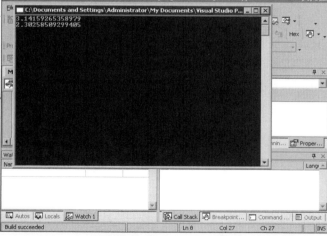

4 Inside a module or class in the code module, type code that accesses a class within the namespace without specifying the namespace.

5 Press F5 to run your project.

■ VB .NET accesses the correct class without specifying the namespace without direct addressing.

CREATE A NAMESPACE

In Visual Basic .NET, all classes and components reside inside a namespace. This convention helps you to locate appropriate classes and eliminate naming conflicts. If you use a large number of classes in your application, you can create namespaces to separate the application into logical sections much like the .NET Framework splits its large number of classes.

A .NET application contains at least one namespace. In VB .NET, a single namespace wraps the entire project and any namespaces inside it. VB .NET creates this namespace automatically when you create the project. The project properties page enables you to modify the name of the root namespace. By default the root namespace is the name of the project.

To create a namespace inside the root namespace, use the Namespace block. Place the name for the namespace following the Namespace keyword. The End Namespace statement marks the end of the namespace in a particular

file. In situations where you want to place classes from multiple files in the same namespace, create a namespace block in each file and use the same name for the namespaces. This enables you to spread classes across multiple files, but still include them in a single namespace.

A class not located in a Namespace block has the full name ProjectRoot.Class. A class you place inside a Namespace block has the full name ProjectRoot. Namespace.Class. To access the class in classes outside of the namespace, you must specify the namespace and the class name. You can place namespaces inside other namespaces to create a hierarchy of components.

The default accessibility for classes inside a namespace is Friend, which lets any other part of your application access the class. When you declare a class inside a namespace as Private, only other classes inside the namespace can access the class.

CREATE A NAMESPACE

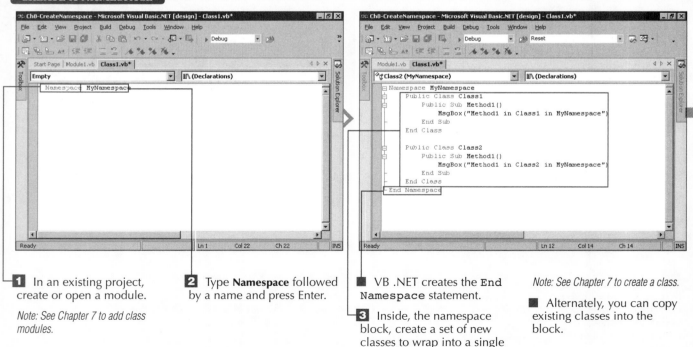

1 In an existing project, create or open a module.

Note: See Chapter 7 to add class modules.

2 Type **Namespace** followed by a name and press Enter.

■ VB .NET creates the **End Namespace** statement.

3 Inside, the namespace block, create a set of new classes to wrap into a single namespace.

Note: See Chapter 7 to create a class.

■ Alternately, you can copy existing classes into the block.

Extra

You can remove the default project root namespace to force the namespaces you create in the application to function as root namespaces. This enables you to bring classes from multiple applications together into the same namespace. However, if you choose to remove the root namespace, you must specify a namespace for each class in your application, including forms. You can specify a namespace hierarchy of your choosing. For example, you can use a namespace MyCompany.MyProduct with various namespaces under that application base. You can then add multiple products under the MyCompany hierarchy. To remove the default root namespace, right-click the project name in the Solution Explorer, and click Properties. In the Root namespace text box, clear the value and then click OK.

Example:
```
Namespace _
MyCompany.MyProduct.MyApplication.Documents
    Class Document
        ...
    End Class
End Namespace
```

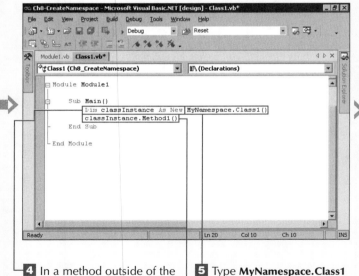

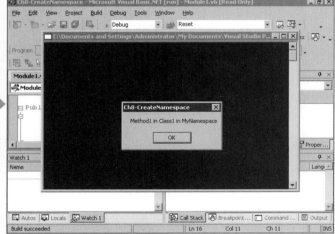

4 In a method outside of the namespace, type **Dim classInstance As New**, replacing classInstance with a variable name.

5 Type **MyNamespace.Class1** (), replacing MyNamespace with the name of the namespace and Class1 () with the name of the class to instantiate.

6 Type necessary code.

7 Press F5 to run your project.

■ Your method accesses the class located inside the namespace.

Note: See the section "Using Namespaces" to work with your namespace.

INHERIT A FORM

Because a `Form` in VB .NET is nothing more than a class, you can inherit a form into a new form using standard inheritance techniques. You can use visual inheritance of forms to create base forms that encourage uniform appearances and easier management. For example, a base form can represent the appropriate size and button placements for the dialogs in the application. Each dialog in the application inherits this base form and builds the interface necessary for the particular dialog, but maintains the same size and button functionality of the base form.

The Windows Forms Designer supports inheritance for forms. On the designer, inherited controls appear with a small icon over them to indicate that they inherit from the base class. You can change properties of the inherited items, but cannot delete them because the base class predefines them. See the section "Inherit from Existing Classes" for more information on inheriting classes.

All of the event handlers you specify in the base form automatically work the same in the inherited form. If a button on the base form specifies an event handler, the inherited form's button calls the event handler in the base class. If you add an event handler in the inherited class for a component on the base class, both event handlers fire. The base class's event handler fires first, followed by the inherited class's event handler.

You can override an event handler in the base form, however. To accomplish this, place the `Overridable` keyword in the definition of the base class's event handler, and then create a new method in the inherited class with the same parameter list. Do not place the `Handles` keyword on the inherited form's override method. If you want to call the base form's event handler inside the overridden method, use the `MyBase` object to access the base form.

INHERIT A FORM

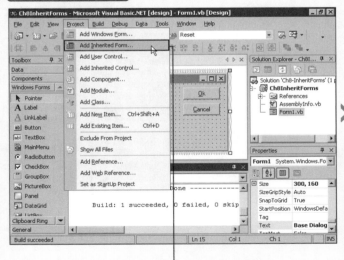

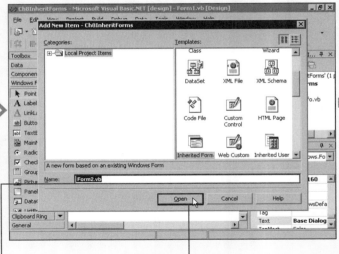

1 Create a new form or open an existing one to act as the base class adding controls as necessary.

Note: See Chapter 1 to build a project.

2 Build the project.

Note: See Chapter 2 to build a project.

3 Click Project ⇨ Add Inherited Form.

■ The Add New Item dialog appears with Inherited Form selected in the template list.

4 Type a name for the inherited form.

5 Click Open.

Extra

Remember that the inheritance of a form is not a one-time operation. Although you inherited from a base form in a particular state, you can always change the base form to add functionality. For example, you can update the base form to replace old controls with new ones that have the same function but a more attractive appearance. Likewise, you can debug the code in the base form and have it automatically update all of the inherited forms. To alter the base form, make sure you close all inherited forms. You then open the base form, make changes, and rebuild the project. When you reopen inherited forms, you see your changes.

When using inheritance on forms, you do not need to inherit controls. You can create a base form that declares useful variables and methods so you do not need to replicate them in each form you create. You can build a very powerful base form that makes programming additional forms quite simple. Make sure to add the `Overridable` keyword, when appropriate, to allow inherited forms to extend the functionality.

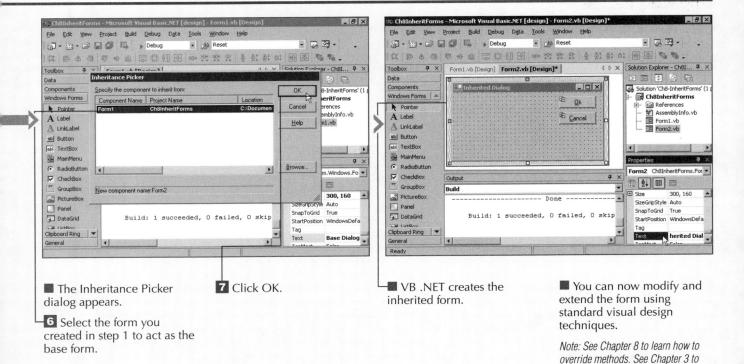

■ The Inheritance Picker dialog appears.

6 Select the form you created in step 1 to act as the base form.

7 Click OK.

■ VB .NET creates the inherited form.

■ You can now modify and extend the form using standard visual design techniques.

Note: See Chapter 8 to learn how to override methods. See Chapter 3 to modify, add controls, and manipulate the form.

CREATE A THREAD

Threads enable multiple parts of your application to execute concurrently. You can use threads to start a calculation or network connection without affecting the usability of the program. For example, when your application performs a search of the file system for the user, you do not want to force the user to stop working in another part of your application while waiting for the search to complete. Instead, you can create a thread to complete the search that runs concurrently with the rest of your application.

Threading in VB .NET operates using a free-threaded system. With free-threading, all threads run in the same memory space in the application. This means you can access all variables, objects, and components available in the program through the thread. Before you create a thread, understand that many complexities arise when multiple parts of code access variables and objects concurrently. See the section "Write Thread-Safe Code" for more information on Visual Basic .NET's synchronization commands.

In VB .NET, a thread runs the code of a single method in a separate thread. The method can call other methods in its thread. To create a new thread, you create a new instance of the `Thread` class. The `System.Threading` namespace contains the `Thread` class. You pass the address of a method to run using the `AddressOf` keyword. For more information on using `AddressOf`, see the section "Using Delegate and AddressOf."

To start the thread, call its `Start` method with no parameters. The thread runs until it meets one of three conditions. The thread stops when the code in the method completes, when the process containing the thread ends (normally meaning your program exits), or when you stop the execution explicitly. See the section "Modify Thread Execution" for more information.

The `Thread.CurrentThread` method returns the currently running thread. You can use this method anywhere, which makes it easy to receive an instance of the thread you create.

CREATE A THREAD

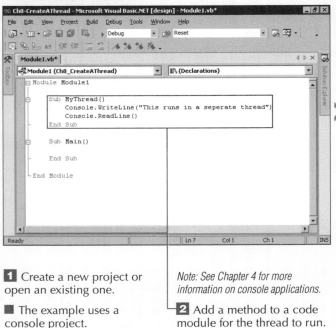

1 Create a new project or open an existing one.

■ The example uses a console project.

Note: See Chapter 4 for more information on console applications.

2 Add a method to a code module for the thread to run.

3 Type **Dim** followed by a variable name.

4 Type **As New System.Threading.Thread ( )**.

5 Inside parentheses, type **AddressOf** followed by the name of the method.

■ The example loads the thread in `Sun Main`.

Extra

Keeping track of a large number of threads consumes significant processor time. If you need to use a large number of threads, for example ten or twenty, you may find that they perform very poorly because the system spends more time switching between threads than running them. Also, if you are using most of the processor time in your process, threads in other processes run less frequently. You can ease the requirements of threading by using the minimum number of threads to accomplish a particular task. For example, you may need to search four different database tables or download ten different Web pages in your application. You know threads enable your application to respond to the user during this operation, but creating all the threads at once for the operation can cause more harm than good, especially on slower computers. Experiment with different numbers of concurrent threads to see which yields the best performance. See the section "Write Thread-Safe Code" to learn how you can start a new thread when one completes using the `Join` method or a `ThreadPool` object. Threadpool allows you to queue an unlimited number of threads and let the system determine how many to run.

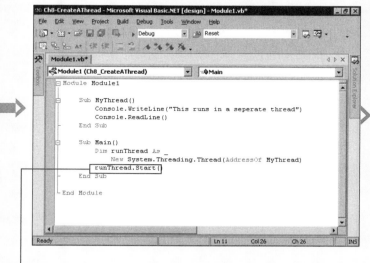

6 On a new line, type the variable name for the thread followed by **.Start()**.

7 Repeat steps 3 through 7 to start as many threads as necessary.

8 Press F5 to run your project.

■ The threads run the code in the method concurrently.

Note: To write thread-safe code for multiple threads or for input and output operations, see the section "Write Thread-Safe Code."

WRITE THREAD-SAFE CODE

Although threading is one of the most difficult and frustrating tasks in modern programming, Visual Basic .NET makes threading simple and easy when you carefully program. The problem with free-threading is that every thread of your application runs in the same memory space, meaning the threads all access the same objects. You must make sure that the threads of your application do not interfere with each other by interacting with the same object. You can use commands in VB .NET to create thread-safe code.

In general, the .NET Framework is not thread-safe, meaning if two threads attempt to access the same object at the same time, the object does not contain code to respond properly. Particularly, the Windows Forms classes cause many problems when not carefully managed.

To make sure you do not have more than one thread access an object, you use the `SyncLock` block. When you use the `SyncLock` statement, you provide VB .NET with an object,

inside parentheses, on which to lock . The `End SyncLock` statement marks the end of the block you want to lock. For example, you may have a list of results that you want to load into a `ListBox` control. However, you do not want more than one thread to access the `ListBox` at once, because the `ListBox` control is not thread-safe. You can provide the `ListBox` control as the `SyncLock` object and place the command to add information to the `ListBox` inside the lock. Then, if another thread runs the same lines of code, VB .NET forces the thread to wait until the previous lock releases.

In some cases, you can start a thread after another completes to avoid synchronizing objects in use by the two threads. Call the `Join()` method and pass another thread object as the parameter to cause the thread to wait until the thread you specify completes. Place this command inside the code of another thread to make it wait for another thread to complete.

WRITE THREAD-SAFE CODE

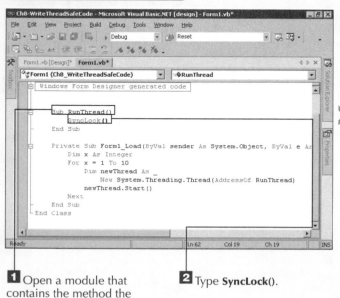

1 Open a module that contains the method the thread runs.

Note: For more information about creating a thread, see the section "Create a Thread."

2 Type **SyncLock()**.

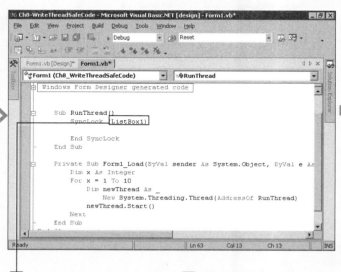

3 Inside the parentheses, type the object on which you want VB .NET to lock.

4 Press Enter to complete the block statement.

■ VB .NET creates the **End SyncLock** statement.

Extra

Because creating a large number of threads can use a significant quantity of resources, VB .NET includes the `ThreadPool` class. This class stores a queue of waiting methods you select to run on a thread independent of the application. The `ThreadPool` automatically manages the number of threads to create depending on the system speed and OS resources in use. For example, if you queue ten methods to run in separate threads, the `ThreadPool` class determines that three threads can run optimally on the system, and starts the first three methods in the queue in unique threads. As methods finish, new methods from the queue begin.

Example:
```
Sub ThreadMe(ByVal state As Object)
          SyncLock (ListBox1)
                  ListBox1.Items.Add("Thread
                      running")
          End SyncLock
End Sub
Private Sub Form1_Load(...) Handles MyBase.Load
      Dim x As Integer
      For x = 1 To 10
              Dim y As New
                  Threading.WaitCallback
                  (AddressOf ThreadMe)
              System.Threading.
                  ThreadPool.
                  QueueUserWorkItem(y)
      Next
End Sub
```

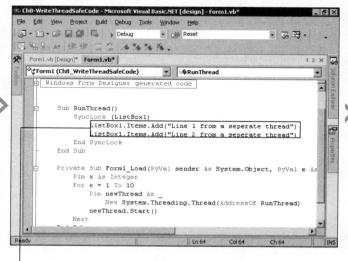

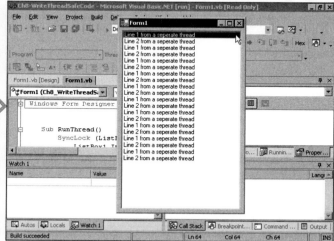

5 Add a call to non-thread-safe object's method or property.

6 Run your project by pressing F5.

■ The non-thread-safe object performs properly and multiple threads access the object.

MODIFY THREAD EXECUTION

The Thread class provides a variety of functions for greater control over threads. You can call these methods to affect the execution of the threads you create. For example, if you execute a complex task in the background, you can provide the ability to pause, resume, and cancel the operation. The thread object has a method for each of these operations.

The Suspend method stops the execution of the thread at a safe time. Use Suspend to pause a thread without danger of crashing the program. The Resume method starts a thread that you suspend where the thread last stopped.

The Sleep method lets a thread wait for data while consuming only minimal CPU cycles. You can use this to make the thread wait for a specified number of milliseconds before resuming execution. You specify the number of milliseconds to wait as the first parameter.

If you set a thread into a wait state, by using the Sleep method, or the Join method explained in "Write Thread-Safe Code," you can interrupt the waiting and cause the thread to resume execution again with the Interrupt method.

To ask a thread to stop execution, call the Abort method. When you call the method, VB .NET issues an exception to the thread. Code in the thread automatically skips out of any Try block and exits the thread. The thread may execute a few commands before exiting, so use the Join command to wait for the thread to stop completely.

The IsAlive property of the Thread object returns True if the thread starts and is not dead. You can also check the ThreadState property for the status of the thread. The property returns a value from the ThreadState enumeration.

MODIFY THREAD EXECUTION

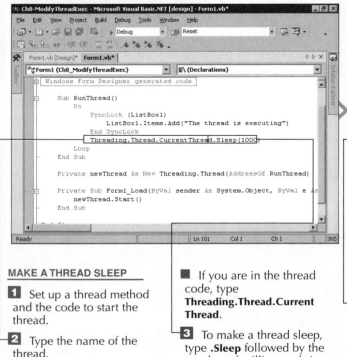

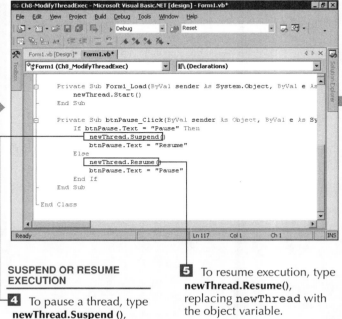

MAKE A THREAD SLEEP

1 Set up a thread method and the code to start the thread.

2 Type the name of the thread.

■ If you are in the thread code, type **Threading.Thread.Current Thread**.

3 To make a thread sleep, type **.Sleep** followed by the number of milliseconds in parentheses.

SUSPEND OR RESUME EXECUTION

4 To pause a thread, type **newThread.Suspend ()**, replacing **newThread** with the object variable for a thread.

5 To resume execution, type **newThread.Resume()**, replacing **newThread** with the object variable.

Extra

You can control various properties that specify how the scheduler, the management the operating system provides to switch between threads on a system, chooses to run a thread. The `IsBackground` property enables or disables background running. If a thread inside your application is a background thread, the thread automatically exits when your program exits. If the thread is a foreground thread, `IsBackground = False`, the program does not exit until the thread completes, just like the main application thread. You can control the priority of a thread in Visual Basic .NET using the `Priority` property. The priority determines how often a thread runs when the system multitasks. You can set the `Priority` property to one of the constants from the `ThreadPriority` enumeration. The values, from highest to lowest in terms of run-time, include: `Highest`, `AboveNormal`, `Normal`, `BelowNormal`, `Lowest`. You can set threads that run in the background, for example an automatic save, to below normal priorities. The default priority is `Normal`. Using priorities above normal gives the thread a majority of processor time at the expense of the user's ability to use the system seamlessly.

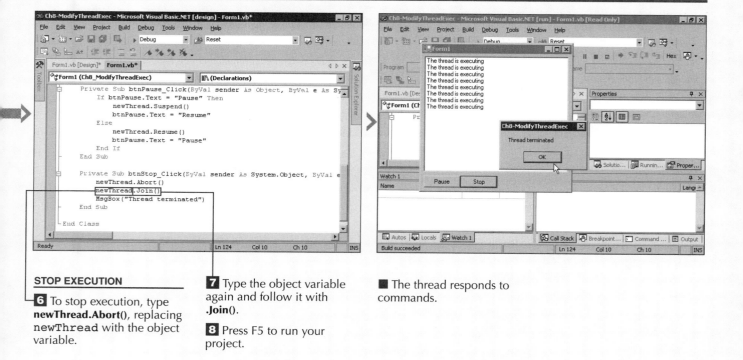

STOP EXECUTION

6 To stop execution, type **newThread.Abort()**, replacing `newThread` with the object variable.

7 Type the object variable again and follow it with **.Join()**.

8 Press F5 to run your project.

■ The thread responds to commands.

AN INTRODUCTION TO DATABASES

One of the most-used functions in the Visual Basic language's history, powerful database support, provides many functions to automate the development of database applications. You can use databases to quickly and efficiently store large or small quantities of information of any type, as well as search, filter, and manipulate that data to suit your needs. In certain cases where you need to store only a small list of data, you can use text files to more easily store the information. For more information on reading and writing to text files, see Chapter 5.

Visual Basic .NET and other Microsoft languages use a database system called ADO.NET. ADO, or Active Data Objects, allows you to wrap a set of standard functionality around any supported database format. For more information on the concepts of ADO.NET, see the section "An Introduction to ADO.NET."

DATABASE SOFTWARE

A variety of programs allow you to create database files, and ADO supports most database formats. Common database packages to use with Visual Basic .NET include Microsoft Access, Microsoft SQL, and Oracle. Make sure the vendor of your database provides a native .NET data provider, or an OLEDB compatible provider. ADO.NET can work with databases that support one of these two providers.

Microsoft Access is best suited for creating small databases that do not need to function under a heavy load. Microsoft SQL Server provides a more powerful database solution for large and high-load applications, such as Web development.

DATABASE STRUCTURE

A database consists of one or more tables, and a table contains one or more records. Each record can have one or more fields that make up its data. Each field in the record contains a single piece of information about that record, such as a string, a number, or a date. For example, you can define a table in a database to store customer information. The table has a field for the customer's first name, last name, address, and phone number. Then you can define individual customers by adding new records to the table.

Database design is a very important part of creating an efficient, powerful, and maintainable application. You should carefully evaluate your data storage needs and create a database that fits those needs while providing flexibility for expansion.

For ADO.NET to access a variety of data sources, it must have a common language that works with a variety of databases. You use Structured Query Language (SQL) to communicate with databases of any format. SQL provides a simple English-like instruction set that can accomplish any action a database supports.

SQL FEATURES

IBM originally developed SQL in a prototype relational database management system, System R, in the mid 1970s. In 1979, Oracle Corporation introduced the first commercially available implementation of SQL. Since then, the entire database industry has adopted SQL to access their databases. With the help of ADO.NET's ability to support different databases seamlessly, SQL enables you to move between different databases with few changes. For example, you can use Microsoft Access to develop your application, but move it to Microsoft SQL Server later.

This introduction to SQL covers a minute part of its abilities. Many books dedicate their entire subject to SQL. SQL provides the ability to combine tables, filter data, and create powerful procedures. This book covers the major SQL commands necessary to retrieve, update, and modify records in a database.

SQL Clauses

You use the WHERE clause to specify records on which the SELECT, UPDATE, and DELETE commands should function. You can use equal, less than, greater than, less than or equal, greater than or equal, or LIKE operators in the clause. When you use LIKE, you specify test string values containing wildcard characters. You can also use AND, OR, and NOT to combine multiple conditions.

Example:
```
WHERE Price < 10.50
WHERE LastName LIKE 'S%'
WHERE FirstName LIKE 'J__n' AND LastName = 'Smith'
```

You use the ORDER BY clause to specify how the SELECT command performs a sort on the data records it returns. After the ORDER BY clause, specify the field on which to sort the records. Place the DESC keyword after the field name to sort in descending order. If you want to sort on one field, then another, separate the sort fields by commas.

Example:
```
SELECT TotalBalance FROM Customers
ORDER BY Price, Quantity DESC
```

Example:
```
SELECT TotalBalance FROM Customers
ORDER BY LastName, FirstName
```

SQL Statements

You can use these four statements throughout this chapter to perform the necessary tasks.

The SELECT statement retrieves information from tables. You specify the fields for the command to retrieve followed by a FROM clause. You follow the FROM clause with the name of the table that you want to use. You can use the optional WHERE statement to retrieve only the necessary data using standard comparison operators.

Example:
```
SELECT TotalBalance
FROM Customers
WHERE LastName = 'Smith'
```

The INSERT statement adds a record into a table. After INSERT, specify INTO followed by the name of the table. After the table name, place the field names to set in parentheses. Then use the VALUES clause with the values for the fields in the same order enclosed in parentheses.

Example:
```
INSERT INTO Customers
(LastName, FirstName, TotalBalance)
VALUES ('Smith', 'John', 150.25)
```

The UPDATE statement changes fields in records that meet a given criteria. Type the table name after the UPDATE statement followed by the SET clause. You then specify field names and new values and use the WHERE clause to identify the records to alter.

Example:
```
UPDATE Customers
SET TotalBalance = 560.50
WHERE LastName = 'Smith'
AND FirstName = 'John'
```

The DELETE statement deletes records from the table that meet given crieteria. After the DELETE statement, type FROM followed by the name of the table. Use the WHERE clause to identify the records to delete.

Example:
```
DELETE Customers
WHERE LastName = 'Smith'
AND FirstName = 'John'
```

VISUAL BASIC .NET

AN INTRODUCTION TO ADO.NET

The latest evolution in Microsoft's database technologies, ADO.NET provides support for new functionality and programming methods. ADO.NET functions inside of the .NET Framework, allowing any .NET application to access its features in a similar way.

FEATURES

Recently, through the evolution of the Internet, many developers now develop new client applications based on the Web application model. Many applications use XML to encode data to pass over network connections. Web applications use HTTP to communicate, and therefore must maintain state between requests. This new model differs from the connected, tightly coupled style of programming where a connection was held open for the duration of the program's lifetime and no special handling of *state*, defined as the persistence of data across parts of an application, was required.

ADO.NET was designed to meet the needs of this new programming model: disconnected data architecture, tight integration with XML, and common data representation with the ability to combine data from multiple and varied data sources, and optimizations for accessing data in different ways.

Consistency

One of its major features, Microsoft database technology can work with multiple data sources consistently, thus providing consistent access to data sources such as Microsoft SQL Server and any data sources exposed via OLE DB. ADO.NET also includes inherent support for XML datasets. You can use ADO.NET to connect to data sources and retrieve, manipulate, and update data.

Powerful Object Model

ADO.NET provides an Object Model with database features. This allows you to use the objects together with a database provider, or individually to work with custom application data.

In addition, you still have the option to work with the database provider using SQL to execute commands and retrieve results directly.

Similarities to ADO

The design for ADO.NET maintains as many similarities to ADO as possible, while still addressing requirements necessary to support new disconnected functions.

ADO.NET coexists with ADO. Although you commonly write new applications with ADO.NET, ADO remains available to the .NET programmer.

Supports N-Tier Programming

ADO.NET provides support for the disconnected, n-tier programming environment for which many Visual Basic .NET programmers need to develop. *N-tier programming* involves developing separate levels of the application — the presentation tier, the business logic tier, the data access and storage tier — that work together to provide the complete user experience.

XML Support

To access data in a standard way, XML serves to encode and format of data into a standards compliant format. A fundamental part of their applications, developers need XML to function as a data source. For this reason, XML builds its support into ADO.NET at a very fundamental level. The core of the entire .NET Framework, the XML class framework allows you to cross between the two libraries easily.

Disconnected Recordsets

Although previous versions of ADO added disconnection as an afterthought, ADO.NET, through major changes in design, focuses its functionality around disconnected data. When you connect to a database, you actually load all of the data in tables of the database into the client application's memory. ADO.NET performs all of the data manipulation to these in-memory copies of the table information. When the user finishes with the form or application, and makes changes to the database, you can reconnect to the database. ADO.NET looks through the in-memory data and makes changes to synchronize the two.

Because of disconnection, you must carefully design your database. Large tables may perform poorly when you load them into memory. To improve speed, you must filter only necessary data down to a particular client. Also, multiple users can connect to a database, retrieve a table, make changes, and update the same records.

Object Model

In ADO.NET, the Object Model recreates all of the functionality present in a database system. The Object Model must replicate the database contents because the database does not stay connected to the client. The DataTable object represents a single table of a database, and consists of DataColumn objects, which define the fields, and DataRow objects, which store the records of the table. A DataTable resides in a DataSet object, which is the main wrapper control, and can hold any number of tables. The DataSet object also allows you to create relationships between tables using DataRelation objects. These objects, the core set of data for storage and manipulation, allow you to bind the data to controls, whether the components connect to an actual database or not.

ADO.NET OBJECTS

The connection and adapter components provide the basic ability for connecting to a database, while the DataSet provides storage in memory for everything that makes up tables and relationships. See the section "Add a Connection to a Form" for more information. The table, row, and column objects provide the underlying data and manipulation abilities for the DataSet object.

DbConnection

To attach a database to your application, you first create a data connection object. Microsoft includes two components that implement the DbConnection interface, OleDbConnection and SqlConnection. The OleDbConnection components allow you to connect to any database that the OLEDB interface supports, and SqlConnection allows you to connect to a Microsoft SQL Server database. This chapter develops database applications using the SQL connection classes, but you can substitute the use of OLEDB classes because they use the same interfaces, methods, and properties.

DataSet

The DataSet component is the major component for retrieving and manipulating information. The DataSet object stores a set of tables from the database, including their field definitions and all of the associated data. Controls can bind to the DataSet or contained tables to view or modify the data.

DataAdapter

A data adapter provides the conduit for connecting a DbConnection to the objects in ADO.NET that actually store and manipulate the database information. For a particular connection component, you must have a specific adapter that understands how to communicate with the connection. Microsoft provides the SqlDataAdapter and the OleDbDataAdapter, depending on which DbConnection you use.

DataTable

The DataTable object represents a single database table. Because the database source disconnects, this object must provide all the abilities of an actual database table. The DataTable object relies on DataColumn objects to define the fields of the table and DataRow objects to store the actual data of the table. See the section "Work with Data Tables" for more information on the DataTable object.

CREATE A DATABASE CONNECTION

To access a database in an application, you must create a connection to it via the Server Explorer. You can attach a number of database formats to your application using ADO.NET, which provides the same interface to multiple formats.

When you open the Server Explorer window in the Development Environment, it presents a list of the current database connections. The Server Explorer also displays a list of servers, which allow you to access remote data objects. From the Server Explorer window, you can access the Data Link Property dialog box. Here, you can create a new connection, tell VB .NET what type of data provider to use, and name the database. For databases that support password protection, you see options to enter the appropriate password, which allows you to connect to the database.

You can access a list of advanced settings when creating the connection. These settings, which depend on the data provider you use, enable you to edit access permissions for the application's connection and specify connection timeouts.

After you create the connection, VB .NET shows you the database in the Server Explorer and lists all of the tables, views, and stored procedures available in the database. You can edit the database contents directly in Visual Basic .NET via the tables in the Server Explorer. This allows you to make quick changes to test data before you complete the entire application interface.

Adding a connection to the Server Explorer does not change your project. The Server Explorer stores database connections independently. Only when you add the connection to a form does the database actually become a part of your project. For more information on adding a connection you create in the Server Explorer to a form, see the section "Add a Connection to the Form."

CREATE A DATABASE CONNECTION

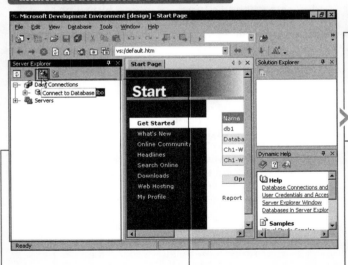

1 Access the Server Explorer window.

Note: Click View ➪ Server Explorer if you do not have the Server Explorer open.

2 Click the Connect to Database button (   ).

■ The Data Link dialog box appears.

3 Click the Provider tab.

4 Select the appropriate database provider for your data.

■ The example uses the Microsoft OLE DB Provider for SQL Server.

5 Click Next.

Extra

The Server Explorer provides the ability to edit and modify table information. The Development Environment includes an entire database editor package. You can use the abilities provided in the Development Environment to add tables, modify designs, and modify data present in a database. To add a new table, right-click the Tables category inside the connected database and click New Table. You can modify the design of an existing table by right-clicking an existing table and clicking Design Table. To edit the data inside an existing table, click Retrieve Data from Table.

You can use the Advanced tab of the Data Link Properties dialog box to specify network protection levels. The protection level determine how and when the client must authenticate with the server to ensure an accurate and untampered connection over the network. The Call setting makes the client authenticate the source of the data on each request. You can use the Connect setting, which requires that the client authenticate at the first connection, to improve the speed of the data connection while maintaining minmimum security. When you select None, no authentication takes place. These settings only appear when you connect to a database over a network, and the database supports these authentication options.

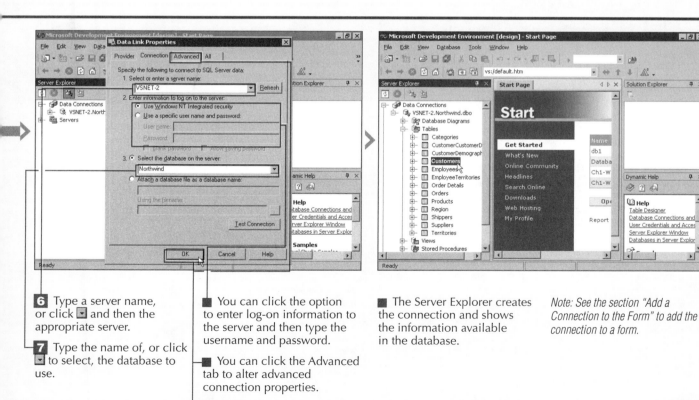

6 Type a server name, or click ▾ and then the appropriate server.

7 Type the name of, or click ▾ to select, the database to use.

■ You can click the option to enter log-on information to the server and then type the username and password.

■ You can click the Advanced tab to alter advanced connection properties.

8 Click OK.

■ The Server Explorer creates the connection and shows the information available in the database.

Note: See the section "Add a Connection to the Form" to add the connection to a form.

207

ADD A CONNECTION TO A FORM

After you set up a database connection, you must add the connection to your application so you can access the database. See the section "Create a Database Connection" for more on connecting to a database. The `OleDbConnection` and `SqlConnection` components hold a connection to a database for a particular form or class. Although the `OleDbConnection` component supports a variety of database connections through the OLEDB database specification, it does not perform as well as the `SqlConnection` due to its layers of compatibility. For that reason, this chapter uses the `SqlAdapter` combined with Microsoft SQL Server 2000. Although this chapter shows the use of `SqlAdapter`, the functionality of the `OleDbAdapter` is the same except for the name of the component.

The connection component provides no ability to access the database directly. Instead, a data adapter component bridges the gap. The `SqlDataAdapter` provides support for `SqlConnection` components. The data adapter component stores the appropriate SQL command text to retrieve,

modify, add, and remove items from the database. With this, the adapter can provide two-way access to the database.

The `DataSet` component provides the final piece required to access the database. A `DataSet` uses the `SqlDataAdapter` to retrieve a set of tables from the database and store them into memory. Then your program can modify the data and write changes back when complete. The `SqlDataAdapter` provides a method, `Fill`, that loads a table of information into a `DataSet`. You provide the `SqlDataAdapter`'s `Fill` method with the instance of the `DataSet` as the first parameter and the table to load as the second parameter.

Visual Basic .NET completes the sequencing of components automatically. When you add the database connection to the form, Visual Basic .NET creates both the connection and adapter components. A wizard enables you to provide the appropriate SQL command for the `SqlDataAdapter`. Another dialog box lets you select the appropriate tables to load into the `DataSet`.

ADD A CONNECTION TO A FORM

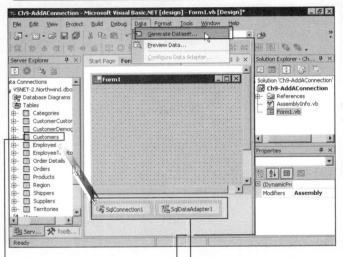

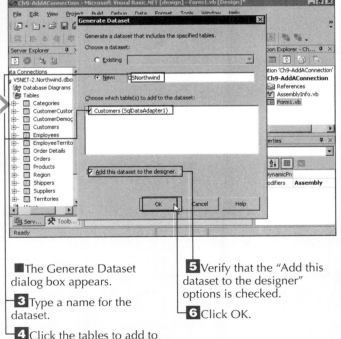

1 Click and drag a table listed in the Server Explorer from a connected database to the form.

Note: To create a database connection, see the section "Create a Database Connection."

■ VB .NET adds an `SqlConnection` control and an `SqlDataAdapter` control to the form.

2 Click Data ➪ Generate Dataset.

Note: If the menu item is disabled, click the form and try again.

■ The Generate Dataset dialog box appears.

3 Type a name for the dataset.

4 Click the tables to add to the dataset.

5 Verify that the "Add this dataset to the designer" options is checked.

6 Click OK.

Apply It

You can create a dataset based off an XML file to bind to controls. You cannot bind controls visually when creating a dataset at runtime, but you can set the `DataSource` property of a `DataGrid` control or add a `DataBindings` object to a simple control. For more information on binding, see the section "Bind a Control on a Form."

TYPE THIS:

```
XMLTEST.XML
<root>
<Companies>
    <CompanyName>Sample Company, Inc.</CompanyName>
    <Products>
        <ProductName>Sample Product 1</ProductName>
        <ProductPrice>99.99</ProductPrice>
    </Products>
    <Products>
        <ProductName>Sample Product 2</ProductName>
        <ProductPrice>49.99</ProductPrice>
    </Products>
</Companies>
</root>

Bind XML To Grid
Dim CompaniesXML As New DataSet("Companies")
CompaniesXML.ReadXml("C:\COMPANIES.XML")
DataGrid1.DataSource = CompaniesXML
```

RESULT:

The DataGrid automatically displays the Companies table and provides a hyperlink to access the related products.

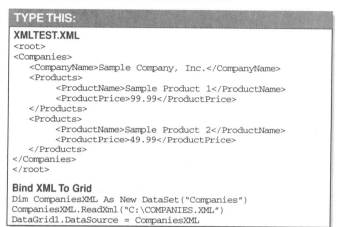

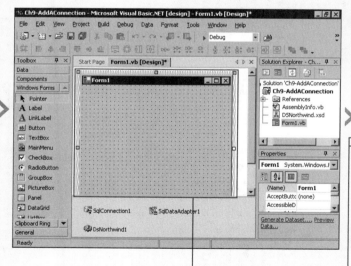

■ VB .NET adds a **DataSet** component to the form. The name consists of your entered name and a number.

7 Double-click the form to open the **Form_Load** event handler.

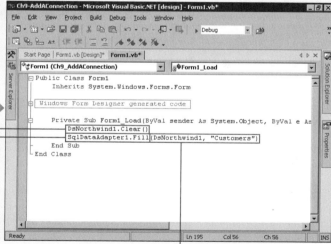

■ The Code Editor opens.

8 Type the name of the dataset followed by **.Clear()**.

9 On a new line, type the data adapter's name followed by **.Fill()**.

10 Inside the parentheses, type the name of the **DataSet**, a comma, and the table to load.

■ You can now close the Code Editor and use the form to hold bound controls.

Note: See the section "Bind a Control on a Form" to bind a control.

WORK WITH DATA TABLES

The DataTable object represents a single table of information. You can use the DataTable object to work with the tables in a DataSet. Much like a table in a database, the DataTable object stores a representation of rows that contain various columns. A DataSet control stores the information it loads from a database table into a DataTable object. This allows the database table to load from the database connection into memory, so the database can then disconnect.

You can access the name of the table represented by the object using the TableName property. The Columns property returns the fields available for each column of the table in a DataColumnCollection object. The PrimaryKey property gets or sets an array of DataColumn objects that act as the primary keys for the table. For more information about the DataColumn object, see the section "Work with Data Columns."

The Rows property returns a DataRowCollection object that allows you to access the individual records. For more

information on the DataRow object, see the section "Work with Data Rows."

The ChildRelations property maintains a DataRelationCollection made up of the list of tables that function as children to this table. The ParentRelations property returns the same object list containing the tables that function as parents to this table. For more information on data-table relationships, see the section "Create a Data Relationships." The Constraints property maintains the list of constraints that the relationship abides by in a ConstraintCollection object.

When you create a DataSet component and have it generate tables for you to access, VB .NET automatically creates an inherited version of this class. This inherited version contains properties and methods that relate to the actual fields and records of that table. For more information on binding controls, adding records, and updating information using the generated tables and the DataSet component, see the section "Bind a Control on a Form."

WORK WITH DATA TABLES

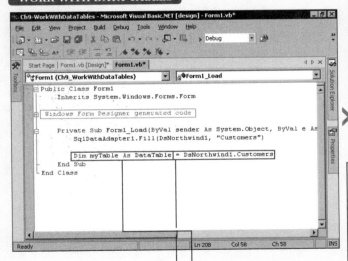

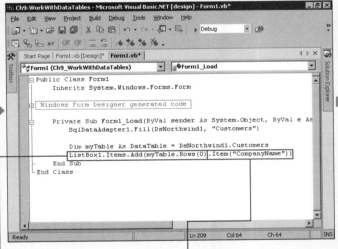

1 Set up a database connection on the form.

Note: See the sections "Create a Database Connect" and "Add a Connection to a Form" to set up a database.

2 In a method of the form, declare a variable of type **DataTable**.

3 Assign an expression formed by the name of the **DataSet** followed by a period and the name of the table to the variable.

4 Type **ListBox1.Items.Add (myTable.Rows(0))**, replacing ListBox1.Items.Add() with a method to display the data, **myTable** with the name of the table, and 0 with the row index to access.

5 Following Rows(0), type **.Item("CompanyName")**, replacing CompanyName with the name of the field to access.

Note: To work with a DataRow, see the section "Work with Data Rows."

A fully functioning standalone component, the `DataTable` object does not need a database adapter connection to an actual database provider. You can declare an instance of a `DataTable`, define its columns using `DataColumn` objects and add `DataRow` objects to the table. Then you can use the `DataTable` to bind to controls as you do with the visual `DataSet` and provider components. See the section "Bind a Control on a Form" for more information.

TYPE THIS:

```
Private Sub Form1_Load(ByVal sender As System.Object, ByVal e As _
System.EventArgs) Handles MyBase.Load
    Dim dt As New DataTable("MyTable")
    dt.Columns.Add("Name", System.Type.GetType("System.String"))
    dt.Columns.Add("Address", System.Type.GetType("System.String"))
    Dim values() As String = {"John Doe", "123 Anytown Rd."}
    dt.Rows.Add(values)
    values(0) = "Aaron Smith"
    values(1) = "456 South Rd."
    dt.Rows.Add(values)
    TextBox1.DataBindings.Add("Text", dt, "Name")
    TextBox2.DataBindings.Add("Text", dt, "Address")
    End Sub
```

RESULT:

TextBox1: John Doe

TextBox2: 123 Anytown Rd.

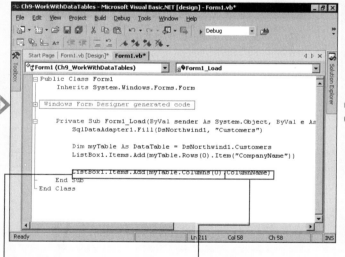

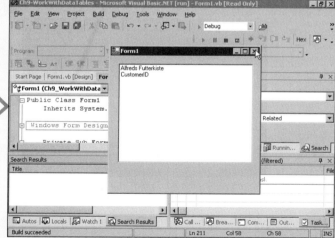

6 Type **ListBox1.Items.Add (myTable.Columns(0))**, replacing `ListBox1.Items.Add()` with the method to display the data, `myTable` with the table name, and 0 with the column index.

7 Following `Columns(0)`, type a period followed by a method or property of the `DataColumn`.

Note: To work with a `DataColumn`, see the section "Work with Data Columns."

8 Press F5 to run your project.

■ The `DataTable` object provides the necessary information about the table contents.

WORK WITH DATA COLUMNS

You define a database table with a set of columns, or fields, which describe sections of data in each record of the table. The `DataColumn` object stores the information of a column in a `DataTable`. You can use the `DataColumn` object, which stores column information in a `DataTable`, to retreive or modify the details of a table. For more information on the `DataTable` control, see the section "Work with Data Tables."

The `Caption` property stores the textual caption for the column. The `ColumnName` property specifies the actual name of the column. A column within a data adapter is equivalent to the column name in the actual database table. To specify the type of the column, you set The `DataType` property.using the `System.Type.GetType` method to return a variable type based on its name. You pass the name as a string for the parameter. For a list of valid data types, search the VB .NET help for the **DataColumn.DataType Property** topic.

The `DefaultValue` property specifies the column's default value when you create a new row. The `MaxLength`

property determines the maximum amount of text the column can hold per row for a string column. The `ReadOnly` property ensures that you cannot change the column after you add the record. When you enable the `AllowDBNull` property, the column accepts blank values, which VB .NET represents with the `DBNull` constant. You can access the table that owns the column using the `Table` property.

You can create the `DataColumn` object and add it to a `DataTable` object to define a table in your application. For the constructor of the `DataColumn`, pass the name of the column followed by a data type for the column as the two parameters. You can add the column to a `DataTable` by calling the `Add` method of the `DataTable.Columns` property.

The example below iterates through the list of columns in a data table and displays information about the columns using a `ListBox` control for display. You can modify the example to work with a specific column instead. You can also substitute any display or manipulation method.

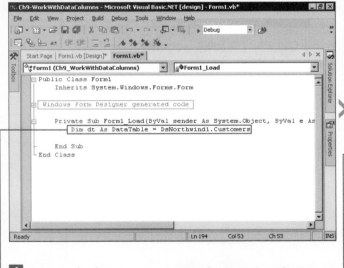

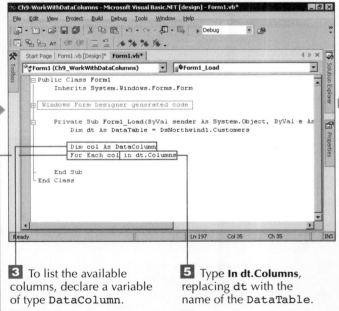

1 Set up a database connection and dataset on the form.

2 In a method of the form, declare a `DataTable` variable and assign a table from the `DataSet`.

Note: See the sections "Create a Database Connect" and "Add a Connection to a Form" to set up a database. See "Work with Data Tables" to access a `DataTable`.

3 To list the available columns, declare a variable of type `DataColumn`.

4 Type **For Each col**, replacing **col** with the variable you define in step 3.

5 Type **In dt.Columns**, replacing **dt** with the name of the `DataTable`.

6 Press Enter.

Extra

You can use the `Expression` property of a `DataColumn` to define a value for the column's contents in each record. You can add this `DataColumn` to an existing `DataTable` that loads from a data adapter. The example adds a `Total` column to the `OrderDetails` table contained in the Northwind database. See the section "Add a Connection to a Form" to set up a dataset that includes the appropriate table. The example assumes you bind the data table to a control such as a `DataGrid`. See the section "Bind a Control on a Form" for more information on binding controls.

TYPE THIS:

```
Dim myColumn As New DataColumn("Total")
Dim dt As System.Type = System.Type.GetType("System.Decimal")
' The expression multiplies the "Price" column by the "Quantity" to create a "Total" column.
myColumn.Expression = "Price * Quantity"
myColumn.ColumnMapping = MappingType.Attribute
' Set various properties.
myColumn.AutoIncrement = False
myColumn.ReadOnly = True
DataSet1.Tables("OrderDetails").Columns.Add(myColumn)
```

RESULT:

PRICE	QUANTITY	TOTAL
10	1	10
10	2	20
20	4	80

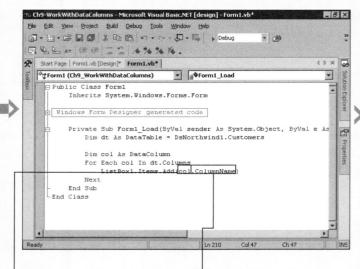

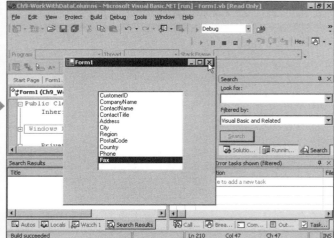

■ The `Next` statement appears automatically.

7 To access a member of the column, type the variable name of the `DataColumn`.

■ To access a column without declaring a variable, you can type `DataTable.Columns(Column)`.

8 Type `.ColumnName`, replacing `ColumnName` with a property or method of the column.

■ You can access any property, such as `DefaultValue` or `Caption`.

9 Press F5 to run your project.

■ The `DataColumn` object retrieves and stores information about a particular field of the database.

WORK WITH DATA ROWS

A table in a database consists of a number of records, or rows. The `DataTable` object uses `DataRow` objects to store records of the database object. You can use the `DataRow` object to manage users' changes to rows and modify or retrieve information from the database. For more information on the `DataTable` object, see the section "Work with Data Tables."

The `DataRow` object maintains an object for each column, or field, of the `DataTable`. You use the `Item` property to access any column of the row. Pass the name of the column as a string, the actual `DataColumn` object, or an `Integer` index to specify the column to retrieve or edit. You can also using the `ItemArray` property to retrieve or modify the entire row at the same time. `ItemArray` returns an `Object` array with the various columns. You access the `DataTable` object that owns the row with the `Table` property.

You can use the `DataRow` object to find and manage errors in data entry. Because the `DataRow` stores in memory, you can use these members to remove errors before trying to write to the database. You use the `HasErrors` property to determine if a row contains an error that prevents it from updating into a database. If `HasErrors` returns `True`, you can retrieve the columns that contain the errors using the `GetColumnsInError` method. The method returns an array of `DataColumn` objects, where each column in the array specifies a field in the row that contains an error. You can retrieve the error associated with a particular column with the `GetColumnError` method. Pass the column name as the only parameter. After you correct all the errors in the row, call the `ClearErrors` method with no parameters to remove the error states from the columns. For more information on managing errors, see the section "Validate Data."

The example in this section iterates through the list of rows in a data table and displays their information with a `ListBox` control. You can modify the code to work with a specific row. You can modify the code to work with a specific row, and you can substitute any display or manipulation method.

WORK WITH DATA ROWS

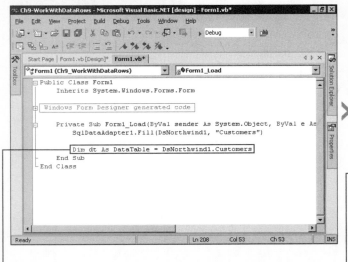

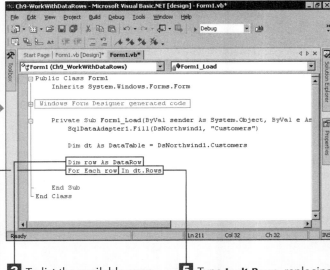

1 Set up a database connection and dataset on the form.

2 Declare a `DataTable` variable and assign a table from the `DataSet`.

Note: See the sections "Create a Database Connection" and "Add a Connection to a Form" to set up a database. See "Work with Data Tables" to access a `DataTable`.

3 To list the available rows, declare a variable of type `DataRow`.

4 Type **For Each row**, replacing `row` with the variable you define in step 3.

5 Type **In dt.Rows**, replacing `dt` with the name of the `DataTable`.

6 Press Enter.

Apply It

You can access a list of `DataRow` objects available in a `DataTable` easily using the `Select` method of the table. The method returns an array of `DataRow` objects in the table. If you pass a filter string as the parameter to `Select`, the array contains only `DataRow` objects that match the criteria. Also, you can pass a sort expression as the second parameter to sort the array.

TYPE THIS:

```
Private Sub GetRowsByFilter()
    Dim dt As DataTable = DsNorthwind1.Tables("Orders")
    ' Get orders from the year 1998 and later.
    Dim Expression As String = "OrderDate >= #1/1/98#"
    Dim SortString As String = "Freight DESC"
    Dim row As DataRow, selectedRows() As DataRow
    selectedRows = dt.Select(Expression, SortString)
    ' Print the freight and name for the shipping address
    ListBox1.Items.Clear()
    For Each row In selectedRows
        ListBox1.Items.Add(row.Item("Freight") & " - " &  row.Item("Ship Name"))
        Next
End Sub
```

RESULT:

830.75 - Save-a-lot Markets

754.26 - Ernst Handel

...

0.17 - Suprêmes délices

0.02 - La corne d'abondance

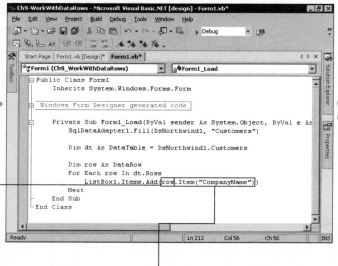

■ VB .NET creates the **Next** statement.

7 To access the member of a row, type the variable name of the `DataRow`.

■ To access a row without declaring a variable, you can type **DataTable.Rows(Row)**.

8 Type **.Item("Company Name")**, replacing **"Company Name"** with the name of the column to access.

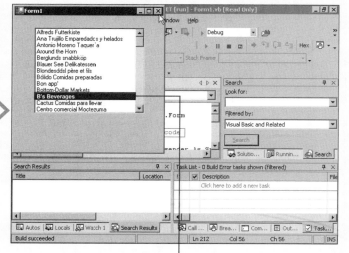

9 Press F5 to run your project.

■ The `DataRow` object retrieves and stores information about a particular row.

ADD A DATAVIEW COMPONENT

The `DataSet` component provides the ability to load multiple tables in a database into memory for use by your application. You can use the `DataView` component to filter and sort a database table before binding to a control. To learn more about binding a control, see the section "Bind a Control on a Form." A `DataView` represents one table of a `DataSet` component. The `Table` property specifies the source table the `DataView` uses.

You can sort the items in the `DataView` by setting the `Sort` property to the field it uses to sort the table. You can specify multiple sort fields by separating them with commas. You can sort the items in descending order by following the field name with the `DESC` SQL keyword. For an introduction to Structured Query Language (SQL), see the section "An Introduction to Databases."

You can use the `DataView` to return a partial set of rows from the full database table and treat it just like a standard table. Use the `RowFilter` property to filter the data table. To form the `RowFilter`, specify the filter field followed by a conditional operator and the value to test each field in the available records. To test a string value, place the value inside single quotes ('). You can also use the `RowStateFilter` property to filter based on the state of a record. You can use this property to filter the `DataView` to expose only new records, or deleted records. The `Count` property returns the number of records in the filtered view.

The `Item` property returns a row from the attached data table. Specify the record index as the parameter. To find an item by the primary key value, use the `Find` method. Pass the key value as the only parameter, and the method returns the row index where the row exists in the table.

ADD A DATAVIEW COMPONENT

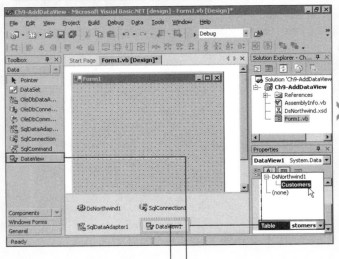

1 Set up a database connection on the form.

Note: See the section "Create a Database Connection."

2 Double-click the **DataView** component in the Data section of the Toolbox.

3 In the Properties window, click the **Table** property [▼] and select the appropriate table.

4 To sort the table, type the name of the field by which you want to sort in the **Sort** property.

■ You can type a space followed by **DESC** to sort in descending order.

5 To filter the data, type a field name followed by a conditional operator and the value to test in the **RowFilter** property.

■ The example uses the filter `ContactName LIKE 'A%'` to retrieve contacts that start with A.

Extra

You can modify the table associated with the `DataView` using provided methods and properties. The `AllowEdit`, `AllowNew`, and `AllowDelete` properties specify whether the `DataView` allows you to edit field values, add new records, and delete records, respectively. You can add a record to the underlying table of the `DataView` using the `AddNew` method. The method returns a new `DataRowView` object. Use this object to edit the individual records of the new row. The `Delete` method deletes a row you specify as the only parameter to the method. When you delete the row, its state changes to `DataViewRowState.Deleted`.

You can use the constants in the `DataViewRowState` enumeration with the `RowStateFilter` property to filter records in the `DataView`.

CONSTANT	DESCRIPTION
`Added`	The rows you added since the last time you saved or accepted changes.
`CurrentRows`	The current rows including unchanged, new, and modified rows.
`Deleted`	The rows you deleted since the last time you saved or accepted changes.
`ModifiedCurrent`	The current version of rows that you have modified.
`ModifiedOriginal`	The original version of rows that you have modified.
`OriginalRows`	All original rows including unchanged and deleted rows.
`Unchanged`	An unchanged row.

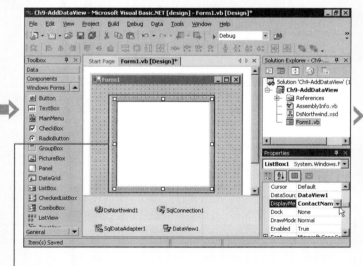

6 Add the appropriate means of viewing the data contained in the `DataView`.

Note: To add a bound control to the form, see the section "Bind a Control on the Form."

■ The example adds a `ListBox` control data bound to the `DataView` component.

■ The `DataView` performs the appropriate sort or filter before making the data available.

BIND A CONTROL ON A FORM

When you access data, you often need to allow the user to edit the data. VB .NET provides functionality in each control to automatically connect its properties to data fields. You can use binding to very quickly connect a form to a database without having to write a significant amount of code.

There are two major types of binding: Simple and complex. Most controls support one or the other type. *Simple binding* connects a single field of a single record to a control property. For example, you can link the LastName field in a database to a text box for viewing and editing. *Complex binding* involves binding an entire set of data, be it a single field from a list of records, or an entire table of data.

Simple binding functions through a property called DataBinding in any control that supports it. The property stores a collection of Binding objects that link a property in the control to a DataSet field. Visual Basic .NET enables

you to create the appropriate Binding object through the control's property page. You simply select the field to bind to the control.

To work with list of records with complex binding, you can use the ListBox, ComboBox, or CheckedListBox. Each displays a list of records that DataSet provides. Set the DataSource property to a valid DataSet and the DataMember property to the field to display. Commonly, you use the ListBox and ComboBox controls to display a list of records to edit. See the section "Move through a Dataset" for information on choosing the active record.

The ErrorProvider control also uses complex binding to monitor a DataSet for errors. This control monitors the data in the field and automatically supplies the error icon beside a control that contains a binding to the field. For more information on ErrorProvider, see the section "Validate Data."

BIND A CONTROL ON A FORM

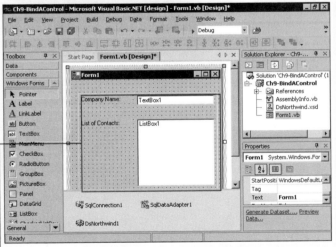

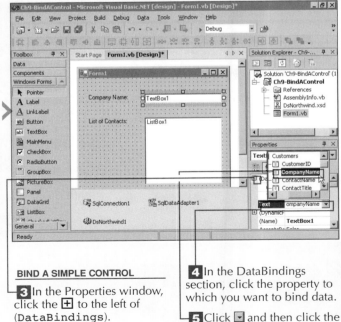

CREATE A FORM

1 Setup a database connection and database on the form.

2 Add appropriate controls to the form.

Note: See the sections "Create a Database Connection" and "Add a Connection to a Form" to set up a database. For more information about adding controls to a form, see Chapter 3.

BIND A SIMPLE CONTROL

3 In the Properties window, click the ⊞ to the left of (DataBindings).

4 In the DataBindings section, click the property to which you want to bind data.

5 Click ▾ and then click the appropriate field to bind.

Extra

If you create a `DataSet`, `DataView`, or `DataTable` component in code without using the visual designer, you may still want to bind it to a control. You can bind the component to the control using the properties discussed in this topic. For a simple object, add a new instance of the `Binding` class to the `DataBindings` collection property.

Example:
```
Dim myDataTable As New DataTable("MyTable")
myDataTable.Columns.Add("MyField")
Dim myData As DataRow = myDataTable.NewRow()
myData.Item("MyField") = "Test"
myDataTable.Rows.Add(myData)
Dim bindText As New Binding("Text", _
    myDataTable, "MyField")
TextBox1.DataBindings.Add(bindText)
```

You can bind complex controls like the `DataGrid` controls to data components without using the designer.

Example:
```
Dim myDataTable As New DataTable("MyTable")
myDataTable.Columns.Add("MyField")
Dim myData As DataRow = _
    myDataTable.NewRow()
myData.Item("MyField") = "Test"
myDataTable.Rows.Add(myData)
Dim myData As DataRow = _
    myDataTable.NewRow()
myData.Item("MyField") = "Test Item 2"
myDataTable.Rows.Add(myData)
DataGrid1.DataSource = myDataTable
```

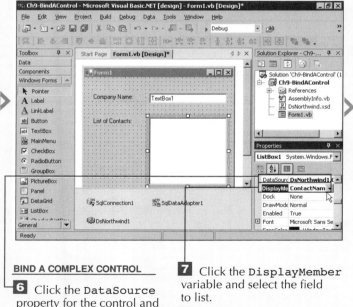

BIND A COMPLEX CONTROL

6 Click the `DataSource` property for the control and select the appropriate table.

7 Click the `DisplayMember` variable and select the field to list.

8 Press F5 to run your project.

■ The controls bind to the data set and display the first available record.

Note: See the section "Move through a Dataset" to allow changes and provide movement to controls.

MOVE THROUGH A DATASET

To effectively use your bound controls, you must give users the ability to move through the available records in the `DataSet`. Typically, a form contains the information for a single record, and back and forward controls normally enable the user to move through the records. For example, a customer database may store all of the information about a customer. The screen provides text boxes to display and allow changes to the data.

To add movement controls to a form, you need to use the `BindingContext` object provided on a form. To access the `BindingContext` for a form, use the

`Me.BindingContext` property. The object holds a list of all bound data sets on the form. You pass the name of the `DataSet` and the name of the table as the two parameters to the method. It returns a `BindingManagerBase` that matches the parameters. A `BindingManagerBase` object synchronizes all `Binding` objects that refer to the same data source. The `Position` property controls the position the bound controls show. The property is zero-based, meaning you access the first available record using `Position = 0`. The `Count` property returns the number of records available in the binding, so to move to the end of the list, set `Position` equal to `Count - 1`.

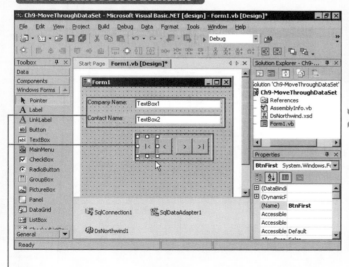

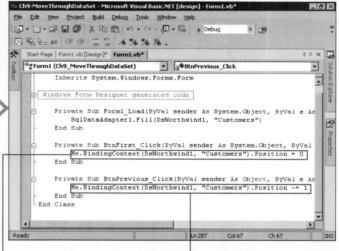

1 Set up a database connection on the form.

2 Place necessary bound input controls on the form.

3 Include a button to go to the first record, go back a record, go forward a record, and go to the last record.

Note: See the section "Bind a Control on a Form" to bind a control.

4 Double-click the appropriate button to add an event handler.

■ The Code Editor opens.

5 For the first record button, type **Me.BindingContext(Ds Northwind1, "Customers"). Position = 0**, replacing DsNorthwind1, "Customers" with the `DataSet` and table.

6 For the previous record button, type **Me.Binding Context (DsNorthwind1, "Customers"). Position –= 1**, replacing DsNorthwind1, "Customers" with the `DataSet` and table.

Apply It

You can enable users to view their current position in a data set using the following procedure. You call this procedure when the data loads initially, and after the user presses a button and you alter the `Position` property.

TYPE THIS:

```
Private Sub ShowPosition()
    Dim recordCount As Integer
    Dim currentPosition As Integer
    recordCount = Me.BindingContext(DsNorthwind1, "Customers").Count
    If recordCount = 0 Then
            Label1.Text = "(No records)"
    Else
            currentPosition = Me.BindingContext(DsNorthwind1, "Customers").Position + 1
            Label1.Text = currentPosition.ToString & " of " & recordCount.ToString
    End If
End Sub
```

RESULT:

5 of 36

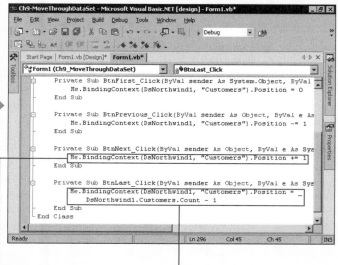

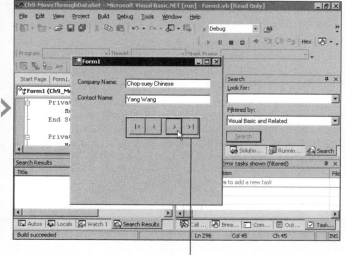

7 For the next record button, type **Me.Binding Context (DsNorthwind1, "Customers") .Position += 1**, replacing `DsNorthwind1, "Customers"` with the `DataSet` and table.

8 For the last record button, type **Me.BindingContext (DsNorthwind1, "Customers") .Position = DsNorthwind1. Customers.Count - 1**, replacing `DsNorthwind1, "Customers"` with the `DataSet` and table, and `.DsNorthwind1.Customers` with the data table.

9 Press F5 to run your project.

■ You can click the buttons to move through the records present in the table.

EDIT DATA USING BOUND CONTROLS

To make your database application truly useful, you can allow the user to not only browse the records, but also update their contents. Using bound controls allows a user to easily add, edit, and update records to the database.

The `DataSet` keeps all changes users make to records in memory. Therefore, to update the actual database, you need to write the changes back to it. The `OleDbDataAdapter` or `SqlDataAdapter` controls access the database and maintain the necessary SQL commands to perform the update. Call the `DataAdapter.Update` method to save changes in the `DataSet`. For the two parameters to the `Update` method, pass the `DataSet` object followed by the name of the table to update as a string. See the section "Validate Data" to learn how to check for errors in the `DataSet`.

When you add a table to a `DataSet` using the designer, the `DataSet` generates custom classes to represent the tables,

creating methods and properties that match the names of the actual tables and fields. In the methods and objects for this section, you replace the `Table` text with the actual name of the table you want to use. To add new records to a table in a `DataSet`, you insert the `AddTableRow` method of the table. For the parameters, you can specify a `TableRow` object, or you can specify a separate parameter for each field to the method. The `NewTableRow` method returns a row setup with the proper default values from the database, so you can use it to pass into the `AddTableRow` method.

For example, if your table is called `Customers`, the designer creates a class called `Customers` inside of the `DataSet` to match the table name. Then, the methods for the `Customers` class include `NewCustomersRow`, `AddCustomersRow`, and so on.

EDIT DATA USING BOUND CONTROLS

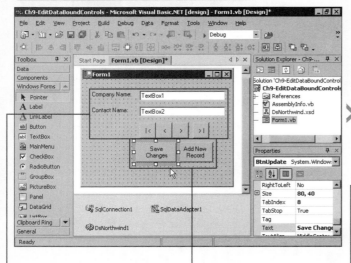

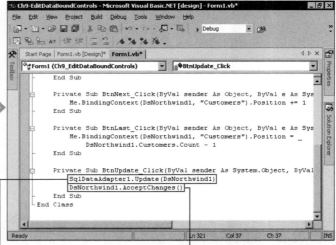

1 Set up a form with appropriate input and movement controls.

Note: To bind a control, see the section "Bind Controls to a Form." To create movement controls, see the section "Move through a Dataset."

2 Place a button on the form for the user to add and update database rows.

3 Double-click a button to go to the code editor and specify the event handler.

■ The Code Editor window appears.

4 To update the database, type **SqlDataAdapter1.Update (DsNorthwind1)**, replacing `SqlDataAdapter1` with the name of the data adapter on the form and `DsNorthwind1` with the `DataSet` that binds the controls.

5 On a new line, type **DsNorthwind1. AcceptChanges()**, replacing `DsNorthwind1` with the name of the `DataSet`.

Extra

To delete a record from a table in the `DataSet`, access the table object and use the method `RemoveTableRow`, replacing `Table` with the name of the table. You must pass the row to delete. You can access a row by index number using the `Rows` property of the table object. Pass the index of the row you wish to delete in parentheses to the `Rows` property, starting from zero, and it returns a `DataRow` object. For more information on `DataTable` objects, see "Work with Data Tables." You need to update the position that the form displays since the row no longer exists. For more information on using `BindingContext`, see "Move through a Dataset."

Example:
```
Dim pos As Integer = Me.BindingContext(DsNorthwind1, "Customers").Position
Dim row As DataRow = DsNorthwind1.Customers.Rows(pos)
DsNorthwind1.Customers.RemoveCustomersRow(row)
Me.BindingContext(DsNorthwind1, "Customers").Position -= 1
```

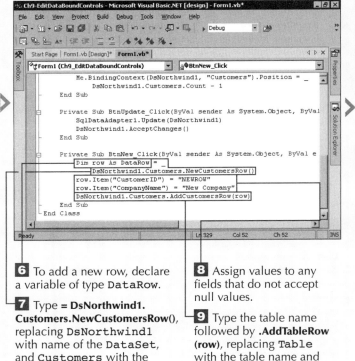

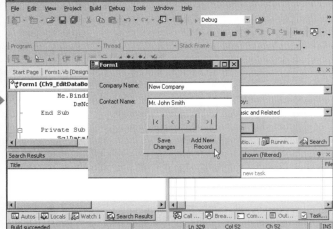

6 To add a new row, declare a variable of type `DataRow`.

7 Type **= DsNorthwind1.Customers.NewCustomersRow()**, replacing `DsNorthwind1` with name of the `DataSet`, and `Customers` with the table's name.

8 Assign values to any fields that do not accept null values.

9 Type the table name followed by **.AddTableRow (row)**, replacing `Table` with the table name and `row` with the variable declared in step 5.

■ When you run the project, you can add, edit, and update information in the database.

VALIDATE DATA

Databases contain specific rules for the data they contain. When users enter data, they may not understand the requirements of the data source. You can prevent errors in Windows applications by validating the data before allowing the user to update it to the database table.

The `ErrorProvider` control manages `DataSet` errors. For information on adding the `ErrorProvider` control to a Windows Form, see Chapter 3. To validate data with the `ErrorProvider` control, set its `DataSource` property to the `DataSet` or `DataTable` you want to monitor. If you use a `DataSet`, you must also set the `DataMember` to the table to watch.

In the form code , you must set the `ContainerControl` property of the `ErrorProvider` control to the form for data validation to occur. To check for validation issues on a control the user edits, use the input control's `Validating` event, which fires when the user leaves the input control.

When you detect an error, you set the event parameter `e.Cancel` to `True` and the control allows the user to reenter the data. You then alert the `DataRow` representing the row that the user made an error. Use the `BindingContext`'s `Position` property to determine the current row. For more information on the `BindingContext` object, see the section "Move through a Dataset."

After you find the appropriate row, call the `SetColumnError` method of the `DataRow` object. Provide the column and the error message as the two parameters. For more information on the `DataRow` object, see the section "Work with Data Rows."

You also need to respond to the control's `Validated` event, where you enter code to run when validation is successful. This event runs only if you do not set `Cancel = True` in the `Validating` event. You remove the error message by using `SetColumnError` again with a blank string for the error message.

VALIDATE DATA

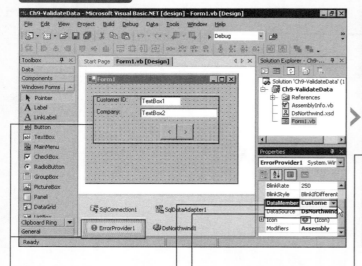

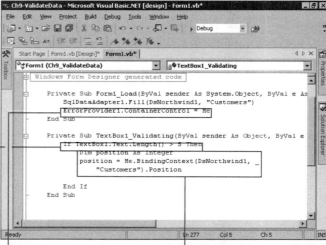

1 Set up a form with input and movement controls, and add an **ErrorProvider** control on the form.

Note: To bind a control, see "Bind Controls to a Form." To create movement controls, see "Move through a Dataset." See Chapter 3 to add an ErrorProvider control.

2 For the **ErrorProvider** control, click the **DataSource** property ⬝ and select the appropriate data set component.

■ For **DataSet**, click the **DataMember** ⬝ and select the appropriate table.

3 In the **Form_Load** event, type **ErrorProvider1.Container Control = Me**, replacing **ErrorProvider1** with the name of the **ErrorProvider** control.

4 In the **Validating** event of an input control, create an **If** statement that performs the validation test.

5 Declare a variable to hold the current record index, assigning the **Position** property of the **BindingContext** to the variable.

Note: See page the section "Move through a Dataset" to use BindingContext.

Extra Instead of validating with the `ErrorProvider`, you can use the `DataTable` object to perform validation on every record in the table with the `ColumnChanging` event. Because the `DataSet` component does not expose the table's events, you must create the event handler manually. The event expects two parameters: `sender`, an `Object` variable, and `e`, a `DataColumnChangeEventArgs` object. You can access the column that fires the event with `e.Column`. To cause a validation error, create a new `Exception` object and pass the constructor an error message. Then use the `Throw` command and pass the exception object.

Example:
```
Private Sub ColumnChanging(ByVal sender As_
   System.Object, ByVal e As_
   System.Data.DataColumnChangeEventArgs) _
   Handles DsNorthwind1.Customers.ColumnChanging
   Dim msg As String = "", control As Object
   Select Case e.Column.ColumnName
      Case "CustomerID"
         control = TextBox1
         If Len(e.ProposedValue) > 5 Then
            msg = "Value cannot be longer than 5 characters"
         End If
      Case "CustomerName"
         ...
   End Select
   e.Row.SetColumnError(e.Column, msg)
   If msg <> "" Then Throw (New Exception(msg))
End Sub
```

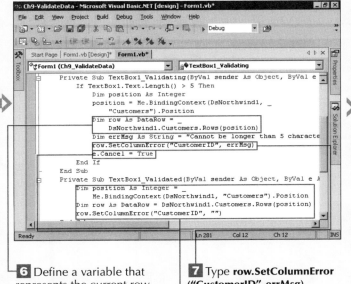

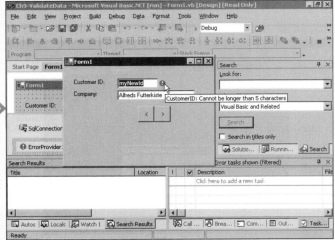

6 Define a variable that represents the current row determined in step 6.

Note: See the section "Work with Data Rows" for more about `DataRow` objects.

7 Type **row.SetColumnError ("CustomerID", errMsg)**, replacing "CustomerID" with the column name, and errMsg with an error string.

8 On a new line, type **e.Cancel = True**.

9 In the `Validated` event of the input control, type the text in step 6 through 8, replacing errMsg with "".

■ When you run the project and enter an invalid value, the error icon appears with a proper description.

CREATE A DATA RELATIONSHIP

I n most cases, a single table of a database does not store all of the information that makes up the necessary data for an application. Various tables store different parts of the information, and you combine the data from the various tables to create an application that allows the user to modify all of the related data in an effective way. You can define data relationships in your Visual Basic .NET application to create complex data displays easily.

For example, if you have a database containing an `Orders` and a `Customers` table, the `Orders` table stores all of the orders that various users make. You can use a data relationship to attach the orders that relate to a particular customer in the `Customers` table. VB .NET allows you to set up the `DataRelation` class visually with the XSD editor. When you create a `DataSet` in your application, an XSD file automatically generates to store the various tables you add to the `DataSet`. For more information on creating

`DataSet` objects, see the section "Add a Connection to the Form."

When you access the Add Relationship dialog box, it enables you to select two tables and the fields between the tables that match to create the relationship. In the previous example, you link the `CustomerID` field in the `Customers` table to the `CustomerID` field in the `Orders` table. You can also set which table functions as the parent table, the table where one record specifies multiple records in the child table. In the example, the `Customers` table is the parent because multiple orders connect to the same single customer.

Once you create a relationship, you can display the parent table in a `DataGrid` control and each record automatically links to child records. For more information on creating a `DataGrid` control, see the section "Add a DataGrid Control."

CREATE A DATA RELATIONSHIP

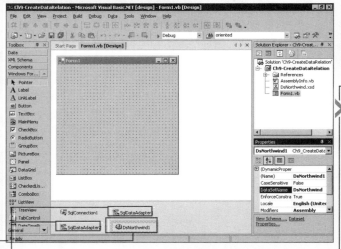

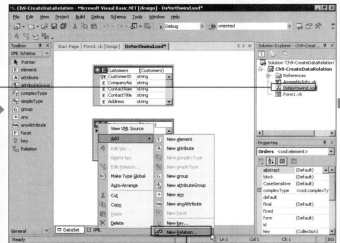

1 Set up two data adapters presenting different tables that relate.

2 When you generate the dataset, add both tables from the adapters to the same `DataSet`.

Note: To create the data connection, see "Create a Database Connection." To add data adapters to the form and set up a `DataSet` object, see "Add a Connect to the Form."

3 Double-click the dataset XSD schema file in the Solution Explorer.

4 Right-click one of the tables and click Add ➪ New Relation.

Extra

To create a `DataRelation` object manually, you create an instance of the class and pass a name for the relation as the first parameter. Pass the column in the parent table to link as the second, and the column in the child table to link as the third parameter. After you create the `DataRelation` object, assign it to the `DataSet.Relations` object using the `Add` method.

To manually retrieve the associated entries from the child table, call the `GetChildRows` method of a `DataRow` with the relationship name as the parameter. The method returns an array of `DataRow` objects that contains the child data associated with the parent record. You can go in the other direction and retrieve the parent rows that relate to a particular child row using the `GetParentRows` method of a `DataRow`.

Example:
```
Dim parentCol As DataColumn =
    DsNorthwind1.Customers.CustomerID

Dim childCol As DataColumn =
    DsNorthwind1.Orders.CustomerID

Dim relCustOrder As DataRelation

relCustOrder = New
    DataRelation("CustomersOrders", parentCol,
    childCol)

DsNorthwind1.Relations.Add(relCustOrder)
```

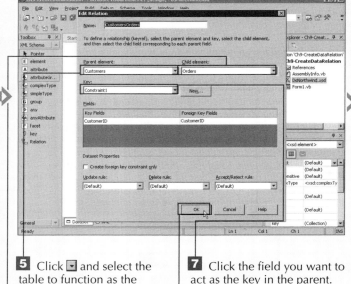

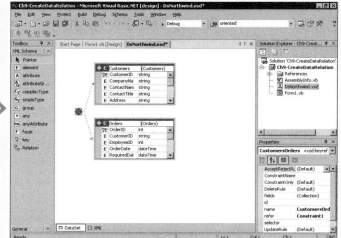

5 Click ▼ and select the table to function as the parent.

6 Click ▼ and select the table to function as the child.

7 Click the field you want to act as the key in the parent.

■ If the dialog box does not properly select the field to act as the child, click the proper field.

8 Click OK.

■ The schema editor creates the relationship.

■ You can save and close the schema as well as add controls to display the relationship.

Note: See the section "Add a DataGrid Control" to add a `DataGrid` *control, which is capable of natively displaying data with relationships.*

ADD A DATA GRID CONTROL

The `DataGrid` control allows you to provide an editable table-like interface to a table or database query. You can use the `DataGrid` to easily provide editing or viewing functionality on a form without creating individual edit controls for each data field. In some cases, however, using a form full of simple controls makes more sense for a table with many fields or lots of records. For information on the `DataGrid` Web Forms control, see Chapter 10.

You find the `DataGrid` control in the Windows Forms section of the Toolbox. You can link the control using the `DataSource` property to a `DataSet`, `DataView`, or a table contained inside a `DataSet`. The grid automatically creates the necessary columns for the bound grid. If you link the grid directly to a `DataSet` component containing multiple tables, each table displays with a hyperlink, which the user can click to access individual tables. Tables containing relationships also provide hyperlinks for each row to access the child records pertaining to the displayed record. A back button appears as necessary at the top of the grid control to move to the parent table. The control also displays information about a parent record when you move to a child relationship in a single scrolling line in the header.

You can sort the grid automatically by clicking the column headers. You do not need to bind to a `DataView` control to support sorting. You can disable sorting with the `AllowSorting` property. You can set a style for the appearance of the grid using the Auto Format dialog.

When the user makes changes to items in the grid, the grid automatically updates the associated `DataTable` inside the `DataSet` of `DataView`. You must save changes to the database manually. For more information on saving changed information to the database, see the section "Move through a Dataset."

ADD A DATA GRID CONTROL

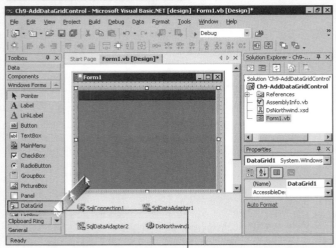

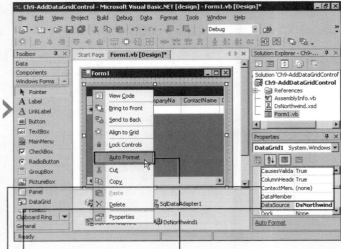

1 Set up a database connection and dataset on the form.

Note: See the sections "Create a Database Connection" and "Add a Connection to a Form" to set up a database.

2 Click and drag the `DataGrid` control from the Windows Forms section of the Toolbox to the form.

3 Click the `DataSource` property ▼ and select the `DataSet` control or table you want to display.

4 Set any necessary properties.

Note: To set properties, see Chapter 2.

5 To format the appearance of the grid, right-click the `DataGrid` control on the form.

6 Click Auto Format.

Extra

You can use the `TableStyles` property to modify the appearance of tables you display in the grid. When you bind the control to a `DataSet`, go to the `TableStyles` property in the Properties window and click the link button (🔘) button. Add a `DataGridTableStyle` object and set the `MappingName` to one of the tables in the `DataGrid`. Then click the `GridColumnStyle` property in the object editor and click 🔘. Here, you can add the columns to display for specified table. Also, by clicking the 🔽 beside Add, you can add text columns or check-box columns. Use the `MappingName` property of each `DataGridColumn` to specify the data column to display, and customize any appropriate properties. You can specify formatting strings using the `Format` property, the width of the column using the `Width` property, and the header text using the `HeaderText` property. You can create multiple `DataGridTableStyle` objects for each table the grid displays, like child relationships. When you run your project and a table appears for which you define a style, and the grid automatically uses the style.

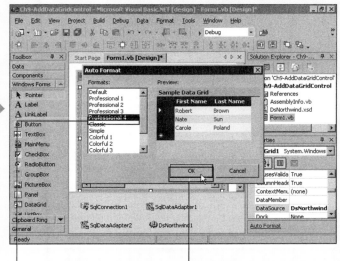

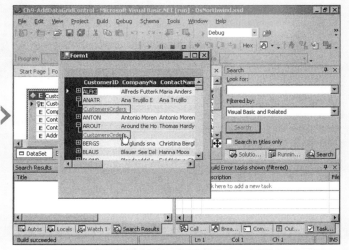

7 Click a style to apply.

■ A preview displays.

8 Click OK to select the style.

9 Press F5 to run your project.

■ The `DataGrid` displays the data in the table and gives hyperlinks to related tables.

AN INTRODUCTION TO WEB FORMS

Web Forms, a new technology in the .NET Framework, provides a visual design tool for ASP.NET applications inside of Visual Basic .NET. You build a Visual Studio Web application around ASP.NET, a platform that includes design-time objects and controls, as well as a runtime for developing and running applications on a Web server.

A part of the .NET Framework, ASP.NET is integrated with the rest of the Framework and can access all of its features. For example, you can create ASP.NET Web applications using any .NET programming language, and then debug with the .NET facilities. You access data using ADO.NET, just like in a standard Windows Forms application. Similarly, you can access operating system and other services using .NET Framework classes.

HOSTING REQUIREMENTS

ASP.NET Web applications run on a Web server configured with Microsoft Internet Information Services (IIS). You do not, however, need to work directly within IIS. Visual Studio handles file management tasks such as creating IIS applications when needed, and provides ways for you to deploy your Web applications to IIS.

Before attempting to host your application on a remote server, make sure the server supports ASP.NET development. To find more information about Microsoft-endorsed ASP.NET hosting solutions, visit www.microsoft.com/asp/ and click the Hosted Applications Partner Directory.

HTML AND CLIENT-SIDE HTML CONTROLS

Because ASP.NET is a universal server-side architecture, it works only with standard HyperText Markup Language (HTML), the standard for transferring web pages over the HyperText Transfer Protocol (HTTP) protocol, for its output. HTML files contain tags consisting of a text command inside angle brackets (<>). You embed these tags in the text to create rich interfaces with fonts, colors, tables, and other layouts. For example, to make a block of text appear bold, you place <b> in front of, and a </b> at the end of the block of text you want to make bold. You can add standard HTML markup to text you include in pages and labels.

To provide interactivity, ASP.NET relies on standard HTML <form> blocks. Client-side HTML controls enable you to accept simple data and send it to the server. You use these controls constantly to login to a Web site and sign up for services. The table lists the available HTML input controls and the similar control in Windows Forms for comparison. Because HTML has few input controls available, you may find it difficult to create complex environments using HTML.

HTML TAG	SIMILAR WINDOWS FORMS CONTROL
`<input type="button">`	`Button` control.
`<input type="checkbox">`	`Checkbox` control.
`<input type="radio">`	`RadioButton` control.
`<input type="text">`	`TextBox` control (single-line only).
`<textarea>`	`TextBox` control (multi-line).
`<input type="password">`	A `TextBox` control with the `PasswordChar` property set.
`<input type="hidden">`	No equivalent; functions like a private variable that the user does not see but sends back to the server.
`<input type="image">`	`PictureBox` control.
`<input type="file">`	No equivalent; allows the user to upload a file to the server.

ASP.NET FRAMEWORK

You build Web Forms pages on the ASP.NET Page Framework. Each Web Forms page, object that derives from the ASP.NET Page class, acts as a container for controls. When users request a Web Forms page, the Page Framework runs the Web Forms page object and all the individual controls on it. The output of the Page class and of all the controls it contains is standard HTML that a Web browser can process. The page consists of a standard <FORM> combined with client-side scripting, if supported, so it can capture user actions and send them back to the server. The Page Framework processes these in a way that lets you treat them as standard events. You can choose from a large selection of controls available in Visual Studio. In addition, you can create your own custom controls.

Despite its many attributes, you may find it very difficult for Web Forms to generate something that works and feels like an application. Web Forms uses the HTTP protocol, which is *stateless*, meaning a connection to a server only lasts long enough to download a page, after which the browser "forgets" about the server until the user presses a link or button. To help, the Page Framework includes facilities for managing state. These include page-based "viewstate" — a method for preserving values in controls — and access to non-page-based state facilities such as Session state (user-specific) and Application state (global to the application).

The Page class is the base class for all of the Web Forms in your application. For more information on using a Web Form, see the section "Using a Web Form."

WEB FORMS EVENT MODEL

The ASP.NET event system contains some very important differences from the version with which you build standard Windows Forms applications. ASP.NET uses the POST method to send information back from the client Web browser to the server using the results of the <Form> block, so all of the controls on the Web Form must exist within the <Form> block. ASP.NET then interprets the form results on the server, and fires the appropriate event in your Page object. Web Forms uses JavaScript for client-side scripting to add more interactivity to hyperlinks and HTML controls.

Limited events

To create a Web application, you must design your application with the smallest possible amount of interaction between the user and the code. Because the client must send information back, or post-back information, to the server when an event occurs, Windows Application events such as MouseMove and KeyPress become impractical and impossible; events that report mouse movement and individual changes in a text box cannot be continually reported back to the server. Most Web Forms events, therefore, consist of simple click events that alert you when a user clicks a particular button or selects a particular item in a box. Most controls add events that cause less performance problems, such as the TextChanged event on the TextBox control, which only fires when the user leaves the TextBox.

Post-back/non-post-back events

The term *post-back* means that the browser requests a new version of the page from the server; the control the user interacts with causes the page to submit back to the server. Except for button controls, the Web server controls do not immediately post-back to the server for all events. These events, called *non-post-back events* by ASP.NET, do not fire on the server until a post-back event occurs. Keep in mind which events need to immediately update the display and which events you can wait to handle until the user presses a button. For example, the SelectIndexChanged event of the ListBox and DropDownList controls do not fire as soon as the user selects an item. Instead, it fires along with a method that uses post-back, like a Button's Click event. This reduces the number of times the page must refresh and prevents interruptions to the user's workflow. You can use properties to enable post-back in the ListBox, ComboBox, and option controls that do not post-back to the server by default.

CREATE A WEB APPLICATION

The Web Application project lets you begin building Web Forms-based applications that use standard HTML to generate a client interface that any user can access with a standard browser. Your Web application automatically maintains information about state, used to create a seamless application that shares information across multiple pages, and connects a full object model to the HTML controls used on the client to let you interact with the controls on the server.

To create a Web Application project, you simply select the ASP.NET Web Application template in the New Project dialog box. The name you specify for the project generates a folder in your standard Visual Studio project directory that contains the solution and project files. Visual Studio also creates a folder given by the project name on the server, sets appropriate security settings for that folder, and creates an IIS application for the folder; this application specifies

that IIS can execute the ASP.NET scripts and runs the files in a separate memory space. The project template also adds a single Web Form to the project, which functions as the main, or default, page. The Web Form is given the name `WebForm1.aspx` by default. Visual Studio stores the code for this Web Form in a separate file named. If IIS runs on your development machine, the Web project directory typically stores in C:\Inetpub\wwwroot\.

When you run a Web Application project, the Visual Studio builds the VB .NET code files into a *dynamic link library* (DLL) that the ASPX files use to perform their operations. The ASPX files contain the HTML necessary to generate the page appearance and the appropriate hooks to access appropriate methods and event handlers in your project DLL file. For more information on working with your Web Form, see the section "Using a Web Form," later in this chapter.

CREATE A WEB APPLICATION

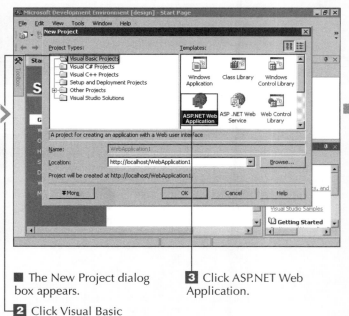

1 Click File ➪ New ➪ Project.

■ If the Start page is visible, click the New Project button.

■ The New Project dialog box appears.

2 Click Visual Basic Projects.

■ The New Project dialog box appears.

3 Click ASP.NET Web Application.

Extra

When Visual Basic .NET creates your project, it creates a standard project file, solution file, and one Web Forms page. The project also contains a number of other files that affect how the project functions and how pages in the project appear. You can use these files to customize the way your project works.

PROJECT FILE	WHAT IT CONTAINS
WebForm1.aspx	The actual ASP.NET Web page that shows in the Solution Explorer to represent your form. Stores all of the controls added to the form and layout information.
WebForm1.aspx.vb	Unlike a Windows Forms application, the Development Studio hides the actual .vb class file from you. When you access the source editor for a Web Forms page, this file appears.
Global.asax	Maintains the entire application space for IIS. The file provides a number of methods you can use to customize your project. The server calls Application_BeginRequest at the beginning of each request for any page in the project, Application_AuthenticationRequest when the user authenticates on a locked directory, and Application_Error when an error occurs in any page. The global asax file contains comments on all of the available methods.
Styles.css	The default cascading style sheet (CSS) for the project. The Development Studio provides a built-in visual editor for style sheets. Most controls provide a CssClass property that enables you to assign a defined class from this file.

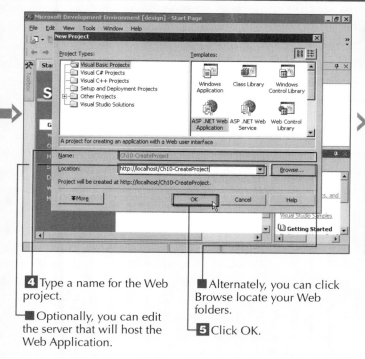

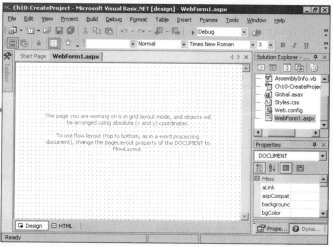

■4 Type a name for the Web project.

■ Optionally, you can edit the server that will host the Web Application.

■ Alternately, you can click Browse locate your Web folders.

■5 Click OK.

■ VB .NET creates the folder on the Web server, loads the new project, and shows the default page.

Note: See the section "Using a WebForm" to work with this page.

USING A WEB FORM

You use a Web Form to develop a page in your ASP.NET application using the Visual Studio Development environment. Web Forms provide visual layout ability, and rich property and event model that function much like their Windows Forms counterparts. Adding controls on a Web Form simplifies building interactive functionality in your Web-based application. Web Forms have some significant differences from Windows Forms-based applications. Unlike Windows Forms, the user can resize and scroll the browser as necessary to view the contents of your Web Form.

You have two options for page layout: *Flow layout* and *Grid layout*. The flow layout functions like a standard Web page in that you add controls, which you place one after the other on the page. Alternately, you can place controls in tables to create the appropriate appearance. The grid layout functions more like an actual Windows Form. You drag and

drop Web controls anywhere on the page and the designer generates CSS positioning code. If you force old browser compatibility, the code generates tables to properly place all of the controls. You can choose the layout for a particular Web Form by altering its `pageLayout` property. You can also change the minimum supported browser for the page using the `targetSchema` property.

You have various properties to change the appearance of your Web Form. You set the title for the page with the `title` property, specify a page description — stored as a `<META>` tag — with the `Description` property, and specify a `<META>` list of keywords with the `keywords` property. You can also add margins around the form to create space from the browser window edges using the `leftMargin`, `rightMargin`, `topMargin`, and `bottomMargin` properties.

USING A WEB FORM

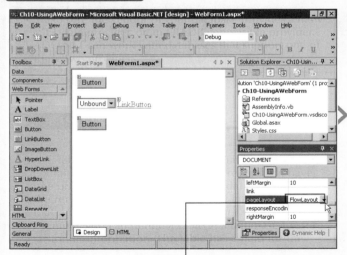

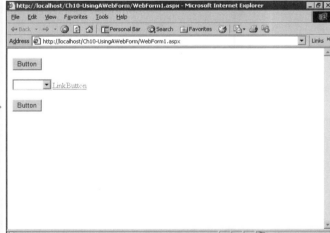

USING A FLOW LAYOUT

1 Create a new Web Application project or open an existing one.

Note: See the section "Create a Web Application" to create a Web Application project.

2 In the Properties window, click the **pageLayout** property's ▾ and select **FlowLayout**.

3 In the toolbox, double-click various Web forms controls to add them to the form.

■ When you run your project by pressing F5, the page displays the controls in a flowing layout that resizes as necessary when the browser resizes.

Extra

You can use properties and events of the `Page` object that your Web Form uses to specify details and provide event handling for the page loading. Below is a partial list of the available members.

PROPERTIES	
`Application`	Provides a reference to the `Application` object associated with the project. The object manages the state for the entire application.
`ClientTarget`	Indicates the capabilities of the browser making the request. ASP.NET uses this information during execution to deliver code depending on the browser.
`ErrorPage`	Set this property to specify the page that the client is sent to if an unhandled exception in your form's code.
`IsPostBack`	Indicates whether the page is being processed in response to a client post-back or whether it is being accessed for the first time.
`IsValid`	Indicates whether page validation succeeded.
`Validators`	A collection of the validation controls on the page.

EVENTS	
`Init`	Fires when the `Page` object loads the first time.
`Load`	Fires each time the user requests the page.
`Unload`	Fires when the `Page` object unloads from memory.

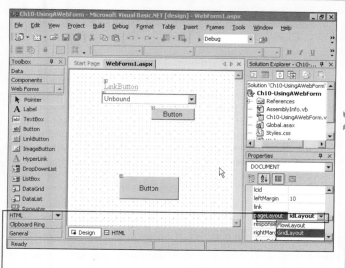

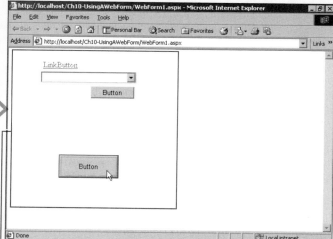

USING A GRID LAYOUT

1 Create a new Web Application project or open an existing one.

2 In the Properties window, click the `pageLayout` property's ▾ and select `GridLayout`.

3 In the toolbox, click a control and then drag the control onto the Web Form in the desired position and size.

4 Run your project by pressing F5.

■ The grid layout maintains the exact position at runtime that you specify in design mode.

ADD A LABEL CONTROL

You can use a `Label` control to display text on your Web Form page. Although you can type text directly onto the page without the `Label` control in Flow layout, using the `Label` control in Grid layout lets you precisely place text; the Grid layout, however, does not support typing text onto the page. To learn more about the Flow and Grid layouts, see the section, "Using a Web Form." Unlike its Windows equivalent, the `Label` control does not support events. In fact, a `Label` control is little more than text you place on the form with standard HTML. To register a click, you must use a `Button` or `HyperLink` control. For more information on the `Button` control, see the section "Add a Button Control."

You access the `Label` and other Web Form controls via the Toolbox. The `Text` property controls the text that appears in the label. Text you place in the `Label` control wraps at the right side, and cannot run outside of the control's

bounds. Visual Studio automatically resizes the control to make the text fit. Because the contents of the `Label` directly outputs to the Web page that ASP.NET generates, you can include HTML formatting tags directly inside the `Text` property.

You can modify the control's appearance with properties similar to the Windows Forms version of the `Label` control. The `BackColor` property specifies the background color to place in the `Label`. You can alter the text's color with `ForeColor` and edit the text's font with the `Font` object.

You can create various borders around the text with the `BorderStyle` property. Available border settings include `NotSet`, which uses the default setting of the page, `None`, `Solid`, `Double`, `Inset`, `Outset`. You can use the `BorderWidth` property to control how large the border draws, and the `BorderColor` alter the border's color.

ADD A LABEL CONTROL

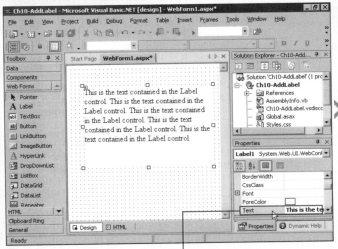

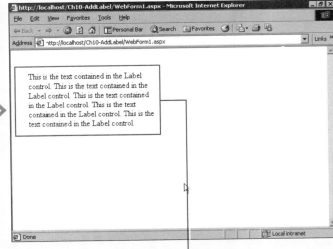

1 Open a Web Application project.

2 In the Toolbox, click and drag the `Label` control to add it to the form.

Note: See the section "Using a Web Form" to add a control to the form.

3 Type text into the `Text` property in the Properties window.

■ You can modify the appearance by clicking the `BorderStyle` property's ▼ and selecting a style or typing a size for the `BorderColor` property.

4 Press F5 to run your project.

■ The text displays on the form appropriately.

ADD A HYPERLINK CONTROL

You can create a hyperlink on an HTML page to link one page to another with the HyperLink. You can link to other forms in your application, to standard Web pages on your server, or to remote server locations.

You can use either text or an image as the object of your link. You set a hyperlink's displayed text with the Text property. If you display an image, you set the ImageUrl property to a valid URL string to an image to load. The control does not display the Text property when you set the ImageUrl property on the page; instead the text displays as a placeholder while the image loads and the user can see the Text as a tooltip when holding the mouse over the image.

You set the URL to which the HyperLink control links using the NavigateUrl property. Because this control contains no events, the link immediately connects to the new page. If you leave the NavigateURL property blank, the browser renders the text as a standard label without a link.

You can change how the link loads into the browser using the Target property. The Target property provides the standard link targets: _blank, _parent, _self, and _top. The _blank target opens a new browser window and loads the linked page. The _parent target loads the link into the immediate parent frame of the current page. The default action, the _self target replaces the current page with the linked page. The _top target renders the content into the current window, and removes any currently displayed framesets. The property also provides one more target, _search, which loads the link into the search sidebar of Microsoft Internet Explorer. If the user's browser does not support the _search target, the page loads into the current frame.

ADD A HYPERLINK CONTROL

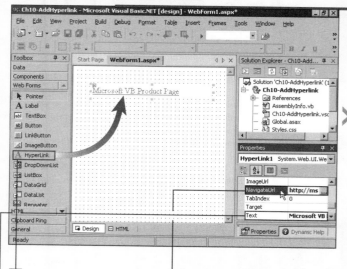

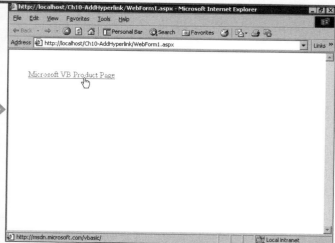

1 Click and drag the **HyperLink** control in the Toolbox of an open Web Application project.

2 Type text into the **Text** property in the Properties window.

■ Set the hyperlink to appear as an image by typing the image's URL into the **ImageUrl** property.

3 Type a URL to link to in the **NavigateUrl** property.

■ Modify the **Target** property by clicking ▼ and selecting a new target for the link.

4 Press F5 to run your project.

■ The hyperlink takes you to the specified URL.

ADD A BUTTON CONTROL

You can create a button, the simplest form of interaction, so that users can perform an action on your Web Form. Most users understand that buttons accept changes they make on a Web page form, thus making your application easier to use.

Button controls on Web Forms can take one of three appearances depending on your needs. The `Button` control creates a standard button control similar to the one you see on any HTML form. The `LinkButton` creates a hyperlink, using JavaScript support in the browser that functions as a button. The `ImageButton` creates an image that the user can click.

To create both the `LinkButton` and `Button` controls, you add the control from the Toolbox onto the form and then set the `Text` property. For an `ImageButton`, you set the `ImageUrl` property to load an image and the `AlternateText` property to specify text if the user does

not load the image. You can modify the style of all three button types using CSS properties. The `BackColor` property controls the background color of the button, while `BorderColor` controls the color to use for the edges of the button. You can alter the style of the border with the `BorderStyle` property. `BorderStyle` supports all standard CSS borders, such as `Dashed`, `Solid`, and `Ridge`. The default is `NotSet`, which means that the HTML file contains no setting and that the browser uses the default appearance. You can assign a keyboard key that the user can press to bring *focus,* or make the control the active control onscreen, to the button using the `AccessKey` property. Set it to a single character, and the user can then press Alt plus the character to focus the button.

When the user presses the button, the browser sends the form request back to the server, and your application fires the `Click` event. When the available event code completes, a new page is sent back to the user.

ADD A BUTTON CONTROL

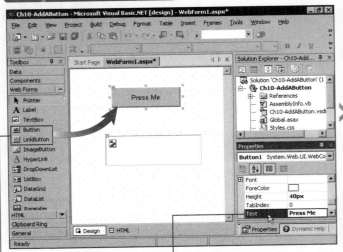

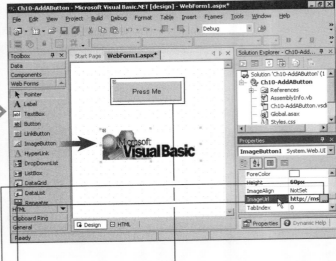

1 In the Toolbox, click the **LinkButton**, **Button**, or **ImageButton** control in the Toolbox and add it to the Web form.

Note: To add a control, see the section "Using a Web Form."

2 For the **Button** control, type a caption into the **Text** property in the Properties window.

■ This example shows a **Button** control and an **ImageButton** control.

3 For the **ImageButton** control, click the **ImageUrl** property and type a URL to a valid image file.

■ You can click the link button (⋯) to browse the IIS project directory for an image.

■ You can type the **AlternateText** for the **ImageButton** to display.

4 Double-click the control.

Apply It

To create a list of buttons that perform together, you can set each of the buttons in the list's `CommandName` property to a single name and set the `CommandArgument` property to a specific value. For example, in a shopping page, you may have ten Add to Cart buttons. You can set the `CommandName` equal to "AddToCart" and set each `CommandArgument` to the ID of the product.

TYPE THIS:

```
Sub HandleCommandAction(ByVal sender As Object, _
    ByVal e As System.Web.UI.WebControls.CommandEventArgs) _
    Handles Button1.Command, Button2.Command

    If e.CommandName = "AddToCart" Then
        Dim productNumber As Integer = CInt(e.CommandArgument)
        Label1.Text = "You chose to buy product #" & productNumber
    End If
End Sub
```

RESULT:

You chose to buy product #145

>

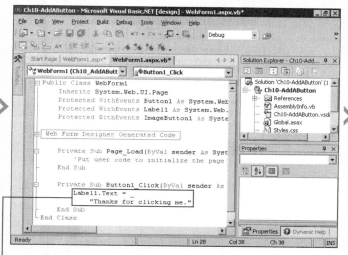

■ The **Click** event loads in the Code Editor.

5 Type code to specify an action for the button.

■ The example changes the text displayed in a label control.

6 Press F5 to run your application.

Note: To work with label controls, see the section "Add a Label Control." For general coding tasks, see Chapter 4.

■ Your Web Application responds to a button-click using your server-side code.

ADD OPTION CONTROLS

You can create `CheckBox` and `RadioButton` controls for users to select on your Web Form. These controls function nearly identically to the controls with the same name in the Windows Forms Framework. The `CheckBox` control enables the user to select multiple check boxes on the form, while a `RadioButton` control allows the user to select only a particular control from the group.

You use the `Text` property to set text for both of the option controls. You can place HTML codes inside the `Text` property to create bold, italics, or various size fonts. The `TextAlign` property specifies if the text displays to the right or left of the check box or radio button, with the default being `Right`. You can use an option control with no text combined with an `Image` to provide selections for graphical items. If you choose an image, the text displays as a tooltip when the mouse rests over the image.

For the `RadioButton` control, the `GroupName` property specifies the name of the group for the control. Specify the same group name for a set of `RadioButton` controls to make them function together. If the user selects one of the items in the group, all of the other items in the group deselect.

For check boxes, you can use the `Checked` property to retrieve or set the check status of the control. If the form submits and the user selected an option control, the `Checked` of that option control property equals `True`.

To create a long set of either check boxes or radio buttons, you can use the `CheckBoxList` or `RadioButtonList` controls, which enable you to create one Web Forms control with an entire set of controls automatically. You can also bind the list control to a database to have a list of items created automatically. For more information, see the section "Work with Option List Controls."

ADD OPTION CONTROLS

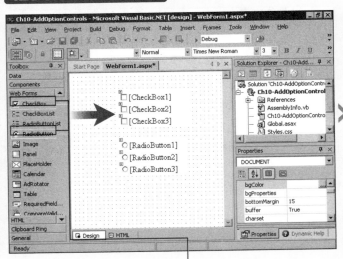

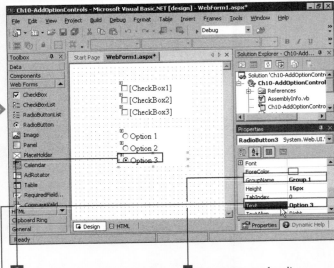

1 Create a new Web Application project or open an existing one.

Note: See the section "Create a Web Application" to create a Web Application project.

2 Click either the `CheckBox` or `RadioButton` control in the Toolbox and add an appropriate number of the control to the form.

Note: See the section "Using a Web Form" to add a control.

3 Click a control to select it.

4 Type a caption into the `Text` property.

5 Set the radio button or check box properties.

■ For a group of radio buttons, type the same group name for each of the controls you create into the `GroupName` property.

Extra

In some cases, you may want to place code for controlling the `RadioButton` or `CheckBox` control inside a separate event, rather than handling it in a button that accepts changes in the form. You can use the `CheckedChanged` event of both controls to monitor changes to the `Checked` property. The event is a non-post-back event, so the event stores and fires as soon as the user invokes an event that requires a server connection, like clicking a button.

You may want to know immediately when the user clicks one of the controls. Normally, VB .NET saves the event and fires it along with a post-back event to cause fewer round-trip connections to the server, which can consume a significant amount of time and interrupt the user. You can use the `AutoPostBack` property to enable post-back behavior for this control. When you set `AutoPostBack` to `True`, the `CheckedChanged` property causes the browser to submit the page to the server, allowing your event to fire and a new page to generate.

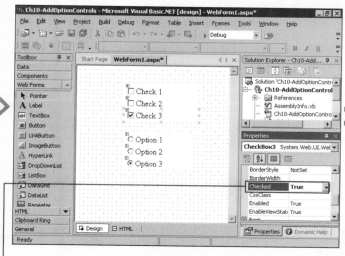

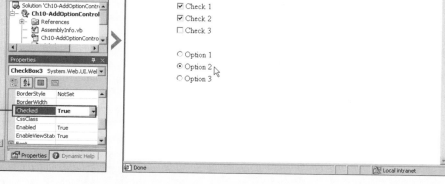

6 Double-click the `Checked` property to toggle it to `True` for appropriate controls.

■ For radio buttons, only one radio in a group can have `Checked = True`.

7 Edit any optional properties.

8 Run your project by pressing F5.

■ The option buttons respond to user input and let you make selections.

WORK WITH OPTION LIST CONTROLS

Option list controls, only available in Web Forms, let you provide a list of multiple check boxes or radio buttons that function as a single control. You can also add and work with individual `CheckBox` and `RadioButton` controls to a page. Working with the controls individually lets you control the layout and appearance of each item, applying separate fonts and colors. The two option lists create a sequence of options easily, and can bind to a database to automatically provide the selection list. The section "Adding Option Controls" provides more information on `CheckBox` and `RadioButton` controls, and "Bind A Field to a List Control" shows how to bind controls to a database.

The `CheckBoxList` and `RadioButtonList` controls create a sequence of `CheckBox` or `RadioButton` controls, respectively. For each `RadioButtonList`, the user may select only one of the controls listed; for each `CheckBoxList`, the user can select any number of items

listed. You can use these lists to generate a selection menu on a form while simplifiying the page. To provide the list, edit the `Items` collection. The List Items Collection Editor lets you specify the caption for each item with the `Name` property, and assign a `Value` to each item to distinguish the items from one another. If you do not set the `Value` property, the control assigns the text in `Name` to the `Value` property.

The `SelectedIndexChanged` event let you handle a selection. A non-post-back event, it stores and fires when the user invokes an event that requires a server connection, such as clicking a button. See the section "An Introduction to Web Forms" for more information on events. For the `RadioButtonList`, access the single selected item using the `SelectedItem` or `SelectedIndex` property. For the `CheckBoxList`, use a `For Each` loop to loop through the `Items` collection. Check each item's `Selected` property to see if the user selected the item.

WORK WITH OPTION LIST CONTROLS

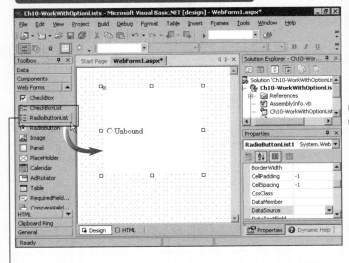

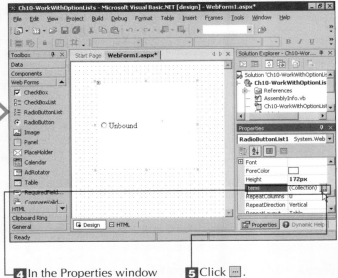

1 Create a new Web Application project or open an existing one.

2 Click either the **CheckBoxList** or **RadioButtonList** control.

3 Add the control to the form.

Note: See "Create a Web Application" to create a Web Application project and "Using a Web Form" to add a control to a Web form.

4 In the Properties window for the control, click the **Items** property.

5 Click ⌐.

Extra

You can use a set of properties provided by both of the option controls to change their default appearance, beyond standard font and color changes. Both the `CheckBoxList` and `RadioButtonList` controls list the options contained in the `Items` collection from top to bottom by default. You can change the `RepeatDirection` property from `Vertical` to `Horizontal` to make the list of items flow from left to right instead of top to bottom. You can set the `RepeatColumns` to have the list control split the items into a number of columns. A value of either zero or one causes the control to show one column, a value of two shows two columns, and so on.

Normally, the option list controls do not fire an event immediately after an item changes. They wait until a control posts back to the server for the event to fire. You can change this default behavior, and cause the option list controls to post back to the server and fire the `SelectedIndexChanged` event immediately. Set the `AutoPostBack` property equal to `True` for this behavior to occur. This requires the user's Web browser to reload the page, which causes performance issues on all but a direct network connection to the Web server.

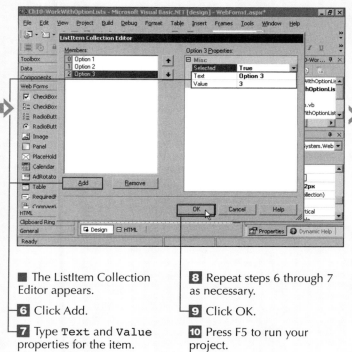

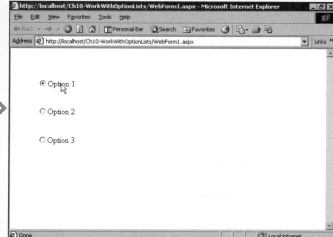

■ The ListItem Collection Editor appears.

6 Click Add.

7 Type **Text** and **Value** properties for the item.

■ If desired, you can set `Selected = True`.

8 Repeat steps 6 through 7 as necessary.

9 Click OK.

10 Press F5 to run your project.

■ The `CheckBoxList` or `RadioButtonList` allows selection of the items it contains.

USING VALIDATION CONTROLS

Validation controls enable you to check the values of user-entered data to ensure the values make sense. The validation controls automatically generate client-side scripts to provide this validation.

Web Forms provide a number of validation controls. The `RequiredFieldValidator` ensures that the user completes in an input control, such as a text box. The `RangeValidator` checks that a user's entry falls in a valid range of values. The `CompareValidator` checks the user's entry in one control against that in another control, or against a string value. For information on the regular expression validation, see the section "Work with Regular Expression Validation." To create a listing of validation errors, see the section "Provide a Validation Summary."

A validation control binds to a single input control on the form that you specify using the `ControlToValidate` property. The `ErrorMessage` property appears in the validation control when the validation fails. The `Display` property controls how the control shows errors. If you set

`Display` to `Static`, the control uses space on the form but remains blank until an error occurs. With the `Dynamic` setting, the control uses no space until an error occurs, and then becomes visible. If you set the page layout to Flow, this moves elements on the page to make space for the validation control. The `EnableClientScipt` property enables the use of JavaScript to perform the validation on the client. Otherwise, the control performs the validation using a round trip to the server.

For the `CompareValidator` control, you set the `ControlToCompare` property or the `ValueToCompare` property against the the text you want to compare. The `Operator` property specifies the comparison. The `Type` property specifies the variable type to use for the comparison.

For the `RangeValidator` control, set the `MinimumValue` and `MaximumValue` properties to the lower bound and upper bound of the acceptable entries. Use `Type` to specify the variable type for the comparison.

USING VALIDATION CONTROLS

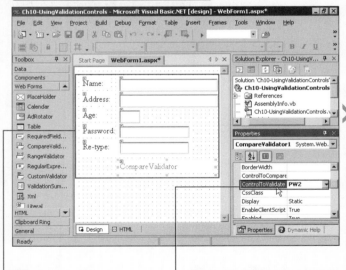

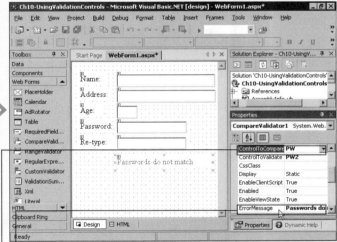

1 Create a new Web Application project or open an existing one.

2 Add necessary input controls to the form and validation controls to the form.

Note: See the sections "Create a Web Application" to create a new project and "Using a Web Form" to add controls.

3 In the Properties window, click the ▼ `ControlToValidate` and click the appropriate input control.

4 Type an error message into the **ErrorMessage** property.

5 For the `CompareValidator`, click `ControlToCompare`'s ▼ and select a control or type a value for the `ValueToCompare` property.

■ If necessary, click the `Operator` ▼ and `Type` to select a value.

Extra

Each of the validation controls, except for the RequiredFieldValidator control, accepts a blank entry without causing a validation error. In the input controls you validate, you may want to perform a test using a RangeValidator or RegularExpressionValidator control but do not want the user to leave the input control blank. For example, a RangeValidator control accepts a blank value even if the range for the validation is from 10 to 100. You can require the user to provide an entry for the input control and then validate the entry by adding a RequiredFieldValidator along with the RangeValidator, RegularExpressionValidator, or other validation control. You then specify the same input control in the ControlToValidate property for each validation control. You can customize the error message appropriately for each validation control using the individual ErrorMessage properties of the two validation controls. To conserve space for the use of two different validation controls relating to a single control, you can add a validation summary control. For more information on the ValidationSummary control, see the section "Provide a Validation Summary."

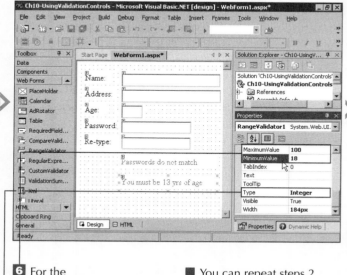

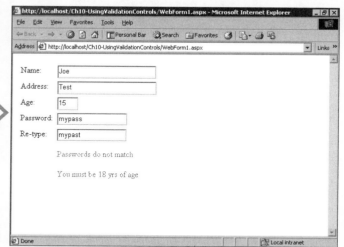

6 For the RangeValidator control, set the MinimumValue and MaximumValue properties.

■ If necessary, click the Type ▾ and select a value .

■ You can repeat steps 2 through 6 as necessary.

7 Press F5 to run your project.

■ The validation controls validate the data in the input controls appropriately.

WORK WITH REGULAR EXPRESSION VALIDATION

A method of testing a string with a complex condition set, a *regular expression* specifies a format that a string must follow. You can use the `RegularExpressionValidator` control on your Web Forms to use a regular expression to validate complex data entries, such as phone numbers, social security numbers, or other strings that follow standard formats. To set up the validation control, you set the `ControlToValidate` property to a valid input control, using the `ErrorMessage` property to specify the message. For more information on the standard properties of validation controls, see the section "Using Validation Controls."

To setup the validator, you assign the regular expression you create to the `ValidationExpression` property. To build a regular expression, determine the test that needs to occur on the input data. To match individual characters other than reserved characters (`. $ ^ { [ ( | ) * + ? \`), type the character into the expression. To use these special characters, place a slash (`\`) in front of them. The period (`.`) matches any character other than a new line character (`\n`).

You place a list of characters that a single character in the tested string must match in block brackets (`[]`). You can also place ranges in the block, for example, A–Z to match any uppercase letter, or 0–9 to match any number. Avoid using separators in the block to separate entries, for example `[A-Za-z]` matches any upper- and lowercase character. You can repeat a character by placing the number of times it should appear in braces (`{ }`). For example, `[0-9]{5}` checks for five digits in a row.

Place a caret (`^`) as the first character in the block to mean *not*. A caret indicates that the character in the test string must not match any characters in the list. For example, `[^aeiou]` matches any non-vowel character.

WORK WITH REGULAR EXPRESSION VALIDATION

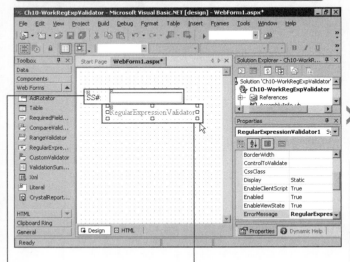

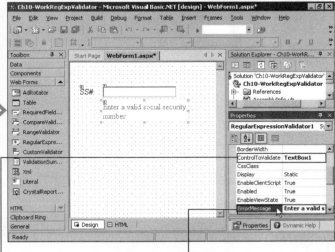

1 Create a new Web Application project or open an existing one.

2 Add the necessary input control to the form.

3 Add a `RegularExpression Validator` control to the form.

Note: See the sections "Create a Web Application" to create a new Web Application project and "Using a Web Form" to add controls.

4 In the Properties window, click the `ControlToValidate` ▾ and select the appropriate input control.

5 Type an appropriate error message into `ErrorMessage`.

Extra

Regular expressions support many expressions, and can represent very advanced strings. You can use the table for more regular expression strings. For more expressions, search Visual Basic .NET help by typing **Regular Expression Language Elements**.

EXPRESSION	DESCRIPTION
.	Matches any character except the line break.
\w	Matches any word character. Same as `[a-zA-Z_0-9]`.
\W	Matches any non-word character. Same as `[^a-zA-Z_0-9]`.
\s	Matches any white-space character.
\S	Matches any non-white-space character.
\d	Decimal digit. Same as `[0-9]`.
\D	Nondigit. Same as `[^0-9]`.
*	Specifies zero or more matches; for example, `\w*` or `(abc)*`. Same as `{0,}`.
+	Specifies one or more matches; for example, `\w+` or `(abc)+`. Same as `{1,}`.
?	Specifies zero or one matches; for example, `\w?` or `(abc)?`. Same as `{0,1}`.
{n}	Specifies exactly n matches; for example, `(pizza){2}`.
{n,}	Specifies at least n matches; for example, `(abc){2,}`.
{n,m}	Specifies at least n, but no more than m, matches.

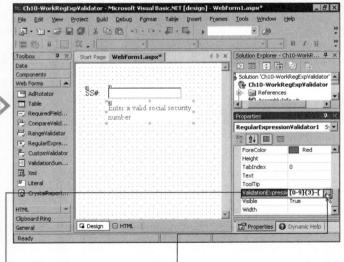

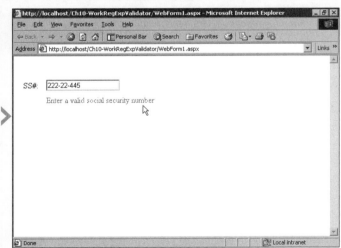

6 Type a regular expression in the `ValidationExpression` property.

■ The example uses the regular expression `[0-9]{3}-[0-9]{2}-[0-9]{4}` to validate a social security number.

■ You can click […] to view a list of commonly used expressions.

■ The regular expression validator checks the input against the regular expression and outputs the error message if they do not match.

PROVIDE A VALIDATION SUMMARY

You can provide one validation summary area on your form instead of having validation for each control display individually. You use the `ValidationSummary` control to integrate validation information on the form into a single area.

The `ValidationSummary` control holds the validation text of all the validation controls on the form. Although it displays the errors only after the user presses a control like a button, the client-side browser performs the validation without a roundtrip to the server. You can disable the `EnableClientScript` property to force validation summary generation to occur on the server. You can set the `CausesValidation` property of a `LinkButton`, `Button`, or `ImageButton` control to `False` to enable the user to click the button without causing a validation. If you disable the client scripting display for the validation summary without disabling the `CausesValidation` property button, the button's click event still does not fire until the user corrects validation errors.

You can use the `DisplayMode` to change the listing style to `BulletList`, `List`, or `SingleParagraph`. The default, `BulletList`, shows one validation error per line, prefaced with bullets. The `List` setting uses the same layout without the bullets. The `SingleParagraph` setting places one error after the other without line breaks, and wraps text when necessary.

Because the summary control displays the list of errors of all the validation controls on the form, you may want to remove the visual display of the various validation controls on the form. To remove the visual interface of each validation control, set its `Display` property to `None`. This hides the individual validation controls but still displays the correct information in the `ValidationSummary` control. On some longer forms, you may want to use both displays, one directly beside the control, and the other as a reference at the top of the page.

PROVIDE VALIDATION SUMMARY

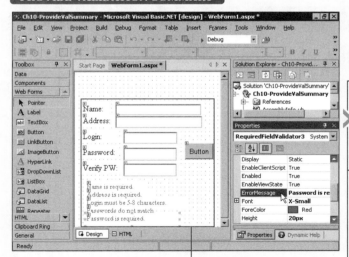

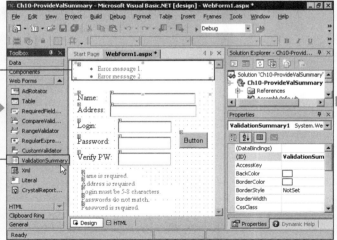

CREATE A VALIDATION FORM

1 Create a new Web Application project or open an existing one.

2 Set up the necessary input and validation controls, adding a post-back control such as a **Button** to generate the summary.

Note: To create a validation control, see the section "Using Validation Controls."

3 Add a **ValidationSummary** control to the Web form.

Note: To add a control, see the section "Using a Web Form."

4 Change any necessary properties.

Extra

The validation summary by default does not display a message at the top of the summary explaining the list of errors. You can place a header on the summary with the `HeaderText` control. The header does not display unless the summary also contains at least one error. For other visual changes, you can change the default red color of the errors with the `ForeColor` property.

Example:
```
ValidationSummary1.HeaderText = _
    "You must enter an appropriate  value " _
    in the following fields:"
```

Your page may not have enough room for the validation summary control. You can cause the validation summary control to display its list of errors as a message box instead of displaying on the page. Assuming the browser supports scripting and `EnableClientScripting` is set to `True`, you can enable the `ShowMessageBox` property, which shows a message box when the user clicks a button containing the list of errors. If you choose to use `ShowMessageBox`, you can disable the standard summary appearance. You can enable or disable the main display of the control with the `ShowSummary` property.

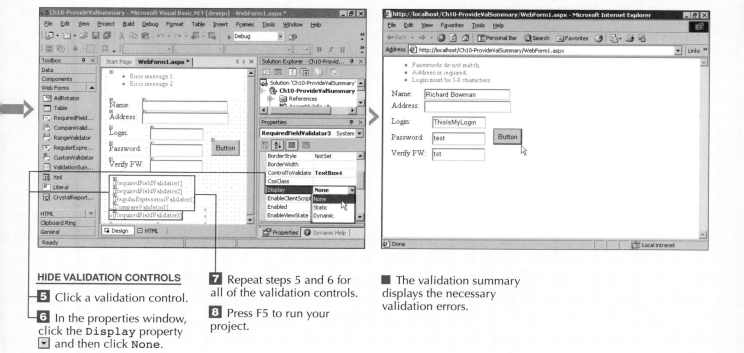

HIDE VALIDATION CONTROLS

5 Click a validation control.

6 In the properties window, click the `Display` property ▼ and then click `None`.

7 Repeat steps 5 and 6 for all of the validation controls.

8 Press F5 to run your project.

■ The validation summary displays the necessary validation errors.

ADD AN ADDITIONAL WEB FORM

You can add multiple Web Forms to a single Web project just like you add multiple Windows Forms to a Windows project. Each form represents a single Web page of the Web site. For example, you may use the initial Web page to display the options in the application, and then a number of pages for each major section of the page. Unlike a Windows Application that compiles into a single executable file with a single entry point, a Web Application is simply a series of individual ASPX files that store the individual forms.

To add a new form, use the Project menu. When you access the Add Item dialog box, you can specify the new form's filename. The Development Environment builds a blank Web Form and adds the necessary files to the Web folder.

You can choose individual settings for the layout details and browser requirements for each Web Form in the project. For instance, you can make the main page of the application support the most browser types possible. Then, for particularly complex pages, you can require a high-level browser. To learn how to edit individual page properties and to set browser requirements, see the section "Using a Web Form."

You can add `HyperLink` controls to link from one page in the project to another. The `HyperLink` control simply adds a standard HTML-based hyperlink to a page. You can use the `Target` property of the `HyperLink` control to make the page load into a separate window if you want to keep the previous page open. For more information on using the hyperlink control, see the section "Add a Hyperlink Control."

ADD AN ADDITIONAL WEB FORM

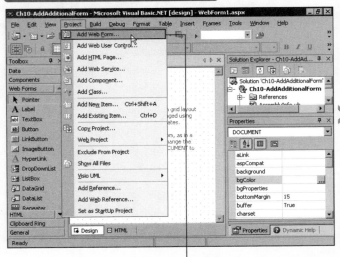

1 Create a new Web Application project or open an existing one.

Note: To create a Web Application project, see the section "Create a Web Application."

2 Click Project ➪ Add Web Form.

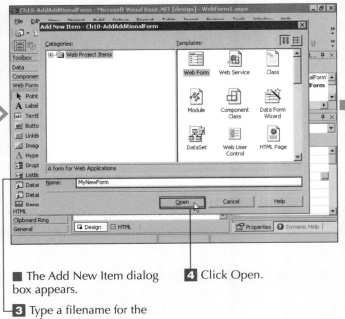

■ The Add New Item dialog box appears.

3 Type a filename for the new form.

4 Click Open.

Extra

Although a hyperlink provides a simple way for the user to move from a page within your project to a location anywhere on the Internet, you can use code to redirect the user without their interactively clicking a hyperlink. You may want to redirect the user when they click a button and need to move on to a new page. For example, the user completes a form of personal information in order to log in to the site. When the user presses Submit, you can add the information to a database and direct the user to the members page. To cause a redirection, call the `Redirect` method of the `Response` object. In parentheses, place the URL to load. You do not need to make the URL a Web Form or something inside of your project. You can use any URL accessible to the client you want.

Example:
```
Private Sub Button1_Click(ByVal sender As System.Object, ByVal e As _
    System.EventArgs) Handles Button1.Click

    Response.Redirect("webform2.aspx")
End Sub
```

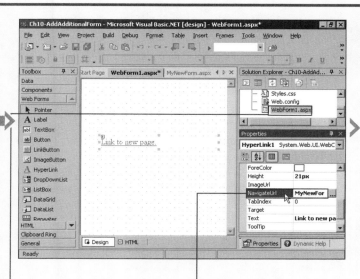

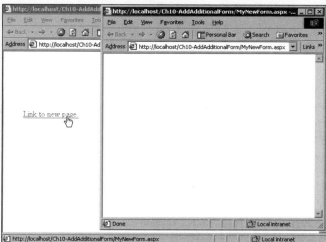

■ VB .NET adds the new Web form to the project.

5 Open a form accessible to the client browser that needs to open the new page.

6 Add a hyperlink control and set the `NavigateUrl` property to the name of the new form.

Note: To create a hyperlink, see the section "Add a Hyperlink Control."

7 Press F5 to run your project.

■ The project builds the new page and displays the default page in the project.

■ You can access the new Web Form by pressing the hyperlink on the main page.

BIND A FIELD TO A LIST CONTROL

You can bind a database field for users to display dynamic database information through the Web Form. Web Forms data binding is read-only, which means a control can load information but does save changes into the data set.

In Web Forms, you most often use list controls for binding. The ListBox, DropDownList, CheckBoxList, and RadioButtonList controls all support data binding explicitly. You can use a list control to display items that read from a data source. Each item in the control corresponds to a row in the data source. The control displays one field from the source and can optionally use a second field as the item value. You optionally set the item value to the unique key field in the database so you can easily locate the record for processing.

To set up a list control, specify the DataSource property to reference a data source, such as a DataSet or DataView

component, for the page. For more information on creating database connections, see Chapter 9.

You specify which data-source fields the control displays with the DataTextField property. Specify the field to function as the item value with DataValueField. If the data source has only one field, you do not set the properties, and the control displays the single field automatically.

To update each of your bound controls, you must call their DataBind method. Alternately, you can call the form's DataBind method, which binds every control on the form that contains a binding. You should only call this method when the page loads and when data changes. To make sure the page does not rebind the data source each time it loads, check the IsPostBack property. If the property is False, the page is loading for the first time, and you need to bind the controls.

BIND A FIELD TO A LIST CONTROL

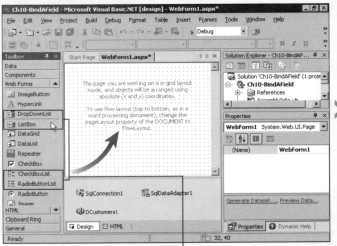

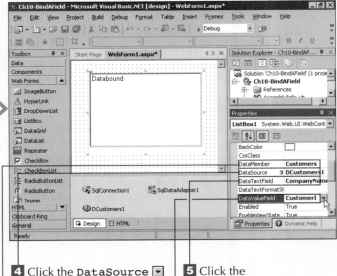

1 Create a new Web Application project or open an existing one.

2 Add a data source to the page.

3 Click the ListBox, DropDownList, CheckBoxList, or RadioButtonList controls in the Toolbox and add it to the form.

Note: To create a database connection, see Chapter 9. See the section "Work with Option List Controls" for more on the CheckBoxList and RadioButtonList controls.

4 Click the DataSource in the Properties Window and select a DataSet or DataView.

■ If the DataSet contains multiple tables, click the DataMember and select the appropriate table.

5 Click the DataTextField and select the field to display.

■ Optionally, click the DataValueField and select a field that specifies values for the items.

6 Double-click the page.

Extra

When the user selects an item in the list controls, the `SelectedIndexChanged` event fires. You can handle this event to load information based on an item the user selects. The `ListBox.SelectedItem.Value` property contains the value ID assigned by the database. The `SelectedIndexChanged` event is not a post-back event for any of the four controls. You can cause the list controls to post back to the server and fire the `SelectedIndexChanged` event immediately by setting the `AutoPostBack` property to True.

Example:
```
Private Sub ListBox1_SelectedIndexChanged(ByVal sender As Object, _
ByVal e As System.EventArgs) Handles ListBox1.SelectedIndexChanged
Dim custID As String                        ' get the selected item's value
custID = ListBox1.SelectedItem.Value        ' to find the entry in the database
' search the database for the selected ID
Dim r As DataRow = DataSet1.Customers.FindByCustomerID(custID)
Label1.Text = r("Address")                  ' display the information from
Label2.Text = r("City")                     ' the database
Label3.Text = r("State")
Label1.Text = r("Zip")
End Sub
```

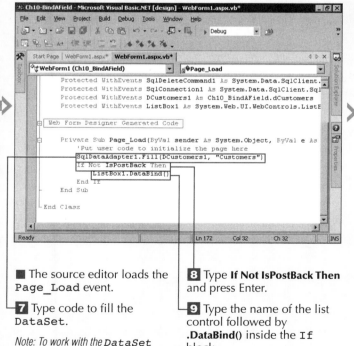

■ The source editor loads the `Page_Load` event.

7 Type code to fill the `DataSet`.

Note: To work with the `DataSet` object, see Chapter 9.

8 Type **If Not IsPostBack Then** and press Enter.

9 Type the name of the list control followed by **.DataBind()** inside the **If** block.

10 Press F5 to run your project.

■ The list Web server control displays the appropriate field of the table.

ADD A DATAGRID CONTROL

You may want to create a Web Application project that displays tables of information, like product listings or a list of articles in a magazine. You can use the DataGrid control to easily display a fully customized table of information from a dataset.

The Web Forms DataGrid control renders a standard HTML table of a set of data. You link the DataSet or DataView component to the grid with the DataSource property. You must fill the data set before using it. See Chapter 9 to learn how to create a database connection.

The Web DataGrid server control only fills when you call its DataBind method. Otherwise, it uses cached data. If you call the method on a post back, for example, if the user selects an item, the event is lost when you call DataBind. For this reason, make sure to only call DataBind in the

Page_Load event when the IsPostBack of the Page is False, meaning the page loaded for the first time.

You use the Property Builder dialog box of the DataGrid, which has five pages, to set up all of its major properties. The first page, General, sets up the data source. You need to set the DataSource property to the DataSet or DataView component that contains the table you want to bind. The DataMember specifies the table to display. Set the DataKeyField to the key field of the database, a field that is unique among the records. You can use the key field to easily find a record in the database that the user selects.

The other property pages enable you to change the appearance and function of the grid. For more information on setting up the appearance and columns of the control, see the section "Change the Appearance of the DataGrid."

ADD A DATAGRID CONTROL

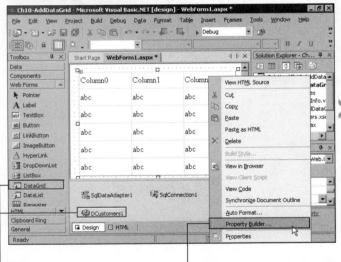

1 Create a new Web Application project or open an existing one.

2 Add an appropriate DataSet or DataView.

3 Click the DataGrid control in the Toolbox and add it to the form.

4 Right-click the control and then click Property Builder.

Note: See Chapter 9 to add a database connection. See the section "Using a Web Form" to add a control.

■ The Property Builder appears.

5 For the DataSource, click ▾ and select the data control.

6 If you use a DataGrid, select the correct table for the DataMember.

7 Select the appropriate unique ID field for Data key field.

8 Click OK.

9 Double-click the Page outside of the grid.

Extra

In most modern applications and Web sites, users expect to sort the different columns in a table. The `DataGrid` can provide hyperlinks on each field name in the header to enable sorting. You can sort by checking the Allow sorting check box on the General property page in the Property Builder. Alternately, you can enable the `AllowSorting` property in the Property tool window. The field to sort automatically returns in the `SortCommand` event, which fires when the user clicks one of the column headers. The event object passes a `SortExpression` property that contains the field to sort. You can alter the sort field a particular column uses in the Property Builder. To provide the sorting capabilities, you must bind the grid to a `DataView` component, not a `DataSet` component, which does not perform any sorting or filtering functions. To create a `DataView` component, see Chapter 9.

Example:
```
Private Sub DataGrid1_SortCommand(ByVal source As Object, _
    ByVal e As System.Web.UI.WebControls.DataGridSortCommandEventArgs) _
    Handles DataGrid1.SortCommand

    DataView1.Sort = e.SortExpression
    DataGrid1.DataBind()
End Sub
```

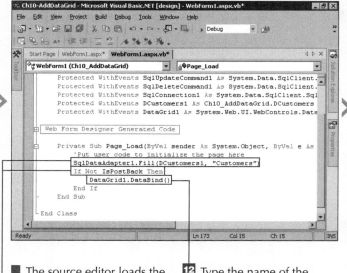

■ The source editor loads the **Page_Load** event.

10 Fill the **DataSet**.

Note: To bind controls, see Chapter 9.

11 Type **If Not IsPostBack Then** and press Enter.

12 Type the name of the **DataGrid** followed by **.DataBind()** inside the **If** block.

13 Press F5 to run your project.

■ The **DataGrid** displays the appropriate table.

Note: See the section "Change the Appearance of a DataGrid" to customize the grid appearance.

CHANGE THE APPEARANCE OF A DATAGRID

A number of properties enable the `DataGrid` to display data effectively and attractively. You can use `DataGrid` properties to set up a color and border scheme, and modify the columns it displays. For more information on adding a `DataGrid` server control to your Web Form, see the section "Add a DataGrid Control."

The `ItemStyle` and `AlternatingItemStyle` determine how items look in the table. If you do not define `AlternatingItemStyle`, all items appear the same. If you set both properties, the items in the table switch between two styles. The `HeaderStyle` determines the appearance of the header and `FooterStyle` determines the appearance of the footer. You can easily edit these properties using the Format page of the Property Builder for the control.

You can set borders for the grid using the `BorderWidth` and `BorderStyle` properties. The `CellPadding` property specifies the amount of space between the edge of a cell

and its contents, and the `CellSpacing` property specifies the space between cells of the table. Alternately, you can also set these properties via the Borders page of the Property Builder.

To automatically add a style to the grid, you use the Auto Format dialog box, which provides a number of pre-made color-coordinated table setups. After you select a style, all properties of the control update to reflect the change.

Use the Columns page of the Property Builder dialog box to specify the columns the table displays. By default, the grid displays all of the columns. The dialog box provides the option "Create columns automatically at runtime" to disable this operation. You can also set the `AutoGenerateColumns` property to `False` in the property tool window. You can then add the columns you want to display. The control contains the list of columns to use in the `Columns` property.

CHANGE THE APPEARANCE OF A DATAGRID

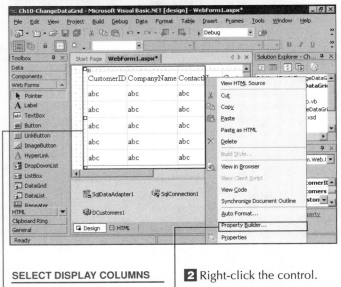

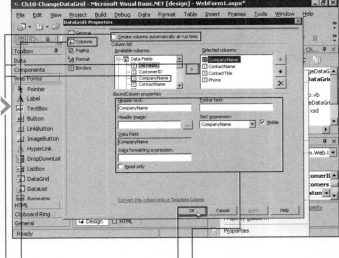

SELECT DISPLAY COLUMNS

1 Configure a `DataGrid` on the Web form.

Note: See the section "Add a DataGrid Control" to add a `DataGrid` control.

2 Right-click the control.

3 Click Property Builder.

■ The DataGrid Property Builder dialog box appears.

4 Click Columns.

5 Click to remove the automatic column headers (☐ changes to ✔).

6 Click a field from the list

7 Click ⊳ to add columns.

■ You can edit the display properties for each column.

8 Click OK.

9 Press F5.

■ The grid generates with the appropriate column headings.

Extra

In a table with a large number of records, you may want to separate the records onto a number of pages. The `DataGrid` control provides paging, which enables you to specify the number of records that display at a time. The `DataGrid` automatically generates a set of links so that the user can jump to another page of items. You enable paging with the `AllowPaging` property. You specify the number of items that display on each page with the `PageSize` property. The default page size is 10. You can modify the appearance of the pager buttons using the `PagerStyle` property. You can change the `PagerStyle.Mode` property to display either a list of pages for the user to click, or a next and previous button. For the paging to work, the `PageIndexChanged` event must set the selected page and update the data grid.

Example:
```
Private Sub DataGrid1_SortCommand(ByVal source_
    As Object, ByVal e As_
    System.Web.UI.WebControls.DataGridSortCommandEventArgs)_
    Handles DataGrid1.SortCommand

    DataView1.Sort = e.SortExpression
    DataGrid1.DataBind()
End Sub
```

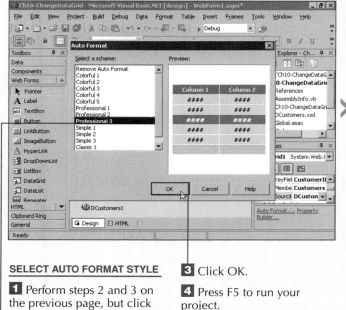

SELECT AUTO FORMAT STYLE

1 Perform steps 2 and 3 on the previous page, but click AutoFormat in step 3.

2 Click a scheme to preview it.

3 Click OK.

4 Press F5 to run your project.

■ The grid generates with the selected style.

EDIT DATA IN A DATAGRID

Y ou may want to provide a table of information to a user, and let them update information in the database directly over the Web. The DataGrid control can automatically provide edit controls for the user to add, edit, and update database records. Because database binding in Web Forms provides only support for reading information form a database, you must add the code to your application to perform the individual adding, editing, and updating actions.

You can add buttons to the DataGrid control to enable the user to edit records. The Property Builder includes, in the list of available columns, a section called Button Column. This section provides a Select column, an Edit column, and a Delete column. Each of these columns consists of a hyperlink or button for each record in the grid.

You add a Select column to the DataGrid to enable the user to select a row. The DataGrid automatically updates the SelectedItem property and raises the SelectedIndexChanged event. The selected item displays using the SelectedItemStyle style.

The Edit row provides a method for the user to update a record. When the user clicks the button, the grid fires the EditCommand event. The edit does not start automatically. You must set the EditItemIndex property of the DataGrid to the appropriate item inside the EditCommand event. You can retreive the item the user selects using the e.Item.ItemIndex property of the event parameters. You must then invoke the DataBind method to update the grid.

When you invoke editing mode, the edit column for that record changes to display a Cancel and an Update button. The grid places TextBox controls for each column in the table. VB .NET raises the CancelCommand and UpdateCommand events when the user selects one of the buttons. To cancel the edit, set the EditItemIndex property to negative one. To save the updates, access each column of the grid using the Cells collection. VB .NET locates the TextBox for each cell in the Controls collection of the TableCell object in position zero.

EDIT DATA IN A DATAGRID

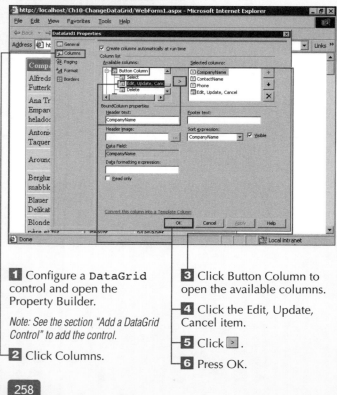

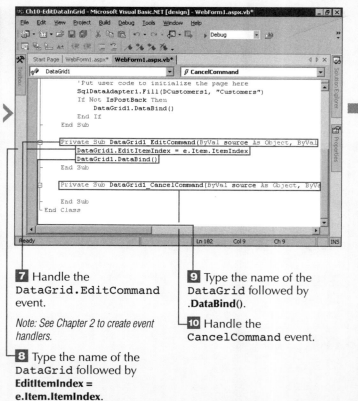

1 Configure a **DataGrid** control and open the Property Builder.

Note: See the section "Add a DataGrid Control" to add the control.

2 Click Columns.

3 Click Button Column to open the available columns.

4 Click the Edit, Update, Cancel item.

5 Click ▶.

6 Press OK.

7 Handle the **DataGrid.EditCommand** event.

Note: See Chapter 2 to create event handlers.

8 Type the name of the **DataGrid** followed by **EditItemIndex = e.Item.ItemIndex**.

9 Type the name of the **DataGrid** followed by **.DataBind()**.

10 Handle the **CancelCommand** event.

Extra

You can use the Delete Button column to allow users to remove items from the database. When the user clicks Delete for a particular row, the grid posts to the server with the `DeleteCommand` event. To delete an item, pass the `e.Item` object from the parameter list to determine the item to remove. If you set the `DataKeyField` to the unique ID of the record, you can access the key data for the entry the user wants to delete with the `DataGrid.DataKeys` collection. To find a `DataRow` in a `DataSet` by a unique ID, the `DataSet` component creates a `FindByFieldName` method, where `FieldName` is the name of the unique field.

Example:
```
Private Sub DataGrid1_DeleteCommand(ByVal source As Object, _
    ByVal e As System.Web.UI.WebControls.DataGridCommandEventArgs) _
    Handles DataGrid1.DeleteCommand

    Dim custID As String = DataGrid1.DataKeys(e.Item.ItemIndex)
    Dim rowInDb As DataRow = _
    DataSet11.Customers.FindByCustomerID(custID)

    DataSet11.Customers.RemoveCustomersRow(rowInDb)
    DataGrid1.DataBind()
End Sub
```

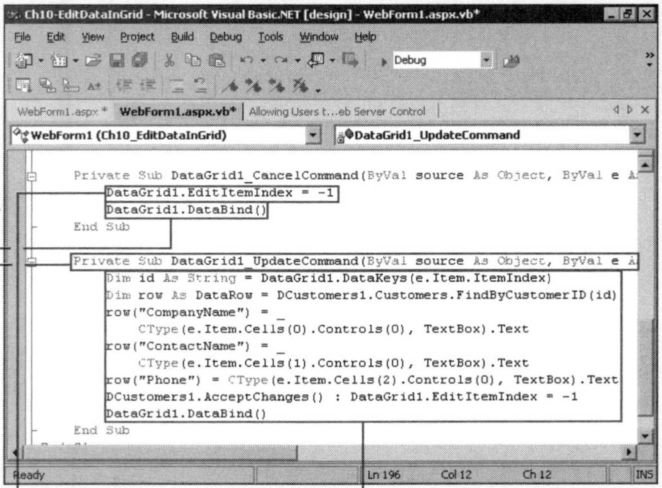

11 Type the name of the `DataGrid` followed by **.EditItemIndex = -1**.

12 To rebind the grid, type the `DataGrid` name and **.DataBind()**.

13 Handle the `UpdateCommand` event.

14 Type code to update the `DataSet`, cancel the edit, and rebind the grid.

Note: See Chapter 9 to update data.

15 Press F5 to run your project.

■ The `DataGrid` provides an editor, and you can cancel edits or update items in the data set.

259

CREATE A WINDOWS SERVICE

When you develop a complex application, you often require functionality to continuously run parts of the application on a server or a client computer. You also often require background code to run continuously when you develop server components — for example, a service that performs continuous maintenance on a server database, or calculates real-time statistics on usage. You can use Windows Services to run code in the background with no interface and without requiring a user to login to the computer and start the executable. For example, the Microsoft Internet Information Services (IIS) Web server runs as a Windows service so that it can serve incoming requests and does not directly provide an interface

To create a Windows service, you use the Windows Service template when you create a new project. Your project consists of a single class that inherits from the `System.ServiceProcess.ServiceBase` class. A *service*

initiates when a user activates it from the Service Manager, or when the system reboots. Your class overrides the `OnStart` method of the `ServiceBase` class. Use this method to add functions to initialize and start the service. Your class overrides the `OnStop` method to provide the ability to stop, either at a user's request or at system shutdown. Provide code to stop functions of the service in this method.

You cannot place the main functionality of the service in the main thread, which needs to remain available for stop requests. You can, however, use a `Timer` component or create a `Thread` that lets your process function. For more information on creating threads, see Chapter 8.

A service does not provide a visual interface. Most services write information and errors to the system's event log. For more information on adding entries to the event log, see the section "Using the Event Log."

CREATE A WINDOWS SERVICE

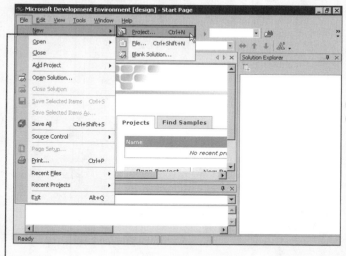

1 Click File ➪ New ➪ Project.

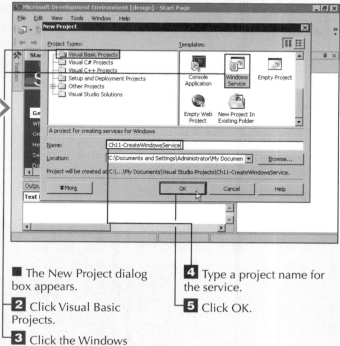

■ The New Project dialog box appears.

2 Click Visual Basic Projects.

3 Click the Windows Service template.

4 Type a project name for the service.

5 Click OK.

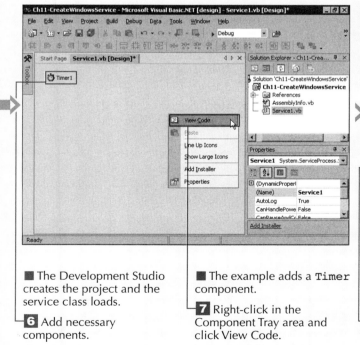

Apply It

In many cases, users want to pause and resume your service to conserve system resources. To support pausing and continuing, you set the `CausePauseAndContinue` property of your class to `True` and override the base class's `OnPause` and `OnContinue` methods. To install and run your service, see the section "Install a Windows Service."

TYPE THIS:

```
Protected Overrides Sub OnStart(ByVal args() As String)
    Timer1.Enabled = True
    System.Diagnostics.EventLog.WriteEntry("MyService", "Starting")
End Sub
Protected Overrides Sub OnStop()
    Timer1.Enabled = False
    System.Diagnostics.EventLog.WriteEntry("MyService", "Stopping")
End Sub
Protected Overrides Sub OnPause()
    Timer1.Enabled = False
    System.Diagnostics.EventLog.WriteEntry("MyService", "Pausing")
End Sub
Protected Overrides Sub OnContinue()
    Timer1.Enabled = True
    System.Diagnostics.EventLog.WriteEntry("MyService", "Resuming")
End Sub
```

RESULT:

MyService - Starting

MyService - Pausing

MyService - Resuming

MyService - Stopping

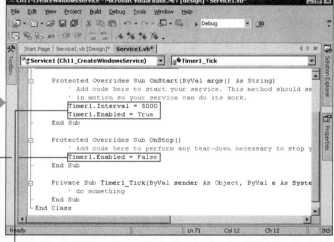

■ The Development Studio creates the project and the service class loads.

─■ 6 Add necessary components.

Note: See Chapters 3 and 4 for information on various components.

■ The example adds a `Timer` component.

─■ 7 Right-click in the Component Tray area and click View Code.

8 Type the necessary code to start the process into `OnStart`.

9 Type in the necessary code to stop the process into `OnStop`.

■ If you rely on the `Timer` control, type code to enable and disable the timer. If you use threads, start and stop the secondary threads.

■ The service is complete.

Note: To install the service, see the section "Install a Windows Service."

USING THE EVENT LOG

Services do not provide visual output through a form or console. Because they run in the background without requiring the user to login, services must run without user interaction. You can use the system event log to provide informational and error messages about your service to the users or system administrators. Although the event log's primary use is for services, any Windows application can access the event logs.

The `System.Diagnostics` namespace provides a variety of classes covering security and debugger abilities. The namespace also includes the `EventLog` class, which enables your application to write logging information to the system event log. Use the `WriteEntry` method to add an item to the event log. A number of overloaded versions of this method exist. One of the available methods expects a

string representing the source of the event, a message to store for the event, and a constant from the `EventLogEntryType` enumeration. The source string typically contains the name of your application. Consider using the same source for each event you add to the log, so the user of the event log can easily determine which events belong to your application or service. For the message string, specify the necessary information or error message that contains the reason for the log entry.

When the method executes, it adds an appropriate entry to the `Application` event log, which is the default for applications and services. You can search the MSDN library by typing **EventLog Class** to find more information on altering the log, adding custom logs, and working with event logs.

USING THE EVENT LOG

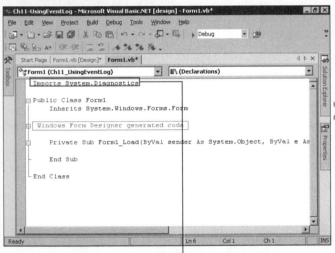

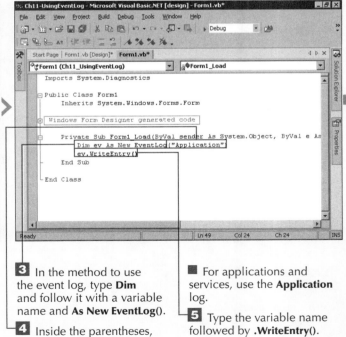

1 Create a new project or open an existing one.

2 In the code module where you need to use the event log, import the `System.Diagnostics` namespace.

Note: To import a namespace, see Chapter 8.

3 In the method to use the event log, type **Dim** and follow it with a variable name and **As New EventLog()**.

4 Inside the parentheses, type the name of the event log to use.

■ For applications and services, use the **Application** log.

5 Type the variable name followed by **.WriteEntry()**.

Extra

You can view event logs using the Event Viewer that the operating system provides. When you sign on as an administrator or a user with access to the event log, in Windows Server versions, click Start ➪ click Programs ➪ Administrative Tools folder, and then click the Event Viewer icon. In Windows Professional versions, click Start ➪ Settings ➪ Control Panel, then double-click the Administrative Tools folder and click the Event Viewer icon.

The following table of `EventLogEntryType` enumerations can help the user distinguish the particular reason for the event entry in an event log. For example, if an error occurs in your application or service, you can use the `Error` constant, which places a red error icon beside the entry in the Event Log viewer.

CONSTANT	DESCRIPTION
Error	An error event. This indicates a significant problem the user should know about such as a loss of functionality or data.
FailureAudit	A failure audit event. This indicates a security event that occurs when an audited access attempt fails such as a failed attempt to open a file.
Information	An information event. This indicates a significant, successful operation.
SuccessAudit	A success audit event. This indicates a security event that occurs when an audited access attempt is successful; for example, logging on successfully.
Warning	A warning event. This indicates a problem that is not immediately significant, but may signify conditions that can cause future problems.

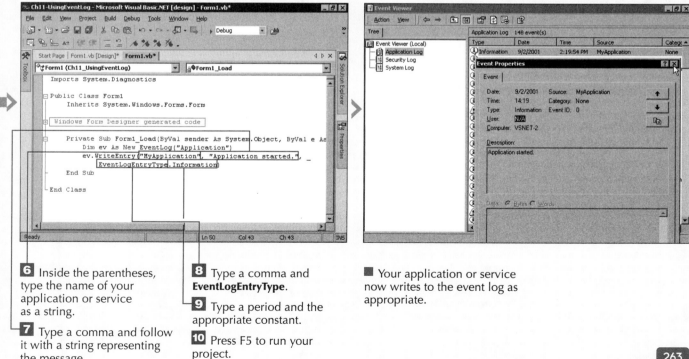

■ **6** Inside the parentheses, type the name of your application or service as a string.

■ **7** Type a comma and follow it with a string representing the message.

■ **8** Type a comma and **EventLogEntryType**.

■ **9** Type a period and the appropriate constant.

■ **10** Press F5 to run your project.

■ Your application or service now writes to the event log as appropriate.

INSTALL A WINDOWS SERVICE

Unlike a regular application, a Windows service cannot install and place icons on the Programs menu because the service must start when the computer starts, and respond to service requests. You can, however, create a specialized class that provides the initialization to install your service onto a system. Creating this class requires a good understanding of classes. For information on classes, member variables, and constructors, see Chapter 7.

You must add a new class to your service project. In the class module, you import the `System.Configuration.Install` and `System.ServiceProcess` namespaces. The `Install` namespace resides in a separate DLL you must reference. See Chapter 12 to add the reference.

In the class definition, you must define the attribute `<RunInstaller(True)>` so that the service installation can find the appropriate class to use. Your class must also inherit from the `Installer` class.

The `ServiceInstaller` and `ServiceProcessInstaller` objects provide the

necessary installation ability. Your class should contain only a *constructor*, which sets up the installer. The `ServiceInstaller` object sets up the service information. The `ServiceName` property of `ServiceInstaller`, which you make identical to the name of the service project, sets the name of the service to install. Set the `StartType` property to a constant from the `ServiceStartType` enumeration.

The `ServiceProcessInstaller` object manages how the process runs. Set the `Account` property to a constant from the `ServiceAccount` enumeration. When utilizing the `User` constant, you must specify a user account to run the service with the `Username` and `Password` properties.

After setting up these two objects, you add them both to the `Installers` collection.

After you build your service into an executable, you can use Visual Basic .NET's `installutil.exe` program to install the service by specifying the path and filename of the service as the command line argument. To uninstall the service from the computer, run the installation utility with `/u` after the executable name.

INSTALL A WINDOWS SERVICE

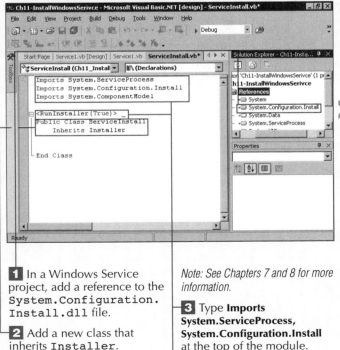

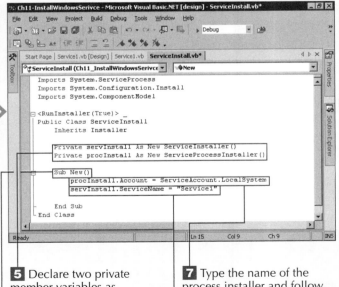

1 In a Windows Service project, add a reference to the `System.Configuration.Install.dll` file.

2 Add a new class that inherits `Installer`.

Note: See Chapters 7 and 8 for more information.

3 Type **Imports System.ServiceProcess, System.Configuration.Install** at the top of the module.

4 Type **<RunInstaller(True)>** before the `Class` keyword.

5 Declare two private member variables as new objects of type `ServiceInstaller` and `ServiceProcess Installer`.

6 Add a constructor with no parameters.

7 Type the name of the process installer and follow it with **.Account =** and an appropriate constant.

8 Type the name of the service installer and follow it with **.ServiceName =** and the name of the service.

Extra

You can use the `ServiceStartType` to specify how the service installs onto the client computer. You can indicate whether you want to start the service automatically, start it manually, or disable it.

CONSTANT	DESCRIPTION
Automatic	Indicates that the operating system starts the service at system start-up. If an automatically started service depends on a manually started service, the manually started service also starts automatically at system startup.
Disabled	Indicates a disabled service that neither a user nor the system can start.
Manual	Indicates that the service starts manually. It can only start when a user or application invokes it.

You can use the `ServiceAccount` enumeration to specify the user account a service uses.

CONSTANT	DESCRIPTION
LocalService	Provides extensive local privileges, and presents the computer's credentials to remote servers.
LocalSystem	Acts as a non-privileged user on the local computer, and presents anonymous credentials to remote servers.
NetworkService	Authenticates using the domain controller's or workgroup Service account.
User	Acts as a non-privileged user on the local computer, and presents the computer's credentials to remote servers.

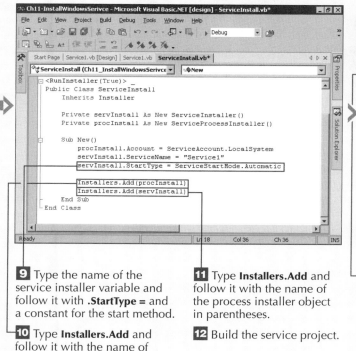

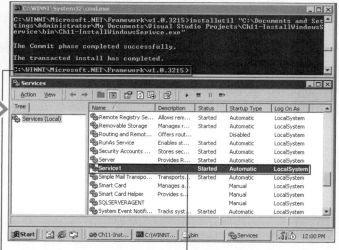

9 Type the name of the service installer variable and follow it with **.StartType =** and a constant for the start method.

10 Type **Installers.Add** and follow it with the name of the service installer object in parentheses.

11 Type **Installers.Add** and follow it with the name of the process installer object in parentheses.

12 Build the service project.

■ You can now run the installutil.exe utility to install the service onto a machine. You can find the program in the C:\WINNT\Microsoft. NET\v\directory where v is the current program version.

■ Use the Services console located in the Administrative Tools in your Programs menu to stop and start the service.

MONITORING A WINDOWS SERVICE

You can monitor and manipulate the state of a Windows service from another application. For example, you can provide a configuration interface that allows the user to configure properties of the service. When the user makes configuration changes, you can stop and restart the service to allow configuration changes to go into effect.

The `ServiceController` component, part of the `System.ServiceProcess` namespace, manipulates running services. You can add this component via the Component section of the Toolbox, or you can create an object instance of the class in code. Two properties specify the service to use. The `MachineName` property sets the machine on which the service runs. You set it to a period (.) if the service runs on the local machine. You set the `ServiceName` property to the name of the service to manipulate.

The `CanPauseAndContinue` property returns a value that determines whether the service can pause and resume. If this value is `True`, you can use the `Pause` method to pause the service and the `Continue` method to resume execution of the service. The `CanStop` property returns a value that determines whether the service can stop after it starts. If you set this to `True`, you can stop the service with the `Stop` method. You can start a service using the `Start` method.

The `Status` property returns the current status of the service. The property returns a constant from the `ServiceControllerStatus` enumeration. If you want your application to wait for the service to reach a particular state, use the `WaitForStatus` method. Pass a constant from the `ServiceControllerStatus` enumeration as the first parameter. Optionally, you can pass a `TimeSpan` object as the second parameter if you want the wait to time out.

MONITORING A WINDOWS SERVICE

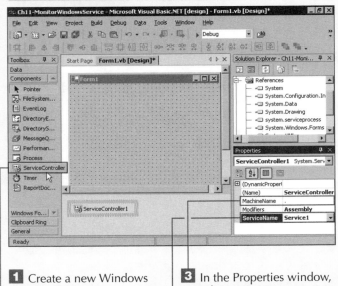

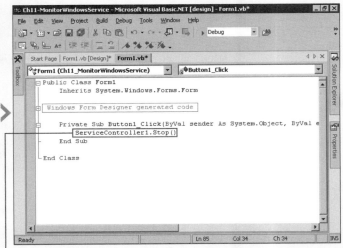

1 Create a new Windows Application project.

2 Click the Components section of the Toolbox and double-click the `ServiceController` component.

3 In the Properties window, type the computer name on which the service runs in the `MachineName` property.

4 Type the name of the service into the `ServiceName` property.

5 In the method of the form to manipulate the service, type the name of the component and follow it with **.Stop()** to stop the service.

■ The example adds three buttons, using `Button1` to stop the service, `Button2` to start it, and `Button3` to check the status.

Extra

You can retrieve a list of the services that are currently running on a machine. You use the `GetDevices` method to return a list of device driver services, and the `GetServices` method to access a list of non-device driver services. Both methods return an array of `ServiceController` classes representing each of the services. To access services on the local computer, you specify no parameters to the methods. For a remote computer, specify the computer name as the only parameter. The `ServicesDependedOn` property returns an array of services on which the service depends. You can use the `ServiceControllerStatus` enumeration to examine the status of the service with the `Status` property.

CONSTANT	DESCRIPTION
ContinuePending	The service is attempting to resume.
Paused	The service is paused.
PausePending	The service is moving to pause state.
Running	The service is running.
StartPending	The service is starting.
Stopped	The service is stopping.
StopPending	The service is not running.

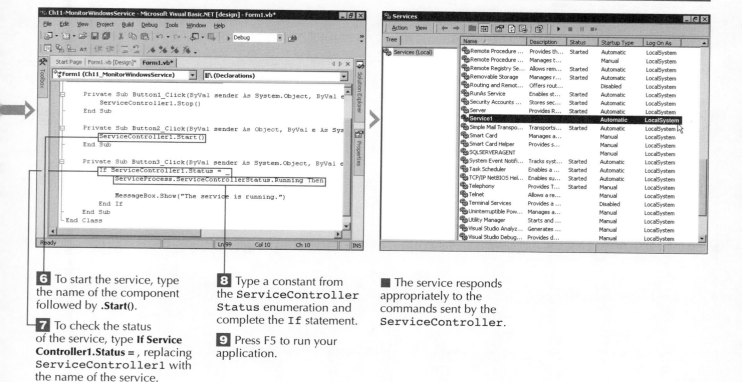

6 To start the service, type the name of the component followed by **.Start()**.

7 To check the status of the service, type **If Service Controller1.Status =** , replacing `ServiceController1` with the name of the service.

8 Type a constant from the `ServiceController Status` enumeration and complete the `If` statement.

9 Press F5 to run your application.

■ The service responds appropriately to the commands sent by the `ServiceController`.

CREATE A WEB SERVICE

A Web service is an ASP.NET file that provides an object with a set of methods that your application can access over an Internet connection. You can create a Web service project and a corresponding set of objects that you can access from any other XML-enabled application over the Web.

To create a Web service project, you select the ASP.NET Web Service template from the New Project dialog box. Upon selection, VB .NET creates one service class and names it the same as the project name given. You use this name to access Web methods of the service.

Each ASMX service class file represents a separate Web service. You can create other classes in the project, but unless you want to make them available over the Internet, do not inherit from the `System.Web.Services.WebService` base class. Only one Web service class can exist in a single code module file. ASP.NET ignores other classes you add to the code module

even if they inherit from the `WebService` base class. Each project can contain multiple ASMX files, with each holding a separate Web service.

A Web service project can contain Web Forms pages as well. You can add Web Forms from the Project menu. For more information on adding a Web Form to a project, see Chapter 10.

To specify the namespace and other properties of the service, you add the attributes to the class identifier, which is the line that specifies the `Class` keyword. Place `WebService()` inside of arrow brackets (< >) as the first entry on the `Class` statement line. Specify properties of the `WebServiceAttribute` class by using the name of the property followed by a colon, an equal sign, and the value.

The `Description` property specifies a textual description that specifies information about the abilities of the service. The `Namespace` property lets you assign a namespace to the Web application.

CREATE A WEB SERVICE

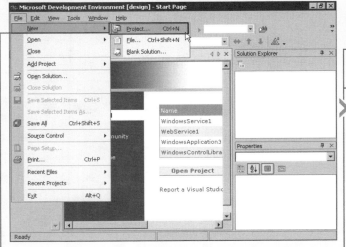

1 Click File ➪ New ➪ Project in the Development Environment.

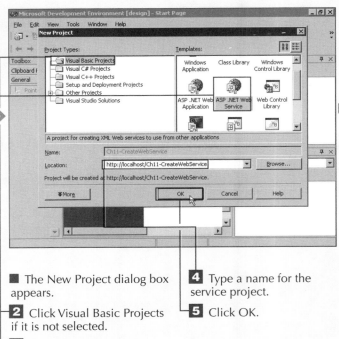

■ The New Project dialog box appears.

2 Click Visual Basic Projects if it is not selected.

3 Click ASP .NET Web Service in the project template list.

4 Type a name for the service project.

5 Click OK.

Extra

You can use namespaces to provide distinct names for your Web service. Distinct names enable clients to easily access the class they want. Namespaces also play an important part in making Web services function. Because of the vastness of the Web, more opportunity exists for classes to fall under the same name. Because of this, Web services require a namespace defined by a *Universal Resource Identifier* (URI). You define a URI much like any Web address except this URI functions only as a naming resource, and does not provide a link to an actual resource available on a server. The URI serves as the default XML namespace for the service. You should make the URI specify a unique domain you own. In fact, you can use the location of the Web service for its namespace identification.

Example:
```
<WebService(Namespace:="http://www.mycomp.com/Webservices/", _
    Description:="This class does something important.")> _
Public Class VBNETWebService
...
End Class
```

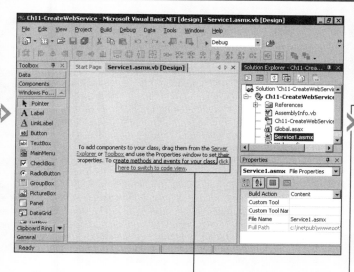

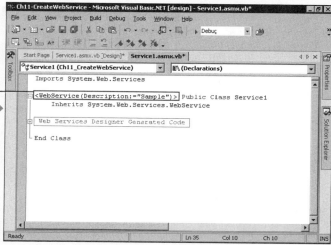

■ The Development Environment creates the project and opens the component view of the service class.

6 Click here to switch to code view link.

■ The Code Editor loads.

■ You can delete the sample code the template displays.

7 On the line of the class declaration, type **<WebService (Description:="Sample")>**, replacing `Sample` with a description of your service.

■ You can now add methods to your service.

Note: See the section "Add a Web Service Method" for more information.

ADD A WEB SERVICE METHOD

The power of a Web service lies in its ability to expose functionality across the Internet through standard communication protocols. To make your service function, you need to provide service methods that consumers of your object can use.

To create a Web method, you define a standard class method inside of a Web service class. For more information on defining methods, see Chapter 4.

To make the method accessible to outside users, you place the WebMethod attribute before the method so the compiler knows which methods it should expose. To do this, on the line where you define the method, you place the WebMethod() attribute inside of left and right arrow brackets (<>). This defines the method as a Web-accessible public method.

The WebMethod attribute contains a number of properties to explain the purpose of your method. Each of the various properties you use with the WebMethod attribute are named parameters, which means that you follow the name

of the parameter you want to use with a colon and an equal sign. After the equal sign, you specify the necessary value. You can use named parameters to specify a partial list of the available parameters.

The MessageName property defines a unique identity for the method if the underlying method is overloaded. By default, MessageName simply equals the name you assign to the class. For example, if you have two Add classes, one for integers, and one for doubles, you must specify unique names, such as AddInteger and AddDouble. You make method names unique to the Web server. For overloaded methods, you must specify the MessageName property to give each method a unique Web method name.

The Description property specifies a textual description for the method, allowing the method to describe its functionality to clients. This description automatically appears on the Service help page. For more information on using the Service help page, see the section "Using the Service Help Interface."

ADD A WEB SERVICE METHOD

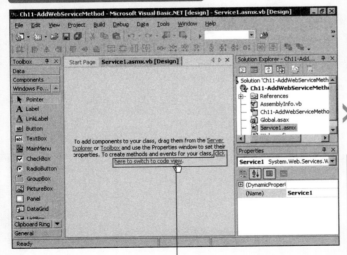

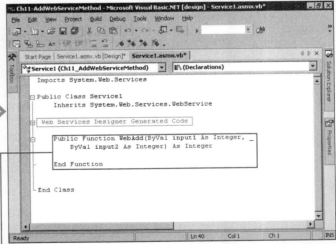

1 Create a new Web Service application or open an existing one.

Note: To create a Web Service application, see the section "Create a Web Service."

2 Click here to switch to code view link.

■ The Code Editor appears.

3 Define a **Public** method.

Note: To define a method, see Chapter 4.

Extra

You can use a number of method attribute properties to specify how the server deals with method calls. The `BufferResponse` property controls whether the method buffers the response information of the method until it completely finishes, or sends the data to the server as soon as possible to send to the client. Normally, `BufferResponse` should equal `True`, which is the default value, because it improves performance. If you plan to send a large quantity of data from the method, you may want to make `BufferResponse = False`.

Example:
```
<WebMethod(BufferResponse := True)> _
Public Sub MyWebMethod()
    ...
End Sub
```

The server can automatically cache results for a particular input to a method. For example, if the method accepts a single integer parameter, and you call the method with a five, it stores the result of the method given an input of five. If another call to the method is made with an input of five, it uses the cache result. To enable caching, set the `CacheDuration` attribute property to the number of seconds to cache the value.

Example:
```
<WebMethod(CacheDuration := 60, MessageName :=_
"ServiceUsage")>_
Public Function MyWebMethod(x As Integer) As Integer
    ...
End Function
```

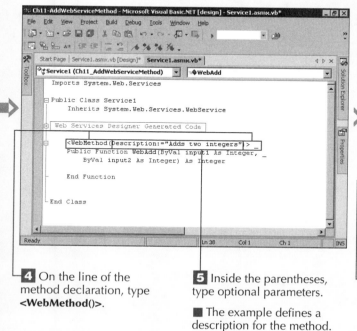

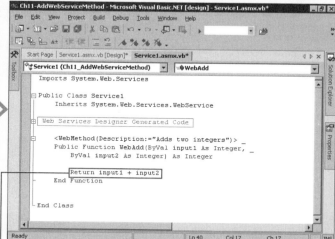

4 On the line of the method declaration, type **<WebMethod()>**.

5 Inside the parentheses, type optional parameters.

■ The example defines a description for the method.

6 Type code in the method to make it perform an appropriate action and return a value.

■ The Web Service method is complete.

■ You can add more methods as necessary.

Note: See the section "Using the Service Help Interface" to test the service.

USING THE SERVICE HELP INTERFACE

Web services enable you to provide a set of objects you can access using the Internet. A Web service, like a Windows service, does not provide an interface for a user to access. Web services do provide an interface you can use to debug the project, however. When you access the URL of a Web service directly, the service invokes the service help page. You can use the page to manipulate and test the various functions of the service to aid in debugging.

The service help page uses the Web service to detect a list of methods that it exposes through Web services. When you start the project from the Development Environment, the help interface appears. The main screen shows the list of methods available in the service as hyperlinks. The descriptions you assign to the class and each method appear on this screen. The page provides a link called

Service Description link where you can view the actual XML that enables the help system to discover the functions of the service. If you want to access this XML in an application, place the query ?WSDL after the URL of the service.

When you click a method, the interface loads a screen that lets you input the parameters the method requires. This page also lists HTML and XML code, which explains return types, and which lets you invoke the method. The page provides bold placeholders, which explains where the method locates particular information. When you click the Invoke button, the XML response of the method appears in a new window. The XML tag that surrounds the response represents the data type the function returns. For example, if the method you call returns a string, the XML response looks like `<string>value</string>`.

USING THE SERVICE HELP INTERFACE

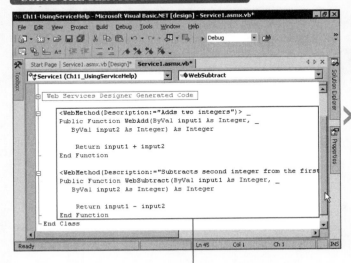

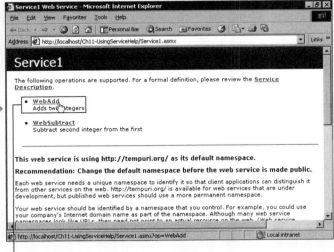

1 Open an existing Web Service project or create a new one.

Note: See the section "Create a Web Service" to create a Web Service.

2 Define necessary methods.

Note: See the section "Add a Web Service Method" to add a method.

3 Press F5 to build the project and start the service interface.

4 Click a method to test.

Extra

The Service Help interface works through the power of Web services to provide an interface to the exported methods. A Web Service is a programmable Web-based application that provides a set of methods, possibly representing application logic, which you can access through any number of systems using Internet standards like XML and HTTP. Web services depend heavily upon the broad acceptance of XML, and other Internet standards, to create an infrastructure that supports application interoperability at a level that solves many of the problems, which previously hindered such attempts. One of the core characteristics of a Web service is the high degree of abstraction that exists between the implementation and consumption of a service. By using XML-based messaging as the mechanism by which you create and access the service, both the Web service client and the Web service provider need no knowledge of each other beyond inputs, outputs, and location. Like the service help interface and the .NET Framework, you can connect different servers and computers, which can work together using the technology of Web services.

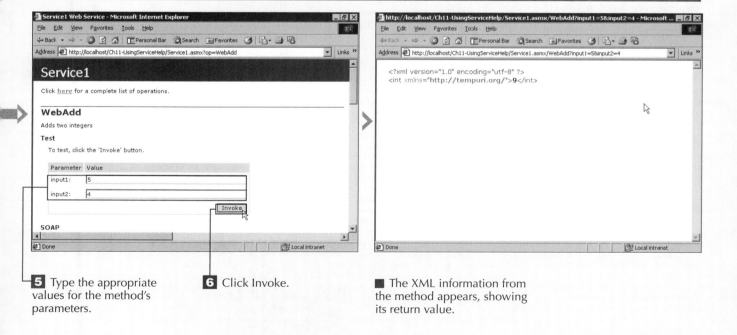

5 Type the appropriate values for the method's parameters.

6 Click Invoke.

■ The XML information from the method appears, showing its return value.

USING WEB SERVICES

When you generate a Web Services class and export methods over the Internet, you need to access those methods. You can invoke Web Service methods in any .NET program ranging from Windows applications to User Controls to Web Form Applications. A Web-enabled object functions like a standard object in other projects.

To use a Web Service in an application, you must first make the service accessible. You can add a reference to a Web Service application in any VB .NET project type. To reference a Web service, you simply need the URL of the service.asmx or service.disco file that contains information about the service. If you reference an asmx file directly, you can only access the specific object contained in that ASP.NET file. If you specify the .disco (discovery) file when referencing the Web service, you can access all Web service classes available in the project.

To create an instance of the object, you simply declare a variable of the class name you define in the Web service. To access the class, you must specify the namespace consisting of the server name. For example, to access a class on the local server named Service1, you declare a variable as Locahost.Service1.

After you declare a new instance of the Web service class, you can access methods exposed by the service. Note that you can access only methods that contain the WebMethod() tag as part of their identifier. You cannot access properties, events, and non-Web enabled methods that exist in the Web service class. Also, connection state does not exist between accesses to the Web method. If you call a method that sets a variable in the Web service class and you call another method that accesses the same variable, the previous value does not store across methods.

USING WEB SERVICES

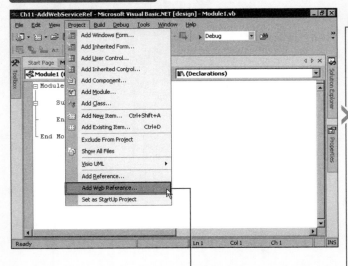

1 Open or create a new project.

■ The example uses a Console Application project.

2 Click Project ⇨ Add Web Reference.

3 Type **http://localhost/Ch11-UsingServiceHelp/Ch11-UsingServiceHelp.vsdisco**, replacing localhost with the server, and Ch11-UsingServiceHelp with the project name.

4 Click the View Contract link on the appropriate Web service.

5 Click Add Reference.

Apply It

A Web service automatically creates asynchronous versions of each Web method you create. You can call an asynchronous version of the Web method and not wait for the method to complete. You then register a function that VB .NET calls when the method completes. For each Web method, the class exports a `BeginMethod` and `EndMethod` method, where `Method` is the name of your Web method.

TYPE THIS

```
Private Sub Button1_Click(ByVal sender As System.Object, ByVal e As _
    System.EventArgs) Handles Button1.Click
    Dim math As New localhost.Service1()
    Dim cb As New AsyncCallback(AddressOf ServiceCallback)
    math.BeginWebAdd(5, 4, cb, cService)
    ListBox1.Items.Add("This code runs first.")   ' Run other code while the web method runs
End Sub
Public Sub ServiceCallback(ByVal ar As IAsyncResult)
    Dim math As localhost.Service1
    Set math = ar.AsyncState                              'Retrieve the class instance
    ListBox1.Items.Add(math.EndLongProcess(ar))          ' Retrieve the results
End Sub
```

RESULT:

This code runs first.

9

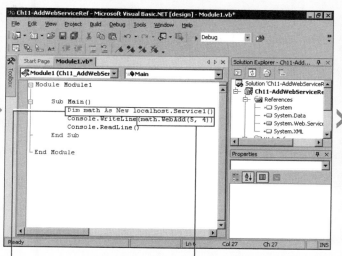

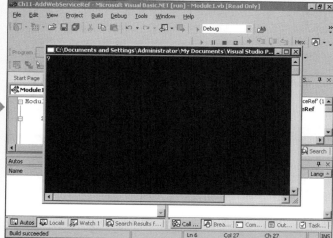

6 Declare a new instance of the Web object by typing in the name of the server, a period, and the name of the service.

■ To find the namespace assigned to the server, you can open the Web References section in the Solution Explorer.

7 Type your variable name and follow it with a period and the method.

8 Press F5 to run your project.

■ The Web Method responds with the appropriate value.

AN INTRODUCTION TO COMPONENT CREATION

V isual Basic .NET enables you to create components that you can use and reuse throughout your Windows, console, Web, and service applications.

Components are classes that work more effectively as design tools in application development.

Ease of Use

You can easily create your own components in code or assemble them from the existing components in the .NET Framework classes, using either Visual Basic .NET or C#. You can use non-visual components and associated features to easily incorporate resources such as message queues, event logs, and performance counters into your applications.

The .NET Framework classes greatly expand the component programming capabilities of Visual Studio .NET. Instead of a limited set of base classes, you have a large library of sophisticated components that you can use to assemble applications, or to derive high-quality components of your own.

Component Visual Development

The new *rapid application development,* or RAD, support makes authoring controls and non-visual components as easy as creating forms. You start with

inheriting from an existing component, and add other components to build in the functionality you need.

COMPONENT TYPES

You can build components that service a variety of purposes based on the needs of a particular project, or for reuse throughout multiple projects. All the components support working within the visual designer of the Development Studio, enabling you to use drag and drop to add components to your projects and to modify properties visually with the Properties window.

You can also create a specialized type of components known as *controls*. You can create controls that offer functionality to a form just like the controls provided by the .NET Framework. You can create both Windows and Web controls that offer their own visual interface and allow you to drag and drop them onto their respective forms.

CREATE A COMPONENT CLASS

Components are a new idea in VB .NET. A basic component lets you create an object very similar to a class, which adds support for the designer. Standard components work in all types of applications, including console applications where no visual interface is available.

You can use components to create objects that offer important functionality to forms, which you manipulate

more easily than a typical class. You can modify the properties of the component visually instead of setting up a class in code. For example, you can easily add the `Timer` control to a form or any other application type and modify its properties in the Properties window, but the `Timer` itself provides no graphical interface.

Project Type

You can add a component to a class library or a Windows Control Library project. You can then build this library and reference it in applications that need to use the component. For information on adding references, see the section "Reference a Library."

Component Base

You create components by inheriting from the `System.ComponentModel.Component` class or implementing the `IComponent` interface. For more information, see the section "Create a Component."

CREATE WINDOWS CONTROLS

You can build a *Windows control,* a specialized type of component, to create custom and reusable graphical interfaces. As with VB .NET and third-party controls, you can create controls that you can drag and drop onto Windows Forms and work with in the Properties window to define their appearance and functionality.

Your control can expose properties and methods, and use a GDI+ drawn graphical interface or use a combination of one or more standard controls. Your

control's properties appear in the Properties tool window, and you can visually manipulate your component in the designer. For example, you can create a custom button control that provides special visual effects. You can build a Windows custom control to create a specialized `ListView` control that displays the contents of a directory.

To add a control to your Windows Application projects, see the section "Create a Windows Forms Control."

Project Type

You can build Windows controls either by creating them directly inside existing Windows Application projects or using a Windows Control Library project.

If you add the control directly to a project, you can use it only within the project. The Windows Control Library builds a DLL that you can reuse across multiple Windows Application projects easily by referencing the library as necessary.

Component Base

VB .NET creates a `UserControl` class that inherits from `System.Windows.Forms.UserControl`. The `UserControl` object provides a design surface to build a complex control easily, and inherits from the `ContainerControl` class to add all of the standard properties and functions you expect in a Windows Forms control.

CREATE WEB CONTROLS

A powerful new feature of VB .NET, Web Forms, lets you create server-side applications that maintain their state and provide advanced functionality. You can create Web User Controls that encapsulate functions of a Web Form for reuse and ease of development.

You can build two types of Web controls. *Web user controls* enable you to define a visual layout combining multiple existing user controls. For example, you can create a Web user control that defines the top border of your Web site and then import the control in the various parts of your site. Web user controls embed into the page at runtime, so you cannot see the control at design time or manipulate its properties using the designer. To

add a control to your project, see the section "Create a Web User Control."

The other type of Web controls, *Web custom controls,* work only in Web Control Library projects. You generate the actual HTML these controls send to the browser and the controls cannot use existing Web controls on which to build. You can reference these controls in a Web Forms project and work with them just like the actual controls provided by the .NET Framework. Custom controls let you drag and drop the control directly onto the form from the Toolbox and use a full set of properties and events. To create custom controls, see the section "Create a Web Control Library."

Project Type

You add Web user controls directly into existing Web Application projects.

You use Web custom controls by building a Web Control Library project and referencing the library in Web Application projects.

Component Base

VB .NET provides a Web Control Library project template, which automatically creates a `WebControl` class that inherits from the `System.Web.UI.WebControls.WebControl` class.

CREATE A COMPONENT

Components provide reusable code in the form of objects. Components are a special type of class that you can add to the Toolbox and manipulate using the designer. Components provide no visual interface on a form and appear in the Component Tray. The ability to work with the component using the designer means the developer can quickly and easily modify component properties in a point-and-click manner.

To create a component, you use the Component Class template provided by the Development Studio. The template provides a constructor and initialization routine for you.

To define a component, you add public methods, properties, and events to the component just like you would with a class. Unlike a normal class, you can define extra information about properties and events of the component that a designer can use when the user manipulates the component at design time. To specify a description for a property, place the attribute `Description()` inside angle brackets (<>) before the

`Property` statement or accessibility keyword with the description as the parameter. You can hide a property by specifying the `Browsable()` attribute with `False` as the parameter.

To add your component to an application after you reference the library that contains the component, you simply double-click the component in the Toolbox. You can then use the Properties window to manipulate public properties of the component. Because the component is a specialized kind of class, you can also create an instance of the component in code using the `New` operator. For more information on specifying which properties are public, how accessibility works, and how to create class instances, see Chapter 7.

When you create a set of components in a library, you can use namespaces to help locate components more easily for reuse. You can see Chapter 8 for information on using and creating namespaces.

CREATE A COMPONENT

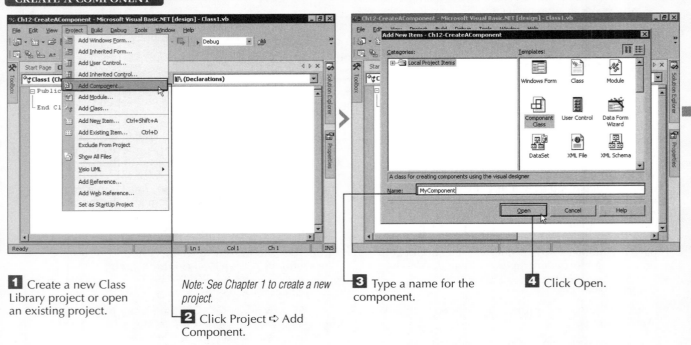

1 Create a new Class Library project or open an existing project.

Note: See Chapter 1 to create a new project.

2 Click Project ➪ Add Component.

3 Type a name for the component.

4 Click Open.

Extra

You can use the various attributes available to components to provide helpful information to the user and provide setup information to the designer. You can separate multiple attributes using commas. You need to import the `System.ComponentModel` namespace for attributes to work.

Example:

```
<Description("Sets the timer " & _
"length."), DefaultValue(1000)> _
Public Property TimerInterval() _
    As Integer
    Get
                    Return mTimerInterval
    End Get
    Set(value As Color)
                mTimerInterval = value
    End Set
End Property
```

ATTRIBUTE	DESCRIPTION
`Browsable(Boolean)`	Specifies whether a property or an event should be displayed in the property browser.
`Category(String)`	Specifies the category to display the property if the user uses the categorical property display.
`Description(String)`	Specifies a description for the component.
`Bindable(Boolean)`	Specifies whether a property is useful to bind a database field.
`DefaultProperty (String)`	Specifies the default property that the designer shows when the user clicks the control. Insert this attribute before the class declaration.
`DefaultValue(Object)`	Specifies a default value for the property of the same type as the property.
`DefaultEventAttribute (String)`	Specifies the default event that is selected in the property browser when a user clicks the component. Insert this attribute before the class declaration.

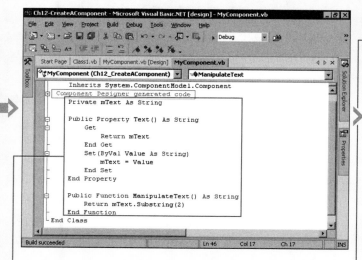

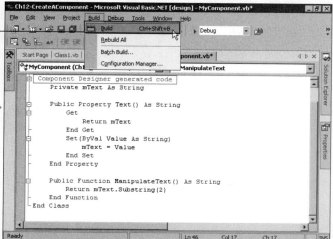

■ The component appears in designer mode.

5 Double-click the designer area.

■ The Code Editor opens.

6 Add any desired properties, methods, and events to the component.

■ This example adds a property to store a text string and a method to manipulate the string.

Note: See Chapter 7 to add properties and events. See Chapter 4 to add methods.

7 Click Build ➪ Build.

■ Visual Basic .NET builds the library.

■ You can now use your component by referencing it in another application and adding the component to the Toolbox.

Note: See Chapter 1 to build a project and the section "Reference a Library" to reference a library.

CREATE A WINDOWS FORMS CONTROL

You can create a Windows Forms user control into which you can add a set of controls for reuse throughout a project. Alternately, you can place the control in a library to use in multiple projects. The `UserControl` object provides the ability to design your own controls.

When you add a user control to a project, the Windows Control Designer, similar to the Windows Forms Designer, gives you a designer space without a title bar. You can use the Toolbox to add any number of controls to the user control. For more information on designing a user control by combining standard Windows form controls, see the section "Using Standard Controls."

You can also use the `UserControl` object's events that the control inherits from to paint onto the service and create your own user control that does not rely on combining other controls. This capability lets you create any sort of control by providing a custom painting method and your own event model. For more information on creating a control without using standard controls, see the section "Create a Control from Scratch."

To name a control that you create, change the `Name` property of the `UserControl` object. The `Name` property modifies the class name, so this name functions as the default name of the control that displays in the Toolbox when you add the user control to a form.

If you want to use a control, or a set of controls, in multiple projects, you can create a Windows Control Library project to hold the controls. When you create this project, VB .NET builds a .NET-compliant DLL that you can reference in other projects. To create a Windows Control Library project, you select the template from the Add Project dialog box. The name you give the project functions as the name of the assembly for referencing. The template provides one `UserControl` automatically, but you can add any number of controls to the project.

CREATE A WINDOWS FORMS CONTROL

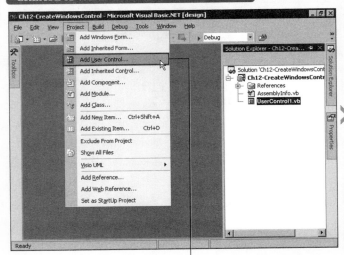

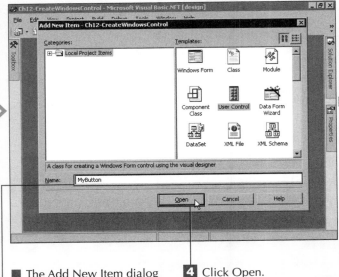

1 Open a Control Library or Windows Application project.

■ To create a Control Library project, select the Windows Control Library template when you create a project.

2 If you are using a Windows Application project, click Project ➪ Add User Control.

■ The Control Library project already contains a **UserControl** you can use.

■ The Add New Item dialog box opens.

3 Type a name for the new user control.

4 Click Open.

Extra

The `UserControl` also contains a number of default properties it inherits from the `ContainerControl` class, which is the class that lets controls contain other controls inside of it. The `ContainerControl` inherits from `ScrollableControl`, which inherits from `Control` to provides the basic functions of all parts of the Windows Forms hierarchy. Properties such as `BackColor`, `ForeColor`, `Tag`, `Enabled`, and `AutoScroll` automatically apply to your user control through the various classes that the `UserControl` inherits. For more information on how to handle and override these built-in properties, see the section "Handle Default Properties."

Unlike Visual Basic 6, you cannot create a `UserControl` that the user utilizes as a container. When developing the `UserControl`, you can add any necessary properties. The user cannot add controls to the `UserControl`, so you cannot replicate the function of a `GroupBox` or `Panel` control. You may want to create your own versions of these container controls directly instead of building a `UserControl`. To inherit from existing controls, search Visual Basic help by typing **Inherit from existing Windows Forms controls**.

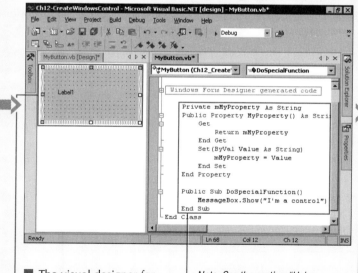

■ The visual designer for the new control appears.

5 Add any necessary controls to the visual designer.

Note: See the section "Using Standard Controls" to add controls to the `UserControl`.

6 In the Code Editor, add necessary members to the control.

Note: See the section "Add a Member" to add class members to the control.

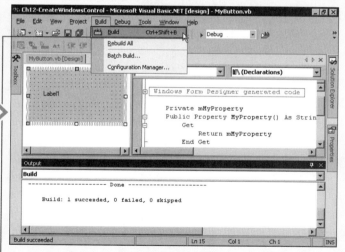

7 Click Build ➪ Build to make the control or library usable.

■ If the control exists in a control project, you can now reference the library. If you created the control in a Windows Application, go to a form and add it to the form.

Note: To reference a Control Library project, see the section "Reference a Library."

HANDLE DEFAULT PROPERTIES

When you create a user control using the Control Designer, VB .NET uses the `UserControl` class to manage many of the details of the control's placement, communication, and architecture requirements for it to function on a form. A user control inherits from the standard `ContainerControl` class that all container controls on a form and the form itself inherit. Because of this, containers of your control can access a number of properties that exist within the `ContainerControl` class without you explicitly defining them. For example, the container can retrieve and modify standard properties like `BackColor`, `Tag` and `Visible`. For some of these properties, such as appearance properties, you can handle changes specially.

Most of the controls you add to a user control automatically respond to formatting changes on the user control. For example, controls, with `BackColor` set to `Control`, contained in the `UserControl` automatically respond to

color changes made by the `UserControl`'s `BackColor` property. If you change the `UserControl` properties in the designer, the container control can still override these settings. To force a particular property value, you need to handle the `OnPropertyChanged` event, where `Property` is the name of the standard property, available in the Base Class Events section of the `UserControl`. If you set a value for the property inside this event handler, the value cannot change.

Another way to handle the base class's properties and methods is to override them. Because your `UserControl` is little more than an inherited version of the class, you can use standard inheritance techniques to override properties and other members. Inside the overridden method or property, do not assign a new value to the property or invoke the method of the same name, because doing that causes an infinite loop. For more information on using inheritance and overriding members of a class, see Chapter 8.

HANDLE DEFAULT PROPERTIES

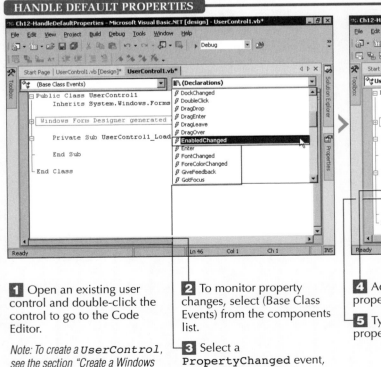

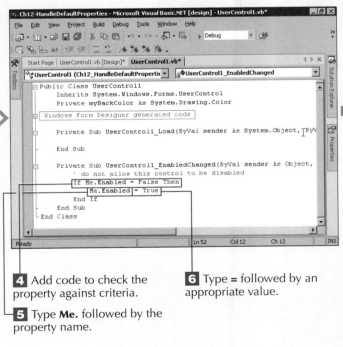

1 Open an existing user control and double-click the control to go to the Code Editor.

Note: To create a UserControl, see the section "Create a Windows Forms Control."

2 To monitor property changes, select (Base Class Events) from the components list.

3 Select a `PropertyChanged` event, where `Property` is the property to monitor.

4 Add code to check the property against criteria.

5 Type **Me.** followed by the property name.

6 Type = followed by an appropriate value.

Extra

As with properties, you can override methods and events of the User Control class. For example, the control provides a Click event that fires whenever the user clicks part of the UserControl that does not contain a constituent control. You may not want the containing application to provide code for clicking in the blank areas of the code. You can override the OnClick method to prevent this event from reaching the parent control.

Example:
```
Protected Overrides Sub OnClick(ByVal e As System.EventArgs)
     ' do nothing... hide the event from the parent.
End Sub
```

You can also use the OnEvent, where Event is the name of a particular event, to modify certain information, and pass the event along as usual. Because the events exist in the Control class, you cannot raise them normally. Instead, you must define the event again in your UserControl class using the Shadows keyword.

Example:
```
Public Shadows Event Click(ByVal sender As Object, ByVal e As System.EventArgs)

Protected Overrides Sub OnClick(ByVal e As System.EventArgs)
     ' perform necessary preprocessing
     '...

     ' raise the normal event
     RaiseEvent Click(Me, e)
End Sub
```

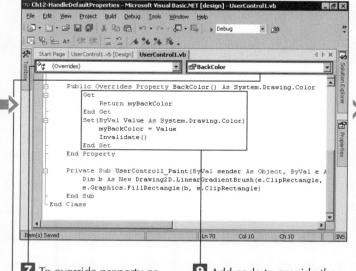

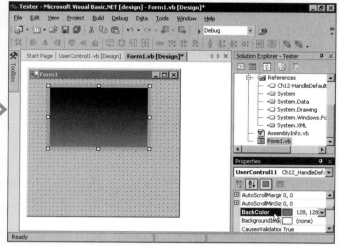

7 To override property or event functionality, select (Overrides) from the components list.

8 Select a property or method to override.

9 Add code to provide the new functionality for the property or method.

■ The example overrides the background color and paints a gradient using the selected color.

10 Click Build ➪ Build to build the project.

■ When you add the control to a form and attempt to modify a property, the appropriate code either monitors or overrides the function.

■ If you use a control library, you must reference the control library.

Note: To reference a control library, see the section "Reference a Library."

ADD A MEMBER

You can provide properties and methods in your user control that interact with its container to customize the appearance and functionality of your control. Similar to the Text property of the Button control, which sets the caption that displays on the button, you can create properties that modify the appearance and functionality of your control. You can also add custom methods, which allow the container to send commands and specify the control's actions.

To add a property to your user control, you access the Code Editor and add the property definition to the existing class that defines the user control. You define properties for your control's container as Public to give the container access to them. For more information on adding a property to a class, see Chapter 7.

To add a method to your user control, define the method inside the existing user control class. Define the

method Public to let the control's container invoke the method. If you want to create an inherited version of the control, make sure that necessary properties contain the Overridable keyword. For more information on adding a method to a class, see Chapter 7.

When you build a control and add it to a Form, you can access the properties you define inside the Properties window. You can also manipulate both the properties and methods in code. The Properties window determines the type of properties and uses the most appropriate selection system. For example, if you create a property of type Color, the Properties window automatically provides a color selector drop-down list for your property. If you have a property of type Size or Point, the designer shows the properties of the object as a subsection of your property.

ADD A MEMBER

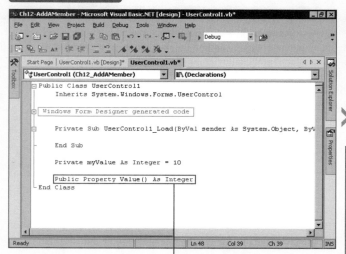

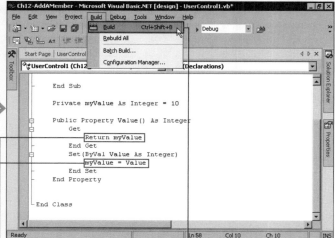

ADD A PROPERTY

1 Open an existing user control, double-click the surface of the user control to go to the Code Editor.

2 Define a private member variable.

Note: To use private member variables, see Chapter 7.

3 On an empty line of the class, type **Public Property** followed by the name of the property.

4 Press Enter.

5 Type code inside the property to set and retrieve the value that the property specifies.

Note: To add properties to a class, see Chapter 7.

6 Click Build ⇨ Build to build the control.

■ You can now add the **UserControl** to a form and access the properties of the control.

Extra

You can add read-only methods to your component, control, or class to provide information to the control's container. If your control maintains a collection of objects, you can use a ReadOnly property to allow access to the items without allowing direct changes to the objects.

Example:
```
Private items As New Collection()
Public ReadOnly Property Item(ByVal index As Integer)
    Get
        Return items(index)
    End Get
End Property
Public Sub Add(ByVal item As Object)
    items.Add(item)
End Sub
```

You can make your property take on a range of values specified by an enumeration of constants using the Enum block. Use the type name of the enumeration block for the property, and the designer loads the list and provides a drop-down list of constants.

Example:
```
Public Enum SelectionStyles
    ByColor
    ByName
End Enum
Public Property SelectionStyle() As
SelectionStyles
...
```

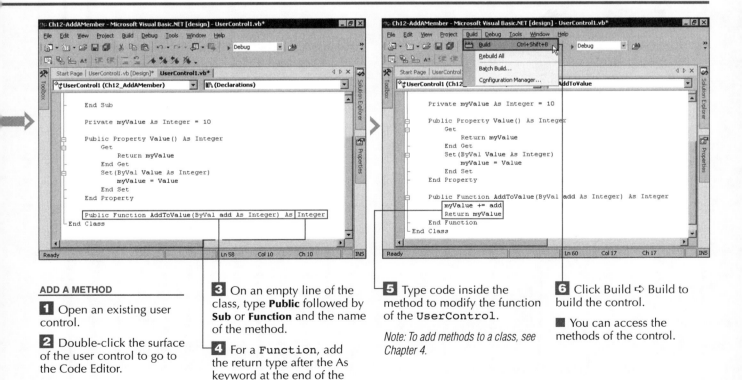

ADD A METHOD

1 Open an existing user control.

2 Double-click the surface of the user control to go to the Code Editor.

3 On an empty line of the class, type **Public** followed by **Sub** or **Function** and the name of the method.

4 For a **Function**, add the return type after the As keyword at the end of the line, and then press Enter.

5 Type code inside the method to modify the function of the **UserControl**.

Note: To add methods to a class, see Chapter 4.

6 Click Build ➪ Build to build the control.

■ You can access the methods of the control.

ADD AN EVENT

You can add events to your user control that the containing form can catch to provide event handlers. You can create custom events that you can raise when necessary. For example, a Button control provides the Click event that raises when the user clicks a button.

To define an event, add a standard event definition in the existing UserControl class's declarations. Define the event as Public to allow the user control's container to handle the event. You raise the event in the container by calling RaiseEvent. For more information on creating events in a class, see Chapter 7.

Because the UserControl inherits from the Control class, it provides a number of events that fire when actions occur on the user control's surface. For example, if the user clicks the UserControl where no control exists, the user control's Click event fires. The UserControl class and

the containing form receive this event automatically. You can override these events to prevent the container from automatically receiving them. See the section "Handle Default Properties" for more information. You can also use these events in a control where you draw on the surface. See the section "Create a Control from Scratch" for more information.

The controls you place on the user control fire events that you can handle inside the control. If you want to pass back a control's event, define an event and raise it in the event handler of the control's UserControl. For example, if your UserControl uses a ListBox control, you can alert the form when the user selects an item in the list. First, create a public event for your user control. Then, in the the ListBox's SelectedIndexChanged event, fire your public event for the user control's container to handle.

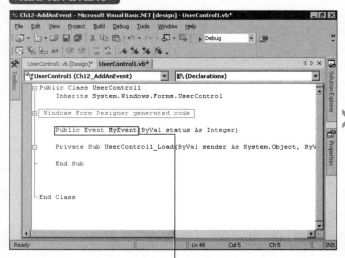

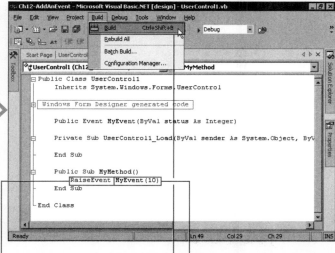

1 Open an existing user control.

Note: To create a UserControl, see the section "Create a Windows Forms Control."

2 Double-click the surface of the user control to go to the Code Editor.

3 Define an event as **Public** for the control.

Note: To define an event, see Chapter 7.

4 Type **RaiseEvent** in the method or internal event handler where you want to raise the event.

■ The example raises the event in a method called **MyMethod**.

5 Type the name of the event you defined followed by necessary parameters in parentheses.

6 Click Build ⇨ Build to build the control.

Extra

You can override the default events the `UserControl` provides to function as events for specific controls you contain in the `UserControl`. For example, the control automatically raises the `Click` event on the `UserControl`'s container when the user clicks the control's blank areas. You can add a `Button` to the user control that fires the `Click` event instead. To do this, you must shadow the existing event in the base `Control` class and then raise your event as necessary. You can disable the default `Click` event on the `UserControl` as well. For more information, see the section "Handle Default Properties."

Example:
```
Public Shadows Event Click(ByVal sender As Object, ByVal e As System.EventArgs)

Private Sub Button1_Click(ByVal sender As System.Object, ByVal e As _
        System.EventArgs) Handles Button1.Click

    ' Raise standard Click event
    RaiseEvent Click(Me, e)
End Sub
Protected Overrides Sub OnClick(ByVal e As System.EventArgs)
        ' hide event from parent
End Sub
```

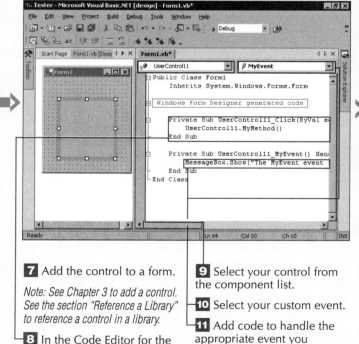

7 Add the control to a form.

Note: See Chapter 3 to add a control. See the section "Reference a Library" to reference a control in a library.

8 In the Code Editor for the form, type code to cause the event to fire.

9 Select your control from the component list.

10 Select your custom event.

11 Add code to handle the appropriate event you created.

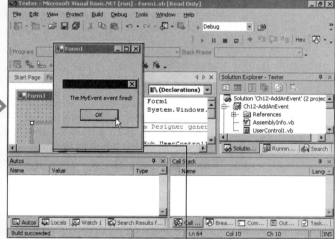

12 Press F5 to run your application.

■ The user control raises the event when necessary and the form the control resides on handles the event.

USING STANDARD CONTROLS

You can build a custom user control with the standard controls available in VB .NET and other custom controls. These composite controls function like a single control when you add them to a form, which enables you to build a layout with certain reusable controls. You can set properties of the controls and they remain constant across various instances of the control you create on forms.

You can use the Windows Control Designer to drag a control onto the surface of the UserControl. Note that you cannot access the properties, events, and other members of controls you add from outside the UserControl. You must decide what members to add to the UserControl to create so that you can replicate, modify, or extend the functionality already available in the controls.

For example, your user control may consist of a button that you modify with a particular color and font to make a standard appearance for your program. But when the user clicks the Button inside the user control, the form does not receive the button's Click event. Your user control receives the event, and you have the choice of adding an event to your user control to alert the form to the event. To alert the form, you need to create an event definition, and in the Button_Click event of the user control, raise the defined public event of the user control.

Keep in mind that you must give a UserControl the ability to resize. You can use the Dock and Anchor properties to make the controls you use on the form resize to the size of the user control. For more information on using Dock and Anchor, see Chapter 2.

USING STANDARD CONTROLS

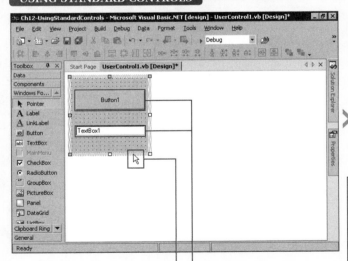

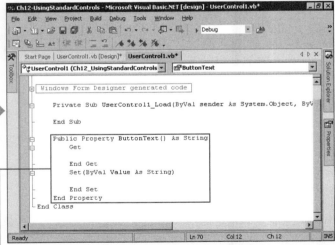

1 Open an existing user control.

Note: To create a UserControl, see "Create a Windows Forms Control."

2 Click controls in the Toolbox and then click and drag the control on the surface of the user control to pick the appropriate size and location.

3 Double-click the surface of the user control.

■ The Code Editor appears.

4 Add a property to the control that relates to a property of a control on the surface.

Note: To add a property to a UserControl, see "Add a Member."

Apply It

You can use standard controls in your project by directly inheriting from them. This provides very specific support for building a control, because you must base your control on a single existing control. You can control functions of an inherited control by overriding their event methods such as `OnPaint`. If you want the base control to perform its function, call `MyBase.OnEvent`, where `Event` is the name of the event in the base to invoke. Follow this with the appropriate parameters. To use your custom control, place it in a control library and then reference the control in a project.

TYPE THIS:

```
Public Class CustomControl1
    Inherits System.Windows.Forms.Button
    Public Sub New()
        MyBase.New()
    End Sub
    Protected Overrides Sub OnPaint(ByVal pe As_
      System.Windows.Forms.PaintEventArgs)
        MyBase.OnPaint(pe)
        ' Draw a red border around the edge of a button.
        pe.Graphics.DrawRectangle(Drawing.Pens.Red, pe.ClipRectangle)
    End Sub
End Class
```

RESULT:

The inherited button draws a red border over the standard border of a button. All functions perform the same.

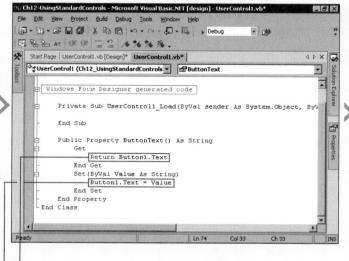

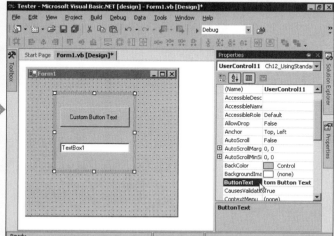

5 Return the property of the control on the `UserControl` in the `Get` routine.

6 Set the property of the control on the `UserControl` in the `Set` routine.

Note: To work with properties, see Chapter 7.

7 Build the control.

Note: To build a project, see Chapter 1.

■ The control is ready for use.

■ You can add it to a form, and alter the property of the control embedded in the `UserControl`.

Note: To add a reference to a control contained in a control library, see the section "Reference a Library."

CREATE A CONTROL FROM SCRATCH

Typically you can simply make a customized version of an existing control to ease development. But in cases where the standard controls do not offer the functionality you want for a control, you can create a control completely from scratch. For example, you can create a highly stylized button control that a standard control cannot provide.

To create a control from scratch, you must rely heavily on the graphics command layer to draw the image of your control on the surface of the `UserControl`. For more information on drawing onto a surface using graphics primitives, see Chapter 6.

Providing interactivity is essential to the usefulness of your control. The `UserControl` provides a number of properties to monitor mouse and keyword actions and movement. For example, to create a customized button, you may want to draw one style for the inactive button, one

for a pressed button, and third for the active button. Add code to paint the surface of the control in the `Paint` event handler. Make sure your `Paint` event uses the dimensions specified by the `UserControl`.

All of the drawing code in the control should exist in the `Paint` event. Placing painting code for interactivity, such as mouse clicks in the mouse events, can cause the control to draw improperly when the control repaints. To avoid this, call the `Invalidate` method the control to fire the `Paint` event and let the control redraw. Make sure to handle the `Resize` event to enable your control to redraw with the new dimensions.

The `UserControl` provides the `Click` event when the user clicks its surface, and the `MouseDown` and `MouseUp` events for the user pressing and releasing the mouse on your control, respectively. You can use `KeyPress`, `KeyDown`, and `KeyUp` events to monitor for key presses.

CREATE A CONTROL FROM SCRATCH

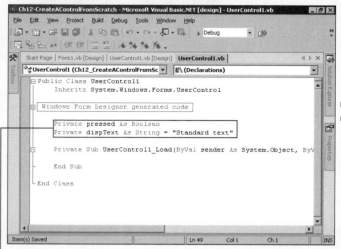

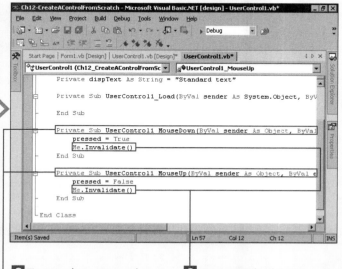

1 In the Code Editor of an existing user control class, add necessary member variables to the control.

Note: To create a `UserControl`, see "Create a Windows Forms Control." See Chapter 7 to add member variables.

2 Type code to respond to any necessary events raised by the `UserControl`.

■ The example adds code to respond to mouse clicks.

3 In any method that changes the appearance of the control, type **Me.Invalidate()**.

Apply It

You can provide drawing functions that appear like the popup style of the `Button` control. To monitor for the user pressing the mouse in the `UserControl`, set a state variable in the `MouseDown` event handler and the `MouseUp` event handler when the user lets go of the mouse button. You can use the `MouseEnter` and `MouseLeave` event to monitor the user entering or exiting the control, which you can use to provide a popup-style appearance.

TYPE THIS:

```
Private Enum ButtonState
    Normal
    Pressed
    Hover
End Enum
Private myState As ButtonState = ButtonState.Normal

Private Sub UserControl1_MouseDown(...) Handles MyBase.MouseDown
    .myState = ButtonState.Pressed: Me.Invalidate()
End Sub
Private Sub UserControl1_MouseEnter(...) Handles MyBase.MouseEnter
    myState = ButtonState.Hover: Me.Invalidate()
End Sub
Private Sub UserControl1_MouseLeave(...) Handles MyBase.MouseLeave
    myState = ButtonState.Normal: Me.Invalidate()
End Sub
Private Sub UserControl1_MouseUp(...) Handles MyBase.MouseUp
    myState = ButtonState.Normal: Me.Invalidate()
End Sub
```

RESULT:

The control responds graphically to the user's mouse.

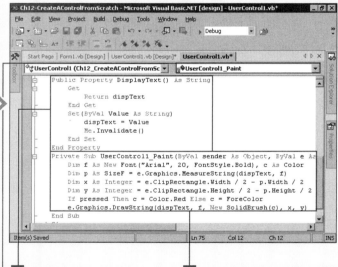

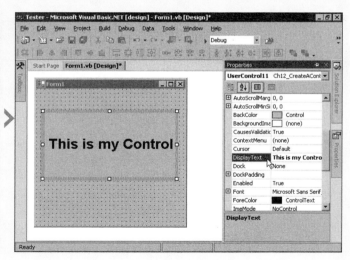

4 Add necessary events, properties, and methods to the control.

5 Select (Base Class Events) in the component list and select the `Paint` event.

6 Type code to paint the control.

7 Build the control.

Note: To add properties and methods, see "Add a Member." To add events, see "Add an Event." To build a project, see Chapter 1.

■ The control draws itself and functions like a standard control when you add it to a form.

Note: To reference a control in a control library, see "Reference a Library."

REFERENCE A LIBRARY

The Windows Control Library project builds a DLL that contains a set of `UserControl` controls, which you can reuse in your applications. The Class Library project also builds a DLL that normally contains components and classes that you can reuse across projects. These projects build the same library type. The template only varies in the type of component it initially provides when you create the project.

To use a library in another project, you indicate the compiled DLL library to reference in your project. Referencing a component library means that you now can access the classes, components, and controls that the library exports. The library is not part of your application, however, and you cannot access private parts of the library.

To reference a component or class library in an application, you use the Add Reference dialog box. A reference makes

all of the classes in the component library available, but you cannot use the controls automatically. You must customize the Toolbox and select from the library which controls and components you want available in the Toolbox.

Each assembly resides within its own namespace. Therefore, to add a library to another application, you must remember your library project's namespace to access the components and controls inside of the library. Unless you change the root namespace of the library project, the namespace is the same as the name of the project.

Because the reference you make saves into the assembly of your application, you can create a setup project that automatically installs the appropriate component library DLL with your application.

REFERENCE A LIBRARY

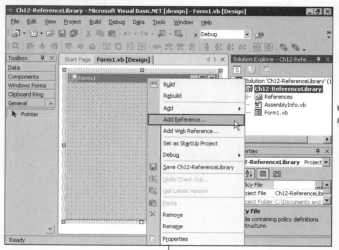

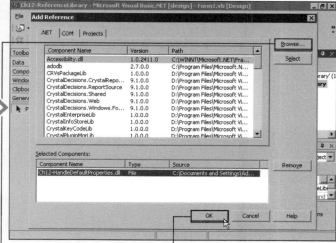

ADD A REFERENCE

■1 Create a new Windows Application project or open an existing one.

■2 Right-click the project in the Solution Explorer.

■3 Click Add Reference.

■ The Add Reference dialog box appears.

■4 Click Browse and select the DLL file.

■ The library project places the built DLL in the `bin\` subdirectory of the project directory.

■5 Click OK.

The .NET component model does not require components to register with the system before you use them in other assemblies. The COM interface, however, does require components to register before use. You can register your .NET components with COM to provide backwards compatibility for other development environments that rely on COM, such as Microsoft Office and ASP applications. To register your library DLL, use the `regasm.exe` utility where the system .NET Framework files install, typically C:\WINNT\Microsoft.NET\ Framework\v\ where v is the version of the software you are using. Run this utility and pass the path and file name of the .NET DLL assembly to register. If you do want to register the file on the current machine, pass `/regfile:` followed by the filename of a registry file to generate. You can then import this file on any computer that contains the DLL.

Example:

Register a Component
```
Regasm.exe MyLibrary.DLL
```

Generate a Registry Import File
```
Regasm.exe MyLibrary.DLL /regfile:MyLibrary.REG
```

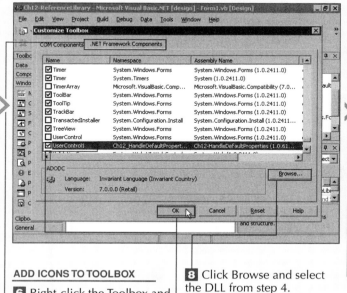

ADD ICONS TO TOOLBOX

6 Right-click the Toolbox and click Customize Toolbox.

■ The Customize Toolbox dialog box appears.

7 Click the .NET Framework Components tab.

8 Click Browse and select the DLL from step 4.

9 Check the appropriate controls and components.

10 Click OK.

11 Add controls or components in the Toolbox to the form of the application.

■ The components load from the library DLL and let you manipulate them like other controls and components.

CREATE A WEB USER CONTROL

Web user controls enable you to generate a control for use on Web Form applications. Like user controls for Windows Forms, you can build a Web control from scratch or insert existing server controls to build a new control. You can also convert an entire ASP.NET page directly into a Web server control, which you can reuse on other pages. Web user controls reside in ASCX files on the server.

You can add Web user controls to existing Web Form applications or create a project that contains a number of server controls for reuse in various controls. For more information on Web Control Library projects, see the section "Using Web Control Libraries."

Because Web Forms generate standard HTML code, a server control must generate HTML code to export to the Web browser on the client. If you build the control out of

existing controls, the controls inside your Web server control generate the HTML automatically. Web controls function in Flow layout mode only, so you add controls adjacent to one another and cannot position the controls precisely. You can type text directly onto the surface of the Web user control.

When you create the control, you can still create methods and properties to modify the functions of the control. For more information on adding methods and properties to the Web control, see the section "Add a Member."

All code runs on the server, not the client, so changed properties do not update until a post-back event occurs. If you add a post-back control, such as a Button to your UserControl, a post-back occurs on the page, and events fire in your control. Non-post-back events raise when the next post-back event occurs.

CREATE A WEB USER CONTROL

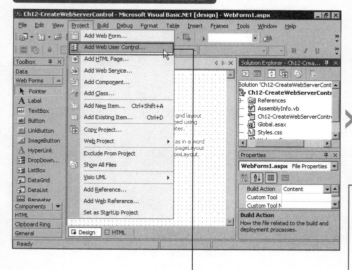

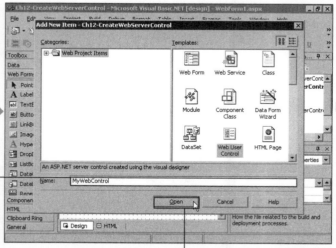

1 Create a new Web Application or Web Control Library project or open an existing one.

Note: To create a Web Control Library, see "Using Web Control Libraries."

2 Click Project ➪ Add Web User Control.

■ The Add New Item dialog box appears.

3 Type a name for the new control.

4 Click Open.

Extra

The Render method lets you generate a completely custom control without the standard Web forms controls. You can generate a client-side script and the appropriate link to make a post-back event occur in your control.

Example:
```
Public Class WebControl1
    Inherits System.Web.UI.UserControl
    Implements IpostBackEventHandler
' ... Web Form Designer Generated Code ...
    Public Sub RaisePostBackEvent(ByVal eventArgument As String) _
        Implements IPostBackEventHandler.RaisePostBackEvent
        If eventArgument = "Action1" Then
            ' do something here
        End If
    End Sub
    Protected Overrides Sub Render(ByVal writer As _
        System.Web.UI.HtmlTextWriter)
        writer.Write("<input type=button value=Action1 OnClick=""jscript:" & _
            Page.GetPostBackEventReference(Me, "Action1") & """><p>")
    End Sub
End Class
```

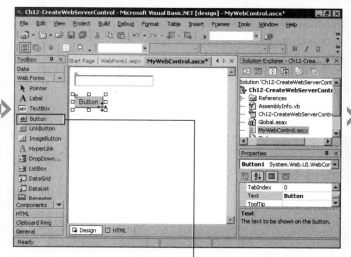

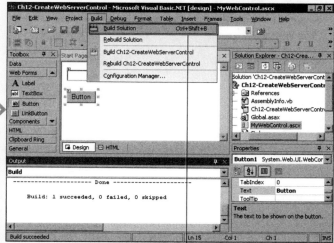

■ The designer for the new control appears.

5 Double-click controls in the Toolbox to add them to the Web user control.

■ You can add necessary properties, methods to the control through the Code Editor by double-clicking the surface of the Web user control.

Note: See "Add a Member" to add properties and methods.

6 Click Build ⇨ Build Solution.

■ The control is complete. You can now use it in a Web Form in the project.

Note: See "Add a Web Control to a Page" to add the control to a Web Form.

ADD A WEB CONTROL TO A PAGE

Web user controls let you create components that you can use throughout a Web Application. Web user controls function much differently than Windows user controls. The server represents each Web user control as a separate ASP.NET file, and by virtue of how Web servers function, the server must *embed* the control onto your form to use it. This means the actual definition of the control simply adds into the design of the Web Form page.

To add a Web user control to a Web page, you drag the ASCX file that represents the control onto a Web form. Web user controls do not appear in the Toolbox. When you add the user control onto your Web form, you cannot view the control in design mode. The control shows as a gray area showing only the name of the control. You cannot control the size or modify any properties from the designer.

When you drag the user control onto the form to embed it, the designer does not automatically create an object reference in code to access the control's properties and methods. You must add a declaration to the Web Form class's base definition. For the Web Form compilation to attach this variable to the Web user control, you must specify the same name that you assign to the control in the designer. For the variable type, use the Web user control's class name.

A good use for a Web user control is to contain functionality to login a user by providing an interface, which you can include on various entry pages to allow logins. The user control can handle all of the login events and functions without the main page needing any logic, except to check a property in the user control.

ADD A WEB CONTROL TO A PAGE

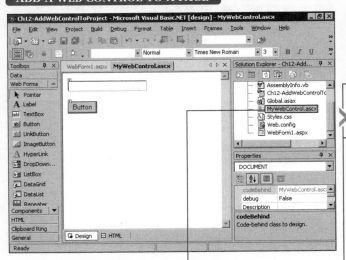

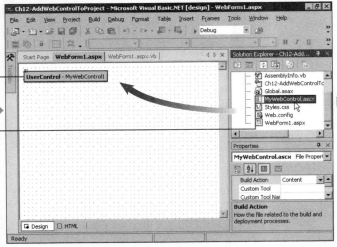

ADD A WEB CONTROL

1 Create a new Web Application project or open an existing one.

2 Add a Web user control to the project.

Note: See "Create a Web User Control" to add a Web user control.

3 Open the page to embed the control.

4 Click the control in the Solution Explorer and drag it to the page.

■ The page shows the embedded control.

■ If the page is in layout mode, you can place the control using tables and lines.

5 Double-click the surface of the Web form.

■ The Code Editor opens.

Extra

You can move events from a user control to the Web Forms page. ASP.NET calls the function bubbling events. You can bubble events from a user control to a form using the `RaiseBubbleEvent` method. In the user control event you want to raise up to the page, call the `RaiseBubbleEvent` method with the first parameter being the source object, and an event argument object. You pass `Nothing` as the second parameter if you do want to pass a second parameter. In the Web Form, you override the `OnBubbleEvent` method. If you have multiple controls raising bubble events, you can use the `Sender` object to check the type. The example assumes the user control contains a `Label` and a `Button` control, and the form contains another `Label` and the `UserControl`.

Example:

Button1_Click in User Control

```
Private Sub Button1_Click(ByVal sender As System.Object, ByVal e As _
    System.EventArgs) Handles Button1.Click

    Label1.Text = "Button1_Click Fired"
    RaiseBubbleEvent(Me, Nothing)
End Sub
```

Code in Web Form

```
Protected Overrides Function OnBubbleEvent(ByVal source As Object, _
    ByVal args As System.EventArgs) As Boolean

    If TypeOf source Is WebUserControl1 Then
        Label1.Text = "Clicked Button in the Web Control"
    End If
End Function
```

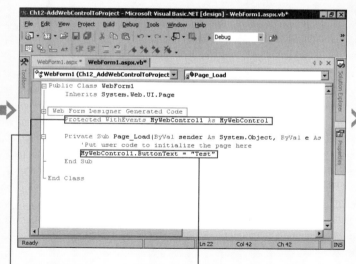

ACCESS CONTROL CODE

6 In the base of the page code module, type **Protected WithEvents MyWebControl1 As MyWebControl**, replacing `MyWebControl1` with the control's variable name, and `MyWebControl` with your user control's class name.

7 In the method to set up the control, set properties and call necessary methods to set up the control.

8 Press F5 to run your project.

■ The control contents appears when the project runs, allowing manipulation.

Note: This example uses the control created in the section "Create a Web User Control."

USING WEB CONTROL LIBRARIES

You can use a Web control project to generate a DLL of Web custom controls for use on Web Forms pages. Unlike a Web user control, you add Web custom controls to a Web control library. These controls appear as actual entries in the Web Forms toolbox and do not reside on an ASP.NET page of a Web project. A Web custom control functions exactly like the existing controls that VB .NET provides.

When you create a custom control, you create your very own custom control, therefore preventing you from combining existing controls like you would in a Web user control. To create a Web custom control, you must specify exactly how the control generates on the Web Form page.

You use standard HTML output to generate the appearance for your control. To output this code, you override the `Render` method provided by the `WebControl` base class. The method has a single parameter of type `HtmlTextWriter`,

which enables you to write to the page with the object's `Write` method.

You define properties, methods, and events like any other class or control. See the section "Add a Member" for information on adding properties and methods to a control. Use private member variables to hold data for the control. The Web Forms system maintains the state of the object automatically.

When you create a Web Control Library project, the template contains one custom control. The control in the template predefines a `Text` property and outputs the text in its `Render` method. You can delete this property and alter the `Render` method, but the template provides a good starting point for building your control. To reference the Web Control library in a Web Application project, add a reference and customize the Toolbox as you might when using a Windows forms control library. For more information on referencing a library, see the section "Reference a Library."

USING WEB CONTROL PROJECTS

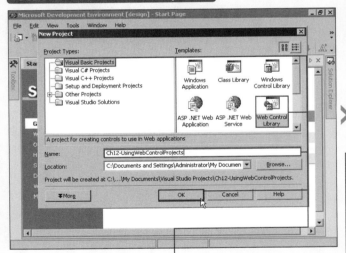

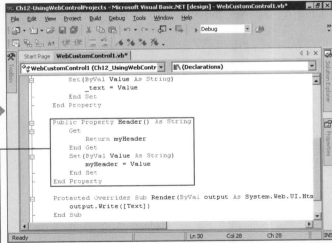

CREATE A WEB CONTROL LIBRARY PROJECT

1 Open the New Project dialog box.

Note: To create a new project, see Chapter 1.

2 Click Visual Basic Projects.

3 Click the Web Control Library template.

4 Type a name for the project.

5 Click OK.

■ The Code Editor appears with a default Web custom control class open.

6 Define properties, methods, and events for the control.

■ If desired, you can remove the code for the default **Text** property and the default code from the **Render** method.

Note: To define methods and properties, see "Add a Member." To define events, see "Add an Event."

Extra

You can add information to your properties for the visual forms designer if you desire. To add template information, use angle brackets (<>) before the definition of either the class or a particular property or event. You can find a reference for most of the standard template properties in the section "Create a Component."

Example:
```
<Bindable(True), Category("Appearance"), DefaultValue("")> _
Property Text() As String
    Get
        Return mText
    End Get

    Set(ByVal Value As String)
        mText = Value
    End Set
End Property
```

The `WebControl` class forms the basis of your custom control in a Web control library. The `WebControl` class exports a number of properties for all controls, much like the Windows forms `Control` class. You can override these properties if you want them to function in a particular way. See "Handle Default Properties" to learn how to override properties and events of the base control. For a reference of the properties a `WebControl`, search Visual Basic .NET help by typing **WebControl members**.

Because you cannot use other controls to build a Web custom control, if you want to post-back for certain events, you must provide the function yourself. For more information on generating post-back events, see the section "Create a Web User Control."

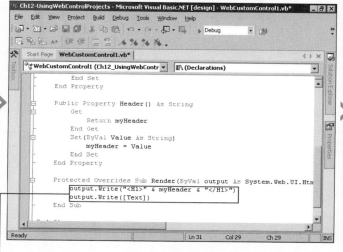

RENDER THE CONTROL

7 In the `Render` method, type **output.Write ()**, replacing `output` with the `HtmlTextWriter` object's variable name and placing a string of data to export from the control inside the parentheses.

■ The default definition declares the variable as `output`.

8 Repeat step 7 as necessary.

9 Build the control library.

Note: To build a project, see Chapter 1.

■ The control is complete.

■ You can reference the control in a Web Application project and add it to the page.

Note: To reference the Web control library, see "Reference a Library." To use Web forms, see Chapter 10.

DEBUG AN APPLICATION

The process of *debugging* an application involves solving problems that cause the application not to compile, or operate properly when it runs. You can use the debugging abilities of the Development Studio to aid in the correction of these problems.

The term *design-time error* describes an error that causes the application not to compile. Normally, design-time errors occur because you mismatch parentheses or spell a method improperly. You can correct a design-time error easily by satisfying the criteria that the error message explains. For example, a common error message may say that you have not defined a particular. For this message, you check to see if you specify the namespace for the object, or import the namespace as necessary. Another common error involves an unexpected end of statement. You correct this error by checking for a missing comma, making sure you enclose strings with quotes properly, and ensuring that underscores

split lines correctly. For more information on building projects and handling design-time errors, see Chapter 1.

Runtime errors can take much longer to correct. A runtime error includes any error that results from logic or design error during programming, and results in a program that builds and runs, but does not function as expected. A runtime error can occur in two different ways. An actual application error that occurs while your program runs is called an exception. In this case, the Development Environment breaks your program and enables you to view the line of code that causes the exception. The other type of error is when your program runs with no errors, but it does not function correctly. When your code seemingly looks correct, you need to look deeper into the execution of your program. For more information on stepping through your application one line at a time and using watch variables, see the section "Monitor Program Execution."

DEBUG AN APPLICATION

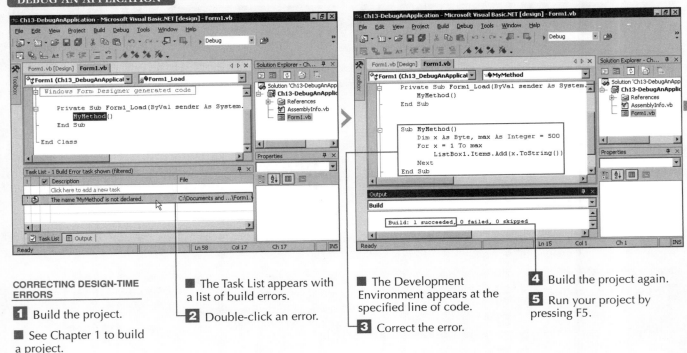

CORRECTING DESIGN-TIME ERRORS

1 Build the project.

■ See Chapter 1 to build a project.

■ The Task List appears with a list of build errors.

2 Double-click an error.

■ The Development Environment appears at the specified line of code.

3 Correct the error.

4 Build the project again.

5 Run your project by pressing F5.

Extra

When an error occurs, the .NET Framework objects use exceptions to make the error message available for handling or debugging. For more information on exceptions and debugging runtime errors, see the section "Monitor Program Execution." You can customize how the debugger manages exceptions. To do so, click the Debug menu and click Exceptions. A dialog appears that lets you modify the default settings. You can have the debugger break the program immediately when the object throws the exception, or have it continue and allow the program to handle the error. You can also make the environment break if your application does not handle the error, or allow the program to continue executing. By default, exceptions continue when an object throws them but break into the debugger if your application does not handle them.

You can use the debugger to attach to any running process on the system and examine its runtime state. To do so, click Debug and then Processes. Select the process to which you want to attach the debugger and click Attach. In the dialog that appears, select the parts of the program that you want to debug and click OK. The debugger loads and lets you monitor the process.

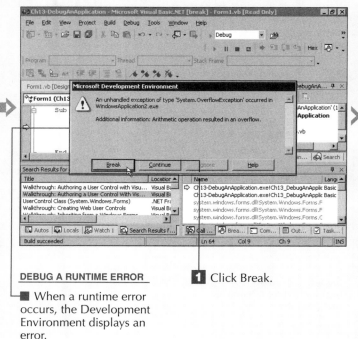

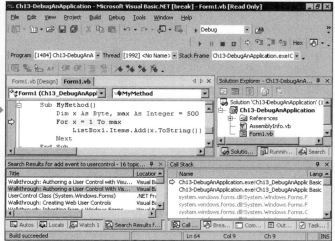

DEBUG A RUNTIME ERROR

■ When a runtime error occurs, the Development Environment displays an error.

1 Click Break.

■ The Development Environment displays the running line in the code editor.

■ You can correct the error and run the project again.

Note: To monitor and setup debugging checkpoints in your code for runtime errors, see "Monitor Program Execution."

MONITOR PROGRAM EXECUTION

You may find yourself unable to correct code, because it looks right but does not work as you expect. You can use the debugging tools that Visual Studio provides to monitor the execution of your program. You can easily debug a runtime error when an exception occurs during program execution. When an exception occurs, Visual Basic .NET breaks and lets you look at the line in question. For more information concerning runtime exception errors, see the section "Debug an Application."

But when no error occurs, yet your program does not work like you expect, you can use the debugger. The debugger provides a feature called *breakpoints*. When the execution of the program reaches a breakpoint, it stops and lets you examine variables and objects that the line accesses. The tool window also lets you find, add, or delete the breakpoints in a project.

When you run your program, and the execution reaches a line that contains a breakpoint, the Development Environment activates and highlights the line on which the execution stops. The Autos Watch tool window at the bottom in the Development Environment provides a list of variables and objects that the line uses. The current value of the various variables appears in the window. The Locals Watch window provides a list of all local variables to the method or property that contains the breakpoint line.

You can examine the flow of an application by setting a breakpoint and stepping through the code as it runs, one line at a time. Use the Step Into command on the Debug menu to execute the current line. If the current line contains methods or properties in your project, the execution steps into those functions. You can use Step Over to skip the execution of a function, run the line, and step to the next line in the same module.

MONITOR PROGRAM EXECUTION

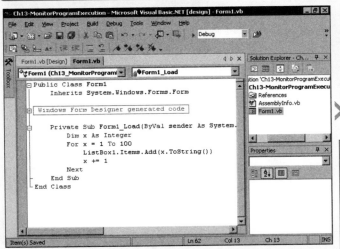

1 Open an existing project and open a code module in the code editor.

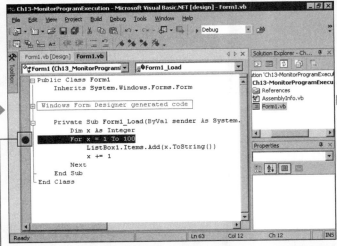

2 Left-click the margin on the left side of the code editor beside the line to place a breakpoint.

■ You cannot place a breakpoint on declaration lines unless the declaration contains an assignment.

Extra

You can inspect any variable in the application in debug mode. Although the Autos and Locals watch window display most of the variables in question for a particular line, you may need to inspect a variable that the debugger did not determine the current line uses. For information not shown in either of these windows, the Watch window lets you enter variables or objects to inspect.

When an error occurs in an object at runtime, it raises an exception to notify your program of the problem. While many objects raise custom exception objects, all exceptions derive from the `Exception` object, and have the same basic set of properties. To retrieve an exception when a runtime error occurs, see the section "Recover from an Error."

SEVERAL OBJECT MEMBERS

`Message`	The `Message` property specifies a `String` containing an error message explaining the problem that causes the exception.
`Source`	The `Source` property holds a `String` representing the object where the error occurs.
`GetType`	The `GetType` method returns a `Type` object specifying the actual type of `Exception` class this object represents. See Visual Basic Help for more information on using the `Type` object.

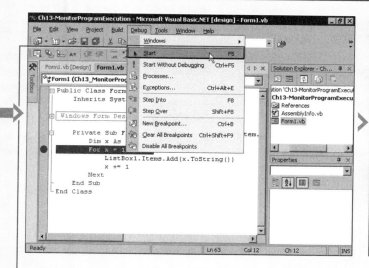

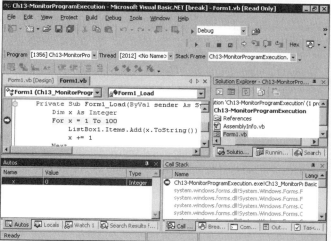

3 Click Debug ⇨ Start to start the project in debug mode.

■ You can also press F5 to start the project in debug mode.

■ The application breaks and allows you to examine variables and objects in memory.

RECOVER FROM AN ERROR

Error handling and recovery is an important part of making an easy-to-use and reliable program. You can use error-checking statements to catch errors and handle them appropriately.

You can catch any error that raises an exception using a special statement block. When an exception occurs, the object raising the error creates an instance of an Exception class, or an inherited version of this class, that contains information about the error. For example, a database object raises an exception when it cannot connect to a database or when it attempts to save data into a database that does not fit the specified characteristics for the field.

You use the Try block to catch errors that occur as the program runs. You terminate the block with the End Try statement. You place the code that may cause an error inside the Try block area. Then, you use the Catch statement to catch exceptions that occur. After the Catch

statement, type a variable name followed by the As keyword and the exception type to catch. You can use multiple Catch statements to catch various kinds of specific exceptions.

You can use the Exception type to catch any sort of exception that occurs. You can test for specific exceptions, like the DataException type, and then use another Catch for other types of errors using the generic Exception type. Using multiple exception tests enables you to handle the various errors that arise in specific ways.

After the Catch statement, add code to handle the error. You should always add some sort of code to either correct the error or at least notify the user of the error.

You can add the Finally block after any Catch statements to run code after the Try block runs and any necessary Catch blocks correct exceptions.

RECOVER FROM AN ERROR

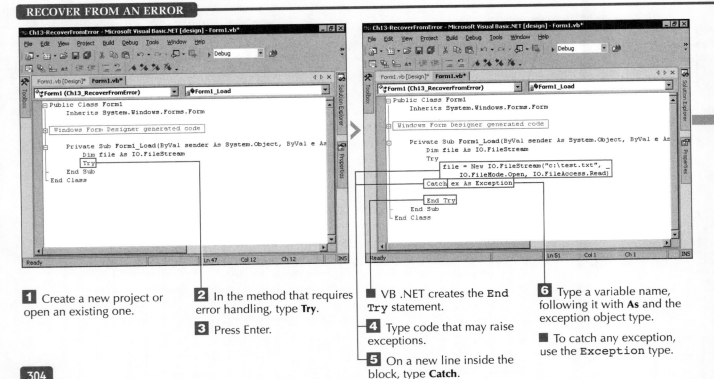

1 Create a new project or open an existing one.

2 In the method that requires error handling, type **Try**.

3 Press Enter.

■ VB .NET creates the **End Try** statement.

4 Type code that may raise exceptions.

5 On a new line inside the block, type **Catch**.

6 Type a variable name, following it with **As** and the exception object type.

■ To catch any exception, use the **Exception** type.

Extra

A `Try` block cannot handle exceptions that occur inside a `Catch` or `Finally` block. If the code you use to correct the error has the potential to cause an error as well, you can nest multiple `Try` blocks inside of each other.

TYPE THIS:

```
Dim file As IO.FileStream
Try
    file = New IO.FileStream("c:\test.txt", IO.FileMode.Open, _
        IO.FileAccess.Read, IO.FileShare.None)
Catch ex As Exception
    Try
        file = New IO.FileStream("c:\backup\test.txt", IO.FileMode.Open, _
            IO.FileAccess.Read, IO.FileShare.None)
    Catch
        Dim msg As String = "Could not find original or backup " & _
            "configuration file. Reinstall the application"
        MessageBox.Show(msg)
        End Try
End Try
If Not (file Is Nothing) Then
    ' configure using the file
    MessageBox.Show("Configuration loaded")
End If
```

RESULT:

```
Could not find original or backup configuration file. Reinstall the application.
```

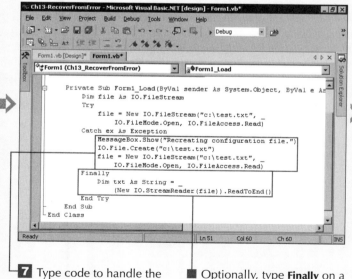

7 Type code to handle the exception.

■ Optionally, type **Finally** on a new line inside the block and add code to run after the rest of the **Try** block completes.

8 Press F5 to run your project.

■ The **Try** block catches an exception and the **Catch** block handles the error gracefully.

USING THE REGISTRY

The Registry provides a universally accessible data storage area for a computer. You can write information to the Registry to remember user preferences and settings. Specific to Win32 machines, the `Registry` class and supplementary classes exist under the `Microsoft.Win32` namespace. To learn how to import a namespace, see Chapter 8.

The `Registry` class provides instances of the `RegistryKey` object representing each of the eight base keys in the registry. The `CurrentUser` property returns a `RegistryKey` representing information stored for the current login. The `LocalMachine` property returns a `RegistryKey` object representing the settings for the local machine, regardless of user. You store software settings for your application in the `SOFTWARE` key inside the `LocalMachine` or `CurrentUser` key, depending on if the application stores separate information for various users.

Use the `OpenSubKey` method to open a subkey. Pass the path of the subkey to open the first parameter. You can load a deeper sublevel by separating the subkeys with back slashes. Pass `True` as the second parameter to enable write support. The method returns a new `RegistryKey` object representing the subkey. To create a subkey, pass the name to the `CreateSubKey` method of a `RegistryKey` object and the method adds the key under the existing key.

You retrieve the value associated with a particular name using the `GetValue` method. Pass a string representing the name of a value in the key and the method returns the data the value holds.

You can add and change values using the `SetValue` keyword. Pass the name as a string for the first parameter, and a value as the second parameter. For the value, you can pass a string or an integer number.

After you make changes to the registry key, invoke the `Flush` method of a `RegistryKey` with no parameters to save the changes.

USING THE REGISTRY

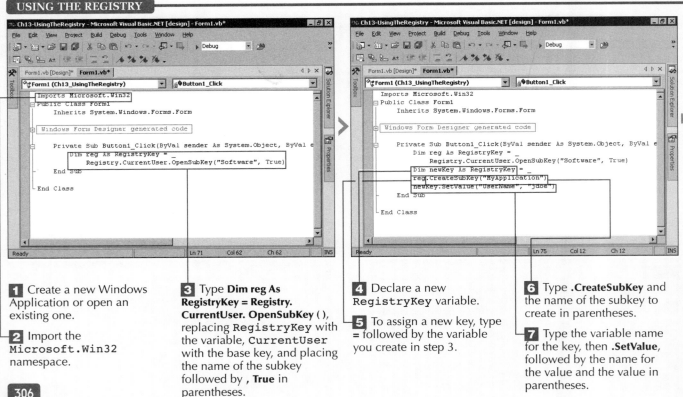

1 Create a new Windows Application or open an existing one.

2 Import the `Microsoft.Win32` namespace.

3 Type **Dim reg As RegistryKey = Registry. CurrentUser. OpenSubKey ( )**, replacing `RegistryKey` with the variable, `CurrentUser` with the base key, and placing the name of the subkey followed by **, True** in parentheses.

4 Declare a new `RegistryKey` variable.

5 To assign a new key, type = followed by the variable you create in step 3.

6 Type **.CreateSubKey** and the name of the subkey to create in parentheses.

7 Type the variable name for the key, then **.SetValue**, followed by the name for the value and the value in parentheses.

Apply It

You can use properties of a `RegistryKey` object to list the available subkeys and values associated with the key. The `SubKeyCount` property returns the number of subkeys the particular key contains and the `ValueCount` property returns the number of values associated with the key. Use the `GetSubKeyNames` method to return an array of strings representing the names of the available subkeys. To get the values associated with a key, use the `GetValueNames` method to return an array of strings representing the available values.

TYPE THIS:

```
Dim regKey As RegistryKey = Registry.LocalMachine.OpenSubKey("SOFTWARE")
Dim keyName As String, valueName As String

Console.WriteLine("Sub Keys:")
For Each keyName In regKey.GetSubKeyNames()

    Console.Write(keyName & ", ")
Next

Console.WriteLine(ControlChars.CrLf & "Values:")
For Each valueName In regKey.GetValueNames()

    Console.Write(valueName & ", ")
Next
Console.ReadLine()
```

RESULT:

Sub Keys:

Classes, Clients, Microsoft, ODBC, Program Groups, Secure, Windows 3.1 Migration Status,

Values:

Description,

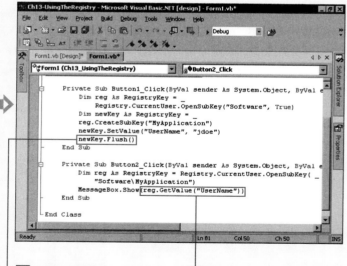

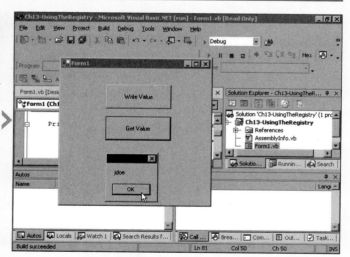

8 To save changes, type the registry key followed by **.Flush()**.

9 To read a key, type the variable name of the key to access, then **.GetValue**, and then the name of the value to retrieve in parentheses.

10 Press F5 to run your project.

■ The application adds and retrieves values from the registry.

PROVIDE ACCESS TO DISABLED USERS

Accessibility aids make it easier for the disabled to use computers. For example, blind people can use screen readers to verbalize the information shown on screen, and people who cannot use a keyboard and mouse can rely on voice input utilities. You can use properties provided in Windows Forms controls to aid disabled users with your application.

To enable users with disabilities to use your application effectively, you need to consider some guidelines that target problem areas an individual may encounter. Always provide a flexible user interface that accommodates the user's needs and preferences. Use color to enhance and emphasize information shown by other means. Do not use color as the only means of using a part of your application. Keyboard access to all parts of your application enables all users, especially disabled users, to use your application more effectively. The size of text and graphics affects both accessibility and usability. You should enable users to size

objects on the screen and follow system metrics for preset user preferences.

All Windows Forms controls inherit an `AccessibleObject` that stores information to use with software- and hardware-based accessibility aids. The `AccessibleDescription` property of the object appears in the Properties window and specifies a description for the control. For example, an Exit button may contain the description "A button with the text Exit." The `AccessibleName` property reports a name for the control to accessibility aids. The `AccessibleRole` property reports the role of the control. In most cases, the designer sets this property correctly. For example, the `AccessiblityRole` of a `Button` control is `AccessibleRole.Button`. In some cases, you may want to change this property. For example, if you use a `PictureBox` control to draw a chart, you can set the role to `AccessibleRole.Chart`.

PROVIDE ACCESS TO DISABLED USERS

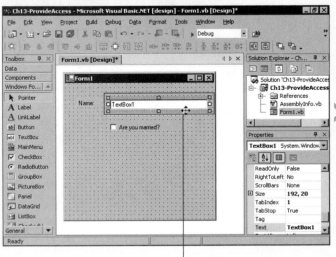

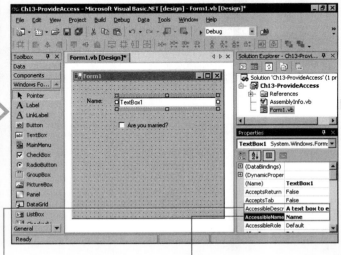

1 Open an existing project.

2 Click a control on a Windows Form.

3 Click the `AccessibleDescription` property in the Properties window and type a description for the particular control.

4 Click `AccessibleName` and type in a name for the control.

Extra

You can use the following list as a partial reference for the accessibility roles available for controls in your application. You can select each of these constants from the enumeration in the Properties window.

CONSTANT	DESCRIPTION
Alert	An alert or condition for a user. You only use this role for objects that have no association with another user interface element, like a message box, graphic, text, or sound.
ButtonDropDown	A button that drops down a list of items.
ButtonDropDownGrid	A button that drops down a grid.
ButtonMenu	A button that drops down a menu.
Character	A cartoon-like graphic object, such as Microsoft Office Assistant, which displays help to users of an application.
Chart	A graphical image used to represent data.
Clock	A control that displays the time.
Diagram	A graphical image used to diagram data.
Dial	A dial or knob, or a read-only visual object like a speedometer.
Equation	A mathematical equation.
Indicator	An indicator, such as a pointer graphic, that points to the current item.
Link	A link, which acts as a connection between a source document and a destination document. You can use this for graphics or labels that act like a button.

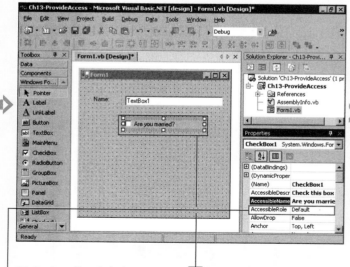

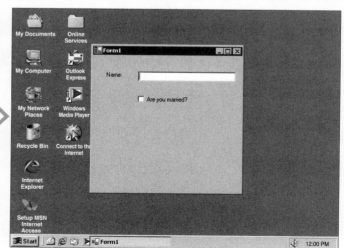

■ Optionally, click the **AccessibleRole** ▾ and select a new role.

5 Repeat for all of the controls on the form.

6 Press F5 to run your project.

■ Your application runs and appears as normal, but accessibility helper applications can use the information to aid disabled users.

CREATE A WINDOWS INSTALLER

When you complete a project, you then need to package the application for distribution. Visual Studio provides tools to develop a setup application for components, applications, and Web projects you create. You can use the tool to build a professional and customized installation program.

The Setup Wizard project enables you to create a project that supports the installation of Windows Application projects, Web Application projects, and component projects. When you add the project to a solution that contains Windows Application and component library projects, a wizard lets you select details for the installation, and then builds a project.

You can also specify for the installation to build a CAB file, which you can provide for download on the Internet. For a Windows machine, the setup project builds a single file with a `.msi` extension that installs using the Windows Installer tool included with recent versions of Windows and Internet Explorer.

With projects that install using the Setup Wizard, the wizard detects dependences necessary for the project to run. For example, if the project requires database support, the setup project automatically includes a database distributable component.

Also included in every project is the .NET redistributable component. After selecting a project, the Setup Wizard asks you which parts of the application you want to distribute. The Primary output selection includes the EXE or DLL file your project outputs. The Localized resource selection includes any resource files you include in your project. You can also include source code and content files associated with the project through the wizard.

After you create the project, you can modify installation details by loading the client file system window and by specifying where files load on the client system. For more information on customizing the installation, see the section "Customize Your Installation."

CREATE A WINDOWS INSTALLER

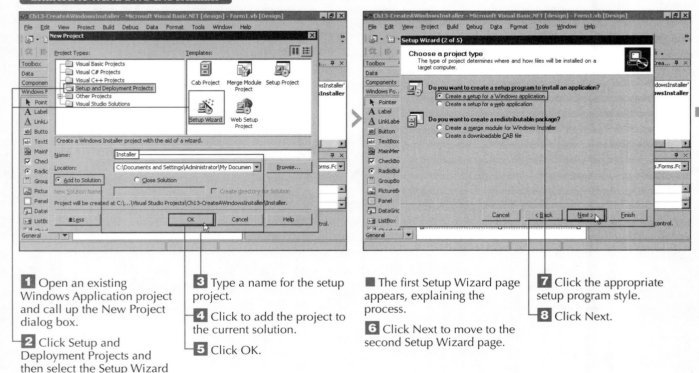

1 Open an existing Windows Application project and call up the New Project dialog box.

2 Click Setup and Deployment Projects and then select the Setup Wizard template.

3 Type a name for the setup project.

4 Click to add the project to the current solution.

5 Click OK.

■ The first Setup Wizard page appears, explaining the process.

6 Click Next to move to the second Setup Wizard page.

7 Click the appropriate setup program style.

8 Click Next.

Extra

You can create a Windows installation program to deploy a Web application onto new servers much like installing a Windows application. When the Setup Wizard begins, you click the Create a setup for a Web application option. Before creating the setup, you must have a Web Forms project open. Then add the setup project to the solution, just like you add an installer for Windows applications in the Introduction. When you run the setup, instead of prompting you for an installation directory, like a Windows application setup, the Web application setup asks for a virtual directory on a local copy of IIS into which it installs the Web application. The setup includes all of the necessary .NET Framework files in case the Web server does not have ASP.NET installed. The File System window contains the same options, although the default folders include only the Global Assembly Class and the Web Application Folder. The Web Application Folder item represents the Web server directory into which the Web application installs. Deploy the server by running the MSI setup file on the server that needs to run the application.

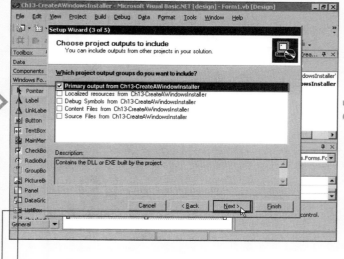

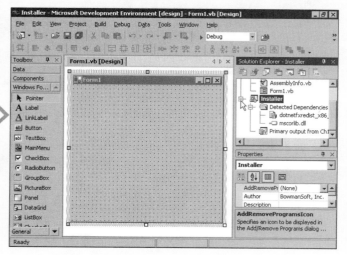

■ **9** Click items from the project to include in the setup.

■ **10** Click Next.

■ **11** On the fourth screen, select any files necessary to include with the setup.

■ **12** Click Next.

■ **13** Click Finish to complete the wizard.

■ The setup project adds to the current solution.

Note: See "Customize Your Installation" to customize and build the setup program.

CUSTOMIZE YOUR INSTALLATION

You can customize the Setup Project to provide various installation capabilities. You can add menu items to the client computer's Start Menu, as well as icons to the Desktop.

To modify the setup appearance, you modify the setup project's properties of the setup project. The `Title` property specifies the title for the installation. The `Author` property specifies the author to show in the installation. `Description` specifies a description to show when setup loads. The `Manufacturer` specifies the company that makes the product. You can optionally specify a URL to make the manufacturer information appear as a hyperlink using the `ManufacturerUrl` property. The `ProductName` property specifies the name of the product the setup program installs. You can specify support information using the `SupportPhone` and `SupportUrl` properties. The `Version` property stores the software version that setup installs. The `DetectNewerInstalledVersion` property determines how setup handles a previously installed version. If setup determines that a newer version already exists and this property is `True`, installation cancels.

To customize the file locations the setup program uses to install the application, you use the File System window in the setup project. In the File System window, four main folders, into which you can place items, appear by default: the Application Folder, the Global Assembly Cache Folder, the User's Desktop, and the User's Program Menu. Although only those four items appear, a multitude of other install paths are available. You can add files to the Windows folder, the System folder, or the user's favorites or application data folders, among others.

You can also specify subfolders in your installation directories to install particular files into particular locations. To move files, you simply drag and drop them.

To add a Start menu item, you go to the User's Programs Menu and add a shortcut. You need to select the primary output file, which automatically links to your project's executable.

CUSTOMIZE YOUR INSTALLATION

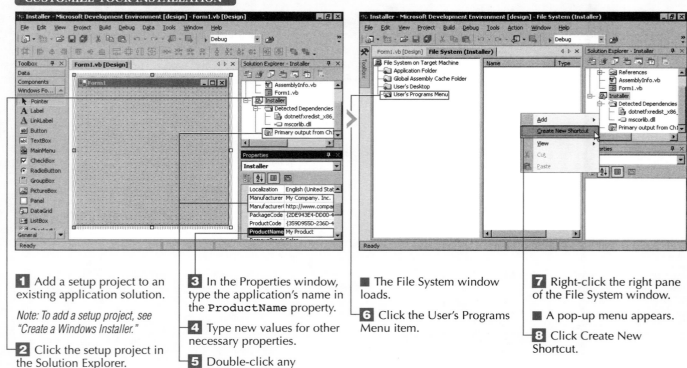

1 Add a setup project to an existing application solution.

Note: To add a setup project, see "Create a Windows Installer."

2 Click the setup project in the Solution Explorer.

3 In the Properties window, type the application's name in the **ProductName** property.

4 Type new values for other necessary properties.

5 Double-click any installation targets.

■ The File System window loads.

6 Click the User's Programs Menu item.

7 Right-click the right pane of the File System window.

■ A pop-up menu appears.

8 Click Create New Shortcut.

Extra

You can view the files that make up the primary output component of the installation by right-clicking the item and then selecting outputs. In some cases, the wizard incorrectly identifies the project files to include with your project. You must modify the files that the setup project automatically determines it should include in this group. You can right-click the primary output item and select `ExcludeFilter`. A dialog box appears, enabling you to specify parts of the project output not to include with your setup application. Common file filters include `*.txt` and `*.vb?`.

For any given list item, such as a file or assembly, you can modify installation properties. You can specify attributes the installation uses to install the file by altering the `System`, `Hidden`, and `ReadOnly` properties. If the file is a DLL or COM component that the installation needs to register, you can set the `Register` property. Only COM-based DLLs and components need to register. Components you create using .NET languages do not need to register. If the component needs to install based on a condition, specify the condition using the `Condition` property. If the condition you enter evaluates to `True`, the setup program installs the file.

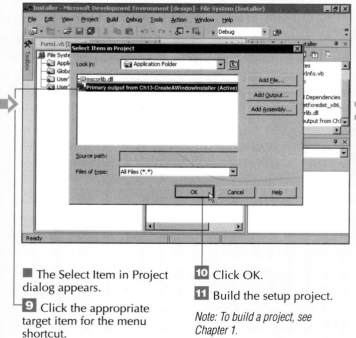

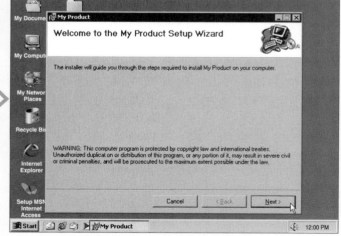

■ The Select Item in Project dialog appears.

9 Click the appropriate target item for the menu shortcut.

10 Click OK.

11 Build the setup project.

Note: To build a project, see Chapter 1.

12 Run the generated installation.

■ The customizations you made appear in the setup project.

WHAT'S ON THE CD-ROM

The CD-ROM included in this book contains many useful files and programs. Before installing any of the programs on the disc, make sure that a newer version of the program is not already installed on your computer. For information on installing different versions of the same program, contact the program's manufacturer. For the latest and greatest information, please refer to the ReadMe file located at the root of the CD-ROM.

SYSTEM REQUIREMENTS

To use the contents of the CD-ROM, your computer must be equipped with the following hardware and software:

- A PC with a Pentium III or faster processor
- Microsoft Windows NT 4.0, Windows 2000, or Windows XP
- Microsoft Visual Studio .NET
- At least 128MB of total RAM installed on your computer
- An eight-speed (8x) or faster CD-ROM drive
- A monitor capable of displaying at least 256 colors or grayscale

AUTHOR'S SOURCE CODE

These files contain all the sample code from the book. You can browse these files directly from the CD-ROM, or you can copy them to your hard drive and use them as the basis for your own projects. To find the files on the CD-ROM, open the D:\Resources\Code folder. To copy the files to your hard drive, just run the installation program D:\Resources\Code\Code.exe. The files will be placed on your hard drive at C:\ProgramFiles\VBNetVB.

ACROBAT VERSION

The CD-ROM contains an e-version of this book that you can view and search using Adobe Acrobat Reader. You cannot print the pages or copy text from the Acrobat files. An evaluation version of Adobe Acrobat Reader is also included on the disc.

INSTALLING AND USING THE SOFTWARE

For your convenience, the software titles appearing on the CD-ROM are listed alphabetically.

Acrobat Reader

Freeware. Acrobat Reader lets you view the online version of this book. For more information on using Adobe Acrobat Reader, see the section "Using the E-Version of This Book." From Adobe Systems, www.adobe.com.

VISUAL BASIC .NET:
Your visual blueprint for building
versatile programs on the .NET Framework

IP*Works.NET

Trial version. IP*Works.NET from /n software, Inc. adds components to your application to support many Internet protocols such as FTP, mail, ping, LDAP, telnet, and more. You can find more information at www.nsoftware.com.

LEADTools for .NET

Demo. LEADTools for .NET from LEAD Technologies, Inc. provides support to your application so you can open and save in 60 graphics formats, perform image manipulation, scan, OCR, print, and more. You can find more information at www.leadtools.com.

UltraWebTree

Demo. UltraWebTree from Infragistics Corp. is a Web control package that enables you to add dynamic menus and trees to your Web applications. You can find more information at www.infragistics.com.

UltraWinListBar

Demo. UltraWinListBar from Infragistics Corp. is a Windows Forms control package that enables you to bring the look of Microsoft Outlook to your applications. You can find more information at www.infragistics.com.

Please note: At the time of publication, the most recent versions of IP*Works.NET, LEADTools for .NET, UltraWebTree, and UltraWinListBar were in the beta process. Please check the Web sites listed in the product description file for updates and current product information.

TROUBLESHOOTING

We tried our best to compile programs that work on most computers with the minimum system requirements. Your computer, however, may differ, and some programs may not work properly for some reason.

The two most likely problems are that you do not have enough memory (RAM) for the programs you want to use, or you have other programs running that are affecting installation or running of a program. If you get error messages like Not enough memory or Setup cannot continue, try one or more of these methods and then try using the software again:

- Turn off any anti-virus software.
- Close all running programs.
- In Windows, close the CD-ROM interface and run demos or installations directly from Windows Explorer.
- Have your local computer store add more RAM to your computer.

If you still have trouble installing the items from the CD-ROM, please call the Hungry Minds Customer Service phone number: 800-762-2974 (outside the U.S.: 317-572-3994). You can also contact Hungry Minds Tech Support by e-mail at techsupdum@hungryminds.com.

USING THE E-VERSION OF THIS BOOK

You can view *Visual Basic .NET: Your visual blueprint for building versatile programs on the .NET Framework* on your screen using the CD-ROM included at the back of this book. The CD-ROM allows you to search the contents of each chapter of the book for a specific word or phrase. The CD-ROM also provides a convenient way of keeping the book handy while traveling.

You must install Adobe Acrobat Reader on your computer before you can view the book on the

CD-ROM. This program is provided on the disc. Acrobat Reader allows you to view Portable Document Format (PDF) files, which can display books and magazines on your screen exactly as they appear in printed form.

To view the content of the book using Acrobat Reader, display the contents of the disc. Double-click the Book folder to display the contents of the folder. In the window that appears, double-click the icon for the chapter of the book you want to review.

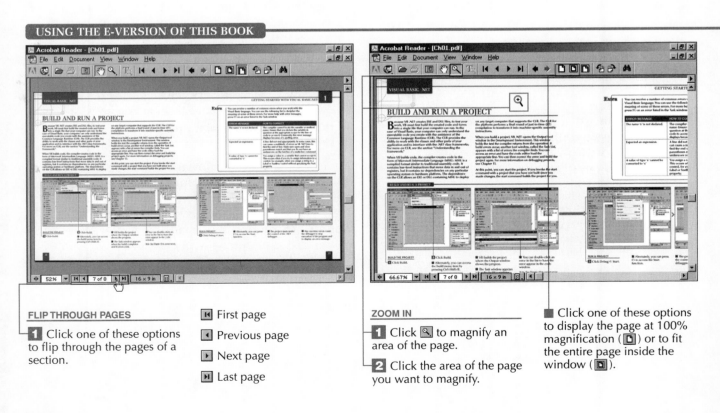

USING THE E-VERSION OF THIS BOOK

FLIP THROUGH PAGES

■1 Click one of these options to flip through the pages of a section.

■ First page

■ Previous page

■ Next page

■ Last page

ZOOM IN

■1 Click 🔍 to magnify an area of the page.

■2 Click the area of the page you want to magnify.

■ Click one of these options to display the page at 100% magnification (■) or to fit the entire page inside the window (■).

VISUAL BASIC .NET:
Your visual blueprint for building
versatile programs on the .NET Framework

Extra

To install Acrobat Reader, insert the CD-ROM into a drive. In the screen that appears, click Software. Click Acrobat Reader and then follow the instructions on your screen to install the program.

You can make searching the book more convenient by copying the .pdf files to your own computer. Display the contents of the CD-ROM and then copy the Book folder from the CD-ROM to your hard drive. This allows you to easily access the contents of the book at any time.

Acrobat Reader is a popular and useful program. There are many files available on the Web that are designed to be viewed using Acrobat Reader. Look for files with the .pdf extension. For more information about Acrobat Reader, visit the `www.adobe.com/products/acrobat/readermain.html` Web site.

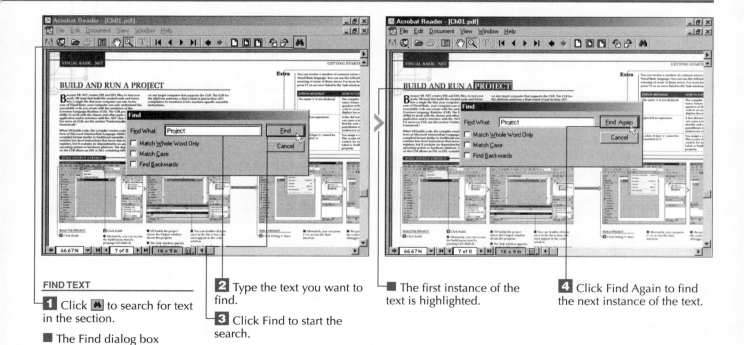

FIND TEXT

1 Click 🔍 to search for text in the section.

■ The Find dialog box appears.

2 Type the text you want to find.

3 Click Find to start the search.

■ The first instance of the text is highlighted.

4 Click Find Again to find the next instance of the text.

HUNGRY MINDS, INC. END-USER LICENSE AGREEMENT

READ THIS. You should carefully read these terms and conditions before opening the software packet(s) included with *Visual Basic .NET: Your visual blueprint for building versatile programs on the .NET Framework*. This is a license agreement ("Agreement") between you and Hungry Minds, Inc. ("HMI"). By opening the accompanying software packet(s), you acknowledge that you have read and accept the following terms and conditions. If you do not agree and do not want to be bound by such terms and conditions, promptly return the Book and the unopened software packet(s) to the place you obtained them for a full refund.

1. License Grant.

HMI grants to you (either an individual or entity) a nonexclusive license to use one copy of the enclosed software program(s) (collectively, the "Software") solely for your own personal or business purposes on a single computer (whether a standard computer or a workstation component of a multi-user network). The Software is in use on a computer when it is loaded into temporary memory (RAM) or installed into permanent memory (hard disk, CD-ROM, or other storage device). HMI reserves all rights not expressly granted herein.

2. Ownership.

HMI is the owner of all right, title, and interest, including copyright, in and to the compilation of the Software recorded on the disk(s) or CD-ROM ("Software Media"). Copyright to the individual programs recorded on the Software Media is owned by the author, or other authorized copyright owner of each program. Ownership of the Software and all proprietary rights relating thereto remain with HMI and its licensers.

3. Restrictions On Use and Transfer.

(a) You may only (i) make one copy of the Software for backup or archival purposes, or (ii) transfer the Software to a single hard disk, provided that you keep the original for backup or archival purposes. You may not (i) rent or lease the Software, (ii) copy or reproduce the Software through a LAN or other network system or through any computer subscriber system or bulletin-board system, or (iii) modify, adapt, or create derivative works based on the Software.

(b) You may not reverse engineer, decompile, or disassemble the Software. You may transfer the Software and user documentation on a permanent basis, provided that the transferee agrees to accept the terms and conditions of this Agreement and you retain no copies. If the Software is an update or has been updated, any transfer must include the most recent update and all prior versions.

4. Restrictions on Use of Individual Programs.

You must follow the individual requirements and restrictions detailed for each individual program in the appendix of this Book. These limitations are also contained in the individual license agreements recorded on the Software Media. These limitations may include a requirement that after using the program for a specified period of time, the user must pay a registration fee or discontinue use. By opening the Software packet(s), you will be agreeing to abide by the licenses and restrictions for these individual programs that are detailed in the appendix and on the Software Media. None of the material on this Software Media or listed in this Book may ever be redistributed, in original or modified form, for commercial purposes.

5. Limited Warranty.

(a) HMI warrants that the Software and Software Media are free from defects in materials and workmanship under normal use for a period of sixty (60) days from the date of purchase of this Book. If HMI receives notification within the warranty period of defects in materials or workmanship, HMI will replace the defective Software Media.

VISUAL BASIC .NET:
Your visual blueprint for building
versatile programs on the .NET Framework

(b) HMI AND THE AUTHOR OF THE BOOK DISCLAIM ALL OTHER WARRANTIES, EXPRESS OR IMPLIED, INCLUDING WITHOUT LIMITATION IMPLIED WARRANTIES OF MERCHANTABILITY AND FITNESS FOR A PARTICULAR PURPOSE, WITH RESPECT TO THE SOFTWARE, THE PROGRAMS, THE SOURCE CODE CONTAINED THEREIN, AND/OR THE TECHNIQUES DESCRIBED IN THIS BOOK. HMI DOES NOT WARRANT THAT THE FUNCTIONS CONTAINED IN THE SOFTWARE WILL MEET YOUR REQUIREMENTS OR THAT THE OPERATION OF THE SOFTWARE WILL BE ERROR FREE.

(c) This limited warranty gives you specific legal rights, and you may have other rights that vary from jurisdiction to jurisdiction.

6. Remedies.

(a) HMI's entire liability and your exclusive remedy for defects in materials and workmanship shall be limited to replacement of the Software Media, which may be returned to HMI with a copy of your receipt at the following address: Software Media Fulfillment Department, Attn.: *VISUAL BASIC .NET: Your visual blueprint for building versatile programs on the .NET Framework*, Hungry Minds, Inc., 10475 Crosspoint Blvd., Indianapolis, IN 46256, or call 1-800-762-2974. Please allow four to six weeks for delivery. This Limited Warranty is void if failure of the Software Media has resulted from accident, abuse, or misapplication. Any replacement Software Media will be warranted for the remainder of the original warranty period or thirty (30) days, whichever is longer.

(b) In no event shall HMI or the author be liable for any damages whatsoever (including without limitation damages for loss of business profits, business interruption, loss of business information, or any other pecuniary loss) arising from the use of or inability to use the Book or the Software, even if HMI has been advised of the possibility of such damages.

(c) Because some jurisdictions do not allow the exclusion or limitation of liability for consequential or incidental damages, the above limitation or exclusion may not apply to you.

7. U.S. Government Restricted Rights.

Use, duplication, or disclosure of the Software for or on behalf of the United States of America, its agencies and/or instrumentalities (the "U.S. Government") is subject to restrictions as stated in paragraph (c)(1)(ii) of the Rights in Technical Data and Computer Software clause of DFARS 252.227-7013, or subparagraphs (c) (1) and (2) of the Commercial Computer Software - Restricted Rights clause at FAR 52.227-19, and in similar clauses in the NASA FAR supplement, as applicable.

8. General.

This Agreement constitutes the entire understanding of the parties and revokes and supersedes all prior agreements, oral or written, between them and may not be modified or amended except in a writing signed by both parties hereto that specifically refers to this Agreement. This Agreement shall take precedence over any other documents that may be in conflict herewith. If any one or more provisions contained in this Agreement are held by any court or tribunal to be invalid, illegal, or otherwise unenforceable, each and every other provision shall remain in full force and effect.

INDEX

VISUAL BASIC .NET:
Your visual blueprint for building versatile
programs on the .NET Framework

INDEX

VISUAL BASIC .NET:
Your visual blueprint for building versatile
programs on the .NET Framework

INDEX

VISUAL BASIC .NET:
Your visual blueprint for building versatile
programs on the .NET Framework

INDEX

O

Object-Oriented
  Concepts, 8
  Programming (OOP), 8, 30
  terms, 26
option
  controls, 58–59, 240
  list control, 242
Oracle, 3
overload, 180–181
override, 182, 194–195
overwrite, 149

P

paint, 32–33, 140, 148
  event, 150, 290–291
  form, 137
  Form1, 152
panels, 49, 61
  control, 78
PaperSize, 125, 127
PaperSource, 127
parent form, 46
path
  create, 154
  graphics, 155
  pens, 155
PDF files, 316
Peek, 112
pens, 190
  create, 144, 148
  curves, 151
  Dim, 144
  object, 144
  overwrite, 149
  parameters, 150, 154
  path, 155
Photoshop, 40
PictureBox, 136–137
pies
  draw, 150, 154
  fill, 150
  graphics, 150
point, 41
  arrays, 148
  objects, 140, 151

polygons, 148, 149
pool thread, 199
pop-up
  button, 50
  menu, 312
  windows, 40
primitives, 148, 149
print, 11, 42
  AllowPaper, 126
  color, 125
  default, 123
  margins, 122
  page setup, 122
  paper size, 125
  preview, 128–129
PrintDialog, 122, 124
PrintDocument, 122–128
printer. *See also* print
  allow, 126
  dialog box, 124–125
  margins, 127
PrinterResolution, 127
PrinterSettings, 125–127
PrintPage, 127
private
  keywords, 10
  method, 181
  operators, 161
  statement, 162
  variables, 186
ProgIDs, 10
programming
  concepts, 18
  multi-thread, 11
properties, 9, 235
  Accept Button, 26
  Accessibility, 30
  AllowPaper, 126
  Anchor, 34, 60–61
  Attributes, 117
  AutoScale, 26
  AutoScroll, 26
  AutoSize, 51
  BackColor, 30
  BackgroundImage, 26, 30, 50, 60

VISUAL BASIC .NET:
Your visual blueprint for building versatile
programs on the .NET Framework

INDEX

VISUAL BASIC .NET:
Your visual blueprint for building versatile
programs on the .NET Framework

INDEX

VISUAL BASIC .NET:
Your visual blueprint for building versatile
programs on the .NET Framework

Read Less – Learn More™

Visual

New Series!

The visual alternative to learning complex computer topics

For experienced computer users developers, network professionals who learn best visually.

Extra

Apply It

"Apply It" and "Extra" provide ready-to-run code and useful tips.

Title	ISBN	Price
Active Server™ Pages 3.0: Your visual blueprint for developing interactive Web sites	0-7645-3472-6	$26.99
HTML: Your visual blueprint for designing effective Web pages	0-7645-3471-8	$26.99
Java™: Your visual blueprint for building portable Java programs	0-7645-3543-9	$26.99
JavaScript™: Your visual blueprint for building dynamic Web pages	0-7645-4730-5	$26.99
JavaServer™ Pages: Your visual blueprint for designing dynamic content with JSP	0-7645-3542-0	$26.99
Linux®: Your visual blueprint to the Linux platform	0-7645-3481-5	$26.99
Perl: Your visual blueprint for building Perl scripts	0-7645-3478-5	$26.99
PHP: Your visual blueprint for creating open source, server-side content	0-7645-3561-7	$26.99
Unix®: Your visual blueprint to the universe of Unix	0-7645-3480-7	$26.99
XML: Your visual blueprint for building expert Web pages	0-7645-3477-7	$26.99

Over 10 million *Visual* books in print!

with these two-color Visual™ guides

The Complete Visual Reference

"Master It" tips provide additional topic coverage

For visual learners
who want an all-in-one
reference/tutorial that
delivers more in-depth
information about a
technology topic.

Title	ISBN	Price
Master Active Directory™ VISUALLY™	0-7645-3425-4	$39.99
Master Microsoft® Access 2000 VISUALLY™	0-7645-6048-4	$39.99
Master Microsoft® Office 2000 VISUALLY™	0-7645-6050-6	$39.99
Master Microsoft® Word 2000 VISUALLY™	0-7645-6046-8	$39.99
Master Office 97 VISUALLY™	0-7645-6036-0	$39.99
Master Photoshop® 5.5 VISUALLY™	0-7645-6045-X	$39.99
Master Red Hat® Linux® VISUALLY™	0-7645-3436-X	$39.99
Master VISUALLY™ Dreamweaver® 4 and Flash™ 5	0-7645-0855-5	$39.99
Master VISUALLY™ FrontPage® 2002	0-7645-3580-3	$39.99
Master VISUALLY™ HTML 4 & XHTML™ 1	0-7645-3454-8	$39.99
Master VISUALLY™ Microsoft® Windows® Me Millennium Edition	0-7645-3496-3	$39.99
Master VISUALLY™ Office XP	0-7645-3599-4	$39.99
Master VISUALLY™ Photoshop® 6	0-7645-3541-2	$39.99
Master VISUALLY™ Windows® 2000 Server	0-7645-3426-2	$39.99
Master Windows® 95 VISUALLY™	0-7645-6024-7	$39.99
Master Windows® 98 VISUALLY™	0-7645-6034-4	$39.99
Master Windows® 2000 Professional VISUALLY™	0-7645-3421-1	$39.99

The Visual™

series is available

wherever books are

sold, or call

1-800-762-2974.

Outside the US, call

317-572-3993

TRADE & INDIVIDUAL ORDERS

Phone: **(800) 762-2974**
or **(317) 572-3993**
(8 a.m.–6 p.m., CST, weekdays)
FAX : **(800) 550-2747**
or **(317) 572-4002**

EDUCATIONAL ORDERS & DISCOUNTS

Phone: **(800) 434-2086**
(8:30 a.m.–5:00 p.m., CST, weekdays)
FAX : **(317) 572-4005**

CORPORATE ORDERS FOR VISUAL™ SERIES

Phone: **(800) 469-6616**
(8 a.m.–5 p.m., EST, weekdays)
FAX : **(905) 890-9434**

Qty	ISBN	Title	Price	Total

Shipping & Handling Charges

	Description	First book	Each add'l. book	Total
Domestic	Normal	$4.50	$1.50	$
	Two Day Air	$8.50	$2.50	$
	Overnight	$18.00	$3.00	$
International	Surface	$8.00	$8.00	$
	Airmail	$16.00	$16.00	$
	DHL Air	$17.00	$17.00	$

Subtotal _____

CA residents add applicable sales tax _____

IN, MA and MD residents add 5% sales tax _____

IL residents add 6.25% sales tax _____

RI residents add 7% sales tax _____

TX residents add 8.25% sales tax _____

Shipping _____

Total _____

Ship to:

Name_____

Address_____

Company_____

City/State/Zip_____

Daytime Phone_____

Payment: □ Check to Hungry Minds (US Funds Only)
□ Visa □ MasterCard □ American Express

Card # _____ Exp. _____ Signature_____

Hungry Minds™

*maran*Graphics®